I0065492

A Celebration of the Ties That Bind Us: Connections between Actuarial Science and Mathematical Finance

Special Issue Editor

Albert Cohen

MDPI • Basel • Beijing • Wuhan • Barcelona • Belgrade

MDPI

Special Issue Editor
Albert Cohen
Michigan State University
USA

Editorial Office
MDPI AG
St. Alban-Anlage 66
Basel, Switzerland

This edition is a reprint of the Special Issue published online in the open access journal *Risks* (ISSN 2227-9091) in 2017 (available at: http://www.mdpi.com/journal/risks/special_issues/actuarial_science).

For citation purposes, cite each article independently as indicated on the article page online and as indicated below:

Lastname, F.M., F.M. Lastname **Year**. Article title. *Journal Name* Article number: page range.

First Edition 2018

ISBN 978-3-03842-733-9 (Pbk)
ISBN 978-3-03842-734-6 (PDF)

Table of Contents

About the Special Issue Editor

Albert Cohen, Academic Specialist, Upon earning his doctorate in mathematical sciences in 2007 from Carnegie Mellon University under the supervision of Dr. David Kinderlehrer, Albert Cohen began his professional career at Michigan State University (MSU). Dr. Cohen has worked at MSU in multiple roles since 2007. In 2010, he was appointed as acting director of the actuarial program, helping to build the undergraduate major in actuarial science. In 2013, Dr. Cohen became the assistant director to Emiliano Valdez, and then to Kevin Clinton in 2015. While teaching and administrating, Dr. Cohen has also grown his research program at the interface between actuarial science and mathematical finance, and he takes great joy in helping to coordinate the program as well as helping support the educational growth of the next generation of actuarial scholars and practitioners.

Preface to "A Celebration of the Ties That Bind Us: Connections between Actuarial Science and Mathematical Finance"

In the nearly thirty years since Hans Buhlmann set out the notion of the Actuary of the Third Kind, the connection between Actuarial Science (AS) and Mathematical Finance (MF) has been continually reinforced. As siblings in the family of Risk Management techniques, practitioners in both fields have learned a great deal from each other. This collection of articles is is set out before the reader in this spirit of cooperation between folks who are, not only experts in both AS and MF, but also those who present diverse perspectives from industry and academia.

Topics from multiple areas, such as Stochastic Modeling, Credit Risk, Monte Carlo Simulation, and Pension Valuation, among others, that were maybe thought to belong to the domain of one type of risk manager are shown time and again to have deep value to other areas of risk management as well.

It is my hope that this special volume will inspire future collaboration between those who seek an interdisciplinary approach to risk management.

In closing, I would like to offer a hearty Thank You to all of the wonderful scholars who contributed to this collection of articles. Your work furthers our understanding of modeling, pricing, and mitigating risk in financial and insurance markets.

Albert Cohen
Special Issue Editor

References

Buhlmann, Hans. 1987. Actuaries of the Third Kind (editorial). ASTIN Bulletin 17: 137–38.

risks

MDPI

Editorial

Editorial: A Celebration of the Ties That Bind Us: Connections between Actuarial Science and Mathematical Finance

Albert Cohen

Department of Mathematics, Michigan State University, East Lansing, MI 48823, USA; albert@math.msu.edu

Received: 5 January 2018; Accepted: 9 January 2018; Published: 15 January 2018

Abstract: In the nearly thirty years since Hans Buhlmann (Buhlmann (1987)) set out the notion of the Actuary of the Third Kind, the connection between Actuarial Science (AS) and Mathematical Finance (MF) has been continually reinforced. As siblings in the family of Risk Management techniques, practitioners in both fields have learned a great deal from each other. The collection of articles in this volume are contributed by scholars who are not only experts in areas of AS and MF, but also those who present diverse perspectives from both industry and academia. Topics from multiple areas, such as Stochastic Modeling, Credit Risk, Monte Carlo Simulation, and Pension Valuation, among others, that were maybe thought to be the domain of one type of risk manager are shown time and again to have deep value to other areas of risk management as well. The articles in this collection, in my opinion, contribute techniques, ideas, and overviews of tools that specialists in both AS and MF will find useful and interesting to implement in their work. It is also my hope that this collection will inspire future collaboration between those who seek an interdisciplinary approach to risk management.

Keywords: actuarial science; mathematical finance; risk management

---

1. Background and Motivation

The construction of this special issue began in 2016, and continued through 2017, while teaching at Michigan State University (MSU) as well as visiting colleagues from the Pacific Northwest to New York City to the Deep South. I had known for some time that I wanted to design an issue that would present cutting edge research in both actuarial science and financial mathematics. In truth, I had been inspired nearly a decade earlier by this strong connection between both fields. As a Ph.D. student at Carnegie Mellon, I had come across Hans Gerber's paper (Gerber (1977)) on the optimal cancellation of policies. At the time, I had begun working on a problem in optimal prediction and was looking for inspiration in solving the problem at hand. When I came across Gerber's paper, I had no previous exposure to actuarial science, but I immediately recognized the power and clarity of his exposition. I was hooked! I did eventually solve the problem in optimal prediction (Cohen (2010)) a few years later, but not without using ideas from Gerber's model of liabilities as an application of optimal prediction to a new kind of risk measure. And so began my education in the overlap of the fields of insurance and financial economics.

2. Overview

This collection you now hold in your hand is crafted in the spirit of Gerber's paper, in that advanced mathematical techniques and risk management go hand in hand to present managers with better information for decision making.

For example, new ideas such as those presented in Peter Carr's work (Carr (2017)) on Bounded Brownian Motion naturally find their place in the modeling of financial instruments, but are perhaps also suitable for insurance models that require such bounded processes. Stephen Mildenhall's paper (Mildenhall (2017)) on Actuarial Geometry combines tools from the classical study of shapes with Levy processes to provide an innovative way to study risks from an insurance perspective. Robert J. Rietz and his group (Rietz et al. (2017)) study the effect of gainsharing (via simulation) on selecting discount rates for defined benefit plans. Gareth W. Peters, Rodrigo S. Targino and Mario V. Wuthrich (Peters et al. (2017)) provide a novel Monte Carlo method to calculate (coherent) capital allocations for a general insurance company. Carolyn W. Chang and Jack S. K. Chang (Chang and Chang (2017)) utilize an approach that integrates commonly used tools from actuarial science and mathematical finance to price a *default-risky* catastrophe reinsurance contract. Daoping Yu and Vytaras Brazauskas (Yu and Brazauskas (2017)) study the impact of model uncertainty on value-at-risk (VaR) estimators. In her paper on predicting prices for high profile tech stocks, Nguyet Nguyen (Nguyen (2017)) applies the Hidden Markov Model (HMM) to forecast stock prices and develop an HMM-based trading strategy. Michael R. Metel, Traian A. Pirvu and Julian Wong (Metel et al. (2017)) investigate the Omega Measure and it's use for assessing portfolio performance, as well as similarities and differences with the Sharpe Ratio when determining the optimal portfolio for different return classes. Finally, Nick Costanzino and I (Cohen and Costanzino (2017)) look at incorporating stochastic recovery into the Black-Cox model of bond pricing, with application to credit default swaps.

3. Conclusions

This collection of articles fits into the greater narrative of collaboration between researchers and practitioners, driven by new and innovative ideas and products in finance and insurance. The connection between AS and MF, for actuaries of the third kind (Buhlmann (1987)) and others who use these tools, will only strengthen with time as the complexity of financial and insurance instruments increases.

Acknowledgments: There are so many colleagues in both finance and actuarial science that I would like to thank for their friendship and guidance. In Actuarial Science, I would like to thank my dear friend Emil Valdez (UConn) for his leadership and dedication to research in the field as well as the education of the next generation of actuaries. I would also like to thank Virginia Young and Kristen Moore at the University of Michigan, and in the East Lansing/MSU community, thank you to all of my students (past and present), Ron and Mary Simon, Mark Wenger, Kevin Clinton, Jacob Geyer, Wellington Ow, Gabor Franciscs, Darren Mason, and Robert J. Rietz for their continued support and mentorship. Thank You to Keith Promislow for bringing me to MSU, and to Yang Wang, now at the Hong Kong University of Science and Technology, for hiring me to help build the major in actuarial science at Michigan State. For his wonderful paper on Actuarial Geometry, I would like to acknowledge Stephen Mildenhall. Stephen's paper is not only an achievement in terms of research, but is also a valuable resource for young researchers in insurance who wish to learn about stochastic processes and geometry from an actuarial perspective. In Finance, thank you to Steven Shreve and Dmitry Kramkov for giving me a solid education in mathematical finance while I was a graduate student at Carnegie Mellon. Also, thank you to all in the field who have extended the hand of friendship and brought me into your community. These include, among many scholars: Peter Carr (NYU-Tandon), Nguyet Nguyen (Youngstown State), Harvey Stein, Sean Hilden, Shlomo Levental (MSU), and Mark Schroder (MSU). I would like to especially thank my friend and research partner Nick Costanzino for his insight and introduction to so many neat areas of cutting edge finance and mathematics. I truly would not be in the position I am now without his continued support. Finally, I would like to thank my family for their support and patience over the last couple years while this special collection of articles took shape. I spent many late nights working on this project while they patiently waited at home for me to come back and spend time with them. To my beautiful wife Jessica and our son Eli, I love you! In closing, I would like to dedicate my work in editing this collection to the memory of my Godfather, Asher Cohen.

Conflicts of Interest: The author declare no conflict of interest.

References

Bühlmann, Hans. 1987. Actuaries of the Third Kind (editorial). *ASTIN Bulletin* 17: 137–38.

Carr, Peter. 2017. Bounded Brownian Motion. *Risks* 5: 61. doi:10.3390/risks5040061.

Chang, Carolyn, and Jack Chang. 2017. An Integrated Approach to Pricing Catastrophe Reinsurance. *Risks* 5: 51. doi:10.3390/risks5030051.

Cohen, Albert, and Nick Costanzino. 2017. Bond and CDS Pricing via the Stochastic Recovery Black-Cox Model. *Risks* 5: 26. doi:10.3390/risks5020026.

Cohen, Albert. 2010. Examples of optimal prediction in the infinite horizon case. *Statistics & Probability Letters* 80: 950–57.

Gerber, Hans U. 1977. On optimal cancellation of policies. *ASTIN Bulletin: The Journal of the IAA* 9: 125–38.

Metel, Michael R., Traian A. Pirvu, and Julian Wong. 2017. Risk Management under Omega Measure. *Risks* 5: 27. doi:10.3390/risks5020027.

Mildenhall, Stephen. 2017. Actuarial Geometry. *Risks* 5: 31. doi:10.3390/risks5020031.

Nguyen, Nguyet. 2017. An Analysis and Implementation of the Hidden Markov Model to Technology Stock Prediction. *Risks* 5: 62. doi:10.3390/risks5040062.

Peters, Gareth W., Rodrigo S. Targino, and Mario V. 2017. Bayesian Modelling, Monte Carlo Sampling and Capital Allocation of Insurance *Risks* 5: 53. doi:10.3390/risks5040053.

Rietz, Robert, Evan Cronick, Shelby Mathers, and Matt Pollie. 2017. Effects of Gainsharing Provisions on the Selection of a Discount Rate for a Defined Benefit Pension Plan. *Risks* 5: 32. doi:10.3390/risks5020032.

Yu, Daoping, and Vytaras Brazauskas. 2017. Model Uncertainty in Operational Risk Modeling Due to Data Truncation: A Single Risk Case. *Risks* 5: 49. doi:10.3390/risks5030049.

risks

MDPI

Article

Bounded Brownian Motion

Peter Carr

Department of Finance and Risk Engineering, Tandon School of Engineering, NYU, 12 MetroTech Center, Brooklyn, NY 11201, USA; pcarr@nyc.rr.com

Academic Editor: Albert Cohen
Received: 12 February 2017; Accepted: 19 October 2017; Published: 17 November 2017

Abstract: Diffusions are widely used in finance due to their tractability. Driftless diffusions are needed to describe ratios of asset prices under a martingale measure. We provide a simple example of a tractable driftless diffusion which also has a bounded state space.

Keywords: standard Brownian motion; Brownian martingale; diffusion coefficient

---

1. Introduction

Standard Brownian motion (SBM) is the most widely studied stochastic process because it serves as a highly tractable model of both a martingale and a Markov process. In finance, the martingale property describes asset prices relative to some numeraire under the assumption of no arbitrage. The Markov property can also describe some asset prices when markets for them are thought to be semi-strong form efficient. However, for limited liability assets, such as stocks, it is well known that SBM cannot describe their prices because prices are non-negative, while the state space of an SBM is the whole real line.

The observation lead Samuelson and Osborne to propose that arbitrage-free asset prices, relative to a numeraire, be modeled as a geometric Brownian martingale (GBM). As is well known, this Markovian martingale is obtained from standard Brownian motion by exponentiating. The convexity of the exponential introduces a positive drift, so one can restore martingality by introducing time decay. One can alternatively create a GBM by starting from a linear Brownian motion with constant drift and then evaluating the scale function of the drifting Brownian motion on the drifting Brownian motion. The resulting GBM has state space $(0, \infty)$, making it suitable to describe arbitrage-free prices of a limited liability asset relative to a numeraire.

While the use of a GBM addresses the lower bound constraint imposed by limited liability, it does not address the upper bound. SBM and GBM can both achieve arbitrarily high positive values. This renders them unsuitable to describe the prices of assets with a finite number of payouts, each of which is bounded above. Examples would include coupon bonds and derivative securities with a finite number of bounded payouts (e.g., a binary option). Exchange rates describe the price of one currency in terms of another and are often legally manipulated by governments to lie between two positive bounds. One may also wish to describe a financial concept other than a price with a stochastic process. For example, stochastic processes are used to describe interest rates, variance rates, and hazard rates. Historical data on these observables is typically confined to a band, which often leads to the imposition of mean reversion in the dynamics. However, it would not be unreasonable to use the historical band as a guide to setting a future band that these rates cannot escape.

Many concepts in probability have evolved into financial concepts. For example, a probability can be used to describe the price of a binary option Taleb (2017), while a correlation is used to describe the swap rate in a correlation swap Jacquier and Slaoui (2010). Since both of these probability concepts are bounded, it becomes natural to consider bounded processes to describe all of these concepts. In this paper, we construct a stochastic process S with the following properties:

1. The process S is obtained by evaluating the scale function of a mean-repelling Ornstein Uhlenbeck (OU) process. As a result, S is a time-homogeneous driftless diffusion. Furthermore, since the scale function can be evaluated in closed form, the transition probabilities of S are known in closed form.
2. The state space of the process S is $(0, H)$, for some $H > 0$. In words, the process S is bounded below and above and its natural boundaries are zero and a positive constant H. Since S has zero drift and can't explode, it is a martingale.
3. The diffusion coefficient of S is positive and bounded above by a positive constant h.
4. Aside from its starting value $S_0 \in (0, H)$, the process S has two free parameters H and h which respectively describe the maximum value and maximum (normal) volatility of S.

Analogous with the term geometric Brownian motion, we christen this process "bounded Brownian motion".

2. Applications

2.1. Managed Currency

Consider a forward exchange rate in a setting when a monetary authority is able to manage the money supply or interest rates such that a given exchange rate stays between two positive barriers over the life of the forward contract. By adding a positive constant to the bounded Brownian motion S, we synthesize the risk-neutral dynamics of the forward exchange rate process. Papers modeling the spot FX process between bands include Carr and Kakuschadze (2017), Hui et al. (2008), Ingersoll (1997), and Rady (1997).

2.2. Correlation Swap

In its simplest form, a correlation swap designates two underlying assets and a fixed maturity date. At maturity, the dollar payoff is affine in the realized correlation of returns between two underlying assets. The slope of this affine relation is the notional of the correlation swap which is determined at inception. The ratio of the intercept to this notional is the correlation swap rate for maturity T, which is also determined at inception. As we move through calendar time, the conditional expected value of the floating leg of a seasoned correlation swap is a martingale fluctuating in the interval $[-1, 1]$. By multiplying S by $\frac{2}{H}$ and subtracting one, we obtain such a process.

2.3. Protection Leg of CDO

The protection leg of a CDO has a nonnegative value that fluctuates in the interval $[0, H]$. The value before the maturity date T is in $(0, H]$, while the value at T is in $[0, H]$. The dynamics presented here fluctuate in the interval $(0, H)$. However, we will show a way to change the domain to $(0, H]$.

3. Genesis

Fix a probability space $(\Omega, \mathcal{F}, \mathbb{Q})$. We will refer to $\mathbb{Q}$ as the risk-neutral measure. Let $X_0 \in \mathbb{R}$ and for positive constants H and h, consider the following[1] mean-repelling OU process:

$$dX_t = \frac{2\pi h^2}{H^2} X_t dt + h dW_t, \qquad t \geq 0, \tag{1}$$

where W is a $\mathbb{Q}$ standard Brownian motion.

[1] The scaling factor 2π in the drift of X is entirely optional, but is inserted here so that the volatility of the bounded Brownian motion can later be expressed in terms of an un-normalized Gaussian function, rather than a normalized one.

Let $S(x) : \mathbb{R} \mapsto \mathbb{R}$ be a C^2 function which solves the linear second order ordinary differential equation (ODE):

$$\frac{h^2}{2} S''(x) + \frac{2\pi h^2}{H^2} x S'(x) = 0, \qquad x \in \mathbb{R}. \tag{2}$$

As this is a linear first order ODE in $S'(x)$, the general solution is given by:

$$S(x) = \int_a^x \exp\left[- \int_b^y \frac{2\pi}{H^2} z dz \right] dy, \tag{3}$$

where the lower integral limits a and b are arbitrary. Since S is increasing in x, it is generally referred to as a scale function of the diffusion process X.

Let $S_H(x)$ denote the particular increasing function obtained when $a = -\infty$ and $b = 0$:

$$S_H(x) \equiv \int_{-\infty}^x \exp\left[- \int_0^y \frac{2\pi}{H^2} z dz \right] dy. \tag{4}$$

Some easy calculus gives:

$$\begin{aligned} S_H(x) &= \int_{-\infty}^x \exp\left[-\frac{1}{2} \frac{2\pi y^2}{H^2} \right] dy \\ &= H \int_{-\infty}^{\frac{\sqrt{2\pi}x}{H}} \frac{\exp[-\frac{z^2}{2}]}{\sqrt{2\pi}} dz \\ &= HN\left(\frac{\sqrt{2\pi}x}{H} \right), \qquad t \geq 0, \end{aligned} \tag{5}$$

where $N(d) : \mathbb{R} \mapsto (0, 1)$ is the standard normal cumulative distribution function (CDF). Since N maps $\mathbb{R}$ to $(0, 1)$, (5) implies that S_H maps $\mathbb{R}$ to $(0, H)$.

Let $\{S_t; t \geq 0\}$ be the stochastic process obtained by evaluating the scale function S_H on the OU process X:

$$S_t \equiv S_H(X_t) = HN\left(\frac{\sqrt{2\pi}X_t}{H} \right), \tag{6}$$

from (5). It is well known that S is a time-homogeneous driftless diffusion. Since the range of the function $S_H(\cdot)$ is bounded, it is clear from (6) that the process S takes values on $(0, H)$. Since S is bounded, it is clearly a martingale and not just a local martingale.

4. Valuing Perpetual Claims Without Knowing Volatility

Consider perpetual claims written on the path of a single underlying asset. In this section, we show that we can value several such claims without knowing the volatility of the underlying asset. The price of the underlying asset will be a continuous martingale, but it need not be the particular continuous martingale S introduced in the last section. To distinguish general results applying to continuous martingales from particular results applying to the driftless bounded diffusion S defined by (6), we will denote the former process by M. We being with some observations about hitting probabilities of S and then generalize to M.

Let ℓ and r be two real-valued constants satisfying:

$$-\infty < \ell < X_0 < r < \infty. \tag{7}$$

In words, ℓ and r are finite and bracket X_0. Let σ_ℓ and σ_r respectively denote the first passage times of X to ℓ and r. Let $S_0 \in (0, H)$ be the initial value of the S process:

$$S_0 \equiv S_H(X_0) = HN\left(\frac{\sqrt{2\pi}X_0}{H}\right), \tag{8}$$

from (6). Let D and U be defined by:

$$D \equiv S_H(\ell) \qquad U \equiv S_H(r). \tag{9}$$

Since $S_H(\cdot)$ is increasing, (7) implies that D and U satisfy:

$$0 < D < S_0 < U < H. \tag{10}$$

In words, D and U are both in $(0, H)$ and bracket S_0. Let τ_u and τ_d respectively denote the first passage times of S to U and D. Since S is a process in natural scale, the probability that S hits U before D starting from S_0 is given by:

$$\mathbb{Q}\{\tau_u < \tau_d | S_0 = S\} = \frac{S - D}{U - D}, \qquad S \in (D, U). \tag{11}$$

In fact, (11) is a standard result that holds for any continuous martingale with unbounded quadratic variation. We will soon discuss results for such processes, but, for now, we confine our explorations to the driftless bounded diffusion S defined by (6).

Consider a claim that pays one dollar if the process S hits U before D and zero otherwise. If interest rates are zero, then (11) gives the value of such a claim as a function of the starting point S of the underlying. Notice that given a direct observation of the starting value S, this value is invariant to the volatility of the process S. Since $\sigma_\ell = \tau_d$ and $\sigma_r = \tau_u$, we can make the corresponding statements for hitting probabilities and claim values when X is the underlying.

In fact, the affine form of the hitting probabilities of S generalize to any continuous martingale M, whose quadratic variation becomes infinite as the horizon become infinite:

$$\lim_{T\uparrow\infty} \langle M \rangle_T = \infty. \tag{12}$$

This condition is needed to rule out continuous martingales which absorb at spatial boundaries placed between the starting value and the barrier of interest. Let $(-\infty, \infty)$ be the state space of the continuous martingale. Suppose again that D and U are both in $(-\infty, \infty)$ and bracket M_0:

$$-\infty < D < M_0 < U < \infty. \tag{13}$$

Consider the random payoff from a "perpetual" claim on M that pays R_d at time τ_d if M hits D first and R_u at time τ_u if M hits U first. Assuming zero interest rates and no dividends from the underlying asset before the first exit, the initial value of this claim is:

$$V_0 = \frac{M_0 - D}{U - D} R_u + \frac{U - M_0}{U - D} R_d. \tag{14}$$

By setting $R_d = 0$ and $R_u = 1$, one obtains the following generalization of (11):

$$\mathbb{Q}\{\tau_u < \tau_d | \mathcal{F}_0\} = \frac{M_0 - D}{U - D}, \tag{15}$$

where we assume that the initial filtration $\mathcal{F}_0$ contains M_0. By setting $R_d = D$ and $R_u = U$, one can interpret R_d and R_u as liquidating dividends from the asset whose price is M. In this case, no assumption on interest rates is needed since the replicating strategy just holds one share.

For the above claims, monitoring of the barriers begins at time $t = 0$. Consider instead a more general claim where monitoring of the exit barriers starts from some fixed time $T \geq 0$. We claim that static positions in European options maturing at T can be used to span this payoff. In particular, consider a butterfly spread with strikes D, K, and U where $-\infty < D < K < U < \infty$. Suppose that the positions in European options are chosen so that the butterfly spread pays off one dollar if $S_T = K$ at T. Then we claim the value of this butterfly spread on M is the joint risk-neutral probability that M hits K after T before it hits D or U after T.

Butterfly spreads can be synthesized using puts or calls. We will use puts and hence let $P_0(K, T)$ denote the initial price of a European put of strike $K \in \mathbb{R}$ and maturity $T \geq 0$. Consider the following butterfly spread payoff:

$$BS_T = \frac{(U - M_T)^+ - (K - M_T)^+}{U - K} - \frac{(K - M_T)^+ - (D - M_T)^+}{K - D}. \tag{16}$$

The initial cost of forming this butterfly spread is:

$$BS_0 = \frac{P_0(U, T) - P_0(K, T)}{U - K} - \frac{P_0(K, T) - P_0(D, T)}{K - D}. \tag{17}$$

Since the payoff in (16) is bounded between 0 and 1, no arbitrage forces the value in (17) to also be bounded between 0 and 1.

Let τ_B^T be the first time after T that the continuous martingale M touches a barrier B. If the martingale never touches B after T, then $\tau_B^T = \infty$. Let $\tau_{DU}^T \equiv \tau_D^T \wedge \tau_U^T$ be the first time after T that the martingale touches either D or U. If the martingale never touches D or U after T, then $\tau_{DU}^T = \infty$.

Theorem 1. No arbitrage and zero interest rates implies:

$$BS_0 = \mathbb{Q}\{\tau_K^T < \tau_{DU}^T\}. \tag{18}$$

Proof. We need to show that BS_0 is the initial cost of a strategy that pays one dollar if $\tau_K^T < \tau_{DU}^T$ and which pays zero otherwise. Consider the following trading strategy. At time 0, the investor buys the butterfly spread by:

1. buying $\frac{1}{U-K}$ puts struck at U
2. selling $\frac{1}{U-K} + \frac{1}{K-D}$ puts struck at K
3. buying $\frac{1}{K-D}$ puts struck at L.

□

The net cost is given in (17). The put portfolio is held static to T. If $S_T < D$ or $S_T > U$, then the portfolio expires worthless. This matches the payoff of the desired claim since if $S_T < D$, then we must have $\tau_K^T \geq \tau_D^T = \tau_{DU}^T$ and similarly, if $S_T > U$, then we must have $\tau_K^T \geq \tau_U^T = \tau_{DU}^T$.

If $S_T \in (D, U)$, then use the payoff from the portfolio to finance the following positions:

1. if $S_T \in (D, K)$ buy $\frac{1}{K-D}$ shares and borrow $\frac{D}{K-D}$ dollars.
2. if $S_T \in (K, U)$ short $\frac{1}{U-K}$ shares and lend $\frac{U}{U-K}$ dollars.

If $\tau_K^T > \tau_{DU}^T$, then at the first exit time τ_{DU}^T of the corridor (D, U), liquidate the stock bond portfolio for zero. Otherwise, if $\tau_K^T < \tau_{DU}^T$, then at the hitting time τ_K^T, liquidate the stock bond portfolio for one dollar. Since the quadratic variation of M grows without bound, the risk-neutral probability that τ_K^T and τ_{DU}^T are both infinite is zero. This concludes the proof. Q.E.D.

There is a second kind of butterfly spread with a probabilistic interpretation. We first consider the simpler spot starting case. Consider a perpetual claim written on the continuous martingale M satisfying both (12) and (13). Suppose again that the claim pays off at τ_{DU}. For $K \in (D, U)$, suppose that the payoff at time τ_{DU} is the *Local Time* of M at time τ_{DU}. Loosely speaking, the payoff at τ_{DU} accumulates over time twice the instantaneous variance experienced by the process M at K until τ_{DU}:

$$L^M_{\tau_{DU}}(K) \equiv 2\int_0^{\tau_{DU}} \delta(M_t - K)d\langle M\rangle_t. \tag{19}$$

From the Tanaka Meyer formula, the cost of creating this payoff is:

$$\hat{G}(M,K) = \begin{cases} 2\frac{(M-D)(U-K)}{U-D}, & -\infty < D < M < K < U < \infty \\ 2\frac{(K-D)(U-M)}{U-D}, & -\infty < D < K < M < U < \infty. \end{cases} \tag{20}$$

This can be written much more succinctly as:

$$\hat{G}(M,K) = 2\frac{[(M \wedge K) - D]^+[U - (K \vee M)]^+}{U - D}. \tag{21}$$

when graphed against either M or K, the function $\hat{G}$ is flat at zero outside (D, U) and triangular in between. When graphed against M, the kinks are at D,K, and U and the change in slope of $\hat{G}$ at K is two. Again, it is remarkable that the claim can be valued without knowledge of the volatility of M.

To value the forward-start version of the above claim, i.e., the claim paying:

$$2\int_T^{\tau^T_{DU}} \delta(M_t - K)d\langle M\rangle_t \tag{22}$$

at τ^T_{DU}, consider the following butterfly spread payoff:

$$BS_T = 2\frac{[(M_T \wedge K) - D]^+[U - (K \vee M_T)]^+}{U - D}. \tag{23}$$

This payoff can be synthesized by:

1. buying $2\frac{U-K}{U-D}$ puts struck at D
2. selling two puts struck at K
3. buying $2\frac{K-D}{U-D}$ puts struck at U.

The initial cost of forming this butterfly spread is:

$$BS_0 = 2\frac{U-K}{K-D}P_0(D,T) - 2P_0(K,T) + 2\frac{K-D}{U-K}P_0(U,T). \tag{24}$$

Suppose that this butterfly spread is held static to maturity. If $M_T < D$ or $M_T > U$, then the butterfly spread expires worthless. This matches the payoff since we already know at T that local time at K cannot increase from zero without M first hitting D or U.

If $M_T \in (D, U)$, then the payoff at T finances the initial position in the following trading strategy in stocks and bonds conducted over the period (T, τ^T_{DU}).

1. if $M_T \in (D, K]$, be long $2\frac{U-K}{U-D}$ shares and borrow $2\frac{U-K}{U-D}D$ dollars
2. if $M_T \in (K, U)$, be short $2\frac{K-D}{U-D}$ shares and lend $2\frac{K-D}{U-D}U$ dollars.

This strategy is self-financing except when the stock price is near the intermediate strike K. Using the Tanaka Meyer formula, one can show that this strategy generates the increase in the local time from T to τ^T_{DU}.

5. Diffusion Coefficient

So far we have been able to value various perpetual claims relative to either the price of the underlying asset or relative to European options written on that asset. For these claims, we have not needed to know the diffusion coefficient of the underlying asset. To value other kinds of claims (e.g., finite lived ones), it will be useful to examine the diffusion coefficient of S as we will show that it appears in the Jacobian when we develop the transition PDF of S.

To obtain the diffusion coefficient of S, we use Itô's formula on (6):

$$dS_t = \sqrt{2\pi}N'\left(\frac{\sqrt{2\pi}X_t}{H}\right)hdW_t, \qquad t \geq 0, \tag{25}$$

as we already know that S is driftless. Since $N'(\cdot)$ and h are positive, so is the diffusion coefficient of S. Evaluating (5) at X_t and inverting implies:

$$\frac{\sqrt{2\pi}X_t}{H} = N^{-1}\left(\frac{S_t}{H}\right), \tag{26}$$

where $N^{-1}(p) : (0,1) \mapsto \mathbb{R}$ is the inverse of the standard normal CDF. Substituting (26) in (25) gives the SDE followed by S:

$$dS_t = a(S_t)dW_t, \qquad t \geq 0, \tag{27}$$

where the diffusion coefficient (normal volatility) of S is given by:

$$a(S) \equiv \sqrt{2\pi}N'\left(N^{-1}\left(\frac{S}{H}\right)\right)h = e^{-\frac{\left[N^{-1}\left(\frac{S}{H}\right)\right]^2}{2}}h. \tag{28}$$

We note from (27) that S is indeed a time-homogeneous driftless diffusion. The diffusion coefficient given in (28) is proportional to a standard Gaussian function of $N^{-1}\left(\frac{S}{H}\right)$. As a consequence, movements in S become more certain when S is near 0 or H:

$$\lim_{S\downarrow 0} a(S) = 0 \qquad \lim_{S\uparrow H} a(S) = 0. \tag{29}$$

Besides its starting value $S_0 \in (0, H)$, the process S has two free parameters H and h. We have already seen that H defines the right end point of the domain of S. As S fluctuates through $(0, H)$, its volatility $\sqrt{2\pi}N'\left(N^{-1}\left(\frac{S_t}{H}\right)\right)h$ evolves as a positive stochastic process. We now show that h defines the right end point of the latter process' domain.

The standard normal density function $N'(\cdot)$ achieves its maximum value when its argument vanishes. The inverse normal CDF $N^{-1}(p)$ vanishes when its argument is $\frac{1}{2}$. Hence, we conclude that volatility is maximized when $S_t = \frac{H}{2}$, i.e., at the midpoint of its domain $(0, H)$. The maximum value of volatility achieved is:

$$\sqrt{2\pi}N'\left(N^{-1}\left(\frac{1}{2}\right)\right)h = h. \tag{30}$$

Now the standard normal probability density function (PDF) is even about zero which implies that its integral, $N(\cdot)$ is the sum of $1/2$ and a function which is odd about zero. It follows that $N^{-1}(\cdot)$ is odd about $1/2$. Since diffusion coefficient of S is proportional to the composition of the even function $N'(\cdot)$ with the function $N^{-1}(\frac{M}{H})$ of S which is odd about $\frac{H}{2}$, the diffusion coefficient of S is symmetric about $\frac{H}{2}$.

The speed density of a diffusion with scale density $s(x)$ and variance rate $\sigma^2(x)$ is $\frac{1}{\sigma^2(x)s(x)}$. Since S is a process in natural scale, $s(x) = 1$ and its speed density is simply the reciprocal of its variance rate. Hence, (27) implies that the speed density of S is given by:

$$m(S) \equiv \frac{1}{2\pi \left[N'\left(N^{-1}\left(\frac{S}{H}\right)\right)\right]^2 h^2} = \frac{e^{\left[N^{-1}\left(\frac{S}{H}\right)\right]^2}}{h^2}, \qquad S \in (0, H). \tag{31}$$

Let τ_{DU} be the first time that S exits the interval $[D, U]$. Suppose we consider how the mean of the random variable τ_{DU} behaves in the limit as we set $D = S - \epsilon$, $U = S + \epsilon$ and let $\epsilon > 0$ shrink down to zero. Clearly, the mean exit time approaches zero, but the question is at what speed. For a process in natural scale such as S, Karlin and Taylor (1981) show on page 197 that the mean exit time $E[\tau_{(S-\epsilon,S+\epsilon)}|S_0 = S]$ approaches zero like $O(\epsilon^2)$, where the coefficient is given by the speed function $m(S)$, i.e.,

$$m(S) = \lim_{\epsilon \downarrow 0} \frac{E[\tau_{(S-\epsilon,S+\epsilon)}|S_0 = S]}{\epsilon^2}. \tag{32}$$

This is the likely origin of the term "speed density". We note that the higher the diffusion coefficient of a process in natural scale, the lower its speed density. This observation prompted Rogers and Williams (1994) to jestingly suggest that $m(\cdot)$ alternatively be called a "sloth density". As indicated in (31), the speed density of the S process is inversely proportional to a Gaussian function of $N^{-1}\left(\frac{S}{H}\right)$. As a consequence, S exits intervals much more slowly on average when it is near zero or H than when it is near $H/2$.

Recall the rough interpretation of the local time of a continuous martingale as the amount of quadratic variation occurring at a point. More precisely, local time captures the stochastic rate at which the quadratic variation experienced below some point in space increases as we increase the point. Loosely speaking, the speed density of a time homogeneous one dimensional diffusion can be interpreted as the expected *calendar time* spent at a point, until the first time that the diffusion exits an interval. This rough interpretation is meant to be contrasted with the expected *quadratic variation* spent at a point until the first exit. Thus the speed density is used to convert the expected local time of a stochastic process into twice the spatial density of the occupation time.

To illustrate these points, let M now denote a time homogeneous one dimensional diffusion martingale:

$$dM_t = a(M_t)dW_t, \qquad t \geq 0. \tag{33}$$

From (19), the local time at K evaluated at the random time τ_{DU} is:

$$L^M_{\tau_{DU}}(K) \equiv 2\int_0^{\tau_{DU}} \delta(M_t - K)a^2(K)dt. \tag{34}$$

In contrast, twice the density of the occupation time at K until τ_{DU} is:

$$2\int_0^{\tau_{DU}} \delta(M_t - K)dt. \tag{35}$$

From the Tanaka Meyer formula, the cost of creating the payoff in (35) is:

$$G(M,K) = \begin{cases} 2\frac{(M-D)(U-K)}{U-D}m(K), & -\infty < D < M < K < U < \infty \\ 2\frac{(K-D)(U-M)}{U-D}m(K), & -\infty < D < K < M < U < \infty. \end{cases} \tag{36}$$

Itô and McKean (1974) refer to this function as the Green's function. One can generalize by starting with a drifting process, but we do not explore that here. For the bounded Brownian Motion S, substituting (31) in (36) implies:

$$G^S(S,K) = \begin{cases} 2\frac{(S-D)(U-K)}{U-D}\frac{\exp\left\{\left[N^{-1}\left(\frac{S}{H}\right)\right]^2\right\}}{h^2}, & -\infty < D < S < K < U < \infty \\ 2\frac{(K-D)(U-S)}{U-D}\frac{\exp\left\{\left[N^{-1}\left(\frac{S}{H}\right)\right]^2\right\}}{h^2}, & -\infty < D < K < S < U < \infty. \end{cases} \tag{37}$$

6. Transition Density

To obtain the transition PDF of the time-homogeneous Markov process S, we first obtain the transition PDF of the process X. Suppose that we write the stochastic differential equation (SDE) (1) as:

$$dX_t = gX_t dt + h dW_t, \qquad t \geq 0, \tag{38}$$

where:

$$g \equiv \frac{2\pi h^2}{H^2} \geq 0 \tag{39}$$

is the expected relative growth rate in X. By standard calculations, one can show that X_T is Gaussian with mean:

$$E_0^{\mathbb{Q}} X_T = X_0 e^{gT}, \tag{40}$$

and variance:

$$V_x = h^2 \frac{e^{2gT}-1}{2g}. \tag{41}$$

We note that both the mean and the variance of X explode as $T \uparrow \infty$. Both results are a consequence of the fact that the process is mean-repelling, i.e., $g > 0$.

To obtain the PDF of S_T, first recall that the scale function $S_H(x)$ is defined in (5) as an increasing map from $\mathbb{R}$ to $(0, H)$. Let $x(S)$ be the inverse map from $(0, H)$ to $\mathbb{R}$:

$$x(S) \equiv \frac{H}{\sqrt{2\pi}} N^{-1}\left(\frac{S}{H}\right), \qquad S \in (0, H). \tag{42}$$

Since $S_H(\cdot)$ is increasing, so is $x(\cdot)$. In fact, from the inverse function theorem:

$$x'(S) = \frac{1}{S_H'(x)} = \frac{1}{\sqrt{2\pi} N'\left(\frac{\sqrt{2\pi}x}{H}\right)} = \frac{1}{\sqrt{2\pi} N'\left(N^{-1}\left(\frac{S}{H}\right)\right)}, \tag{43}$$

from (5). Using the definition of the standard normal density function $N'(\cdot)$, (43) simplifies to:

$$x'(S) = \exp\left\{\frac{1}{2}\left[N^{-1}\left(\frac{S}{H}\right)\right]^2\right\}, \tag{44}$$

for $S \in (0, H)$.

Let:

$$q(S_0, S; T) \equiv \frac{\mathbb{Q}\{S_T \in dS | S_0\}}{dS}, \qquad S \in (0, H), \tag{45}$$

be the transition PDF of S_T. Also let:

$$g(X_0, x; T) \equiv \frac{\mathbb{Q}\{X_T \in dx\}}{dx} = \frac{e^{-\frac{[x - X_0 e^{gT}]^2}{2V_x}}}{\sqrt{2\pi V_x}}, \qquad x \in \mathbb{R}, \tag{46}$$

be the transition PDF of X_T. By the change of variables theorem for densities:

$$q(S_0, S; T) = g(X_0, x(S); T)|x'(S)|, \qquad S \in (0, H). \tag{47}$$

Substituting (46) and (44) in (47) implies that the PDF of S_T is known in closed form:

$$\begin{aligned} q(S_0, S; T) &= \frac{e^{-\frac{[x(m)-X_0 e^{gT}]^2}{2V_x}}}{\sqrt{2\pi V_x}} e^{\frac{1}{2}[N^{-1}(\frac{S}{H})]^2} \\ &= \frac{e^{-\frac{H^2}{4\pi V_x}\left[N^{-1}(\frac{m}{H})-N^{-1}(\frac{S_0}{H})e^{gT}\right]^2+\frac{1}{2}[N^{-1}(\frac{S}{H})]^2}}{\sqrt{2\pi V_x}}, \qquad S \in (0, H), \end{aligned} \tag{48}$$

from (42), where g and V_x are given in (39) and (41) respectively. Not surprisingly, the horizon length T enters the PDF of S_T only through the mean and variance of X_T.

The future level S enters the PDF of S_T only through the variable $N^{-1}\left(\frac{S}{H}\right)$. When the PDF of S_T is considered as a function of this latter variable, (48) indicates that it is proportional to the ratio of two Gaussian densities. The mean and standard deviation of the numerator Gaussian both increase with T, while the denominator Gaussian is a standard normal PDF. At short maturities, the graph of q against $N^{-1}\left(\frac{S}{H}\right)$ is dominated by the numerator Gaussian. Hence, the graph of q against S is an upside down U. As T increases, the numerator Gaussian tends to a uniform density. Hence, as T increases, the graph of q against $N^{-1}\left(\frac{S}{H}\right)$ tends to the reciprocal of a standard normal PDF.

An abrupt change in the shape of the PDF occurs at the maturity for which:

$$\frac{H^2}{4\pi V_x} = \frac{1}{2}. \tag{49}$$

Using (41), this critical level of T is easily found to be:

$$T^* = \frac{1}{2g} \ln\left(1 + \frac{gH^2}{\pi h^2}\right). \tag{50}$$

For $T < T^*$, the net coefficient of the quadratic in the argument of the exponential is negative. As a result, the graph of q against $N^{-1}\left(\frac{S}{H}\right)$ is Gaussian while the graph of q against S is an upside down U. When $T = T^*$, the coefficient on the quadratic vanishes and the PDF becomes exponential in the variable $N^{-1}\left(\frac{S}{H}\right)$ rather than Gaussian. When $T > T^*$, the coefficient on the quadratic becomes positive. As a result, the graph of q against $N^{-1}\left(\frac{S}{H}\right)$ is the reciprocal of a Gaussian while the graph of q against S is U shaped.

Consider a movie of the graph of the PDF q against the forward spatial variable S. As T increases, all of the probability mass moves out from around S_0 to around zero and around H. Intuitively, since S is a martingale, the mean of S_T must remain constant at S_0 while the variance of S_T must increase with the horizon length T. Since S is bounded, the only way its PDF can accommodate this behavior is to become U shaped in the interior.

Suppose one starts the martingale away from $H/2$ and stops it when it first hits $H/2$. When $S_0 = H/2$, the PDF of S is even in S about $H/2$. As a result, one knows the PDF and absorption probability of the stopped martingale. Hence if one wants a tractable bounded process with a lower natural barrier at zero and an absorbing upper barrier, simply start S in $(0, H/2)$ and stop it when it first hits $H/2$. This would describe the value of the protection leg of a CDO. Conversely, if one wants a tractable bounded process with an upper natural barrier and an absorbing lower barrier, simply start S in $(H/2, H)$ and stop it when it first hits $H/2$. This could describe a variation on the Black and Cox (1976) model for describing the dynamics of the value of a firm's assets when default is possible. Let S be the firm's asset value and suppose that H is a natural upper boundary. As in Black and Cox, we also suppose that default and liquidation occur at the first time that S hits $H/2$. It would be straightforward to value contingent claims written on the stopped process.

It is interesting to compare q with the lognormal PDF. If S is lognormally distributed, then in the lognormal PDF, $\ln(S/1)$ plays the same role as $N^{-1}\left(\frac{S}{H}\right)$ in q. The log function maps $\mathbb{R}^+$ to $\mathbb{R}$, while $N^{-1}(\cdot)$ maps $(0,1)$ to $\mathbb{R}$. Both functions asymptote to $\pm\infty$ at the endpoints of their domain. The standard parametrization of the PDF of geometric Brownian motion expresses the lognormal PDF in terms of the mean and variance of the corresponding drifting Brownian motion. Analogously, the above parametrization of the PDF of bounded Brownian motion expresses the PDF in terms of the mean and variance of the corresponding OU process.

A geometric Brownian martingale has a stability property. Specifically, the probability that the terminal level of the process is below any given positive level approaches one as the time horizon becomes arbitrarily large. We speculate that for bounded Brownian motion, the almost sure convergence is to the union of the two sets $(0,\epsilon)$ and $(H-\epsilon)$ for any $\epsilon > 0$.

Acknowledgments: I thank two anonymous referees at Risks, the editor Albert Cohen, and Roy Demeo, David Eliezer, Alexey Polischuk, Nassim Taleb, and Arun Verma, for comments. They are not responsible for any errors.

Conflicts of Interest: The author declares no conflict of interest.

References

Black, Fischer, and John C. Cox. 1976. Valuing corporate securities: Some effects of bond indenture provisions. *Journal of Finance* 31: 351–67.

Carr, Peter P., and Zura Kakushadze. 2017. FX options in target zones. *Quantitative Finance* 10: 1477–86.

Hui, Cho-Hoi, Chi-Fai Lo, Vincent Yeung, and Laurence Fung. 2008. Valuing foreign currency options with a mean-reverting process: A study of the Hong Kong dollar. *International Journal of Finance and Economics* 13: 118–34.

Ingersoll, Jonathan. 1997. Valuing foreign exchange rate derivatives with a bounded exchange process. *Review of Derivatives Research* 1: 159–81.

Itô, Kiyosi, and Henry McKean. 1974. *Diffusion Processes and Their Sample Paths*. Berlin: Springer.

Jacquier, Antoine, and Saad Slaoui. 2010. Variance dispersion and correlation swaps. *arXiv*. arXiv:1004.0125.

Karlin, Samuel, and Howard Taylor. 1981. *A Second Course in Stochastic Processes*. New York: Academic Press.

Rady, Sven. 1997. Option pricing in the presence of natural boundaries and a quadratic diffusion term. *Finance and Stochastics* 1: 331–44.

Rogers, L. Chris G., and David Williams. 1994. *Diffusions, Markov Processes and Martingales*, 2nd ed. New York: John Wiley & Sons, vol. I.

Taleb, Nassim Nicholas. 2017. Election Predictions as Martingales: An Arbitrage Approach. NYU Tandon School Working Paper. New York, NY, USA: New York University.

risks

MDPI

Article

Actuarial Geometry

Stephen J. Mildenhall

St. John's University, Peter J. Tobin College of Business, 101 Astor Place, New York, NY 10003, USA; mildenhs@stjohns.edu; Tel.:+1-312-961-8781

Academic Editor: Albert Cohen
Received: 12 April 2017; Accepted: 2 June 2017; Published: 16 June 2017

Abstract: The literature on capital allocation is biased towards an asset modeling framework rather than an actuarial framework. The asset modeling framework leads to the proliferation of inappropriate assumptions about the effect of insurance line of business growth on aggregate loss distributions. This paper explains why an actuarial analog of the asset volume/return model should be based on a Lévy process. It discusses the impact of different loss models on marginal capital allocations. It shows that Lévy process-based models provide a better fit to the US statutory accounting data, and identifies how parameter risk scales with volume and increases with time. Finally, it shows the data suggest a surprising result regarding the form of insurance parameter risk.

Keywords: capital; capital allocation; capital determination; diversification; homogeneous; insurance; insurance pricing; Lévy process; parameter risk; risk measure; risk theory

1. Introduction

Geometry is the study of shape and change in shape. Actuarial Geometry[1] studies the shape and evolution of shape of actuarial variables, in particular the distribution of aggregate losses, as portfolio volume and composition changes. It also studies the shape and evolution paths of variables in the space of all risks. Actuarial variables are curved across both a volumetric dimension as well as a temporal dimension. Volume here refers to expected losses per year, x, and temporal to the duration, t, for which a given volume of insurance is written. Total expected losses are xt—just as distance = speed × time. Asset variables are determined by a curved temporal return distribution but are flat in the volumetric (position size) dimension. Risk, and hence economic quantities like capital, are intimately connected to the shape of the distribution of losses, and so actuarial geometry is inextricably linked to capital determination and allocation.

Actuarial geometry is especially important today because risk and probability theory, finance, and actuarial science are converging after prolonged development along separate tracks. There is now general agreement that idiosyncratic insurance risk matters for pricing, and as a result we need to appropriately understand, model, and reflect the volumetric and temporal diversification of insurance risk. These are the central topics of the paper.

The paper makes two research contributions both linked to the use of Lévy processes in actuarial science. The first contribution is theoretical. It is to explain precisely how insurance losses diversify as

[1] Actuarial Geometry was originally presented to the 2006 Risk Theory Seminar in Richmond, Virginia, Mildenhall (2006). This version is largely based on the original, with some corrections and clarifications, as well as more examples to illustrate the theory. Since 2006 the methodology it described has been successfully applied to a very wide variety of global insurance data in Aon Benfield's annual Insurance Risk Study, ABI (2007, 2010, 2012, 2013, 2014, 2015), now in its eleventh edition. The findings have remained overwhelmingly consistent. Academically, the importance of the derivative and the gradient allocation method has been re-confirmed in numerous papers since 2006. Applications of Lévy processes to actuarial science and finance have also greatly proliferated. However, the new literature has not touched on the clarification between "direction" in the space of asset return variables and in the space of actuarial variables presented here.

volume increases and to compute the impact of this diversification compared to an asset portfolio model where risk is independent of position size. In particular we show that even when insurance losses and an asset portfolio have the same distribution of outcomes for a particular volume, the agreement is that of two lines crossing at an angle. It is not a first order tangency and so any risk allocation involving derivatives—which almost all do—will produce different results. The picture we make precise is shown in Figure 1. In the figure k is the distribution of values of an asset portfolio with initial value x, modeled as $k(x) = xX$ for a fixed return variable X. The map m represents aggregate losses from an insurance portfolio with expected losses x. Even though $X = m(1) = k(1)$ the tangent vector, $\dot{m}(1)$, to the embedding m at $x = 1$ is not the same as the tangent vector $\dot{k}(1)$. We have drawn m as a straight line because it will naturally capture the idea of "growth in the direction X". The full rationale behind Figure 1 is described in Section 6.

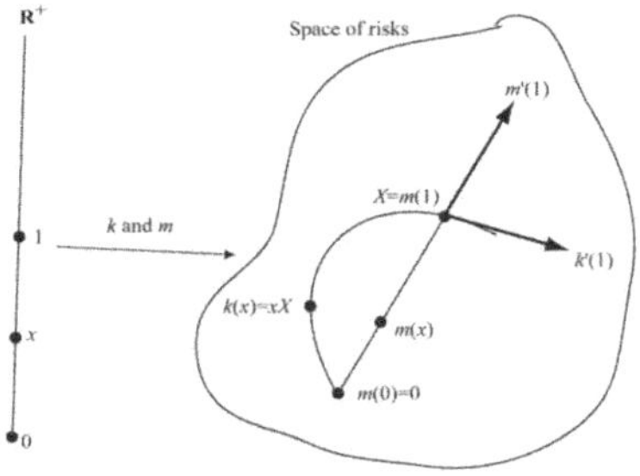

Figure 1. Lévy process and homogeneous embeddings of $\mathbb{R}_+$ into the space of risks, **L**. The Lévy process embedding corresponds to the straight line m and the asset embedding to the curved line k.

The second contribution is empirical. It uses US statutory accounting data to determine a Lévy process based model for insurance losses by line of business that reflects their observed volumetric and temporal properties. The analysis compares four potential models and determines that only one is consistent with the data. The analysis produces specific line of business measures of non-diversifiable parameter risk that vary substantially but that have been consistent over time. It also provides an explicit form for the distribution of parameter risk, even though parameter risk cannot be directly observed. Most papers on risk measures take the actual distribution of losses as given. And much work done by companies to quantify risk is regarded as proprietary and is not published. The explicit quantification we provide should therefore be useful as a benchmark for both academics and practicing actuaries.

The remainder of the paper is organized as follows.

Section 2 describes the how actuaries and academics came to agree, over the last century, that idiosyncratic insurance risk matters for pricing. This agreement provides an important motivation for our theoretical and empirical work.

Section 3 defines a risk measure and explains how the allocation problem naturally leads to the derivative and gradient of a risk measure.

Section 4 presents two motivating examples that it is instructive to keep in mind through the rest of the paper, and which also illustrate Figure 1.

Section 5 defines Lévy processes and gives some basic examples. It then defines four Lévy process-based loss models that will be used as candidate models for aggregate losses, as well as an alternative asset-based model, and it establishes some of their basic properties.

Section 6 is the technical heart of the paper. It investigates the definition of derivative for a real function and considers how it could be defined on more general spaces, such as the space of random variables. It explains how Lévy processes can be used to define "direction" and how the infinitesimal generator of a Lévy process relates to derivatives. This allows us to pin-point the difference between the derivatives of an insurance process and of an asset process.

Section 7 is contains all the empirical results in the paper. It shows how we can effectively quantify parameter risk, even though it cannot be observed directly. It then determines the amount and shape of parameter risk across many lines of business. Finally, it addresses the differences between temporal and volumetric growth.

The paper covers topics from a variety of viewpoints befitting an article in this special edition celebrating the connections between actuarial science and mathematical finance. As a result it is quite long. Readers more interested in the theoretical findings can focus on Sections 4, 5.1, 5.2 and 6. Readers more interested in the empirical analysis can focus on Sections 5.1, 5.2 and 7.

2. Why Idiosyncratic Insurance Risk Matters

In its early years property-casualty actuarial science in the US largely ignored risk theory in rate making because of the dominance of bureau-based rates. Property rates were made to include a 5% profit provision and a 1% contingency provision; they were priced to a 94% combined ratio Magrath (1958). Lange (1966) describes a 5% provision for underwriting and contingencies as "constant for all liability insurance lines in most states". Kallop (1975) states that a 2.5% profit and contingency allowance for workers' compensation has been in use for at least 25 years and that it "contemplates additional profits from other sources to realize an adequate rate level". The higher load for property lines was justified by the possibility of catastrophic losses—meaning large conflagration losses rather than today's meaning of hurricane or earthquake related, severity driven events.

Regulators and actuaries started to consider improvements to these long-standing conventions in the late 1960s. Bailey (1967) introduced actuaries to the idea of including investment income in profit. Ferrari (1968) was the first actuarial paper to include investment income and to consider return on investor equity as well as margin on premium. During the following dozen years actuaries developed the techniques needed to include investment income in ratemaking. At the same time, finance began to consider how to determine a fair rate of return on insurance capital. The theoretical results they derived, summarized as of 1987 in Cummins and Harrington (1987), focused on the use of discounted cash flow models using CAPM-derived discount rates for each cash flow, including taxes. Since CAPM only prices systematic risk, a side-effect of the financial work was to de-emphasize details of the distribution of ultimate losses in setting the profit provision.

At the same time option and contingent claim theoretic methods, (Doherty and Garven 1986; Cummins 1988), were developed as another approach to determining fair premiums. Interest in option theoretic models was motivated in part by the difficulty of computing appropriate βs. These papers applied powerful results from option pricing theory using a geometric Brownian motion to model losses, possibly with a jump component. Cummins and Phillips (2000) and D'Arcy and Doherty (1988) contain a summary of the CAPM and contingent claims approaches from a finance perspective and D'Arcy and Dyer (1997) contains a more actuarial view.

The CAPM-based theories failed to explain the observed fact that insurance companies charged for specific risk. A series of papers, beginning in the early 1990s, developed a theoretical explanation of this based around agency, taxation and regulatory costs of capital, certainty in capital budgeting, costly external capital for opaque intermediaries, contracting under asymmetric information, and adverse selection, see Cummins (2000); Froot and O'Connell (2008); Froot and Stein (1998); Froot et al. (1993); Froot (2007); Merton and Perold (2001); Perold (2001); Zanjani (2002).

At the same time banking regulation led to the development of robust risk measures and an axiomatic theory of risk measures, including the idea of a coherent measure of risk Artzner et al. (1999). Risk measures are sensitive to the particulars of idiosyncratic firm risk, unlike the CAPM-based pricing methods which are only concerned with systemic risks.

The next step was to develop a theory of product pricing for a multiline insurance company within the context of costly firm-specific risk and robust risk measures. This proceeded down two paths. Phillips et al. (1998) considered pricing in a multiline insurance company from a complete-market option theoretic perspective, modeling losses with a geometric Brownian motion and without allocating capital. They were concerned with the effect of firm-wide insolvency risk on individual policy pricing.

The second path, based around explicit allocation of capital, was started by Myers and Read (2001). They also worked in a complete market setting and used expected default value as a risk measure, determined surplus allocations by line, and presented a gradient vector, Euler theorem based allocation assuming volumetrically homogeneous losses—but making no other distributional assumptions. This thread was continued by Tasche (1999), Denault (2001) and Fischer (2003). Sherris (2006) takes the view that, in a complete market setting, only the default put has a canonical allocation and that there is no natural allocation of the remaining capital—a view echoed by Gründl and Schmeiser (2007). Kalkbrener (2005) and Delbaen (2000a) used directional derivatives to clarify the relationship between risk measures and allocations.

Concepts from banking regulation, including an own risk solvency assessment, have been adopted by insurance regulators and have led to increased academic interest in technical aspects of risk measurement, capital allocation and risk based pricing. A focus on catastrophe reinsurance pricing following the US hurricanes of 2004 and 2005 and the development of a robust capital market alternative to traditional reinsurance has also motivated research. As a result there is now a very rich literature around this nexus, including the following.

- Technical and axiomatic characterization of risk measures: (Dhaene et al. 2003; Furman and Zitikis 2008; Laeven and Stadje 2013).
- Capital allocation and its relationship with risk measurement: (Dhaene et al. 2003; Venter et al. 2006; Bodoff 2009; Buch and Dorfleitner 2008; Dhaene et al. 2012; Erel et al. 2015; Furman and Zitikis 2008; Powers 2007; Tsanakas 2009).
- The connection between purpose and method in capital allocation: (Dhaene et al. 2008; Zanjani 2010; Bauer and Zanjani 2013b; Goovaerts et al. 2010).
- Questioning the need for capital allocation in pricing: Gründl and Schmeiser 2007.

Recent summaries include Venter (2009) and Bauer and Zanjani (2013a).

With the confluence of these different theoretical threads, and, in particular, in light of the importance of firm-specific risk to insurance pricing, the missing link—and the link considered in this paper—is a careful examination of the underlying actuarial loss distribution assumptions. Unlike traditional static distribution-based pricing models, such as standard deviation and utility, modern marginal and differential methods require explicit *volumetric* and *temporal* components. The volumetric and temporal geometry are key to the differential calculations required to perform risk and capital allocations. All of the models used in the papers cited are, implicitly or explicitly, volumetrically homogeneous and geometrically flat in one dimension. For example, in a geometric Brownian motion model losses at time t are of the form $S_t = S_0 \exp(\mu t + \sigma B_t)$ where B_t is a Brownian motion. Changing volume, S_0, simply scales the whole distribution and does not affect the shape of the random component. The jump-diffusion model in Cummins (1988) is of the same form. There are essentially no other explicit loss models in the papers cited. Mildenhall (2004) and Meyers (2005b) show volumetric homogeneity is not an appropriate assumption. This paper provides further evidence and uses insurance regulatory data to explore more appropriate models.

3. Risk Measures, Risk Allocation and the Ubiquitous Gradient

3.1. Definition and Examples of Risk Measures

A risk measure, ρ, is a real valued function defined on a space of risks $\mathbf{L} = L^0(\Omega, \mathcal{F}, \mathbb{P})$. Here Ω is the sample space, $\mathcal{F}$ is a sigma-algebra of subsets of Ω, and $\mathbb{P}$ is a probability measure on $\mathcal{F}$. The space L^0 consists of all real valued random variables, that is, measurable functions $X : \Omega \to \mathbb{R}$, defined up to equivalence (identify random variables which differ on a set of measure zero). As Delbaen (2000b) points out there are only two L^p spaces which are invariant under equivalent measures, L^0 and L^∞, the space of all essentially bounded random variables. Since it is desirable to work with a space invariant under change of equivalent measure, but not to be restricted to bounded variables, we work with L^0. Kalkbrener (2005) works on L^0. Risk measures are a large and important topic, but their details are not central this paper. For more details see Föllmer and Schied (2011) and Dhaene et al. (2006).

Given a risk $X \in \mathbf{L}$, $\rho(X)$ is the amount of capital required to support the risk. Examples of risk measures include value at risk at a percentile α (the inverse of the distribution of X, defined as $\inf\{x \mid \Pr(X \leq x) \geq \alpha\}$), tail value at risk (the average of the worst $1-\alpha$ outcomes), and standard deviation $\rho(X) = \alpha \mathrm{SD}(X)$.

3.2. Allocation and the Gradient

At the firm level, total risk X can be broken down into a sum of parts X_i corresponding to different lines of business. Since it is costly for insurers to hold capital Froot and O'Connell (2008) it is natural to ask for an attribution of total capital $\rho(X)$ to each line X_i. One way to do this is to consider the effect of a marginal change in the volume of line i on total capital. For example, if the marginal profit from line i divided by the marginal change in total capital resulting from a small change in volume in line i exceeds the average profit margin of the firm then it makes sense to expand line i. This is a standard economic optimization that has been discussed in the insurance context by many authors including Tasche (1999), Myers and Read (2001), Denault (2001), Meyers (2005b) and Fischer (2003).

The need to understand marginal capital leads us to consider

$$\frac{\partial \rho}{\partial X_i} \tag{1}$$

which, in a sense to be made precise, represents the change in ρ as a result of a change in the volume of line i, or more generally the gradient vector of ρ representing the change across all lines. Much of this paper is an examination of exactly what this equation means.

Tasche (1999) shows that the gradient vector of the risk measure ρ is the only vector suitable for performance measurement, in the sense that it gives the correct signals to grow or shrink a line of business based on its marginal profitability and marginal capital consumption. Tasche's framework is unequivocally financial. He considers a set of basis asset return variables X_i, $i = 1, \dots, n$ and then determines a portfolio as a vector of asset position sizes $x = (x_1, \dots, x_n) \in U \subset \mathbb{R}^n$. The portfolio value distribution corresponding to x is simply

$$X(x) = X(x_1, \dots, x_n) = \sum_{i=1}^{n} x_i X_i. \tag{2}$$

A risk measure on $\mathbf{L}$ induces a function $\rho : \mathbb{R}^n \to \mathbb{R}$, $\rho(x_1, \dots, x_n) \mapsto \rho(\sum_i x_i X_i)$. Rather than being defined on a space of random variables, the induced ρ is defined on (a subset of) Euclidean space $\mathbb{R}^n$ using the correspondence between x and a portfolio. In this context $\partial\rho/\partial X_i$ is simply the usual limit

$$\frac{\partial \rho}{\partial x_i} = \lim_{\epsilon \to 0} \frac{\rho(x_1, \dots, x_i + \epsilon, \dots, x_n) - \rho(x_1, \dots, x_n)}{\epsilon}. \tag{3}$$

Equation (3) is a powerful mathematical notation and it contains two implicit assumptions. First, the fact that we can write $x_i + \epsilon$ requires that we can add in the domain. If ρ were defined on a more general space this may not possible—or it may involve the convolution of measures rather than addition of real numbers. Second, and more importantly, adding ϵ to x in the ith coordinate unambiguously corresponds to an increase "in the direction" of the ith asset. This follows directly from the definition in Equation (2) and is unquestionably correct in a financial context.

Numerous papers work in an asset/volume model framework, either because they are working with assets or as a simplification of the real insurance world, for example (Myers and Read 2001; Panjer 2001; Erel et al. 2015; Fischer 2003). The resulting risk process homogeneity is essential to all Euler-based "adds-up" results: in fact the two are equivalent for homogeneous risk measures (Mildenhall 2004; Tasche 2004). However, it is important to realize that risk can be measured appropriately with a homogeneous risk measure, that is one satisfying $\rho(\lambda X) = \lambda\rho(X)$, even if the risk process itself is not homogeneous, that is $X(\lambda x) \neq \lambda X(x)$. The compound Poisson process and Brownian motion are examples of non-homogeneous processes.

In order to consider alternatives to the asset/return framework, we now discuss the meaning of the differential and examine other possible definitions. The differential represents the best linear approximation to a function at a particular point in a given direction. Thus the differential to a function f, at a point x in its domain, can be regarded as a linear map Df_x which takes a direction, i.e., a tangent vector at x, to a direction at $f(x)$. Under appropriate assumptions, the differential of f at $\mathbf{x}$ in direction $\mathbf{v}$, $D_{\mathbf{x}}f(\mathbf{v})$, is defined by the property

$$\lim_{\mathbf{v}\to\mathbf{0}} \frac{\|f(\mathbf{x}+\mathbf{v}) - f(\mathbf{x}) - D_{\mathbf{x}}f(\mathbf{v})\|}{\|\mathbf{v}\|} = 0, \tag{4}$$

see Abraham et al. (1988) or Borwein and Vanderwerff (2010). The vector $\mathbf{v}$ is allowed to tend to $\mathbf{0}$ from any direction, and Equation (4) must hold for all of them. This is called Fréchet differentiability. There are several weaker forms of differentiability defined by restricting the convergence of $\mathbf{v}$ to $\mathbf{0}$. These include the Gâteaux differential, where $\mathbf{v} = t\mathbf{w}$ with $t \in \mathbb{R}$, $t \to 0$, the directional differential, where $\mathbf{v} = t\mathbf{w}$ with $t \in \mathbb{R}$, $t \downarrow 0$, and the Dini differential, where $\mathbf{v} = t\mathbf{w}'$ for $t \in \mathbb{R}$, $t \downarrow 0$, and $\mathbf{w}' \to \mathbf{w}$. The function $f(x,y) = 2x^2y/(x^4+y^4)$ if $(x,y) \neq (0,0)$ and $f(0,0) = 0$ is not differentiable at $(0,0)$, in fact it is not even continuous, but all directional derivatives exist at $(0,0)$, and f is Gâteaux differentiable. The Gâteaux differential need not be linear in its direction argument.

Kalkbrener (2005) applied Gâteaux differentiability to capital allocation. The Gâteaux derivative can be computed without choosing a set of basis asset return-like variables, that is without setting up a map from $\mathbb{R}^n \to \mathbf{L}$, provided it is possible to add in the domain. This is the case for $\mathbf{L}$ because we can add random variables. The Gâteaux derivative of ρ at $Y \in \mathbf{L}$ in the direction $X \in \mathbf{L}$ is defined as

$$\frac{\partial\rho}{\partial X} = D\rho_Y(X) = \lim_{\epsilon\to 0} \frac{\rho(Y+\epsilon X) - \rho(Y)}{\epsilon}. \tag{5}$$

Kalkbrener shows that if the risk measure ρ satisfies certain axioms then it can be associated with a unique capital allocation. He shows that the allocation is covariance-based if risk is measured using standard deviation and a conditional measure approach when risk is measured by expected shortfall—so his method is very natural.

We have shown that notions of differentiability are central to capital allocation. The next section will present two archetypal examples and that show the asset/return and insurance notions of growth do not agree, setting up the need for a better understanding of "direction" for actuarial random variables. We will see that Lévy processes provide that understanding.

4. Two Motivating Examples

This section presents two examples illustrating the difference between an asset/return model and a realistic insurance growth model.

Let $X(u)$ be a Poisson random variable with mean u. Consider two functions, $k(u) = uX(1)$ and $m(u) = X(u)$. The function k defines a random variable with mean u and standard deviation u. The function m also defines a random variable with has mean u, but it has standard deviation $u^{1/2}$. The variable k defines a homogeneous family, that is $k(\lambda u) = \lambda k(u)$, and correctly models the returns from a portfolio of size u in an asset with an (unlikely) Poisson(1) asset return distribution. The variable m is more realistic for a growing portfolio of insurance risks with expected annual claim count u.

If we measure risk using the standard deviation risk measure $\rho(X) = \mathrm{SD}(X)$, this example shows that although $k(1) = m(1) = \mathrm{Poisson}(1)$ have the same distribution the marginal risk for k is $\partial\rho(k(u))/\partial u = 1$ whereas the marginal risk for m is $\partial\rho(m(u))/\partial u = 1/(2u^{1/2})$. For m risk decreases as volume increases owing to portfolio effects whereas for k there is no diversification.

Next we present a more realistic example, due to Meyers (2005a), where Kalkbrener's "axiomatic" allocation produces a different result than a marginal business written approach that is based on a more actuarial set of assumptions. Meyers calls his approach "economic" since it is motivated by the marginal increase in business philosophy discussed in Section 3.2. This example has also been re-visited recently by Boonen et al. (2017).

In order to keep the notation as simple as possible the example works with $n = 2$ independent lines of business and allocates capital to line 1 . The risk measure is standard deviation $\rho(X) = \mathrm{SD}(X)$ for $X \in \mathbf{L}$. Losses $X_i(x_i)$ are modeled with a mixed compound Poisson variable

$$X_i(x_i) = S_{i,1} + \cdots + S_{i,N_i(x_i)} \tag{6}$$

where $N_i = N_i(x_i)$ is a C_i-mixed Poisson, so the conditional distribution $N \mid C_i$ is Poisson with mean $x_i C_i$ and the mixing distribution C_i has mean 1 and variance c_i. Meyers calls c_i the contagion. The mixing distributions are often taken to be gamma variables, in which case each N_i has a negative binomial distribution. The $S_{i,j}$, $i = 1,2$ are independent, identically distributed severity random variables. For simplicity, assume that $\mathrm{E}(S_i) = 1$, so that $\mathrm{E}(X_i(x_i)) = \mathrm{E}(N_i(x_i))\mathrm{E}(S_i) = x_i$. Since $t = 1$ the model only considers volumetric diversification and not temporal diversification.

We can compute $\rho(X_i(x_i))$ as follows:

$$\begin{aligned}
\rho(X_i(x_i))^2 &= \mathrm{Var}(X_i(x_i))\\
&= \mathrm{Var}(N_i)\mathrm{E}(S_i)^2 + \mathrm{E}(N_i)\mathrm{Var}(S_i)\\
&= x_i(1 + c_i x_i) + x_i(\mathrm{E}(S_i^2) - 1)\\
&= c_i x_i^2 + x_i \mathrm{E}(S_i^2)\\
&= c_i x_i^2 + g_i x_i
\end{aligned}$$

where $g_i = \mathrm{E}(S_i^2)$. Note that $\rho(kX) = k\rho(X)$ for any constant k.

Kalkbrener's axiomatic capital is computed using the Gâteaux directional derivative. Let $\rho_i(x_i) = \rho(X_i(x_i))$ and note that $\rho((1+\epsilon)X_i(x_i)) = (1+\epsilon)\rho_i(x_i)$. Then, by definition and the independence of X_1 and X_2, the Gâteaux derivative of ρ at $X_1(x_1) + X_2(x_2)$ in the direction $X_1(x_1)$ is

$$\begin{aligned}
\frac{\partial\rho}{\partial X_1} &= \lim_{\epsilon\to 0} \frac{\rho(X_1(x_1) + X_2(x_2) + \epsilon X_1(x_1)) - \rho(X_1(x_1) + X_2(x_2))}{\epsilon}\\
&= \lim_{\epsilon\to 0} \frac{\sqrt{(1+\epsilon)^2\rho_1(x_1)^2 + \rho_2(x_2)^2} - \sqrt{\rho_1(x_1)^2 + \rho_2(x_2)^2}}{\epsilon}\\
&= \frac{\rho_1(x_1)^2}{\rho(X_1(x_1) + X_2(x_2))}\\
&= \frac{c_1 x_1^2 + g_1 x_1}{\rho(X_1(x_1) + X_2(x_2))}.
\end{aligned} \tag{7}$$

This whole calculation has been performed without picking an asset return basis, but it can be replicated if we do. Specifically, use the $X_i(x_i)$ as a basis and define a linear map of $\mathbb{R}$-vector spaces $k : \mathbb{R}^n \to \mathbf{L}$, by $(y_1, \ldots, y_n) \mapsto \sum_i y_i X_i(x_i)$. Let ρ_k be the composition of k and ρ,

$$\rho_k(y_1, \ldots, y_n) = \rho(k(y_1, \ldots, y_n)) = \rho\Big(\sum_i y_i X_i(x_i)\Big)$$
$$= \sqrt{\sum_i y_i^2 (c_i x_i^2 + g_i x_i)}.$$

Then

$$\left.\frac{\partial \rho_k}{\partial y_1}\right|_{(1,1)} = \frac{c_1 x_1^2 + g_1 x_1}{\rho(X_1(x_1) + X_2(x_2))} \tag{8}$$

agreeing with Equation (7). It is important to remember that $yX_i(x_i) \neq X_i(yx_i)$ for $y \neq 1$.

Given the definition of $X_i(x_i)$, we can also define an embedding $m : \mathbb{R}^n \to \mathbf{L}$, by $(x_1, \ldots, x_n) \mapsto \sum_i X_i(x_i)$. The map m satisfies $m(x+y) = m(x) + m(y)$ but it is *not* a linear map of real vector spaces because $m(kx) \neq km(x)$. In fact, the image of m will generally be an infinite dimensional real vector subspace of $\mathbf{L}$. The lack of homogeneity is precisely what produces a diversification effect. As explained in Section 3.2, an economic view of capital requires an allocation proportional to the gradient vector at the margin. Thus capital is proportional to $x_i \partial \rho_m / \partial x_i$ where $\rho_m : \mathbb{R}^n \to \mathbb{R}$ is the composition of m and ρ,

$$\rho_m(x_1, x_2) = \rho(m(x_1, x_2)) = \sqrt{\sum_i c_i x_i^2 + g_i x_i}. \tag{9}$$

Since $\rho_m : \mathbb{R}^2 \to \mathbb{R}$ a real function, we can compute its partial derivative using standard calculus:

$$\frac{\partial \rho_m}{\partial x_1} = \frac{2c_1 x_1 + g_1}{2\rho(X_1(x_1) + X_2(x_2))}. \tag{10}$$

There are two important conclusion: (1) the partial derivatives of ρ_m and ρ_k (which is also the Gâteaux derivative of ρ) give different answers, Equations (7) and (10), and (2) the implied allocations

$$\frac{c_1 x_1^2 + g_1 x_1}{\rho(X_1(x_1) + X_2(x_2))} \quad \text{and} \quad \frac{c_1 x_1^2 + g_1 x_1/2}{\rho(X_1(x_1) + X_2(x_2))} \tag{11}$$

are also different. This is Meyers' example.

5. Lévy process Models of Insurance Losses

We define Lévy processes and discuss some of their important properties. We then introduce four models of insurance risk which we will analyze in the rest of the paper.

5.1. Definition and Basic Properties of Lévy processes

Lévy processes are fundamental to actuarial science, but they are rarely discussed explicitly in basic actuarial text books. For example, there is no explicit mention of Lévy processes in Bowers et al. (1986); Beard et al. (1969); Daykin et al. (1994); Klugman et al. (1998); Panjer and Willmot (1992). However, the fundamental building block of all Lévy processes, the compound Poisson process, is well known to actuaries. It is instructive to learn about Lévy processes in an abstract manner as they provide a very rich source of examples for modeling actuarial processes. There are many good textbooks covering the topics described here, including Feller (1971) volume 2, Breiman (1992), Stroock (1993), Bertoin (1996), Sato (1999), and Barndorff-Nielsen et al. (2001), and Applebaum (2004).

Definition 1. *A Lévy process is a stochastic process $X(t)$ defined on a probability space $(\Omega, \mathcal{F}, \mathbb{P})$ satisfying*

LP1. $X(0) = 0$ *almost surely;*
LP2. X *has independent increments, so for* $0 \leq t_1 \leq \cdots \leq t_{n+1}$ *the variables* $X(t_{j+1}) - X(t_j)$ *are independent;*
LP3. X *has stationary increments, so* $X(t_{j+1}) - X(t_j)$ *has the same distribution as* $X(t_{j+1} - t_j)$*; and*
LP4. X *is stochastically continuous, so for all* $a > 0$ *and* $s \geq 0$

$$\lim_{t \to s} \Pr(|X(t) - X(s)| > a) = 0. \tag{12}$$

Based on the definition it is clear that the sum of two Lévy processes is a Lévy process. Lévy processes are in one-to-one correspondence with the set of infinitely divisible distributions, where X is infinitely divisible if, for all integers $n \geq 1$, there exist independent, identically distributed random variables Y_i so that X has the same distribution as $Y_1 + \cdots + Y_n$. If $X(t)$ is a Lévy process then $X(1)$ is infinitely divisible since $X(1) = X(1/n) + (X(2/n) - X(1/n)) + \cdots + (X(1) - X(n-1/n))$, and conversely if X is infinitely divisible there is a Lévy process with $X(1) = X$. In an idealized world, insurance losses should follow an infinitely divisible distribution because annual losses are the sum of monthly, weekly, daily, or hourly losses. Bühlmann Bühlmann (1970) discusses infinitely divisible distributions and their relationship with compound Poisson processes. The Poisson, normal, lognormal, gamma, Pareto, and Student t distributions are infinitely divisible; the uniform is not infinitely divisible, nor is any distribution with finite support, nor any whose moment generating function takes the value zero, see Sato (1999).

Example 1 (Trivial process). $X(t) = kt$ *for a constant* k *is a trivial Lévy process.*

Example 2 (Poisson process). *The Poisson process* $N(t)$ *with intensity* λ *has*

$$\Pr(N(t) = n) = \frac{(\lambda t)^n}{n!} e^{-\lambda t} \tag{13}$$

for $n = 0, 1, \ldots$ *is a Lévy process.*

Example 3 (Compound Poisson process). *The compound Poisson process* $X(t)$ *with severity component* Z *is defined as*

$$X(t) = Z_1 + \cdots + Z_{N(t)} \tag{14}$$

where $N(t)$ *is a Poisson process with intensity* λ*. The compound Poisson processes is the fundamental building block of Lévy processes in the sense that any infinitely divisible distribution is the limit distribution of a sequence of compound Poisson distributions, see Sato (1999) Corollary 8.8*

Example 4 (Brownian motion). *Brownian motion is an example of a continuous Lévy process.*

Example 5 (Operational time). *Lundberg introduced the notion of operational time transforms in order to maintain stationary increments for compound Poisson distributions. Operational time is a risk-clock which runs faster or slower in order to keep claim frequency constant. It allows seasonal and daily effects (rush hours, night-time lulls, etc.) without losing stationary increments. Operational time is an increasing function* $\tau : [0, \infty) \to [0, \infty)$ *chosen so that* $X(\tau(t))$ *becomes a Lévy process.*

Example 6 (Subordination). *Let* $X(t)$ *be a Lévy process and let* $Z(t)$ *be a subordinator, that is, a Lévy process with non-decreasing paths. Then* $Y(t) = X(Z(t))$ *is also a Lévy process. This process is called subordination and* Y *is subordinate to* X*.* Z *is called the directing process.* Z *is a random operational time.*

The characteristic function of a random variable X with distribution μ is defined as $\phi(z) = \mathrm{E}(e^{izX}) = \int e^{izx} \mu(dx)$ for $z \in \mathbb{R}$. The characteristic function of a Poisson variable with mean λ is $\phi(z) = \exp(\lambda(e^{iz} - 1))$. The characteristic function of a compound Poisson process $X(t) = Z_1 + \cdots + Z_{N(t)}$ is

$$\phi(z) = \mathrm{E}(e^{izX(t)}) = \mathrm{E}(\mathrm{E}(e^{izX(t)} \mid N(t))) \tag{15}$$

$$= \mathrm{E}\exp\left(N(t)\log\int e^{izw}\nu(dw)\right) \tag{16}$$

$$= \exp\left(\lambda t\int(e^{izw} - 1)\nu(dw)\right) \tag{17}$$

where ν is the distribution of severity Z_i. The characteristic equation of a normal random variable is $\phi(z) = \exp(i\mu z - \sigma^2 z^2/2)$.

We now quote an important result in the theory of Lévy processes that allows us to identify an infinitely divisible distribution, and hence a Lévy process, with a measure ν on $\mathbb{R}$, and two constants $\sigma > 0$ and γ.

Theorem 1 (Lévy-Khintchine). *If the probability distribution μ is infinitely divisible then its characteristic function has the form*

$$\exp\left(-\sigma^2 z^2 + \int_{\mathbb{R}}(e^{izw} - 1 - izw1_{\{|w|\le 1\}}(w))\nu(dw) + i\gamma z\right) \tag{18}$$

where ν is a measure on $\mathbb{R}$ satisfying $\nu(0) = 0$ and $\int_{\mathbb{R}}\min(|w|^2, 1)\nu(dw) < \infty$, and $\sigma > 0, \gamma \in \mathbb{R}$. The representation by (σ, ν, γ) is unique. Conversely given any such triple (σ, ν, γ) there exists a corresponding infinitely divisible distribution.

See Breiman (1992) or Sato (1999) a proof. In Equation (18), σ is the standard deviation of a Brownian motion component, and ν is called the Lévy measure. The indicator function $1_{\{|w|\le 1\}}$ is present for technical convergence reasons and is only needed when there are a very large number of very small jumps. If $\int_{-1}^{1}\min(|w|, 1)\nu(dw) < \infty$ it can be omitted and the resulting γ can be interpreted as a drift. In the general case γ does not have a clear meaning as it is impossible to separate drift from small jumps. The indicator can therefore also be omitted if $\nu(\mathbb{R}) < \infty$, and in that case the inner integral can be written as

$$\nu(\mathbb{R})\int_{\mathbb{R}}(e^{izw} - 1)\tilde{\nu}(dw) \tag{19}$$

where $\tilde{\nu} = \nu/\nu(\mathbb{R})$ is a distribution. Comparing with Equation (17) shows this term corresponds to a compound Poisson process.

The triples (σ, ν, γ) in the Lévy-Khintchine formula are called Lévy triples. The Lévy process $X(t)$ corresponding to the Lévy triple (σ, ν, γ) has triple $(t\sigma, t\nu, t\gamma)$.

The Lévy-Khintchine formula helps characterize all subordinators. A subordinator must have a Lévy triple $(0, \nu, \gamma)$ with no diffusion component (because Brownian motions take positive and negative values) and the Lévy measure ν must satisfy $\nu((-\infty, 0)) = 0$, i.e., have no negative jumps, and $\int_0^\infty \min(x, 1)\nu(dx) < \infty$. In particular, there are no non-trivial continuous increasing Lévy processes.

The insurance analog of an asset return portfolio basis becomes a set of Lévy processes representing losses in each line of business and "line" becomes synonymous with the Lévy measure that describes the frequency and severity of the jumps, i.e., of the losses. Unless the Lévy process has an infinite number of small jumps the Lévy measure can be separated into a frequency component and a severity component. Patrik et al. (1999) describes modeling with Lévy measures, which the authors call a loss frequency curve.

5.2. Four Temporal and Volumetric Insurance Loss Models

We now define four models describing how the total insured loss random variable evolves volumetrically and temporally. Let the random variable $A(x,t)$ denote aggregate losses from a line with expected annual loss x that is insured for a time period t years. Thus $A(x,1)$ is the distribution of annual losses. The central question of the paper is to describe appropriate models for $A(x,t)$ as x and t vary. A Lévy process $X(t)$ provides the appropriate basis for modeling $A(x,t)$. We consider four alternative insurance models.

IM1. $A(x,t) = X(xt)$. This model assumes there is no difference between insuring given insureds for a longer period of time and insuring more insureds for a shorter period.

IM2. $A(x,t) = X(xZ(t))$, for a subordinator $Z(t)$ with $\mathrm{E}(Z(t)) = t$. Z is an increasing Lévy process which measures random operational time, rather than calendar time. It allows for systematic time-varying contagion effects, such as weather patterns, inflation and level of economic activity, affecting all insureds. Z could be a deterministic drift or it could combine a deterministic drift with a stochastic component.

IM3. $A(x,t) = X(xCt)$, where C is a mean 1 random variable capturing heterogeneity and non-diversifiable parameter risk across an insured population of size x. C could reflect different underwriting positions by firm, which drive systematic and permanent differences in results. The variable C is sometimes called a mixing variable.

IM4. $A(x,t) = X(xCZ(t))$.

All models assume severity has been normalized so that $\mathrm{E}(A(x,t)) = xt$. Two other models suggested by symmetry, $A(x,t) = X(Z(xt))$ and $A(x,t) = X(Z(xCt))$, are already included in this list because $X(Z(t))$ is also a Lévy process.

An important statistic describing the behavior of $A(x,t)$ is the coefficient of variation

$$v(x,t) := \frac{\sqrt{\mathrm{Var}(A(x,t))}}{xt}. \tag{20}$$

Since insurance is based on the notion of diversification, the behavior of $v(x,t)$ as $x \to \infty$ and as $t \to \infty$ are both of interest. The variance of a Lévy process either grows with t or is infinite for all t. If $X(\cdot)$ has a variance, then for IM1, $v(x,t) \propto (xt)^{-1/2} \to 0$ as t or $x \to \infty$ or as $t \to \infty$

Definition 2. *For $v(x,t)$ in Equation (20):*

1. *If $v(x,t) \to 0$ as $t \to \infty$ we will call $A(x,t)$ temporally diversifying.*
2. *If $v(x,t) \to 0$ as $x \to \infty$ we will call $A(x,t)$ volumetrically diversifying.*
3. *A process which is both temporally and volumetrically diversifying will be called diversifying.*

If $X(x)$ is a standard compound Poisson process whose severity component has a variance then IM1 is diversifying.

Models IM1-4 are all very different to the asset model

AM1. $A(x,t) = xX(t)$

where $X(t)$ is a return process, often modeled using a geometric Brownian motion (Hull 1983; Karatzas and Shreve 1988). AM1 is obviously volumetrically homogeneous, meaning $A(kx,t) = kA(x,t)$. Therefore it has no volumetric diversification effect whatsoever, since $\Pr(A(kx,t) \le ky) = \Pr(A(x,t) \le y)$ and

$$v(x,t) = \frac{\sqrt{\mathrm{Var}(X(t))}}{t} \tag{21}$$

is independent of x.

Next we consider some properties of the models IM1-4 and AM1. In all cases severity is normalized so that $E(A(x,t)) = xt$. Define σ and τ so that $\mathrm{Var}(X(t)) = \sigma^2 t$ and $\mathrm{Var}(Z(t)) = \tau^2 t$.

Practical underwritten loss distributions will have a variance or will have limits applied so the distribution of insured losses has a variance, so this is not a significant restriction.

Models IM3 and IM4 no longer define Lévy processes because of the common C term. Each process has conditionally independent increments given C. Thus, these two models no longer assume that each new insured has losses independent of the existing cohort. Example 6 shows that IM2 is a Lévy process.

Table 1 lays out the variance and coefficient of variation v of these five models. It also shows whether each model is volumetrically (resp. temporally) diversifying, that is whether $v(x,t) \to 0$ as $x \to \infty$ (resp. $t \to \infty$). The calculations follow easily by conditioning. For example

$$\begin{aligned}\mathrm{Var}(X(xZ(t))) &= \mathrm{E}_{Z(t)}(\mathrm{Var}(X(xZ(t)))) + \mathrm{Var}_{Z(t)}(\mathrm{E}(X(xZ(t)))) \\ &= \mathrm{E}(\sigma^2 xZ(t)) + \mathrm{Var}(xZ(t)) \\ &= \sigma^2 xt + x^2\tau^2 t = xt(\sigma^2 + x\tau^2).\end{aligned}$$

Table 1. Variance of IM1-4 and AM.

Model	Variance	$v(x,t)$	Diversifying	
			$x \to \infty$	$t \to \infty$
IM1: $X(xt)$	$\sigma^2 xt$	$\frac{\sigma}{\sqrt{xt}}$	Yes	Yes
IM2: $X(xZ(t))$	$xt(\sigma^2 + x\tau^2)$	$\sqrt{\frac{\sigma^2}{xt} + \frac{\tau^2}{t}}$	No	Yes
IM3: $X(xCt)$	$xt(\sigma^2 + cxt)$	$\sqrt{\frac{\sigma^2}{xt} + c}$	No	No
IM4: $X(xCZ(t))$	$x^2t^2\left(\frac{(c+1)\tau^2}{t} + c\right) + \sigma^2 xt$	$\sqrt{\frac{\sigma^2}{xt} + \frac{\tau'^2}{t} + c}$	No	No
AM1: $xX(t)$	$x^2\sigma^2 t$	$\sigma/\sqrt{t}$	Const.	Yes

In IM4, $\tau' = (1+c)\tau$.

The characteristics of each model will be tested against regulatory insurance data in Section 7.

The models presented here are one-dimensional. A multi-dimensional version would use multi-dimensional Lévy processes. This allows for the possibility of correlation between lines. In addition, correlation between lines can be induced by using correlated mixing variables C. This is the common-shock model, described in Meyers (2005b).

6. Defining the Derivative of a Risk Measure and Directions in the Space of Risks

This section is the technical heart of the paper. It investigates the definition of derivative for a real function and considers how it could be defined on more general spaces, such as the space of random variables. It explains how Lévy processes can be used to define "direction" and how the infinitesimal generator of a Lévy process relates to derivatives. This allows us to pin-point the difference between the derivatives of an insurance process and of an asset process.

6.1. Defining the Derivative

When $\rho : \mathbb{R}^n \to \mathbb{R}$ the meaning of $\partial\rho/\partial X_i$ is clear. However we want to consider $\rho : \mathbf{L} \to \mathbb{R}$ where $\mathbf{L}$ is the more complicated space of random variables. We need to define the derivative mapping $D\rho_X$ as a real-valued linear map on tangent vectors or "directions" at $X \in \mathbf{L}$. Meyers' example shows the asset/return model and an insurance growth model correspond to different directions.

A direction in $\mathbf{L}$ can be identified with the derivative of a coordinate path $x : U \to \mathbf{L}$ where $U \subset \mathbb{R}$. Composing ρ and x results in a real valued function of a real variable $\rho_x := \rho \circ x : U \to \mathbb{R}$, $u \mapsto \rho(x(u))$, so standard calculus defines $d\rho_x/du$. The derivative of ρ at $x(u)$ in the direction defined by the derivative $\dot{x}(u)$ of $x(u)$ is given by

$$D\rho_{x(u)}(\dot{x}(u)) := \frac{d\rho_x}{du} \tag{22}$$

The surprise of Equation (22) is that the two complex objects on the left combine to the single, well-understood object on the right. The exact definitions of the terms on the left will be discussed below.

Section 4 introduced two important coordinates. The first is $k : \mathbb{R} \to \mathbf{L}$, $k(u) = uX$ for some fixed random variable $X \in \mathbf{L}$. It is suitable for modeling assets: u represents position size and X represents the asset return. The second coordinate is $m : [0, \infty) \to \mathbf{L}$, $m(u) = X_u$, where X_u is a compound Poisson distribution with frequency mean $u\lambda$ and severity component Z. It is suitable for modeling aggregate losses from an insurance portfolio. (There is a third potential coordinate path $w(u) = B_u$ where B_u is a Brownian motion, but because it always takes positive and negative values it is of less interest for modeling losses.)

An issue with the asset coordinate in an insurance context is the correct interpretation of uX. For $0 < u \leq 1$, uX can be interpreted as a quota share of total losses, or as a coinsurance provision. However, uX for $u < 0$ or $u > 1$ is generally meaningless due to policy provisions, laws on over-insurance, and the inability to short insurance. The natural way to interpret a doubling in volume ("$2X$") is as $X_1 + X_2$ where X, X_1, X_2 are identically distributed random variables, rather than as a policy paying \$2 per \$1 of loss. This interpretation is consistent with doubling volume since $\mathrm{E}(X_1 + X_2) = 2\mathrm{E}(X)$. Clearly $X + X$ has a different distribution to $X_1 + X_2$ unless X_1 and X_2 are perfectly correlated. The insurance coordinate has exactly this property: $m(2) = X_{2u}$ is the sum of two independent copies of X_u because of the additive property of the Poisson distribution.

To avoid misinterpreting uX it is safer to regard insurance risks as probability measures (distributions) μ on $\mathbb{R}$. The measure μ corresponds to a random variable X with distribution $\Pr(X \leq x) = \mu(-\infty, x]$. Now there is no natural way to interpret 2μ. Identify $\mathbf{L}$ with $M(\mathbb{R})$, the set of probability measures on $\mathbb{R}$. We can combine two elements of $M(\mathbb{R})$ using convolution: the distribution of the sum of the corresponding random variables. Since the distribution if $X + Y$ is the same as the distribution of $Y + X$ order of convolution does not matter. Now $2X$ in our insurance interpretation, $X_1 + X_2$, corresponds to $\mu \star \mu := \mu^{\star 2}$, where $\star$ represents convolution, and we are not led astray.

We still have to define "directions" in $\mathbf{L}$ and $M(\mathbb{R})$. Directions should correspond to the derivatives of curves. The simplest curves are straight lines. A straight line through the origin is called a ray. Table 2 shows several possible characterizations of a ray $\mathbb{R}^n$ each of which uses a different aspect of the rich mathematical structure of $\mathbb{R}^n$, and which could be used as characterizations in $\mathbf{L}$.

Table 2. Possible characterizations of a ray in $\mathbb{R}^n$.

Characterization of Ray	Required Structure on $\mathbb{R}^n$
α is the shortest distance between $\alpha(0)$ and $\alpha(1)$	Notion of distance in $\mathbb{R}^n$, differentiable manifold
$\alpha''(t) = 0$, constant velocity, no acceleration	Very complicated on a general manifold.
$\alpha(t) = t\mathbf{x}$, $\mathbf{x} \in \mathbb{R}^n$.	Vector space structure
$\alpha(s + t) = \alpha(s) + \alpha(t)$	Can add in domain and range, semigroup structure only.

The first two use properties of $\mathbb{R}^n$ that require putting a differential structure on $\mathbf{L}$, which is very complicated. The third corresponds to the asset volume/return model and uses the identification of the set of possible portfolios with the $\mathbb{R}$ vector space $\mathbb{R}^n$. This leaves the fourth approach: a ray is characterized by the simple relationship $\alpha(s + t) = \alpha(s) + \alpha(t)$. This definition only requires the ability to add for the range space, which we have on $\mathbf{L}$. It is the definition adopted in Stroock (2003).

Therefore rays in **L** should correspond to families of random variables satisfying $X_s + X_t = X_{s+t}$ (or, equivalently, in $M(\mathbb{R})$ to families of measures μ_s satisfying $\mu_s \star \mu_t = \mu_{s+t}$), i.e., to Lévy processes. Since $X_0 = X_{0+0} = X_0 + X_0$ a ray must start at 0, the random variable taking the value 0 with probability 1. Straight lines correspond to translations of rays: a straight line passing through the point $Y \in \mathbf{L}$ is a family $Y + X_t$ where X_t is a ray (resp. passing thought $\nu \in M(\mathbb{R})$ is $\nu \star \mu_t$ where μ_t is a ray.) Directions in **L** are determined by rays. By providing a basis of directions in **L**, Lévy processes provide the insurance analog of individual asset return variables.

We now think about derivatives in a more abstract way. Working with functions on $\mathbb{R}^n$ obscures some of the complication involved in working on more general spaces (like **L**) because the set of directions at any point in $\mathbb{R}^n$ can naturally be identified with a point in $\mathbb{R}^n$. In general this is not the case; the directions live in a different space. A familiar non-trivial example of this is the sphere in $\mathbb{R}^3$. At each point on the sphere the set of directions, or tangent vectors, is a plane. The collection of different planes, together with the original sphere, can be combined to give a new object, called the tangent bundle over the sphere. A point in the tangent bundle consists of a point on the sphere and a direction, or tangent vector, at that point.

There are several different ways to define the tangent bundle. For the sphere, an easy method is to set up a family of local charts, where a chart is a differentiable bijection from a subset of $\mathbb{R}^2$ to a neighborhood of each point. Charts must be defined at each point on the sphere in such a way that they overlap consistently, producing an atlas, or differentiable structure, on the sphere. Charts move questions of tangency and direction back to functions on $\mathbb{R}^2 \to \mathbb{R}^2$ where they are well understood. This is called the coordinate approach.

Another way of defining the tangent bundle is to use curves, or coordinate paths, to define tangent vectors: a direction becomes the derivative of a curve. The tangent space can be defined as the set of curves through a point, with two curves identified if they are tangent (agree to degree 1). In the next section we will apply this approach to **L**. A good general reference on the construction of the tangent bundle is Abraham et al. (1988).

Figure 2 is an illustrative schematic. The sphere S is used as a proxy for **L**, an object with more complex geometry than flat Euclidean space. The two paths m and k are shown as the red and blue lines, passing through the same point (distribution) x on the sphere at $t = 1$. The red line is part of a great circle geodesic—the analog of a straight line on a sphere—whereas the blue line is not. Above x is the tangent plane (isomorphic to $\mathbb{R}^2$) to the sphere at x, TS_x; π is the projection from the tangent bundle TS to S. The derivative of ρ at x is a linear map $D\rho : TS_x \to T\mathbb{R}$. For Euclidean spaces we can identify the tangent bundle with the space so $T\mathbb{R} = \mathbb{R}$. Although $k(1) = m(1) = x$ they have different derivatives (define different vectors in TS_x), $\dot{m} \neq \dot{k}$ at $t = 1$.

The derivative of a risk measure ρ, $\partial\rho/\partial X$, is the evaluation of the linear differential $D\rho$ on a tangent vector in the direction X. Meyer's embedding m corresponds to $\partial(\rho \circ m)/\partial t|_{t=1} = D\rho_X(\dot{m}(1))$ whereas Kalkbrener's corresponds to $\partial(\rho \circ k)/\partial t|_{t=1} = D\rho_X(\dot{k}(1))$. As demonstrated in Section 4 these derivatives are not the same—just as the schematic leads us to expect—because the direction $\dot{m}(1)$ is not the same as the direction $\dot{k}(1)$.

The difference between $\dot{k}(1)$ and $\dot{m}(1)$ is a measure of the diversification benefit given by m compared to k. The embedding k maps $x \mapsto xX$ and so offers no diversification to an insurer. Again, this is correct for an asset portfolio (you don't diversify a portfolio by buying more of the same stock) but it is *not* true for an insurance portfolio. We will describe the analog of TS_x next.

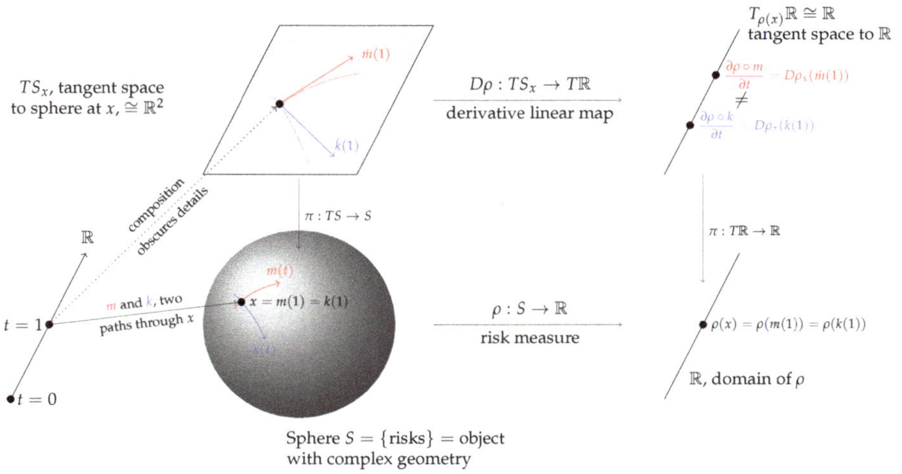

Figure 2. Schematic of the Kalkbrener-Meyers example, using the sphere to illustrate the more complex space **L**.

6.2. Directions in the Space of Actuarial Random Variables

We now show how Lévy processes provide a description of "directions" in the space **L**. The analysis combines three threads:

1. The notion that directions, or tangent vectors, live in a separate space called the tangent bundle.
2. The identification of tangent vectors as derivatives of curves.
3. The idea that Lévy processes, characterized by the additive relation $X(s+t) = X(s) + X(t)$, provide the appropriate analog of rays to use as a basis for insurance risks.

The program is to compute the derivative of the curve $t \mapsto X(t) \in \mathbf{L}$ defined by a Lévy process family of random variables (or $t \mapsto \mu_t \in M(\mathbb{R})$ defined by an additive family of probability distributions on $\mathbb{R}$). The ideas presented here are part of a general theory of Markov processes. The presentation follows the beautiful book by Stroock (2003). We begin by describing a finite sample space version of **L** which illustrates the difficulties involved in regarding it as a differentiable manifold.

To see that the construction of tangent directions in **L** may not be trivial, consider the space M of probability measures on $\mathbb{Z}/n$, the integers $\{0, 1, \dots, n-1\}$ with $+$ given by addition modulo n. An element $\mu \in M$ can be identified with an n-tuple of non-negative real numbers $p_0, \dots, p_{n-1}$ satisfying $\sum_i p_i = 1$. Thus elements of M are in one to one correspondent with elements of the $n-1$ dimensional simplex $\Delta_{n-1} = \{(x_0, \dots, x_{n-1}) \mid \sum_i x_i = 1\} \subset \mathbb{R}^n$. Δ_n inherits a differentiable structure from $\mathbb{R}^{n+1}$ and we already know how to think about directions and tangent vectors in Euclidean space. However, even thinking about $\Delta_2 \subset \mathbb{R}^3$ shows M is not an easy space to work with. Δ_2 is a plane triangle; it has a boundary of three edges and each edge has a boundary of two vertices. The tangent spaces at each of these boundary points is different and different again from the tangent space in the interior of Δ_2. As n increases the complexity of the boundary increases and, to compound the problem, every point in the interior gets closer to the boundary. For measures on $\mathbb{R}$ the boundary is dense.

Let $\delta_x \in M(\mathbb{R})$ be the measure giving probability 1 to $x \in \mathbb{R}$. We will describe the space of tangent vectors to $M(\mathbb{R})$ at δ_0. By definition, all Lévy processes $X(t)$ have distribution δ_0 at $t = 0$. Measures $\mu_t \in M(\mathbb{R})$ are defined by their action on functions f on $\mathbb{R}$.

Let $\langle f, \mu \rangle = \int_{\mathbb{R}} f(x)\mu(dx) = \mathrm{E}(f(X))$, where X has distribution μ. In view of the fundamental theorem of calculus, the derivative $\dot{\mu}_t$ of μ_t should satisfy

$$\langle f, \mu_t \rangle - \langle f, \mu_0 \rangle = \int_0^t \dot{\mu}_\tau f d\tau, \tag{23}$$

with $\dot{\mu}_t$ a linear functional acting on f, i.e., $\dot{\mu}_t(f) \in \mathbb{R}$ and $f \mapsto \dot{\mu}_t(f)$ is linear in f. Converting Equation (23) to its differential form suggests that

$$\dot{\mu}_0 f = \lim_{t \downarrow 0} \frac{\langle f, \mu_t \rangle - \langle f, \mu_0 \rangle}{t} \tag{24}$$

$$= \lim_{t \downarrow 0} \frac{\mathrm{E}(f(X(t))) - \mathrm{E}(f(X(0)))}{t} \tag{25}$$

where $X(t)$ has distribution μ_t.

We now consider how Equation (25) works when $X(t)$ is related to a Brownian motion or a compound Poisson—the two building block Lévy processes. Suppose first that $X(t)$ is a Brownian motion with drift γ and standard deviation σ, so $X(t) = \gamma t + \sigma B(t)$ where $B(t)$ is a standard Brownian motion. Let f be a function with a Taylor's expansion about 0. Then

$$\dot{\mu}_0 f = \lim_{t \downarrow 0} [\mathrm{E}(f(0) + X(t)f'(0) + \frac{X(t)^2 f''(0)}{2} + o(t)) - f(0)]/t \tag{26}$$

$$= \lim_{t \downarrow 0} [\gamma t f'(0) + \frac{\sigma^2 t f''(0)}{2} + o(t))]/t \tag{27}$$

$$= \gamma f'(0) + \frac{\sigma^2 f''(0)}{2}, \tag{28}$$

because $\mathrm{E}(B(t)) = 0$ and $\mathrm{E}(B(t)^2) = t$ and so $\mathrm{E}(X(t)) = \mathrm{E}(\gamma t + \sigma B(t)) = \gamma t$ and $\mathrm{E}(X(t)^2) = \gamma^2 t^2 + \sigma^2 t$. Thus $\dot{\mu}_0$ acts as a second order differential operator evaluated at $x = 0$ (because we assume $\mu_0 = \delta_0$):

$$\dot{\mu}_0 f = \gamma \frac{df}{dx}(0) + \frac{\sigma^2}{2} \frac{df^2}{dx^2}(0). \tag{29}$$

Next suppose that $X(t)$ is a compound Poisson distribution with Lévy measure ν, $\nu(\{0\}) = 0$ and $\lambda = \nu(\mathbb{R}) < \infty$. Let J be a variable with distribution ν/λ, so, in actuarial terms, J is the severity. The number of jumps of $X(t)$ follows a Poisson distribution with mean λt. If t is very small then the axioms characterizing the Poisson distribution imply that in the time interval $[0, t]$ there is a single jump with probability λt and no jump with probability $1 - \lambda t$. Conditioning on the occurrence of a jump, $\mathrm{E}(f(X(t))) = (1 - \lambda t)f(0) + \lambda t \mathrm{E}(f(J))$ and so

$$\dot{\mu}_0 f = \lim_{t \downarrow 0} \frac{\mathrm{E}(f(X(t))) - \mathrm{E}(f(X(0)))}{t} \tag{30}$$

$$= \lim_{t \downarrow 0} \frac{\lambda t(\mathrm{E}(f(J)) - f(0))}{t} \tag{31}$$

$$= \lambda(\mathrm{E}(f(J)) - f(0)) \tag{32}$$

$$= \int (f(y) - f(0))\, \nu(dy) \tag{33}$$

This analysis side-steps some technicalities by assuming that $\nu(\mathbb{R}) < \infty$. For both the Brownian motion and the compound Poisson if we are interested in tangent vectors at $\mu_0 = \delta_x$ for $x \neq 0$ then we replace 0 with x because $\langle f, \mu_0 \rangle = \mathrm{E}(f(x + X_0)) = f(x)$. Thus Equation (33) becomes

$$\dot{\mu}_0 f = \int (f(x + y) - f(x))\, \nu(dy) \tag{34}$$

for example. Combining these two results makes the following theorem plausible.

Theorem 2 (Stroock (2003) Thm 2.1.11). *There is a one-to-one correspondence between Lévy triples and rays (continuous, additive maps) $t \in [0,\infty) \to \mu_t \in M(\mathbb{R})$. The Lévy triple (σ, ν, γ) corresponds to the infinitely divisible map $t \mapsto \mu_t^{(\sigma,\nu,\gamma)}$ given by the Lévy process with the same Lévy triple. The map is $t \mapsto \mu_t^{(\sigma,\nu,\gamma)}$ is differentiable and*

$$\dot{\mu}_t^{(\sigma,\nu,\gamma)} f = \dot{\mu}_t f = \langle L^{(\sigma,\nu,\gamma)} f, \mu_t \rangle. \tag{35}$$

where $L^{(\sigma,\nu,\gamma)}$ is a pseudo differential operator, see Applebaum (2004); Jacob (2001 2002 2005), given by

$$L^{(\sigma,\nu,\gamma)} f(x) = \gamma \frac{df}{dx} + \frac{1}{2}\sigma^2 \frac{d^2 f}{dx^2} + \int_{\mathbb{R}} f(y+x) - f(x) - \frac{df}{dx}\frac{y}{1+|y|^2}\nu(dy). \tag{36}$$

If $t \mapsto \mu_t \in \mathbf{L}$ is a differentiable curve and $\mu_0 = \delta_x$ for some $x \in \mathbb{R}$ then there exists a unique Lévy triple (σ, ν, γ) such that $\dot{\mu}_0$ is the linear operator acting on f by

$$\dot{\mu}_0 f = L^{(\sigma,\nu,\gamma)} f(x) = \langle L^{(\sigma,\nu,\gamma)} f, \mu_0 \rangle. \tag{37}$$

Thus $T_{\delta_x}(M(\mathbb{R}))$, the tangent space to $M(\mathbb{R})$ at δ_x, can be identified with the cone of linear functionals of the form $f \mapsto L^{(\sigma,\nu,\gamma)} f(x)$ where (σ, ν, γ) is a Lévy triple.

Just as in the Lévy-Khintchine theorem, the extra term in the integral is needed for technical convergence reasons when there is an infinite number of very small jumps. Note that $\dot{\mu}_0 f \in \mathbb{R}$ is a number, $L^{(\sigma,\nu,\gamma)} f$ is a function and its value at x, $L^{(\sigma,\nu,\gamma)} f(x) \in \mathbb{R}$ is a number. The connection between μ_t and x is $\mu_0 = \delta_x$ is the measure concentrated at $x \in \mathbb{R}$.

At this point we have described tangent vectors to $\mathbf{L} = M(\mathbb{R})$ at degenerate distributions δ_x. To properly illustrate Figures 1 and 2 we need a tangent vector at a more general μ. Again, following (Stroock 2003, sct. 2.11.4), define a tangent vector to $M(\mathbb{R})$ at a general μ to be a linear functional of the form $\Lambda_\mu f = \langle Lf, \mu \rangle$ where $L = L^{(\sigma(x),\nu(x),\gamma(x))}$ is a continuous family of operators L determined by x. We will restrict attention to simpler tangent vectors where $L = L^{(\sigma,\nu,\gamma)}$ does not vary with x. If μ_t is the Lévy process corresponding to the triple (σ, ν, γ) and f is bounded and has continuously bounded derivatives, then, by independent and stationary increments

$$\begin{aligned}
\dot{\mu}_u f &= \langle L^{(\sigma,\nu,\gamma)} f, \mu_t \rangle && (38)\\
&= \lim_{s\downarrow 0} \mathrm{E}\left(\frac{f(X_{s+u}) - f(X_u)}{s}\right) && (39)\\
&= \lim_{s\downarrow 0} \mathrm{E}_{X_u}\left(\frac{\mathrm{E}_{X_s}(f(X_s + X_u) - f(X_u))}{s}\right) && (40)\\
&= \mathrm{E}_{X_u}\left(\lim_{s\downarrow 0} \frac{\mathrm{E}_{X_s}(f(X_s + X_u) - f(X_u))}{s}\right) && (41)\\
&= \mathrm{E}_{X_u}\left(\langle L^{(\sigma,\nu,\gamma)} f(X_u)\right) && (42)
\end{aligned}$$

by dominated convergence. The tangent vector is an average of the direction at all the locations that X_u can take.

6.3. Examples

We present a number of examples to illustrate the theory. Test functions f are usually required to be bounded and twice continuously and boundedly differentiable to ensure that all relevant integrals exist. However, we can apply the same formulas to unbounded differentiable functions for particular μ_t if we know relevant integrals converge. Below we will use $f(x) = x^2$ as a example, with distributions having a second moment.

Example 7 (Brownian motion). *Let X_t be a standard Brownian motion, corresponding to Lévy triple $(\sigma, \nu, \gamma) = (1, 0, 0)$ and $f(x) = x^2$. The density of X_t is $g(x,t) = (2\pi t)^{-1/2} \exp(-x^2/2t)$ and let l_t be the associated measure. We can compute $\dot{l}_t f$ in three ways. First, using Stroock's theorem Equation (37)*

$$\dot{l}_t f = \langle L^{(1,0,0)} f, l_t \rangle = \langle \frac{1}{2}\frac{\partial^2 f}{\partial x^2}, l_t \rangle = \langle 1, l_t \rangle = 1. \tag{43}$$

Second, using $\dot{l}_t f = d/dt \langle f, l_t \rangle$ and the fact that $\langle f, l_t \rangle = \mathrm{E}(X_t^2) = t$ again gives $\dot{l}_t f = 1$. Thirdly, differentiating $d/dt\langle f, l_t \rangle$ through the integral gives

$$\frac{d}{dt}\langle f, l_t \rangle = \int_{\mathbb{R}} f(x) \frac{\partial g}{\partial t}(x,t) dx \tag{44}$$

$$= \int_{\mathbb{R}} \frac{1}{\sqrt{2\pi t}} e^{-x^2/2t} x^2 \left(\frac{x^2}{2t^2} - \frac{1}{2t} \right) dx \tag{45}$$

$$= \frac{\mathrm{E}(X_t^4)}{2t^2} - \frac{\mathrm{E}(X_t^2)}{2t} \tag{46}$$

$$= 1 \tag{47}$$

since $\mathrm{E}(X_t^4) = 3t^2$ and $\mathrm{E}(X_t^2) = t$.

Example 8 (Gamma process). *Let X_t be a gamma process, (Sato 1999, p. 45), Barndorff-Nielsen (2000), meaning X_t has law $l_t = \Gamma(t\lambda, \alpha)$ with density $\alpha^{t\lambda}/\Gamma(t\lambda) x^{t\lambda - 1} e^{-\alpha x}$ and Lévy measure $\nu(dx) = (\lambda/x) e^{-\alpha x} dx$, $\gamma = \sigma = 0$ on $x \geq 0$. We have*

$$\mathrm{E}(X_t) = \frac{\lambda t}{\alpha},\ \mathrm{E}(X_t^2) = \frac{\lambda t(\lambda t + 1)}{\alpha^2},\ \textit{and}\ \mathrm{Var}(X_t) = \frac{\lambda t}{\alpha^2}. \tag{48}$$

Notice that $\nu([0\infty)) = \infty$ so this example is not a compound Poisson process because it has infinitely many small jumps. But it is a limit of compound Poisson processes. For $f(x) = x^2$, $\langle f, l_t \rangle = \mathrm{E}(X_t^2) = \lambda t(\lambda t + 1)/\alpha^2$ so

$$\frac{d}{dt}\langle f, l_t \rangle = \frac{2\lambda^2 t + \lambda}{\alpha^2}. \tag{49}$$

On the other hand, using Equation (37) with $L^{(0,\nu,0)}$ gives

$$L^{(0,\nu,0)} f(x) = \int (f(x+y) - f(x)) \frac{\lambda}{y} e^{-\alpha y} dy \tag{50}$$

$$= \frac{2\lambda x}{\alpha} + \frac{\lambda}{\alpha^2}, \tag{51}$$

so $\dot{l}_t f = \langle L^{(0,\nu,0)} f, l_t \rangle = (2\lambda^2 t + \lambda)/\alpha^2$, agreeing with Equation (49).

Example 9 (Laplace process). *Let X_t be a Laplace process with law l_t, (Sato 1999, p. 98), and (Kotz et al. 2001, p. 47) . X_1 has density $\alpha \exp(-\alpha|x|)/2$ and Lévy measure $\nu(dx) = \exp(-\alpha|x|)/|x| dx$. X_t can be represented as the difference of two $\Gamma(t, \alpha)$ variables. $\mathrm{E}(X_t) = 0$, $\mathrm{Var}(X_t) = \mathrm{E}(X_t^2) = \langle f, l_t \rangle = 2t/\alpha^2$ and hence*

$$\frac{d}{dt}\langle f, l_t \rangle = \frac{2}{\alpha^2}. \tag{52}$$

On the other hand

$$L^{(0,\nu,0)}f(x) = \int (f(x+y) - f(x))\frac{1}{|y|}e^{-\alpha|y|}dy \tag{53}$$

$$= \int (2xy + y^2)\frac{1}{|y|}e^{-\alpha|y|}dy \tag{54}$$

$$= 2\int_0^\infty ye^{-\alpha y}dy = \frac{2}{\alpha^2} \tag{55}$$

as the first term in the middle equation is odd and hence zero.

6.4. Application to Insurance Risk Models IM1-4 and Asset Risk Model AM1

We now compute the difference between the directions implied by each of IM1-4 and AM1 to quantify the difference between $\dot{m}(1)$ and $\dot{k}(1)$ in Figures 1 and 2. In order to focus on realistic insurance loss models we will assume $\gamma = \sigma = 0$ and $\nu(\mathbb{R}) < \infty$. Assume the Lévy triple for the subordinator Z is $(0, \rho, 0)$. Also assume $\mathrm{E}(C) = 1$, $\mathrm{Var}(C) = c$, and that C, X and Z are all independent.

For each model we can consider the time derivative or the volume derivative. There are obvious symmetries between these two for IM1 and IM3. For IM2 the temporal derivative is the same as the volumetric derivative of IM3 with $C = Z(t)$.

Theorem 2 gives the direction for IM1 as corresponding to the operator Equation (37) multiplied by x or t as appropriate. If we are interested in the temporal derivative then losses evolve according to the process $\tilde{X}_t = X_{xt}$, which has Levy triple $(0, x\nu, 0)$. Therefore, if $\mu_0 = \delta_z$, $z \in \mathbb{R}$, then the time direction is given by the operator

$$\dot{\mu}_0 f = \int f(z+y) - f(z)(x\nu)(dy) = x\int f(z+y) - f(z)\nu(dy). \tag{56}$$

The temporal derivative of IM2, $X(xZ(t))$, is more tricky. Let K have distribution $\rho/\rho(\mathbb{R})$, the severity of Z. For small t, $Z(t) = 0$ with probability $1 - \rho(\mathbb{R})t$ and $Z(t) = K$ with probability $\rho(\mathbb{R})t$. Thus

$$\dot{\mu}_0 f = \rho(\mathbb{R})\mathrm{E}(f(z + X(xK)) - f(z)) \tag{57}$$

$$= \int_{(0,\infty)}\int_{(0,\infty)} f(z+xy) - f(z)\nu^{xk}(dy)\rho(dk) \tag{58}$$

where ν^k is the distribution of $X(k)$. This has the same form as IM1, except the underlying Lévy measure ν has been replaced with the mixture

$$\nu'(B) = \int_{(0,\infty)} \nu^k(B)\rho(dk). \tag{59}$$

See (Sato 1999, chp. 6, Thm 30.1) for more details and for the case where X or Z includes a deterministic drift.

For IM3, $X(xCt)$, the direction is the same as for model IM1. This is not a surprise because the effect of C is to select, once and for all, a random speed along the ray; it does not affect its direction. By comparison, in model IM2 the "speed" is proceeding by jumps, but again, the direction is fixed. If $\mathrm{E}(C) \neq 1$ then the derivative would be multiplied by $\mathrm{E}(C)$.

Finally the volumetric derivative of the asset model is simply

$$\dot{\mu}_0 f = X(t)\frac{df}{dx}(z). \tag{60}$$

Thus the derivative is the same as for a deterministic drift Lévy process. This should be expected since once $X(t)$ is known it is fixed regardless of volume x. Comparing with the derivatives for IM1-4 expresses the different directions represented schematically in Figure 2 analytically. The result is also reasonable in light of the different shapes of tZ and $\sqrt{t}Z$ as $t \to 0$, for a random variable Z with mean and standard deviation equal to 1. For very small t, tZ is essentially the same as a deterministic $t\mathrm{E}(Z)$, whereas $\sqrt{t}Z$ has a standard deviation $\sqrt{t}$ which is much larger than the mean t. Its coefficient of variation $1/\sqrt{t} \to \infty$ as $t \to 0$. The relative uncertainty in $\sqrt{t}Z$ grows as $t \to 0$ whereas for tZ it disappears see Figure 3.

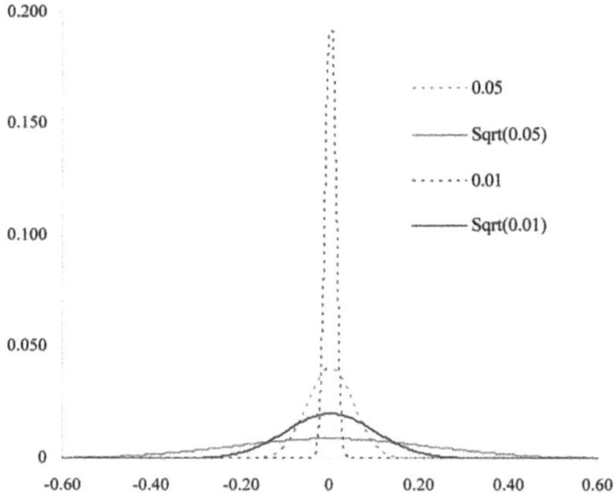

Figure 3. Illustration of the difference between tZ and $\sqrt{t}Z$ for Z a standard normal as $t \to 0$.

Severity uncertainty is also interesting. Suppose that claim frequency is still λ but that severity is given by a family of measures $\tilde{\nu}_V$ for a random V. Now, in each state, the Lévy process proceeds along a random direction defined by $V(\omega)$, so the resulting direction is a mixture

$$\dot{\mu}_0 = \int \dot{\mu}_{0,v} dv. \tag{61}$$

We can interpret these results from the perspective of credibility theory. Credibility is usually associated with repeated observations of a given insured, so t grows but x is fixed. For models IM1-4 severity (direction) is implicitly known. For IM2-4 credibility determines information about the fixed (C) or variable ($Z(t)$) speed of travel in the given direction. If there is severity uncertainty, V, then repeated observation resolves the direction of travel, rather than the speed. Obviously both direction and speed are uncertain in reality.

Actuaries could model directly with a Lévy measure ν and hence avoid the artificial distinction between frequency and severity as Patrik et al. (1999) suggested. Catastrophe models already work in this way. Several aspects of actuarial practice could benefit from avoiding the artificial frequency/severity dichotomy. The dichotomy is artificial in the sense it depends on an arbitrary choice of one year to determine frequency. Explicitly considering the claim count density of losses by size range helps clarify the effect of loss trend. In particular, it allows different trend rates by size of loss. Risk adjustments become more transparent. The theory of risk-adjusted probabilities for compound Poisson distributions (Delbaen and Haezendonck 1989; Meister 1995), is more straightforward if loss rate densities are adjusted without the constraint of adjusting a severity curve and frequency separately. This approach can be used to generate state price densities directly from catastrophe model output. Finally, the Lévy measure is equivalent to the log of the aggregate distribution, so convolution of aggregates corresponds to a pointwise addition of Lévy measures, facilitating combining losses from portfolios with different policy limits. This simplification is clearer when frequency and severity are not split.

6.5. Higher Order Identification of the Differences Between Insurance and Asset Models

We now consider whether Figure 1 is an exaggeration by computing the difference between the two operators $\dot{k}$ and $\dot{m}$ acting on test functions. We first extend k slightly by introducing the idea of a homogeneous approximation.

Let X be an infinitely divisible distribution with associated Lévy process $u \mapsto X_u$. As usual, we consider two coordinate maps $\mathbb{R}^+ \to \mathbf{L}$: the asset return model $k : \mathbb{R}^+ \to \mathbf{L}$, $u \mapsto k(u) = uX_1$, and the insurance model $m : \mathbb{R}^+ \to \mathbf{L}$, $u \mapsto m(u) = X_u$. These satisfy $k(1) = m(1) = X_1$, but in general $\dot{k}_u \neq \dot{m}_u$ at $u = 1$. We use u rather than t as the argument to avoid giving the impression that the index represents time: remember it represents the combination of time and volume.

Obviously there is no need to restrict k to be an approximation of X_1. For general $u = u_0$ we can construct a homogeneous approximation to $m(u_0)$ at u_0 by $k(u) = (u/u_0)X_{u_0}$. The name homogeneous approximation is apt because $k(u_0) = m(u_0)$, and k is homogeneous: $k(su) = (su/u_0)X_{u_0} = sk(u)$, for real $s > 0$. For a general Lévy process X, X_{xt} does not have the same distribution as xX_t, so m is not homogeneous. For example if X is stable with index α, $0 < \alpha < 2$ then $X_{xt} \overset{d}{=} x^{1/\alpha}X_t$ (Brownian motion is stable with $\alpha = 2$). This section will compare $\dot{k}$ and $\dot{m}$ by computing the linear maps corresponding to $\dot{k}$ and $\dot{m}$ and showing they have a different form. We will compute the value of these operators on various functions to quantify how they differ. In the process we will recover Meyers' Meyers (2005a) example of "axiomatic capital" vs. "economic capital" from Section 4.

Suppose the Lévy triple defining X_u is (σ, ν, γ), where σ is the standard deviation of the continuous term and ν is the Lévy measure. Let $L^{(\sigma,\nu,\gamma)}$ be the pseudo-differential operator defined by Theorem 2 and let μ_u be the law of X_u. Using the independent and additive increment properties of an Lévy process and (Sato 1999, Theorem 31.5) we can write

$$\dot{\mu}_u f = \langle L^{(\sigma,\nu,\gamma)} f, \mu_u \rangle = E_{X_u}\left[\lim_{s \downarrow 0} s^{-1} \mathrm{E}_{X_s}(f(X_u + X_s)|X_u) - f(X_u)\right] \tag{62}$$

where $f : \mathbb{R} \to \mathbb{R}$ is a doubly differentiable, bounded function with bounded derivatives.

Regarding k as a deterministic drift at a random (but determined once and for all) speed X_{u_0}/u_0, we can apply Equation (62) with $\gamma = X_{u_0}/u_0$ and average over X_{u_0} to get

$$\dot{k}_u f = \mathrm{E}_{X_{u_0}}(\langle Lf, k_u \rangle) = \mathrm{E}[X_{u_0}/u_0 f'(uX_{u_0}/u_0)]. \tag{63}$$

We can see this equation is consistent with Equation (23):

$$\int_0^u \dot{x}_v dv = \int_0^u \mathrm{E}[X_{u_0}/u_0 f'(vX_{u_0}/u_0)]dv \tag{64}$$

$$= \int_0^u \int x/u_0 f'(vx/u_0)\mu_{u_0}(dx)dv \tag{65}$$

$$= \int \int_0^{ux/u_0} f'(y)dy \mu_{u_0}(dx) \tag{66}$$

$$= \int f(ux/u_0) - f(0)\mu_{u_0}(dx) \tag{67}$$

$$= \mathrm{E}[f(uX_{u_0}/u_0)] - f(0), \tag{68}$$

where l_t is the law of X_t.

Suppose that the Lévy process X_t is a compound Poisson process with jump intensity λ and jump component distribution J. Suppose the jump distribution has a variance. Then, using Equation (62), and conditioning on the presence of a jump in time s, which has probability λs, gives

$$\dot{m}_u f = \lambda E_{X_u}[\mathrm{E}(f(X_u + J)) - f(X_u)]. \tag{69}$$

Now let $f(x) = x$. Usually test functions are required to be bounded. We can get around this by considering $\min(f, n)$ for fixed n and letting $n \to \infty$ and only working with relatively thin tailed distributions—which we do through our assumption the severity J has a variance. Since $\mathrm{E}(X_u) = \lambda u \mathrm{E}(J)$, Equations (63) and (69) give $\dot{k}_u f = \mathrm{E}(X_{u_0}/u_0) = \lambda \mathrm{E}(J)$ and $\dot{m}_u f = \lambda \mathrm{E}(J)$ respectively so the homogeneous approximation has the same derivative in this case.

If $f(x) = x^2$ then since $\mathrm{E}(X_u^2) = \lambda^2 u^2 \mathrm{E}(J)^2 + \lambda u \mathrm{E}(J^2)$ we get

$$\dot{k}_u f = 2\lambda^2 u \mathrm{E}(J)^2 + 2\lambda u \mathrm{E}(J^2)/u_0. \tag{70}$$

On the other hand

$$\dot{m}_u f = 2\lambda^2 u \mathrm{E}(J)^2 + \lambda \mathrm{E}(J^2). \tag{71}$$

Thus

$$\dot{k}_{u_0} f = 2\lambda^2 u_0 \mathrm{E}(J)^2 + 2\lambda \mathrm{E}(J^2) = 2\lambda \mathrm{E}(X_{u_0})\mathrm{E}(J) + 2\lambda \mathrm{E}(J^2) \tag{72}$$

$$\dot{m}_{u_0} f = 2\lambda^2 u_0 \mathrm{E}(J)^2 + \lambda \mathrm{E}(J^2) = 2\lambda \mathrm{E}(X_{u_0})\mathrm{E}(J) + \lambda \mathrm{E}(J^2). \tag{73}$$

The difference $\dot{k}_{u_0} f - \dot{m}_{u_0} f = \lambda \mathrm{E}(J^2)$ is independent of u_0 and so the relative difference decreases as u_0 increases, corresponding to the fact that X_{u_0} changes shape more slowly as u_0 increases. If J has a second moment, which we assume, then the relative magnitude of the difference depends on the relative size of $\mathrm{E}(J^2)$ compared to $\lambda \mathrm{E}(J)^2$, i.e., the variance of J offset by the expected claim rate λ.

In general, if $f(x) = x^n$, $n \geq 3$ then

$$\dot{k}_{u_0} f = \mathrm{E}(n X_{u_0}^n / u_0). \tag{74}$$

On the other hand

$$\dot{m}_u f = \lambda \mathrm{E}_{X_u} \left[\sum_{i=1}^{n} \binom{n}{i} X_u^{n-i} \mathrm{E}(J^i) \right] \tag{75}$$

$$= \lambda \sum_{i=1}^{n} \binom{n}{i} \mathrm{E}(X_u^{n-i}) \mathrm{E}(J^i). \tag{76}$$

Let $\kappa_n(u)$ be the nth cumulant of X_u and $\mu_n'(u) = \mathrm{E}(X_u^n)$ be the nth moment. Recall $\kappa_n(u) = u \int x^n \nu(dx) = \lambda u \mathrm{E}(J^n)$ and the relationship between cumulants and moments

$$\kappa_n = \mu_n' - \sum_{k=1}^{n-1} \binom{n-1}{k-1} \kappa_k \mu_{n-k}'. \tag{77}$$

Combining these facts gives

$$\mathrm{E}(X_u^n) = \lambda u \mathrm{E}(J^n) + \sum_{i=1}^{n-1} \binom{n-1}{i-1} \lambda u \mathrm{E}(J^i) \mathrm{E}(X_u^{n-i}) \tag{78}$$

and hence

$$
\begin{aligned}
\dot{k}_{u_0}f - \dot{m}_{u_0}f &= \mathrm{E}(nX_{u_0}^n/u_0) - \lambda\sum_{i=1}^{n}\binom{n}{i}\mathrm{E}(J^i)\mathrm{E}(X_{u_0}^{n-i}) \\
&= \lambda(n\mathrm{E}(J^n) + n\sum_{i=1}^{n-1}\binom{n-1}{i-1}\mathrm{E}(J^i)\mathrm{E}(X_{u_0}^{n-i}) - \sum_{i=1}^{n}\binom{n}{i}\mathrm{E}(J^i)\mathrm{E}(X_{u_0}^{n-i})) \\
&= \lambda((n-1)\mathrm{E}(J^n) + \sum_{i=1}^{n-1}\left(n\binom{n-1}{i-1} - \binom{n}{i}\right)\mathrm{E}(J^i)\mathrm{E}(X_{u_0}^{n-i})) \\
&= \lambda\sum_{i=2}^{n}(i-1)\binom{n}{i}\mathrm{E}(J^i)\mathrm{E}(X_{u_0}^{n-i}).
\end{aligned} \tag{79}
$$

As for $n = 2$, the $\mathrm{E}(J^n)$ term is independent of u_0 whereas all the remaining terms grow with u_0. For $n = 3$ the difference is $3\lambda\mathrm{E}(J^2)\mathrm{E}(X) + 2\mathrm{E}(J^3)$.

In the case of the standard deviation risk measure we recover same results as Section 4. Let $\rho(\mu_u) = (\langle x^2, \mu_u\rangle - \langle x, \mu_u\rangle^2)^{1/2}$ be the standard deviation risk measure. Using the chain rule, the derivative of ρ in direction $\dot{k}$ at $u = u_0$, where $m(u_0) = k(u_0)$, is

$$
D\rho_{m(u_0)}(\dot{k}) = \frac{\dot{k}_{u_0}(x^2) - 2\langle x, x_{u_0}\rangle\dot{k}_{u_0}(x)}{2\rho(k_{t_0})} \tag{80}
$$

and similarly for direction $\dot{m}$. Thus

$$
D\rho(\dot{k}) - D\rho(\dot{m}) = \frac{\lambda\mathrm{E}(J^2)}{2\rho(m_{u_0})}, \tag{81}
$$

which is the same as the difference between Equations (7) and (10) because here $c_i = 0$, $g = \mathrm{E}(J^2)$ and, since we are considering equality at u_0 where frequency is $x = \lambda u_0$, and we are differentiating with respect to u we pick up the additional λ in Equation (10).

This section has shown there are important local differences between the maps k and m. They may agree at a point, but the agreement is not first order—the two maps define different directions. Since capital allocation relies on derivatives—the ubiquitous gradient—it is not surprising that different allocations result. Meyer's example and the failure of gradient based formulas to add-up for diversifying Lévy processes are practical manifestations of these differences.

The commonalities we have found between the homogeneous approximation k and the insurance embedding m are consistent with the findings of Boonen et al. (2017) that although insurance portfolios are not linearly scalable in exposure the Euler allocation rule can still be used in an insurance context. Our analysis pinpoints the difference between the two and highlights particular ways it could fail and could be more material in applications. Specifically, it is more material for smaller portfolios and for portfolios where the severity component has a high variance: these are exactly the situations where aggregate losses will be more skewed and will change shape most rapidly.

7. Empirical Analysis

7.1. Overview

Next we test different loss models against US statutory insurance data. Aon Benfield's original Insurance Risk Study ABI (2007) was based on the methodology described in this paper and the exhibits below formed part of its backup. The Risk Study has been continued each year since, see ABI (2012, 2013, 2014, 2015) for the most recent editions. The 2015 Tenth Edition provides a high-level analysis using regulatory insurance data from 49 countries that together represent over 90% of global P & C premium. The conclusions reported here hold across a very broad range of geographies and lines of business.

The original analysis ABI (2007) focused on the US and used National Association of Insurance Commissioners (NAIC) data. The NAIC is an umbrella organization for individual US state regulators. The NAIC statutory annual statement includes an accident year report, called Schedule P, showing ten years of premium and loss data by major line of business. This data is available by insurance company and insurance group. The analysis presented here will use data from 1993 to 2004 by line of business. We will model the data using IM1-4 from Section 5.2. The model fits can differentiate company effects from accident year pricing cycle effects, and the parameters show considerable variation by line of business. The fits also capture information about the mixing distribution C.

We will show the data is consistent with two hypotheses:

H1. The asymptotic coefficient of variation or volatility as volume grows is strictly positive.
H2. Time and volume are symmetric in the sense that the coefficient of variation of aggregate losses for volume x insured for time t only depends on xt.

H1 implies that insurance losses are *not* volumetrically diversifying. Based on Table 1, H1 is only consistent with IM3 or IM4. H2 is only consistent with IM1 and IM3. Therefore the data is only consistent with model IM3 and not consistent with the other models. IM3 implies that diversification over time and volume follows a symmetric modified square root rule, $v(x,t) = \sqrt{(\sigma^2/xt) + c}$.

7.2. Isolating the Mixing Distribution

We now show that the mixing distribution C in IM3 and IM4 can be inferred from a large book of business even though it cannot be directly observed.

Consider an aggregate loss distribution with a C-mixed Poisson frequency distribution, per Equation (6) or IM3, 4. If the expected claim count is large and if the severity has a variance then particulars of the severity distribution diversify away in the aggregate. Any severity from a policy with a limit obviously has a variance. Moreover the variability from the Poisson claim count component also diversifies away, because the coefficient of variation of a Poisson distribution tends to zero as the mean increases. Therefore the shape of the normalized aggregate loss distribution, aggregate losses divided by expected aggregate losses, converges in distribution to the mixing distribution C.

This assertion can be proved using moment generating functions. Let X_n be a sequence of random variables with distribution functions F_n and let X be another random variable with distribution F. If $F_n(x) \to F(x)$ as $n \to \infty$ for every point of continuity of F then we say F_n converges weakly to F and that X_n converges in distribution to X.

Convergence in distribution is a relatively weak form of convergence. A stronger form is convergence in probability, which means for all $\epsilon > 0$ $\Pr(|X_n - X| > \epsilon) \to 0$ as $n \to \infty$. If X_n converges to X in probability then X_n also converges to X in distribution. The converse is false. For example, let $X_n = Y$ and X be binomial 0/1 random variables with $\Pr(Y = 1) = \Pr(X = 1) = 1/2$. Then X_n converges to X in distribution. However, since $\Pr(|X - Y| = 1) = 1/2$, X_n does not converge to X in probability.

X_n converges in distribution to X if the moment generating functions (MGFs) $M_n(z) = \mathrm{E}(e^{zX_n})$ of X_n converge to the MGF of M of X for all z: $M_n(z) \to M(z)$ as $n \to \infty$, see (Feller 1971, vol. 2, chp. XV.3 Theorem 2). We can now prove the following proposition.

Proposition 1. *Let N be a C-mixed Poisson distribution with mean n, C with mean 1 and variance c, and let X be an independent severity with mean x and variance $x(1+\gamma^2)$. Let $A_n = X_1 + \cdots + X_N$ and $a = nx$. Then the normalized loss ratio A_n/a converges in distribution to C, so*

$$\Pr(A_n/a < \alpha) \to \Pr(C < \alpha) \tag{82}$$

as $n \to \infty$. Hence the standard deviation of A_n/a satisfies

$$\sigma(A_n/a) = \sqrt{c + \frac{x(1+\gamma^2)}{a}} \to \sqrt{c}. \tag{83}$$

Proof. The moment generating function $M_{A_n}(z)$ of A_n is

$$M_{A_n}(z) = M_C(n(M_X(z) - 1)) \tag{84}$$

where M_C and M_X are the moment generating functions of C and X. Using Taylor's expansion we can write

$$\begin{aligned}
\lim_{n\to\infty} M_{A_n/a}(z) &= \lim_{n\to\infty} M_{A_n}(z/a) \\
&= \lim_{n\to\infty} M_C(n(M_X(z/nx) - 1)) \\
&= \lim_{n\to\infty} M_C(n(M'_X(0)z/nx + R(z/nx))) \\
&= \lim_{n\to\infty} M_C(z + nR(z/nx))) \\
&= M_C(z)
\end{aligned}$$

for some remainder function $R(z) = O(z^2)$. The assumptions on the mean and variance of X guarantee $M'_X(0) = x = \mathrm{E}(X)$ and that the remainder term in Taylor's expansion is $O(z^2)$. The second part is trivial. □

Proposition 1 is equivalent to a classical risk theory result of Lundberg describing the stabilization in time of portfolios in the collective, see (Bühlmann 1970, sct. 3.3). It also implies that if the frequency distribution is actually Poisson, so the mixing distribution is $C = 1$ with probability 1, then the loss ratio distribution of a very large book will tend to the distribution concentrated at the expected.

Figures 4 and 5 illustrate the proposition, showing how the aggregate distributions change shape as expected counts increase. In Figure 4, $C = 1$ and the claim count is Poisson. Here the scaled distributions get more and more concentrated about the expected value (scaled to 1.0). In Figure 5, C has a gamma distribution with variance 0.0625 (asymptotic coefficient of variation of 0.25). Now the scaled aggregate distributions converge to C.

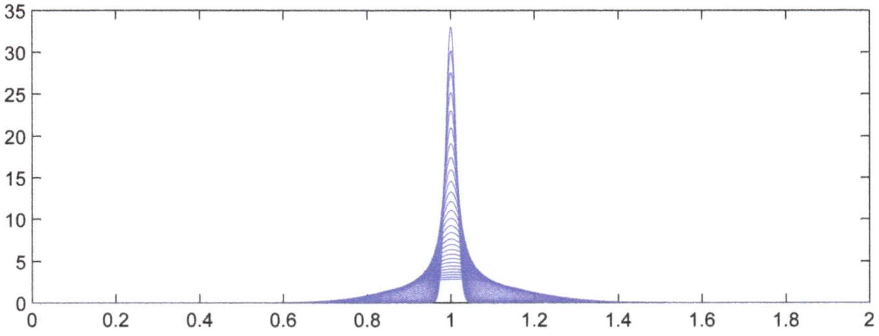

Figure 4. Theoretical distribution of scaled aggregate losses with no parameter or structure uncertainty and Poisson frequency.

Proposition 1 shows that in many realistic insurance situations severity is irrelevant to the shape of the distribution of aggregate losses for a large book of business. This is an irritating but important result. Severity distributions are relatively easy to estimate, particularly when occurrence severity is limited by policy terms and conditions. Frequency distributions, on the other hand, are much more difficult to estimate. Proposition 1 shows that the single most important variable for estimating the shape of A is the mixing distribution C. Problematically, C is never independently observed! The power of the proposition is to suggest a method for determining C: consider the loss ratio distribution of large books of business.

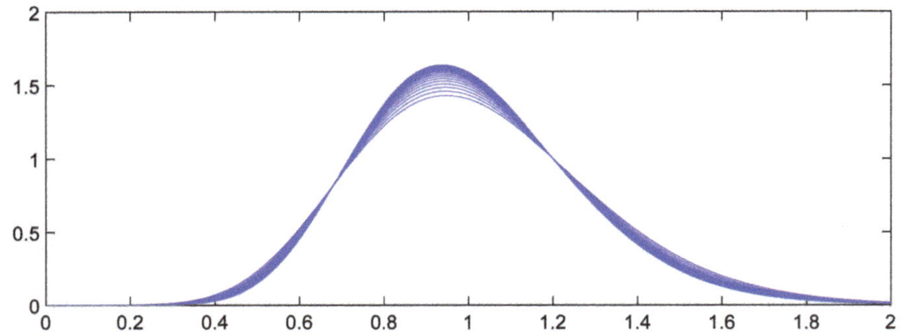

Figure 5. Theoretical distribution envelope of scaled aggregate losses with a gamma mixed Poisson frequency with mixing variance $c = 0.0625$.

The mixing distribution C can be thought of as capturing parameter risk or systematic insurance risks since its effect does not diversify away in a large book of business. In our context C is capturing a number of non-diversifiable risk elements, including variation the type of insured or coverage within a given classification, variation in the weather or other macro-risk factor over a long time frame (for example, the recent rise in distracted driving or changes in workplace injuries driven by the business cycle) as well as changes in the interpretation of policy coverage. We will estimate expected losses using premium and so the resulting C also captures inter-company pricing effects, such as different expense ratios, profit targets and underwriting appetites, as well as insurance pricing cycle effects (both of which are controlled for in our analysis). Henceforth we will refer to C as capturing parameter risk rather than calling it the mixing distribution.

7.3. Volumetric Empirics

We use NAIC annual statement data to determine an appropriate distribution for C (or $Z(1)$), providing new insight into the exact form of parameter risk. In the absence of empirical information, mathematical convenience usually reigns and a gamma distribution is used for C; the unconditional claim count is then a negative binomial. The distribution of C is called the structure function in credibility theory Bühlmann (1970).

Schedule P in the NAIC annual statement includes a ten accident-year history of gross, ceded and net premiums and ultimate losses by major line of business. We focus on gross ultimate losses. The major lines include private passenger auto liability, homeowners, commercial multi-peril, commercial auto liability, workers compensation, other liability occurrence (premises and operations liability), other liability claims made (including directors and officers and professional liability but excluding medical), and medical malpractice claims made. These lines have many distinguishing characteristics that are subjectively summarized in Table 3 as follows.

- **Heterogeneity** refers to the level of consistency in terms and conditions and types of insureds within the line, with high heterogeneity indicating a broad range. The two Other Liability lines are catch-all classifications including a wide range of insureds and policies.
- **Regulation** indicates the extent of rate regulation by state insurance departments.
- **Limits** refers to the typical policy limit. Personal auto liability limits rarely exceed $300,000 per accident in the US and are characterized as low. Most commercial lines policies have a primary limit of $1M, possibly with excess liability policies above that. Workers compensation policies do not have a limit but the benefit levels are statutorily prescribed by each state.
- **Cycle** is an indication of the extent of the pricing cycle in each line; it is simply split personal (low) and commercial (high).

- **Cats** (i.e., catastrophes) covers the extent to which the line is subject to multi-claimant, single occurrence catastrophe losses such as hurricanes, earthquakes, mass tort, securities laddering, terrorism, and so on.

  The data is interpreted in the light of these characteristics.

Table 3. Characteristics of Various Lines of Insurance

Insurance Line	Heterogeneity	Regulation	Limits	Cycle	Cats
Personal Auto	Low	High	Low	Low	No
Commercial Auto	Moderate	Moderate	Moderate	High	No
Workers Compensation	Moderate	High	Statutory	High	Possible
Medical Malpractice	Moderate	Moderate	Moderate	High	No
Commercial Multi-Peril	Moderate	Moderate	Moderate	High	Moderate
Other Liability Occurrence	High	Low	High	High	Yes
Homeowners Multi-Peril	Moderate	High	Low	Low	High
Other Liability Claims Made	High	Low	High	High	Possible

In order to apply Proposition 1 we proxy a "large" book as one with more than \$100M of premium in each accident year. Figure 6 shows how the volatility of loss ratio by line varies with premium size. It is computed by bucketing Schedule P loss ratios by premium size band and computing the volatilities in each bucket. Each inset chart shows the same data on a log/log scale. The figure shows three things.

1. The loss processes are not volumetrically diversifying, that is the volatility does not decrease to zero with volume.
2. Below a range \$100M-1B (varying by line) there are material changes in volatility with premium size.
3. \$100M is a reasonable threshold for large, in the sense that there is less change in volatility beyond \$100M.

The second point means that the inhomogeneity in a loss portfolio is very material in the \$10–100M premium range where most companies would try to set profit targets by line or business unit. This is consistent with Mildenhall (2004).

We now determine C by line by applying Proposition 1. The data consists of observed schedule P gross ultimate loss ratios $\lambda_{c,y}$ by company c and accident year $y = 1993, \ldots, 2004$. The observation $\lambda_{c,y}$ is included if company c had gross earned premium $\geq$ \$100M in year y. The data is in the form of an unbalanced two-way ANOVA table with at most one observation per cell. Let $\lambda_{.,.}$ denote the average loss ratio over all companies and accident years, and $\lambda_{c,.}$ (resp. $\lambda_{.,y}$) the average loss ratio for company c over all years (resp. accident year y over all companies). Each average can be computed as a straight arithmetic average of loss ratios or as a premium-weighted average. With this data we will determine four different measures of volatility.

Res1. Raw loss ratio volatility across all twelve years of data for all companies. This volatility includes a pricing cycle effect, captured by accident year, and a company effect.

Res2. Control for the accident year effect $\lambda_{.,y}$. This removes the pricing cycle but it also removes some of the catastrophic loss effect for a year—an issue with the results for homeowners in 2004.

Res3. Control for the company effect $\lambda_{c,.}$. This removes spurious loss ratio variation caused by differing expense ratios, distribution costs, profit targets, classes of business, limits, policy size and so forth.

Res4. Control for both company effect and accident year, i.e., perform an unbalanced two-way ANOVA with zero or one observation per cell. This can be done additively, modeling the loss ratio $\lambda_{c,y}$ for company c in year y as

$$\hat{\lambda}_{c,y} = \lambda_{.,.} + (\lambda_{c,.} - \lambda_{.,.}) + (\lambda_{.,y} - \lambda_{.,.}), \tag{85}$$

or multiplicatively as

$$\hat{\lambda}_{c,y} = \lambda_{.,.}(\lambda_{c,.}/\lambda_{.,.})(\lambda_{.,y}/\lambda_{.,.}). \tag{86}$$

The multiplicative approach is generally preferred as it never produces negative fit loss ratios. The statistical properties of the residual distributions are similar for both forms.

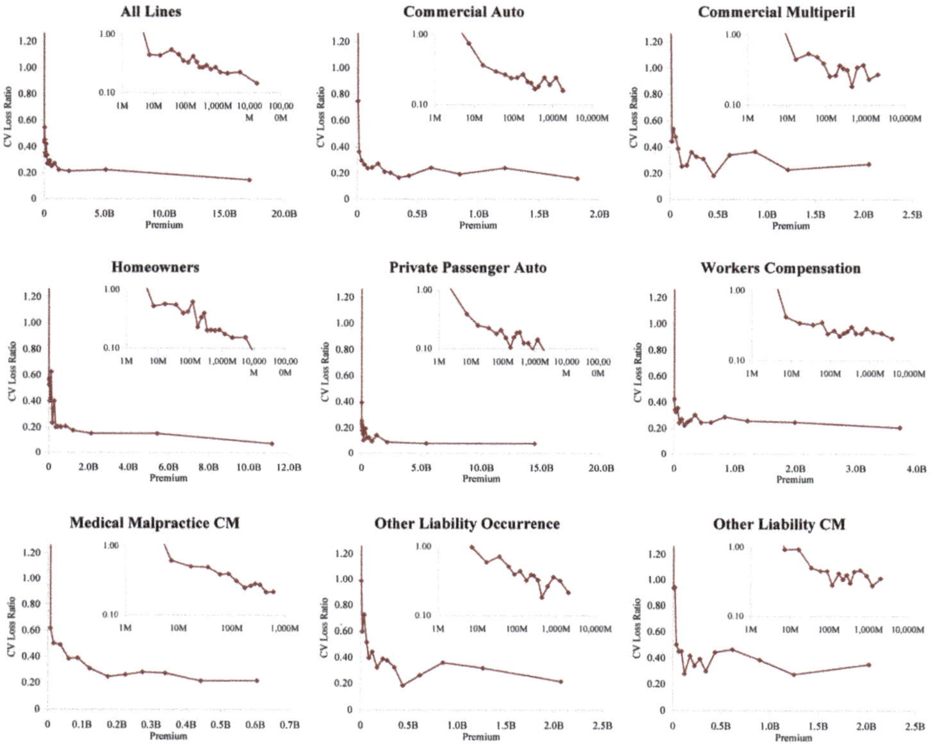

Figure 6. The relationship between raw loss ratio volatility, measured as coefficient of variation of loss ratios, and premium volume, using data from accident years 1993–2004. Each inset graph plots the same data on a log/log scale, showing that the volatility continues to decrease materially for premium volumes in the \$100Ms. The total line is distorted by changing mix of business by volume; the largest companies are dominated by private passenger auto liability which is the lowest volatility line.

Using Proposition 1 we obtain four estimates for the distribution of C from the empirical distributions of $\lambda_{c,y}/\hat{\lambda}_{.,.}$, $\lambda_{c,y}/\hat{\lambda}_{.,y}$, $\lambda_{c,y}/\hat{\lambda}_{c,.}$ and $\lambda_{c,y}/\hat{\lambda}_{c,y}$ for suitably large books of business. The additive residuals $\lambda_{c,y} - \hat{\lambda}_{c,y}$ also have a similar distribution (not shown).

Figures 7–9 show analyses of variance for the model described by Equation (85). Because the data is unbalanced, consisting of at most one observation per cell, it is necessary to perform a more subtle ANOVA than in the balanced case. We follow the method described in (Ravishanker and Dey 2002, sct. 9.2.2). The idea is to adjust for one variable first and then to remove the effect of this adjustment before controlling for the other variable. For example, in the extreme case where there is only one observation for a given company, that company's loss ratio is fit exactly with its company effect and the loss ratio observation should not contribute to the accident year volatility measure. Both the accident year effect and the company effect are highly statistically significant in all cases, except the unadjusted company effect for homeowners and the adjusted company effect for other liability claims made. The R^2 statistics are in the 50–70% range for all lines except homeowners. As discussed above, the presence of catastrophe losses in 2004 distorts the homeowners results.

Additive ANOVA for Commercial Auto, $100M Threshold

Source of Variation	Sum of Squares	D of F	Mean Squares	F Ratio	p Value	
Unadjusted Accident Year	6.3446	11	0.5768	37.2271	6.70E-55	***
Adjusted Company Effect	4.9147	56	0.0878	5.6645	3.44E-26	***
Residual	5.7658	407	0.0142			
Std. Deviation			11.9%			
Total (about mean)	17.0251	474	0.0359			
Std. Deviation			19.0%			
R2	0.6613					
Adjusted Accident Year	5.0773	11	0.4616	29.7914	8.48E-46	***
Unadjusted Company Effect	6.1819	56	0.1104	7.1250	3.14E-34	***
Tukey's Test for Interactions						
SSA	0.0035		F statistic	0.2443		
SSB	5.7658		p Value	0.621		
SSR	5.7624					

Additive ANOVA for Commercial Multiperil, $100M Threshold

Source of Variation	Sum of Squares	D of F	Mean Squares	F Ratio	p Value	
Unadjusted Accident Year	7.3649	11	0.6695	21.3469	1.85E-34	***
Adjusted Company Effect	7.9119	67	0.1181	3.7650	5.72E-17	***
Residual	12.0741	420	0.0287			
Std. Deviation			17.0%			
Total (about mean)	27.3509	498	0.0549			
Std. Deviation			23.4%			
R2	0.5585					
Adjusted Accident Year	9.4834	11	0.8621	27.4873	4.09E-43	***
Unadjusted Company Effect	5.7934	67	0.0865	2.7569	3.68E-10	***
Tukey's Test for Interactions						
SSA	0.0277		F statistic	0.9668		
SSB	12.0741		p Value	0.326		
SSR	12.0464					

Additive ANOVA for Homeowners, $100M Threshold

Source of Variation	Sum of Squares	D of F	Mean Squares	F Ratio	p Value	
Unadjusted Accident Year	3.0722	11	0.2793	3.1671	3.67E-04	***
Adjusted Company Effect	12.9407	78	0.1659	1.8813	3.39E-05	***
Residual	42.7530	488	0.0876			
Std. Deviation			29.6%			
Total (about mean)	58.7659	577	0.1018			
Std. Deviation			31.9%			
R2	0.2725					
Adjusted Accident Year	12.9724	11	1.1793	13.3729	1.97E-22	***
Unadjusted Company Effect	3.0405	78	0.0390	0.4420	1.00E+00	
Tukey's Test for Interactions						
SSA	0.0001		F statistic	0.0008		
SSB	42.7530		p Value	0.977		
SSR	42.7529					

Figure 7. Adjusted analysis of variance (ANOVA) for commercial auto, commercial multiperil and homeowners.

Tukey's test for interactions in an ANOVA with one observation per cell (Miller and Wichern 1977, sct. 4.11) does not support an interaction effect for any line at the 5% level. This is consistent with a hypothesis that all companies participate in the pricing cycle to some extent.

Additive ANOVA for Medical Malpractice CM, $100M Threshold

Source of Variation	Sum of Squares	D of F	Mean Squares	F Ratio	p Value	
Unadjusted Accident Year	5.7299	11	0.5209	8.9928	7.43E-11	***
Adjusted Company Effect	3.2898	29	0.1134	1.9584	7.88E-03	***
Residual	3.9561	97	0.0408			
Std. Deviation			20.2%			
Total (about mean)	12.9758	137	0.0947			
Std. Deviation			30.8%			
R2	0.6951					
Adjusted Accident Year	4.9819	11	0.4529	7.8189	1.49E-09	***
Unadjusted Company Effect	4.0377	29	0.1392	2.4037	7.46E-04	***
Tukey's Test for Interactions						
SSA	0.1502		F statistic	3.8683		
SSB	3.9561		p Value	0.052		
SSR	3.8059					

Additive ANOVA for Other Liability CM, $100M Threshold

Source of Variation	Sum of Squares	D of F	Mean Squares	F Ratio	p Value	
Unadjusted Accident Year	8.6215	11	0.7838	17.0633	6.97E-21	***
Adjusted Company Effect	2.1244	31	0.0685	1.4919	6.22E-02	
Residual	5.0512	138	0.0366			
Std. Deviation			19.1%			
Total (about mean)	15.7971	180	0.0878			
Std. Deviation			29.6%			
R2	0.6802					
Adjusted Accident Year	2.9908	11	0.2719	5.9192	7.73E-08	***
Unadjusted Company Effect	7.7551	31	0.2502	5.4463	1.49E-12	***
Tukey's Test for Interactions						
SSA	0.0566		F statistic	1.5756		
SSB	5.0512		p Value	0.211		
SSR	4.9945					

Additive ANOVA for Other Liability Occurrence, $100M Threshold

Source of Variation	Sum of Squares	D of F	Mean Squares	F Ratio	p Value	
Unadjusted Accident Year	10.5218	11	0.9565	16.9844	4.71E-27	***
Adjusted Company Effect	9.6707	59	0.1639	2.9104	5.08E-10	***
Residual	19.5477	362	0.0540			
Std. Deviation			23.2%			
Total (about mean)	39.7401	432	0.0920			
Std. Deviation			30.3%			
R2	0.5081					
Adjusted Accident Year	10.4953	11	0.9541	16.9416	5.47E-27	***
Unadjusted Company Effect	9.6972	59	0.1644	2.9184	4.56E-10	***
Tukey's Test for Interactions						
SSA	0.0042		F statistic	0.0779		
SSB	19.5477		p Value	0.780		
SSR	19.5435					

Figure 8. Adjusted ANOVA for medical malpractice claims made and other liability claims made and occurrence.

Figure 10 shows the indicated volatilities for commercial auto, commercial multi-peril, homeowners, other liability occurrence, private passenger auto liability and workers compensation for the four models Res1-4 and Equation (86). The right hand plot shows the impact of the pricing (accident year) effect and the firm effect on total volatility. This Figure shows two interesting things. On the left it gives a ranking of line by volatility of loss ratio from private passenger auto liability, 14% unadjusted and 8% adjusted, to homeowners and other liability occurrence, 41% and 36% unadjusted and 30% and 23% adjusted, respectively. The right hand plot shows that personal lines have a lower pricing cycle effect (28% and 32% increase in volatility from pricing) than the commercial lines (mostly over 50%). This is reasonable given the highly regulated nature of pricing and the lack of underwriter schedule credits and debits. These results are consistent with the broad classification in Table 3.

Additive ANOVA for Private Passenger Auto, $100M Threshold

Source of Variation	Sum of Squares	D of F	Mean Squares	F Ratio	p Value	
Unadjusted Accident Year	1.3640	11	0.1240	20.9565	1.55E-37	***
Adjusted Company Effect	6.1637	101	0.0610	10.3137	1.11E-90	***
Residual	4.5636	786	0.0058			
Std. Deviation			7.6%			
Total (about mean)	12.0913	898	0.0135			
Std. Deviation			11.6%			
R2	0.6226					
Adjusted Accident Year	6.2189	11	0.5654	95.5466	9.70E-137	***
Unadjusted Company Effect	1.3088	101	0.0130	2.1900	2.86E-09	***
Tukey's Test for Interactions						
SSA	0.0022		F statistic	0.3720		
SSB	4.5636		p Value	0.542		
SSR	4.5615					

Additive ANOVA for Workers Compensation, $100M Threshold

Source of Variation	Sum of Squares	D of F	Mean Squares	F Ratio	p Value	
Unadjusted Accident Year	13.9945	11	1.2722	68.2576	1.94E-96	***
Adjusted Company Effect	5.1661	86	0.0601	3.2229	1.00E-16	***
Residual	9.5719	569	0.0168			
Std. Deviation			13.0%			
Total (about mean)	28.7325	666	0.0431			
Std. Deviation			20.8%			
R2	0.6669					
Adjusted Accident Year	6.1297	11	0.5572	29.8973	1.08E-49	***
Unadjusted Company Effect	13.0309	86	0.1515	8.1295	2.58E-57	***
Tukey's Test for Interactions						
SSA	0.0133		F statistic	0.7954		
SSB	9.5719		p Value	0.373		
SSR	9.5586					

Figure 9. Adjusted ANOVA for private passenger auto liability and workers compensation.

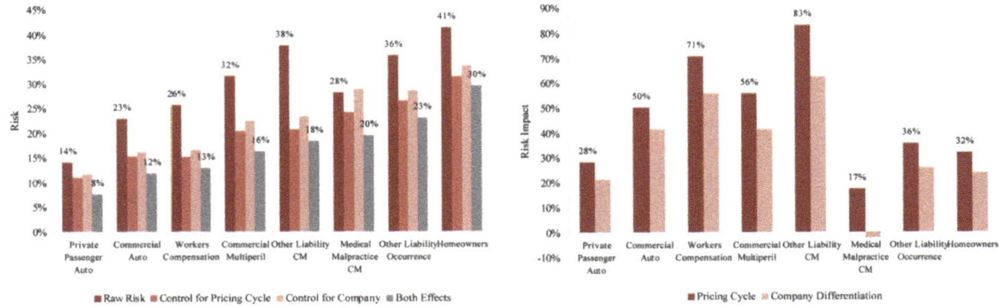

Figure 10. **Left** plot shows the loss ratio volatility by line for companies writing $100M or more premium each year based on Schedule P accident year ultimate booked gross loss ratios, from 1993–2004. The graph shows the effect of adjusting the loss ratio for an accident year pricing effect, a company effect, and both effects (i.e., Res1-4). The **right** hand plot shows the differential impact of the pricing effect and company effect by line. Each bar shows the increase in volatility of the unadjusted loss ratios compared to the adjusted.

Figures 11–14 show the histograms of normalized loss ratio distributions corresponding to Res1-4 for the same eight lines of business. These give a direct estimate of the distribution of C. There are four plots shown for each line.

The top left plot shows the distribution of normalized Schedule P accident year ultimate booked gross loss ratios for companies writing $100M or more premium, for 1993–2004. The distributions are shown for each of the four models Res1-4. LR indicates the raw model Res1, AY Avg adjusts for accident year or pricing cycle effect Res 2, Co Avg adjusts for company effect Res 3, and Mult Both Avg adjusts for both Res 4, per Equation (86). All residuals are computed using the multiplicative model.

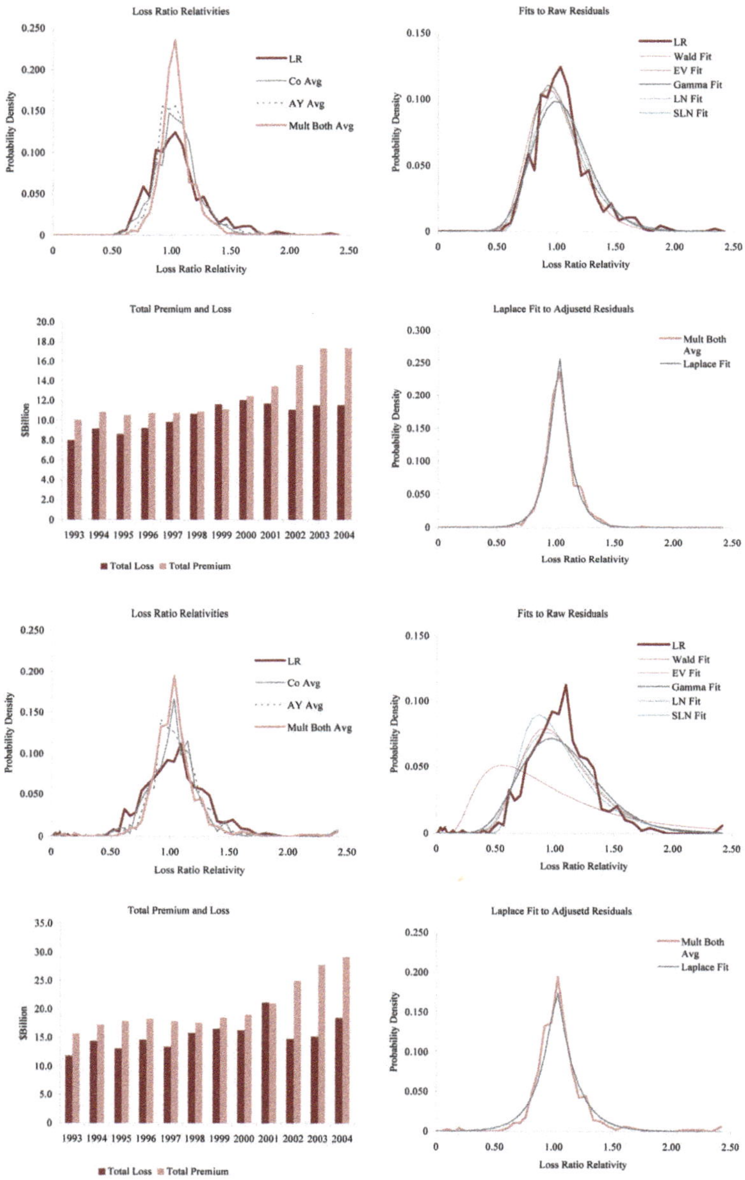

Figure 11. Commercial auto liability (**top four plots**) and commercial multiperil volatility (**bottom four plots**). Note 9/11 loss effect in the lower-left plot. See text for a description of the plots.

The top right hand plot shows five parametric distribution fits to the raw residuals, Res1. The distributions are described in Table 4. The shifted lognormal distribution has three parameters and so would be expected to fit better. The raw residuals, Res1, are typically more skewed than Res4 and do not have the same peaked shape. The commonly-assumed gamma distribution fit is shown in bold grey; the adequacy of its fit varies from line to line.

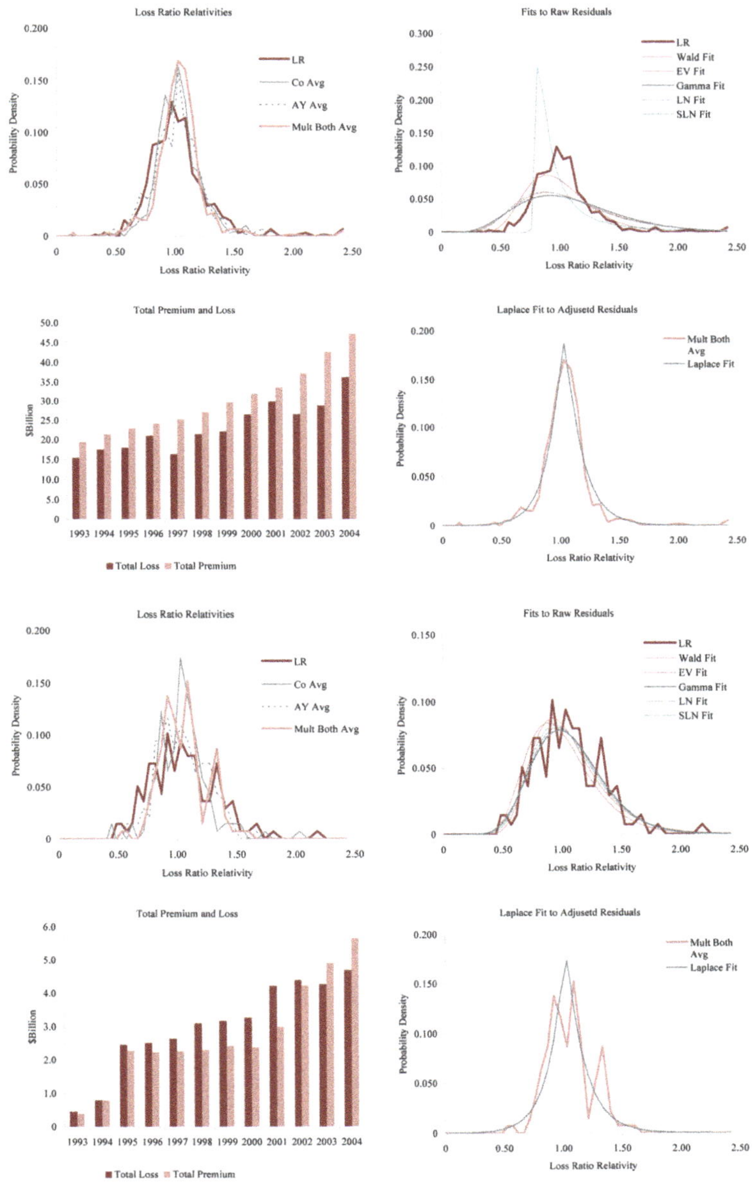

Figure 12. Homeowners (**top four plots**) and medical malpractice claims made volatility (**bottom four plots**). Note the 2004 homowners catastrophe losses. See text for a description of the plots.

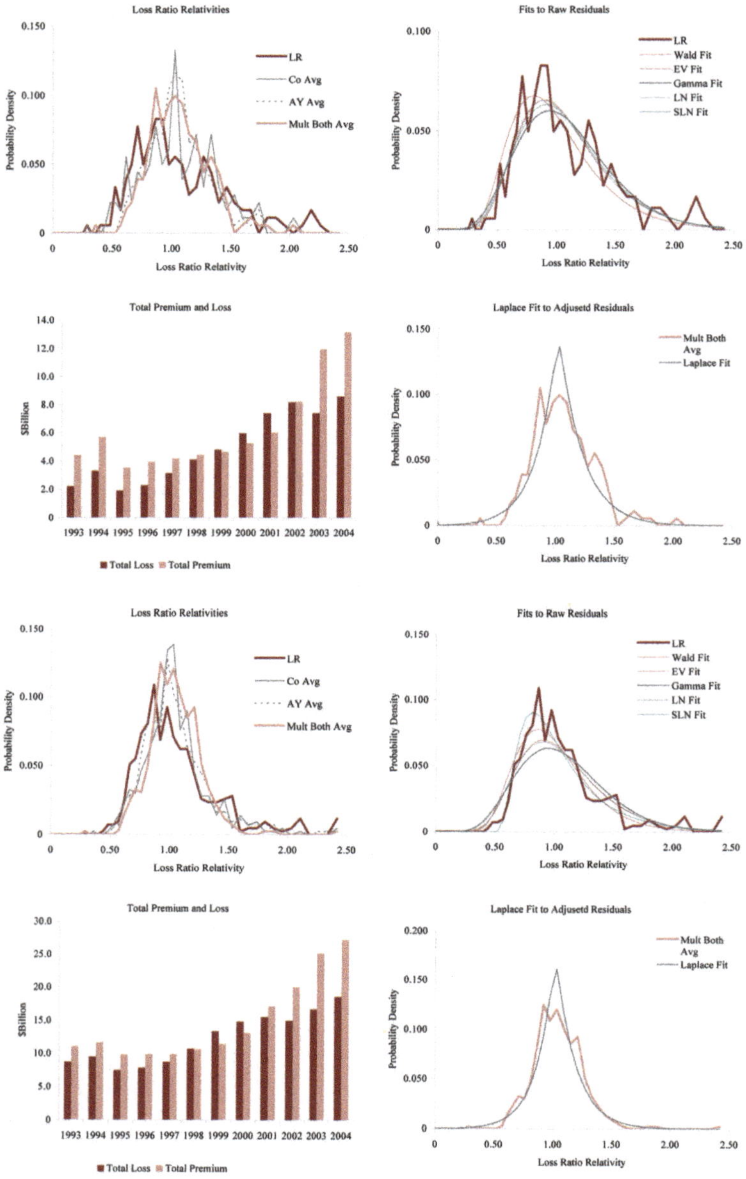

Figure 13. Other liability claims made (**top four plots**) and occurrence volatility (**bottom four plots**). See text for a description of the plots.

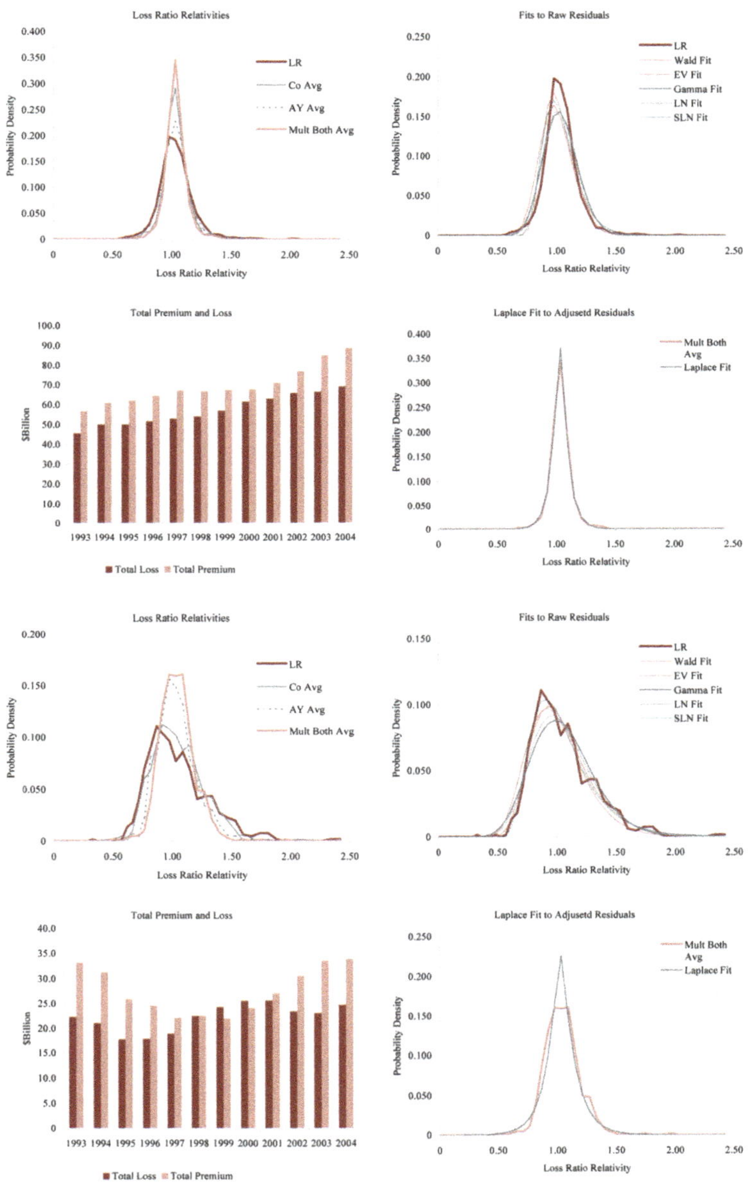

Figure 14. Private passenger auto liability (**top four plots**) and workers compensation volatility (**bottom four plots**). Note vertical scale on private passenger auto loss ratios and the visibly higher volatility of premium than loss in the lower left hand plot. See text for a description of the plots.

Table 4. Summary of distributions fit to C in Figures 11–14.

Abbreviation	Parameters	Distribution	Fitting Method
Wald	2	Wald (inverse Gaussian)	Maximum likelihood
EV	2	Frechet-Tippet extreme value	Method of moments
Gamma	2	Gamma	Method of moments
LN	2	Lognormal	Maximum likelihood
SLN	3	Shifted lognormal	Method of moments

The lower right hand plot shows the residuals adjusted for both pricing cycle and company effects, Res4, and it includes a maximum likelihood Laplace fit to the multiplicative model Equation (86). This plot strongly supports the choice of a Laplace distribution for C in the adjusted case. This is a very unexpected result as the Laplace is symmetric and leptokurtic (peaked). The Laplace distribution has the same relationship to the absolute value difference that the normal distribution has to squared difference; median replaces mean. One could speculate that a possible explanation for the Laplace is the tendency of insurance company management to discount extreme outcomes and take a more median than mean view of losses. The Laplace can be represented as a subordinated Brownian motion, introducing operational time as in IM2 and IM4. The subordinator has a gamma distribution. The Laplace is also infinitely divisible and its Lévy measure has density $\nu(x) = |x|^{-1}e^{-|x|/s}$ explored in Example 13. See Kotz et al. (2001) for a comprehensive survey of the Laplace distribution.

The lower left hand plot shows the premium and loss volume by accident year. It shows the effect of the pricing cycle and the market hardening since 2001 in all lines.

The analysis in this section assumes $t = 1$. Therefore it is impossible to differentiate models IM2-4. However, the data shows that losses are not volumetrically diversifying, Figure 6. The data suggests that C (or $Z(1)$) has a right-skewed distribution when it includes a company and pricing cycle effect and strongly suggests a Laplace distribution when adjusted for company and pricing cycle effects.

Subsequent analyses, conducted after 2006 when the bulk of this paper was written, confirm the parameter estimates shown in Figure 10 are reasonably stable over time. Volatility for liability lines has increased since 2004 driven by loss development from the soft market years that has dispersed loss ratios further as they emerged to ultimate, but the relative ordering is unchanged. Interestingly the Global Financial Crisis had very little impact on insurance volatility other than for Financial Guarantee.

Table 5 and (ABI 2010, p. 6) show a comparison of Solvency II premium risk factors with the risk factors computed here. Finally, Table 6 and (ABI 2012, p. 6) show a comparison of the individual line of business parameters based on data 1992–2011 vs. the original study 1992–2004. See (ABI 2015, p. 52) for a further update of the underwriting cycle effect on volatility by line.

Table 5. Comparison of risk factors with Solvency II premium risk factors.

Dimension	Actuarial Geometry	Solvency II
Time horizon	to ultimate	one year
Catastrophe risk	included	excluded
Size of company	large	average

Table 6. Coefficient of variation of gross loss ratio, Source: Aon Benfield Insurance Risk Study, 7th Edition, used with permission.

Line	1st Edition	7th Edition	Change
Private Passenger Auto	14%	14%	0%
Commercial Auto	24%	24%	0%
Workers' Compensation	26%	27%	1%
Commercial Multi Peril	32%	34%	2%
Medical Malpractice: Claims-Made	33%	42%	9%

Table 6. *Cont.*

Line	1st Edition	7th Edition	Change
Medical Malpractice: Occurrence	35%	35%	0%
Other Liability: Occurrence	36%	38%	2%
Special Liability	39%	39%	0%
Other Liability: Claims-Made	39%	41%	2%
Reinsurance Liability	42%	67%	25%
Products Liability: Occurrence	43%	47%	4%
International	45%	72%	27%
Homeowners	47%	48%	1%
Reinsurance: Property	65%	85%	20%
Reinsurance: Financial	81%	93%	12%
Products Liability: Claims-Made	102%	100%	−2%

7.4. Temporal Empirics

We now investigate the behavior of the coefficient of variation of a book with volume x insured for t years, $v(x,t)$ for different values of t. The analysis is complicated by the absence of long-term, stable observations. Multi-year observations include strong pricing cycle effects, results from different companies, different terms and conditions (for example the change from occurrence to claims made in several lines), and the occurrence of infrequent shock or catastrophe losses. Moreover, management actions, including reserve setting and line of business policy form and pricing decisions, will affect observed volatility.

Reviewing Table 1, and comparing with Figure 6, shows IM2-4 are consistent with the data analyzed so far. The difference between IM2 and IM4 compared to IM3 is the presence of a separate time effect in $v(x,t)$. Both models IM2 and IM4 should show a lower volatility from a given volume insurance when that insurance comes from multiple years, whereas model IM3 will not. This suggests a method to differentiate IM2/4 from IM3. First, compute $v(x,1)$, from the data underling Figure 6. Then combine two years of premium and losses, from the same company and line, and recompute volatilities. This computes $v(x/2,2)$—total volume is still x but it comes from two different years. Similarly, combining 4, 6 or 12 years of data (divisors of the total 12 years of data available) gives estimates of $v(x/4,4)$, $v(x/6,6)$, and $v(x/12,12)$. Normalizing the data to a constant loss ratio across accident years prior to performing the analysis will remove potentially distorting pricing-cycle effects.

Figure 15 shows the results of performing this analysis for private passenger auto liability. Private passenger auto liability is used because it has very low inherent process risk and low parameter risk, and so provides the best opportunity for the delicate features we are analyzing to emerge. In the figure, the second column shows $v(x,1)$ and the last four show $v(x/t,t)$ for $t = 2,4,6,12$. The average volume in each band is shown as average premium in the first column. Below the data we show the averages and standard deviations of v for broader volume bands. Clearly the differences in means are insignificant relative to the standard deviations, and so a crude analysis of variance would not reject the hypothesis that $v(x/t,t)$ is independent of t. This data implies that models IM2 and IM4 do not provide a good fit to the data—unless τ is very small. However, if τ is small then IM2 and IM4 degenerate to IM1, which has already been rejected since it is volumetrically diversifying.

Average Premium	Coefficient of Variation Loss Ratio Computed From				
	1 Year	2 Years	4 Years	6 Years	12 Years
473	1.085	0.819	0.520	0.471	0.550
1,209	0.580	0.428	0.449	0.419	0.438
1,680	0.448	1.455	0.684	0.342	0.245
2,410	1.927	0.451	1.238	0.423	0.383
3,458	0.294	0.299	0.204	0.187	0.376
4,790	0.369	0.286	0.347	0.312	0.346
6,809	0.475	0.292	0.310	0.267	0.350
9,526	0.272	0.346	0.311	0.236	0.248
13,501	0.290	0.623	0.246	0.521	0.212
19,139	0.191	0.227	0.303	0.204	0.211
26,649	0.244	0.195	0.183	0.292	0.196
37,481	0.188	0.191	0.223	0.171	0.155
54,287	0.173	0.183	0.297	0.239	0.264
73,882	0.191	0.154	0.166	0.167	0.219
108,762	0.158	0.169	0.170	0.122	0.159
153,233	0.137	0.185	0.147	0.204	0.175
213,224	0.127	0.152	0.172	0.146	0.102
307,833	0.186	0.129	0.141	0.116	0.152
439,136	0.117	0.125	0.146	0.174	0.085
606,457	0.110	0.182	0.090	0.136	0.137
845,813	0.092	0.102	0.145	0.126	0.137
1,215,551	0.132	0.103	0.124	0.112	0.101
1,725,327	0.115	0.088	0.111	0.125	0.071
2,362,126	0.068	0.130	0.101	0.089	0.135
3,597,590	0.042	0.111	0.080	0.085	0.082
8,430,433	0.079	0.073	0.094	0.087	0.079
Avg. \$3M-20M	0.315	0.345	0.287	0.288	0.291
Std.Dev. \$3M-20M	0.097	0.141	0.052	0.123	0.075
Avg. \$21M-200M	0.182	0.179	0.198	0.199	0.195
Std.Dev. \$21M-200M	0.037	0.015	0.055	0.060	0.042
Avg >\$200M	0.107	0.120	0.120	0.120	0.108
Std.Dev. >\$200M	0.040	0.032	0.030	0.029	0.030

Figure 15. Coefficient of variation of loss ratio by premium volume for private passenger auto liability, computed using bucketed xt for $t = 1, 2, 4, 6, 12$.

Finally, Figures 16 and 17 provide a graphical representation of the same data for homeowners, private passenger auto, commercial auto, workers' compensation, commercial multi-peril and other liability occurrence (other liability claims made and medical malpractice lack the necessary volume). The left hand plot shows the same data as Figure 6 on a log/linear scale and a fit of $v(x, t)$ by $\sqrt{(\sigma^2/xt) + c}$. In the fit, c is estimated from the observed asymptotic volatility and σ is estimated using minimum squared distance. The right hand plot overlays $v(x/t, t)$ for $t = 2, 4, 6, 12$ using the method described above. Thus the private passenger auto liability plot shows the data in Figure 15. These plots are consistent with the hypothesis that $v(x/t, t)$ is independent of t as there is no clear trend with t. (The case $t = 12$ is subject to higher estimation error owing to the lower number of observations.)

We conclude that of the models IM1-4 and AM1 only model IM2 of has volumetric and temporal properties consistent with the data in the NAIC annual statement database.

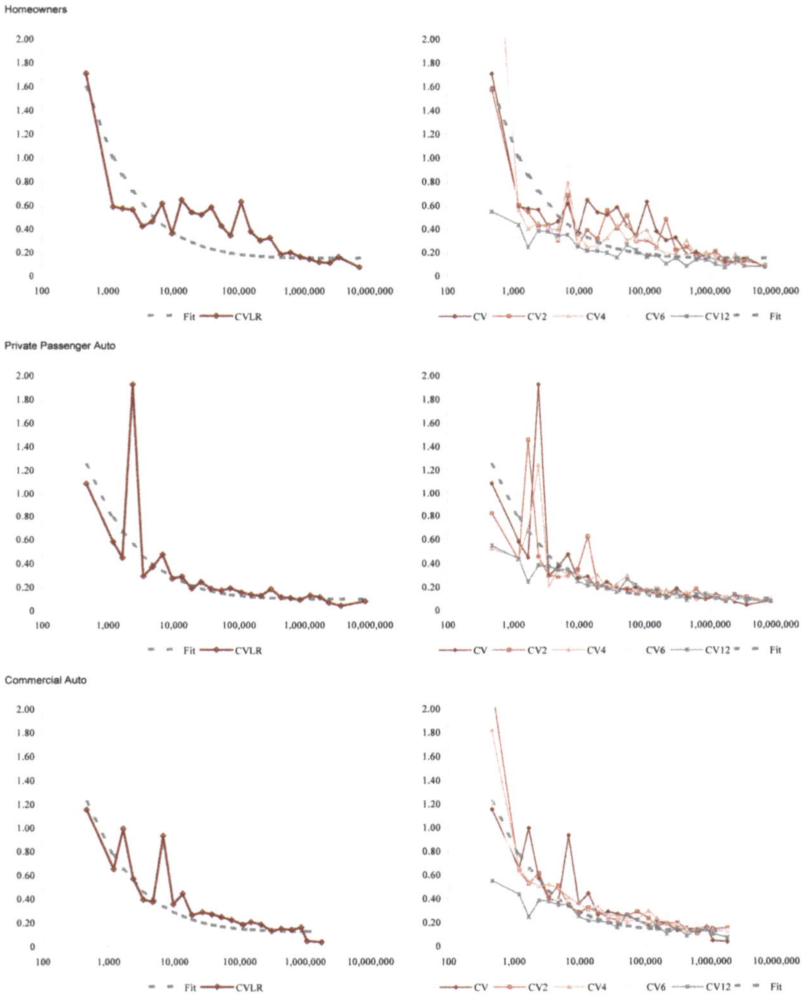

Figure 16. Fit of $\sqrt{\frac{\sigma^2}{xt} + c}$ to volatility by volume, xt, for homeowners, private passenger auto and commercial auto. **Left hand plot** shows data based on a single year $t = 1$; **right hand plot** shows the same data for $t = 1, 2, 4, 6, 12$.

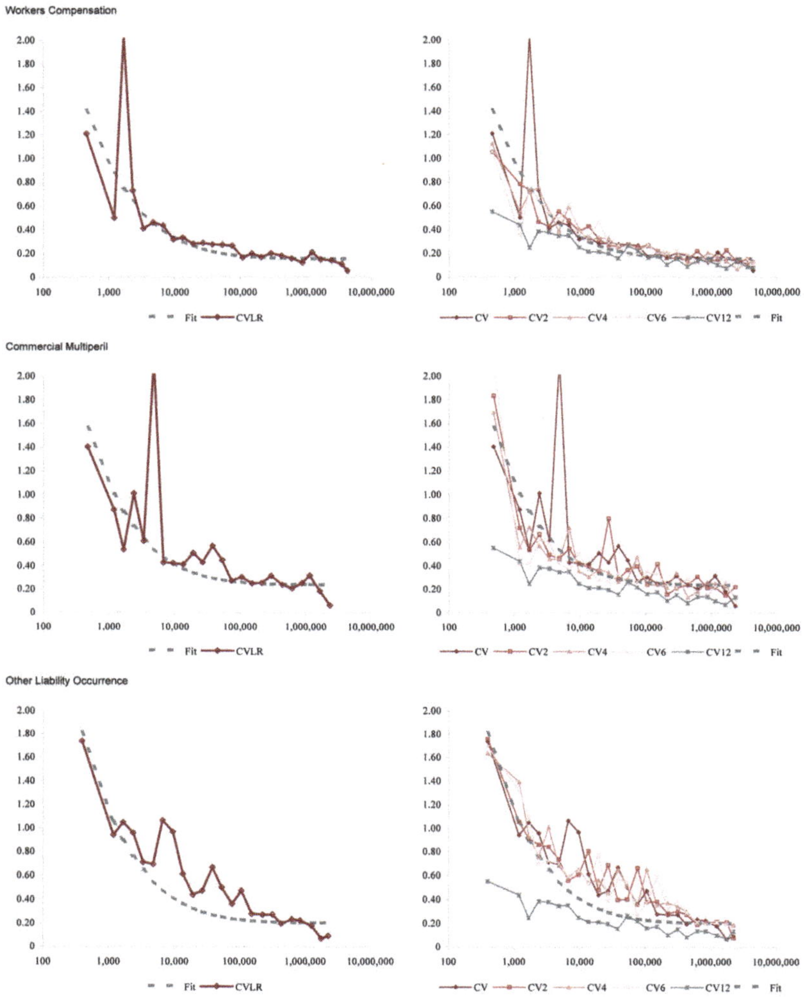

Figure 17. Fit of $\sqrt{\frac{\sigma^2}{xt} + c}$ to volatility by volume, xt, for workers compensation, commercial multiperil and other liability occurrence. **Left hand plot** shows data based on a single year $t = 1$; **right hand plot** shows the same data for $t = 1, 2, 4, 6, 12$.

8. Conclusions

The difference between asset geometry and actuarial geometry reflects a fundamental difference between an individual security, or asset, and a line of insurance. A line is analogous to a mutual fund specializing in an asset class and not to an individual asset. The choice of coordinate used to differentiate risk measures must reflect these differences.

We have provided an introduction to the actuarial use of Lévy processes to model aggregate losses. The Lévy process model reflects the realities of insurance: it is curved in both the volume and time dimensions. Asset returns, in contrast, are volumetrically flat. We have clarified the notion of a "direction" in the space of risks and used it to explain two different allocation results derived using the gradient of a risk measure.

US NAIC annual statement data is used to demonstrate that insurance liabilities do not diversify volumetrically or temporally. We reviewed four models of aggregate losses based on Lévy processes—models with a long risk-theoretic pedigree, it should be noted—and showed that only model IM2 is consistent with the NAIC data. We also show how parameter risk can be explicitly quantified at a *distributional* level even though it is unobservable. Volume-related parameter risk, adjusted for company and pricing cycle effects, is shown to have a Laplace distribution—a surprising result.

In conclusion, this paper is a call-to-arms. Finance now provides a theoretical justification for pricing company-specific risk. Risk theory provides a rigorous approach to evaluating and attributing risk to line using risk measure gradients. Regulation and Enterprise Risk Management, both of which depend crucially on an accurate quantification of aggregate loss distributions, demand accurate and realistic modeling. It is time to satisfy that demand with a fully data-grounded model for losses, including appropriate parameter risk.

Conflicts of Interest: The author declares no conflict of interest.

References

Insurance Risk Study. First Edition. Chicago: Aon Re Global, 2007.

Insurance Risk Study. Fifth Edition. Chicago: Aon Benfield, 2010.

Insurance Risk Study. Seventh Edition. Chicago: Aon Benfield, 2012.

Insurance Risk Study. Eighth Edition. Chicago: Aon Benfield, 2013.

Insurance Risk Study. Ninth Edition Chicago: Aon Benfield, 2014.

Insurance Risk Study. Tenth Edition Chicago: Aon Benfield, 2015.

Abraham, Ralph, Jerrold E. Marsden, and Tudor Ratiu. 1988. *Manifolds, Tensor Analysis, and Applications*, 2nd ed. New York: Springer Verlag.

Applebaum, David. 2004. *Lévy Processes and Stochastic Calculus*. Cambridge: Cambridge University Press.

Artzner, Philippe, F. Delbaen, J.M. Eber, and D. Heath. 1999. Coherent Measures of Risk. *Mathematical Finance* 9: 203–28.

Bühlmann, Hans. 1970. *Mathematical Models in Risk Theory*. Berlin: Springer Verlag.

Bailey, Robert A. 1967. Underwriting Profits From Investments. *Proceedings of the Casualty Actuarial Society* LIV: 1–8.

Barndorff-Nielsen, Ole E., Thomas Mikosch, and Sidney I. Resnick, eds. 2001. *Lévy Proceeses—Theory and Applications*. Boston: Birkhäuser.

Barndorff-Nielsen, Ole Eiler. 2000. *Probability Densities and Lévy Densities*. Aarhus: University of Aarhus. Centre for Mathematical Physics and Stochastics (MaPhySto), vol. MPS RR 2000-8.

Bauer, Daniel, and George Zanjani. 2013a. The Marginal Cost of Risk in a Multi-Period Risk Model. *preprint*, November.

Bauer, Daniel, and George H. Zanjani. 2013b. Capital allocation and its discontents. In *Handbook of Insurance*. New York: Springer, pp. 863–80.

Beard, R. E., T. Pentikäinen, and E. Pesonen. 1969. *Risk Theory—The Stochastic Basis of Insurance*, 3rd ed. London: Chapman and Hall.

Bertoin, Jean. 1996. *Lévy Processes*. Cambridge: Cambridge University Press.

Bodoff, Neil M. 2009. Capital Allocation by Percentile Layer. 2007 ERM Symposium. Available online: www.ermsymposium.org/2007/pdf/papers/Bodoff.png (accessed on 13 June 2017).

Boonen, Tim J., Andreas Tsanakas, and Mario V. Wüthrich. 2017. Capital allocation for portfolios with non-linear risk aggregation. *Insurance: Mathematics and Economics* 72: 95–106.

Borwein, Jonathan M., and Jon D. Vanderwerff. 2010. *Convex Functions: Constructions, Characterizations and Counterexamples*. Cambridge: Cambridge University Press, vol. 109.

Bowers, Newton, Hans Gerber, James Hickman, Donald Jones, and Cecil Nesbitt. 1986. *Actuarial Mathematics*. Schaumburg: Society of Actuaries.

Breiman, Leo. 1992. *Probability, Volume 7 of Classics in Applied Mathematics*. Philadelphia: Society for Industrial and Applied Mathematics (SIAM).

Buch, Arne, and Gregor Dorfleitner. 2008. Coherent risk measures, coherent capital allocations and the gradient allocation principle. *Insurance: Mathematics and Economics* 42: 235–42.

Cummins, J. David, and Scott E. Harrington, eds. 1987. *Fair Rate of Return in Property-Liability Insurance*. Boston: Kluwer-Nijhoff.

Cummins, J. David, and Richard D. Phillips. 2000. Applications of Financial Pricing Models in Property-Liability Insurance. In *Handbook of Insurance*. Edited by G. Dionne. Boston: Kluwer Academic.

Cummins, J. David. 1988. Risk-Based Premiums for Insurance Guarantee Funds. *Journal of Finance* 43: 823–39.

Cummins, J. David. 2000. Allocation of Capital in the Insurance Industry. *Risk Management and Insurance Review* 3: 7–27.

D'Arcy, Stephen P., and Neil A. Doherty. 1988. *The Financial Theory of Pricing Property Liability Insurance Contracts*. SS Huebner Foundation for Insurance Education, Wharton School, University of Pennsylvania; Homewood: Irwin.

D'Arcy, Stephen P., and Michael A. Dyer. 1997. Ratemaking: A Financial Economics Approach. *Proceedings of the Casualty Actuarial Society* LXXXIV: 301–90.

Daykin, Chris D., Teivo Pentikäinen, and Martti Pesonen. 1994. *Practical Risk Theory for Actuaries*. London: Chapman and Hall.

Delbaen, F., and J. Haezendonck. 1989. A martingale approach to premium calculation principles in an arbitrage free market. *Insurance: Mathematics and Economics* 8: 269–77.

Delbaen, Freddy. 2000a. Coherent Risk Measures. *Monograph, Pisa: Scoula Normale Superiore*.

Delbaen, Freddy. 2000b. *Coherent Risk Measures on General Probability Spaces*. Advances in finance and stochastics. Berlin: Springer, 2002. 1–37

Denault, Michel. 2001. Coherent allocation of risk capital. *Journal of Risk* 4: 1–34.

Dhaene, Jan, Mark J. Goovaerts, and Rob Kaas. 2003. Economic capital allocation derived from risk measures. *North American Actuarial Journal* 7: 44–56.

Dhaene, Jan, Steven Vanduffel, Marc J. Goovaerts, Rob Kaas, Qihe Tang, and David Vyncke. 2006. Risk Measures and Comonotonicity: A Review. *Stochastic Models* 22: 573–606.

Dhaene, Jan, Roger JA Laeven, Steven Vanduffel, Gregory Darkiewicz, and Marc J. Goovaerts. 2008. Can a coherent risk measure be too subadditive? *Journal of Risk and Insurance* 75: 365–86.

Dhaene, Jan, Andreas Tsanakas, Emiliano A. Valdez, and Steven Vanduffel. 2012. Optimal Capital Allocation Principles. *Journal of Risk and Insurance* 79: 1–28.

Doherty, Neil A., and James R. Garven. 1986. Price Regulation in Property-Liability Insurance: A Contingent Claims Approach. *Journal of Finance* XLI: 1031–50.

Erel, Isil, Stewart C. Myers, and James A. Read. 2015. A theory of risk capital. *Journal of Financial Economics* 118: 620–635.

Föllmer, Hans, and Alexander Schied. 2011. *Stochastic Finance: An Introduction in Discrete Time*. Berlin: Walter de Gruyter.

Feller, William. 1971. *An Introduction to Probability Theory and Its Applications, Two Volumes*, 2nd ed. New York: John Wiley and Sons.

Ferrari, J. Robert. 1968. The relationship of underwriting, investment, leverage, and exposure to total return on owners' equity. *Proceedings of the Casualty Actuarial Society* LV: 295–302.

Fischer, Tom. 2003. Risk Capital Allocation by Coherent Risk Measures Based on One-Sided Moments. *Insurance: Mathematics and Economics* 32: 135–146.

Froot, Kenneth A., and Paul GJ O'Connell. 2008. On the pricing of intermediated risks: Theory and application to catastrophe reinsurance. *Journal of Banking and Finance* 32: 69–85.

Froot, Kenneth A., and Jeremy C. Stein. 1998. Risk management, capital budgeting, and capital structure policy for inancial institutions: an integrated approach. *Journal of Financial Economics* 47: 52–82.

Froot, Kenneth A., David S. Scharfstein, and Jeremy C. Stein. 1993. Risk Management: Coordinating Corporate Investment and Financing Policies. *Journal of Finance* XLVIII: 1629–58.

Froot, Kenneth A. 2007. Risk management, capital budgeting, and capital structure policy for insurers and reinsurers. *Journal of Risk and Insurance* 74: 273–299.

Furman, Edward, and Riardas Zitikis. 2008. Weighted risk capital allocations. *Insurance: Mathematics and Economics* 43: 263–69.

Goovaerts, Marc J., Rob Kaas, and Roger JA Laeven. 2010. Decision principles derived from risk measures. *Insurance: Mathematics and Economics* 47: 294–302.

Gründl, Helmut, and Hato Schmeiser. 2007. Capital allocation for insurance companies—what good is it? *Journal of Risk and Insurance* 74: 301–17.

Hull, John. 1983. *Options Futures and Other Derivative Securities*, 2nd ed. Englewood Cliffs: Prentice-Hall.

Jacob, Niels. 2001. *Pseduo Differential Operators & Markov Processes: Fourier Analysis and Semigroups*. London: Imperial College Press, vol. I.

Jacob, Niels. 2002. *Pseduo Differential Operators & Markov Processes: Generators and Their Potential Theory*. London: Imperial College Press, vol. II.

Jacob, Niels. 2005. *Pseduo Differential Operators & Markov Processes: Markov Processes and Applications*. London: Imperial College Press, vol. III.

Kalkbrener, Michael. 2005. An axiomatic approach to capital allocation. *Mathematical Finance* 15: 425–37.

Kallop, R. H. 1975. A current look at workers' compensation ratemaking. *Proceedings of the Casualty Actuarial Society* LXII: 62–81.

Karatzas, Ioannis, and Steven Shreve. 1988. *Brownian Motion and Stochastic Calculus*. New York: Springer-Verlag.

Klugman, Stuart A., Harry H. Panjer, and Gordon E. Willmot. 1998. *Loss Models, from Data to Decisions*. New York: John Wiley and Sons.

Kotz, Samuel, Tomasz Kozubowski, and Krzysztof Podgorski. 2001. *The Laplace Distribution and Generalizations*. Boston: Birkhauser.

Laeven, Roger JA, and Mitja Stadje. 2013. Entropy coherent and entropy convex measures of risk. *Mathematics of Operations* 38: 265–93.

Lange, Jeffrey T. 1966. General liability insurance ratemaking. *Proceedings of the Casualty Actuarial Society* LIII: 26–53.

Magrath, Joseph J. 1958. Ratemaking for fire insurance. *Proceedings of the Casualty Actuarial Society* XLV: 176–95.

Meister, Steffen. 1995. *Contributions to the Mathematics of Catastrophe Insurance Futures*. Unpublished Diplomarbeit, ETH Zurich.

Merton, Robert C., and Andre Perold. 2001. Theory of Risk Capital in Financial Firms. In *The New Corporate Finance, Where Theory Meets Practice*. Edited by Donald H. Chew. Boston: McGraw-Hill, pp. 438–54.

Meyers, G. 2005a. Distributing capital: another tactic. *Actuarial Rev* 32: 25–26. with on-line technical appendix.

Meyers, G. 2005b. The Common Shock Model for Correlated Insurance Losses. *Proc. Risk Theory Society*. Available online: http://www.aria.org/rts/proceedings/2005/Meyers%20-%20Common%20Shock.png (accessed on 13 June 2017).

Mildenhall, Stephen J. 2004. A Note on the Myers and Read Capital Allocation Formula. *North American Actuarial Journal* 8: 32–44.

Mildenhall, Stephen J. 2006. Actuarial Geometry. *Proc. Risk Theory Society*. Available online: http://www.aria.org/rts/proceedings/2006/Mildenhall.png (accessed on 13 June 2017).

Miller, Robert Burnham, and Dean W. Wichern. 1977. *Intermediate Business Statistics: Analysis of Variance, Regression and Time Series*. New York: Holt, Rinehart and Winston.

Myers, Stewart C., and James A. Read Jr. 2001. Capital Allocation for Insurance Companies. *Journal of Risk and Insurance* 68: 545–80.

Panjer, Harry H., and Gordon E. Willmot. 1992. *Insurance Risk Models*. Schaumburg: Society of Actuaries.

Panjer, Harry H. 2001. *Measurement of Risk, Solvency Requirements and Allocation of Capital Within Financial Conglomerates*. Waterloo: University of Waterloo, Institute of Insurance and Pension Research.

Patrik, Gary, Stefan Bernegger, and Marcel Beat Rüegg. 1999. The Use of Risk Adjusted Capital to Support Business Decision-Making. In *Casualty Actuarial Society Forum, Spring*. Baltimore: Casualty Actuarial Society, pp. 243–334.

Perold, Andre F. 2001. *Capital Allocation in Financial Firms*. HBS Competition and Strategy Working Paper Series, 98-072. Boston: Harvard Business School.

Phillips, Richard D., J. David Cummins, and Franklin Allen. 1998. Financial Pricing of Insurance in the Multiple-Line Insurance Company. *The Journal of Risk and Insurance* 65: 597–636.

Powers, Michael R. 2007. Using Aumann-Shapley values to allocate insurance risk: the case of inhomogeneous losses. *North American Actuarial Journal* 11: 113–27.

Ravishanker, Nalini, and Dipak K. Dey. 2002. *A First Course in Linear Model Theory*. Boca Raton: Chapman & Hall/CRC.

Sato, K. I. 1999. *Lévy Processes and Infinitely Divisible Distributions*. Cambridge: Cambridge University Press.

Sherris, M. 2006. Solvency, Capital Allocation and Fair Rate of Return in Insurance. *Journal of Risk and Insurance* 73: 71–96.

Stroock, Daniel W. 1993. *Probability Theory, an Analytic View*. Cambridge: Cambridge University Press.

Stroock, Daniel W. 2003. *Markov Processes from K. Itô's Perspective*. Annals of Mathematics Studies. Princeton: Princeton University Press.

Tasche, Dirk. 1999. Risk Contributions and Performance Measurement. *Report of the Lehrstuhl für Mathematische Statistik*, . München: TU München.

Tasche, Dirk. 2004. Allocating portfolio economic capital to sub-portfolios. In *Economic Capital: A Practitioner's Guide*. London: Risk Books, pp. 275–302.

Tsanakas, Andreas. 2009. To split or not to split: Capital allocation with convex risk measures. *Insurance: Mathematics and Economics* 1: 1–28.

Venter, Gary G., John A. Major, and Rodney E. Kreps. 2006. Marginal Decomposition of Risk Measures. *ASTIN Bulletin* 36: 375–413.

Venter, Gary G. 2009. Next steps for ERM: valuation and risk pricing. In Proceedings of the 2010 Enterprise Risk Management Symposium, Chicago, IL, USA, 12–15 April.

Zanjani, George. 2002. Pricing and capital allocation in catastrophe insurance. *Journal of Financial Economics* 65: 283–305.

Zanjani, George. 2010. An Economic Approach to Capital Allocation. *Journal of Risk and Insurance* 77: 523–49.

risks

MDPI

Article

Bayesian Modelling, Monte Carlo Sampling and Capital Allocation of Insurance Risks

Gareth W. Peters [1,2,3,*], Rodrigo S. Targino [4] and Mario V. Wüthrich [5]

1 Department of Statistical Science, University College London, London WC1E 6BT, UK
2 Oxford-Man Institute, Oxford University, Oxford OX1 2JD, UK
3 System Risk Center, London School of Economics, London WC2A 2AE, UK
4 Fundação Getulio Vargas, Escola de Matemática Aplicada, Botafogo, RJ 22250-040, Brazil; rodrigo.targino@fgv.br
5 RiskLab, Department of Mathematics, ETH Zurich, 8092 Zurich, Switzerland; mario.wuethrich@math.ethz.ch
* Correspondence: garethpeters78@gmail.com; Tel.: +44-20-7679-1238

Received: 3 May 2017; Accepted: 31 August 2017; Published: 22 September 2017

Abstract: The main objective of this work is to develop a detailed step-by-step guide to the development and application of a new class of efficient Monte Carlo methods to solve practically important problems faced by insurers under the new solvency regulations. In particular, a novel Monte Carlo method to calculate capital allocations for a general insurance company is developed, with a focus on coherent capital allocation that is compliant with the Swiss Solvency Test. The data used is based on the balance sheet of a representative stylized company. For each line of business in that company, allocations are calculated for the one-year risk with dependencies based on correlations given by the Swiss Solvency Test. Two different approaches for dealing with parameter uncertainty are discussed and simulation algorithms based on (pseudo-marginal) Sequential Monte Carlo algorithms are described and their efficiency is analysed.

Keywords: capital allocation; premium and reserve risk; Solvency Capital Requirement (SCR); Sequential Monte Carlo (SMC); Swiss Solvency Test (SST)

1. Introduction

Due to the new risk based solvency regulations (such as the Swiss Solvency Test FINMA (2007) and Solvency II European Comission (2009)), insurance companies must perform two core calculations. The first one involves computing and setting aside the risk capital to ensure the company's solvency and financial stability, and the second one is related to the *capital allocation* exercise. This exercise is a process of splitting the (economic or regulatory) capital amongst its various constituents, which could be different lines of business (LoBs), types of exposures, territories or even individual products in a portfolio of insurance policies. One of the reasons for performing such an exercise is to utilize the results for a risk-reward management tool to analyse profitability. The amount of capital (or risk) allocated to each LoB, for example, may assist the central management's decision to further invest in or discontinue a business line.

In contrast to the quantitative risk assessment, where there is an unanimous view shared by regulators world-wide that it should be performed through the use of *risk measures*, such as the Value at Risk (VaR) or Expected Shortfall (ES), there is no consensus on how to perform capital allocation to sub-units. In this work we follow the Euler allocation principle (see, e.g., Tasche (1999) and (McNeil et al. 2010, sct. 6.3)), which is briefly revised in the next section. For other allocation principles we refer the reader to Dhaene et al. (2012).

Under the Euler principle the allocation for each one of the portfolio's constituents can be calculated through an expectation conditional on a rare event. Even though, in general, these expectations are not available in closed form, some exceptions exist, such as the multivariate Gaussian model, first discussed in this context in Panjer (2001) and extended to the case of multivariate elliptical distributions in Landsman and Valdez (2003) and Dhaene et al. (2008); the multivariate gamma model of Furman and Landsman (2005); the combination of the Farlie-Gumbel-Morgenstern (FGM) copula and (mixtures of) exponential marginals from Bargès et al. (2009) or (mixtures of) Erlang marginals Cossette et al. (2013); and the multivariate Pareto-II from Asimit et al. (2013).

In this work we develop algorithms to calculate the marginal allocations for a generic model, which, invariably, leads to numerical approximations. Although simple Monte Carlo schemes (such as rejection sampling or importance sampling) are flexible enough to be used for a generic model, they can be shown to be computationally highly inefficient, as the majority of the samples do not satisfy the necessary conditioning event (which is a rare event). We build upon ideas developed in Targino et al. (2015) and propose an algorithm based on methods from Bayesian Statistics, namely a combination of Markov Chain Monte Carlo (for parameter estimation) and (pseudo-marginal) Sequential Monte Carlo (SMC) for the capital allocation.

As a side result of the allocation algorithm, we are able to efficiently compute both the company's overall Value at Risk (VaR) and also its Expected Shortfall (ES), (partially) addressing one of the main concerns of Embrechts et al. (2014): For High Confidence Levels, e.g., 95% and beyond, the "*statistical quantity*" VaR Can only Be Estimated with Considerable Statistical, as well as Model Uncertainty. Even though the issue of model uncertainty is not resolved, our algorithm can, at least, help to reduce the 'statistical uncertainty", measured by a variance reduction factor taking as basis a standard Monte Carlo simulation with comparable computational cost.

The proposed allocation procedure is described for a fictitious general insurance company with 9 LoBs (see Table 1 and Section 8). Further, within each LoB we also allocate the capital to the one-year reserve risk (due to claims from previous years) and the one-year premium risk.

Table 1. Initial synthetic balance sheet.

LoB	Reserves	Premium
1 MTPL	2391.64	503.14
2 Motor Hull	99.08	573.26
3 Property	449.26	748.76
4 Liability	870.27	299.73
5 Workers Compensation (UVG)	1104.66	338.63
6 Commercial Health	271.54	254.21
7 Private Health	7.32	7.20
8 Credit and Surety	49.50	34.64
9 Others	67.64	46.28
Total	5310.92	2805.87

In order to study the premium risk we follow the framework prescribed by the Swiss Solvency Test (SST) in (FINMA 2007, sct. 4.4). In this technical document, given company-specific quantities, the distribution of the premium risk is deterministically defined and no parameter uncertainty is involved. For the reserve risk, we use a fully Bayesian version of the gamma-gamma chain ladder model, analysed in Peters et al. (2017). As this model is described via a set of unknown parameters, two different approaches to capital allocation are proposed: a *marginalized* one, where the unknown parameters are marginalized prior to the allocation process and a *conditional* one, which is performed conditional on the unknown parameters and the parameter is integrated out numerically ex-poste.

The remainder of this paper is organized as follows. Section 2 formally describes marginal risk contributions (allocations) under the marginalized and conditional models. Section 3 reviews concepts of SMC algorithms and how they can be used to compute the quantities described in Section 2. We set the notation used for claims reserving in Section 4, before formally defining the models for the reserve risk (Section 5) and the premium risk (Section 6); these are merged together through a copula in Section 7. Sections 8 and 9 provide details of the synthetic data used, the inferential procedure for the unknown parameters and the implementation of the SMC algorithms. Results and conclusions are presented, respectively, in Sections 10 and 11.

2. Risk Allocation for the Swiss Solvency Test

In this section we follow the Euler allocation principle (see, e.g., Tasche (1999) and (McNeil et al. 2010, sct. 6.3)) and discuss how the risk capital that is held by an insurance company can be split into different risk triggers. As stochastic models for these risks involve a set of unknown parameters, we present an allocation procedure for a marginalized model (which arises when the parameter uncertainty is resolved beforehand) and a conditional model (which is still dependent on unknown parameters).

Although we postpone the construction of the specific claims payments model to Section 5 we now assume its behaviour is given by a Bayesian model depending on a generic parameter vector $\boldsymbol{\theta}$, for which a prior distribution is assigned. Probabilistic statements, such as the calculation of the risks allocated to each trigger, have to be made based on the available data, described by the filtration $\{\mathcal{F}(t)\}_t$ and formally defined in Section 4. This requirement implies that the uncertainty on the parameter values needs to be integrated out, in a process that must typically be performed numerically.

Therefore, to calculate the risk allocations we approximate the stochastic behaviour of functions of future observations, with the functions defined in Section 4. For the moment, let us denote by $\overline{\mathbf{Z}}$ a multivariate function of $\mathcal{F}(t+1)$, the future data, and $\boldsymbol{\theta}$ the vector of model parameters. On the one hand, in the *conditional model*, we approximate the distribution of the components of the vector $\overline{\mathbf{Z}} \mid \boldsymbol{\theta}, \mathcal{F}(t)$. On the other hand, in the *marginalized model*, the approximation is performed after the parameter uncertainty has been integrated out (i.e., marginalized). In this later framework, we approximate the distribution of the components of $\mathbf{Z} \mid \mathcal{F}(t)$, where the random vector $\mathbf{Z}$ is defined as $\mathbf{Z} = \mathbb{E}[\overline{\mathbf{Z}} \mid \mathcal{F}(t)]$, with expectation taken with respect to $\boldsymbol{\theta} \mid \mathcal{F}(t)$. Note that, given $\mathcal{F}(t)$, $\mathbf{Z}$ is a random variable, as it depends on future information, i.e., $\mathcal{F}(t+1)$. Both in the conditional and in the marginalized models we use moment matching and log-normal distributions for the approximations and couple the distributions via a Gaussian copula.

Suppressing the dependence on the available information, $\mathcal{F}(t)$, these two models (marginalized and conditional) are defined through their probability density functions (p.d.f.'s), $f_{\mathbf{Z}}(z)$ and $f_{\overline{\mathbf{Z}}|\boldsymbol{\theta}}(\overline{z} \mid \boldsymbol{\theta})$, respectively, which are both assumed to be combinations of log-normal distributions and a gaussian copula. For the conditional model, as we work in a Bayesian framework, the unknown parameter vector $\boldsymbol{\theta}$ has a (posterior) distribution with p.d.f. $f_{\boldsymbol{\theta}}(\boldsymbol{\theta})$. This is, then, combined with the likelihood $f_{\overline{\mathbf{Z}}|\boldsymbol{\theta}}(\overline{z} \mid \boldsymbol{\theta})$ to construct $f_{\overline{\mathbf{Z}}}(\overline{z})$, the density used for inference under the conditional model.

For the methodology discussed in this work, the important features of these two models are that $f_{\mathbf{Z}}(z)$ is known in closed form, whilst $f_{\overline{\mathbf{Z}}}(\overline{z})$ is not.

In summary, the two models presented in Sections 4 to 7 are defined as

$$\text{Marginalized model: } \mathbf{Z} \sim f_{\mathbf{Z}}(z); \tag{1}$$

$$\text{Conditional model: } \overline{\mathbf{Z}} \sim f_{\overline{\mathbf{Z}}}(\overline{z}) = \int f_{\overline{\mathbf{Z}}\,|\,\boldsymbol{\theta}}(\overline{z} \mid \boldsymbol{\theta}) f_{\boldsymbol{\theta}}(\boldsymbol{\theta}) d\boldsymbol{\theta}. \tag{2}$$

Remark 1. *As the "original" model for claims payments is a Bayesian model, we use the Bayesian nomenclature for both the marginalized and the conditional model. For the former, the Bayesian structure of prior and likelihood is hidden in Equation (1), as the parameter $\boldsymbol{\theta}$ has already been marginalized (with respect to its posterior distribution). For the later, we explicitly make use of the posterior distribution of $\boldsymbol{\theta}$ in Equation (2). Another strategy, followed in Wüthrich (2015), is to use an "empirical Bayes" approach, fixing the value of the unknown parameter vector $\boldsymbol{\theta}$, for example at its maximum likelihood estimator (MLE).*

Under the marginalized model we define $S = \sum_{i=1}^{d} Z_i$ as the company's overall risk. The SST requires the total capital to be calculated as the 99% ES of S, given by

$$\rho(S) = \mathbb{E}[S \mid S \geq \text{VaR}_{99\%}(S)]. \tag{3}$$

In turn, the Euler allocation principle states that the contribution of each component Z_i to the total capital in Equation (3) is given by

$$\rho_i = \mathbb{E}[Z_i \mid S \geq \text{VaR}_{99\%}(S)], \quad \forall i = 1, \ldots, d. \tag{4}$$

The allocations for the conditional model follows the same structure, with Z_i and S replaced, respectively, by $\overline{Z}_i$ and $\overline{S}$ in Equation (4) and reads as

$$\overline{\rho}_i = \mathbb{E}[\overline{Z}_i \mid \overline{S} \geq \text{VaR}_{99\%}(\overline{S})], \quad \forall i = 1, \ldots, d, \tag{5}$$

with $\overline{S} = \sum_{i=1}^{d} \overline{Z}_i$. For the models discussed below the density of $f_{\overline{\mathbf{Z}}}(\overline{\mathbf{z}})$ is not known in closed form, adding one more layer of complexity to the proposed method.

Remark 2. *Observe that the log-normal approximations are done at different stages in the marginalized and the conditional models. Therefore, we expect that the results will differ.*

Although computing ρ_i and $\overline{\rho}_i$ is a *static* problem, for the sake of transforming the Monte Carlo estimation into an efficient computational framework, we embed the calculation of these quantities into a sequential procedure, where at each step we solve a simpler problem, through a relaxation of the rare-event conditioning constraint to a sequence of less extreme rare-events. In the next section we discuss the methodological Monte Carlo approach used to perform this task. The reader familiar with the concepts of Sequential Monte Carlo methods may skip Section 3.1.

3. SMC Samplers and Capital Allocation

For the marginalized and conditional models presented in Sections 4 to 7 the marginal contributions in Equations (4)) and (5) cannot be calculated in analytic form for a generic model, so a simulation technique needs to be employed. In the sequel we provide a brief overview of a class of Monte Carlo methods, named Sequential Monte Carlo (SMC). For a recent survey in the topic, with focus on economics, finance and insurance applications the reader is referred to Creal (2012) and Del Moral et al. (2013). For a generic introductory review we refer the reader to Doucet and Johansen (2009).

3.1. A Brief Introduction to SMC Methods

The class of Sequential Monte Carlo (SMC) algorithms, also called Particle Filters, has its roots in the fields of engineering, probability and statistics where it was primarily used for sampling from a sequence of distributions (see, e.g., Gordon et al. (1993) and Del Moral (1996)). In the context of state-space models, SMC methods can be used to sequentially approximate the filtering distributions of non-linear and non-Gaussian state space models, solving the same problem as the Kalman filter—a technique with a long-standing tradition in actuarial mathematics (see, e.g., De Jong and Zehnwirth (1983) and Verrall (1989)).

The general context of a standard SMC method is that one wants to approximate a (often naturally occurring) sequence of p.d.f.'s $\{\widetilde{\pi}_t\}_{t\geq 1}$ with the support of each function in this sequence is given by $supp(\widetilde{\pi}_t) = \mathbb{R}^d \times \ldots \times \mathbb{R}^d = \mathbb{R}^{d\times t}$, for $t \geq 1$, where t can be any artificial ordering of the sequence that is problem specific. We assume that $\widetilde{\pi}_t$ is (only) known up to a normalizing constant, and we write

$$\widetilde{\pi}_t(\mathbf{z}_{1:t}) = \mathcal{Z}_t^{-1}\widetilde{\gamma}_t(\mathbf{z}_{1:t}),$$

where $\mathbf{z}_{1:t} = (\mathbf{z}_1, \ldots, \mathbf{z}_t) \in \mathbb{R}^{d\times t}$.

3.1.1. SMC Algorithm

Procedurally, we initialize the algorithm sampling a set of N independent particles (as the samples are denoted in the literature) from the distribution $\widetilde{\pi}_1$ and set normalized weights to $W_1^{(j)} = 1/N$, for all $j = 1, \ldots, N$. If it is not possible to sample directly from $\widetilde{\pi}_1$, one should sample from an importance distribution $\widetilde{q}_1$ and calculate its weights accordingly. Then the particles are sequentially propagated through each distribution $\widetilde{\pi}_t$ in the sequence via three main processes: mutation, correction (incremental importance weighting) and resampling. In the first step (mutation) we propagate particles from time $t-1$ to time t, in the second one (correction) we calculate the new importance weights of the particles.

Without resampling, this method can be seen as a sequence of importance sampling (IS) steps, where the target distribution at each step t is $\widetilde{\gamma}_t$ (the unnormalized version of $\widetilde{\pi}_t$) and the importance distribution is given by

$$\widetilde{q}_t(z_{1:t}) = \widetilde{q}_1(z_1) \prod_{j=2}^{t} K_j(z_{j-1}, z_j), \tag{6}$$

where $K_j(z_{j-1}, \cdot)$ is the mechanism used to propagate particles from time $t-1$ to t, known as the mutation kernel. Therefore, after the mutation step each particle $j = 1, \ldots, N$ has (unnormalized) importance weight given by

$$w_t^{(j)} = \frac{\widetilde{\gamma}_t(z_{1:t}^{(j)})}{\widetilde{q}_t(z_{1:t}^{(j)})} = w_{t-1}^{(j)} \underbrace{\frac{\widetilde{\gamma}_t(z_{1:t}^{(j)})}{\widetilde{\gamma}_{t-1}(z_{1:t-1}^{(j)}) K_t(z_{t-1}^{(j)}, z_t^{(j)})}}_{\text{incremental weight: } \alpha_t^{(j)}} = w_{t-1}^{(j)} \alpha_t^{(j)}. \tag{7}$$

These importance weights can be normalized to create a set of (normalized) weighted particles $\{z_{1:t}^{(j)}, W_t^{(j)}\}_{j=1}^N$, with normalized weights $W_t^{(j)} = \frac{w_t^{(j)}}{\sum_{k=1}^N w_t^{(k)}}$. In this case, from the Law of Large Numbers,

$$\sum_{j=1}^{N} W_t^{(j)} \varphi(z_{1:t}^{(j)}) \longrightarrow \mathbb{E}_{\widetilde{\pi}_t}[\varphi(\mathbf{Z}_{1:t})] = \int_{\mathbb{R}^{d \times t}} \varphi(z_{1:t}) \widetilde{\pi}_t(z_{1:t}) dz_{1:t}, \tag{8}$$

$\widetilde{\pi}_t$–almost surely as $N \to \infty$, for any test function φ such that the expectation of φ under $\widetilde{\pi}_t$ exists (see Geweke (1989)).

Remark 3. *The reader should note that the knowledge of $\widetilde{\pi}_t$ up to a normalizing constant is sufficient for the implementation of a generic SMC algorithm, since the normalized weights $W_t^{(j)}$ are the same for both $\widetilde{\pi}_t$ and $\widetilde{\gamma}_t$.*

In simple implementations of the SMC algorithm (such as the one discussed above), when the algorithmic time t increases, the estimates in Equation (8) become, eventually, effectively a function of one sample point $\{z_t^{(j)}, W_t^{(j)}\}$; what is observed, in practice, is that for some particle j, $W_t^{(j)} \approx 1$ and for all the others the normalized weights are negligible. This degeneracy is measured using the Effective Sample Size (ESS) defined in Liu and Chen (1995) and Liu and Chen (1998) as

$$\text{ESS}_t = \left[\sum_{j=1}^{N} (W_t^{(j)})^2 \right]^{-1} \in [1, N].$$

This quantity has the interpretation that ESS_t is maximized when $\{W_t^{(j)}, z_t^{(j)}\}_{j=1}^N$ forms a uniform distribution on $\{z_t^{(j)}\}_{j=1}^N$ and minimized when $W_t^{(j)} = 1$ for some j. One may also use the Gini index or the entropy as a degeneracy measure, as discussed, for example, in Martino et al. (2017).

One way to tackle this degeneracy problem is to unbiasedly resample the whole set of weighted particles, for example, choosing (with replacement) N samples from the system where each $z_t^{(j)}$ is selected with probability weight $W_t^{(j)}$. In our algorithms we propose to resample the whole set of weighted samples whenever it is "too degenerate" and our degeneracy threshold is $\text{ESS}_t < N/2$. Many different resampling schemes have been suggested in the literature and for a comparison between them we refer the reader to Douc and Cappé (2005) and Gandy and Lau (2015).

Although the resample step alleviates the degeneracy problem, its successive reapplication at each stage of the sampler produces the so-called sample impoverishment, where the number of distinct particles is extremely small. In Gilks and Berzuini (2001) it was proposed to add a "move" step with any kernel such that the target distribution is invariant with respect to it in order to rejuvenate the system. This kernel may be, for example, as a Markov Chain Monte Carlo (MCMC) kernel, which would begin with equally chosen weighted samples from the target distribution and then perturb them under a single step of a Metropolis Hastings acceptance-rejection mechanism. Note that in this case the samples start exactly in the target distribution's stationary regime. Therefore, a single step of the Metropolis-Hastings accept-reject mutation is strictly valid and no burn-in is required.

More precisely, we can apply any kernel $M(\widehat{z}_{1:t}^{(j)}, z_{1:t}^{(j)})$ that leaves $\widetilde{\pi}_t$ invariant to move the sample $\widehat{z}_{1:t}^{(j)}$ to $z_{1:t}^{(j)}$ (the hat denotes a sample *after* the resample step but *before* the "move" step), i.e.,

$$\widetilde{\pi}_t(z_{1:t}) = \int M(\widehat{z}_{1:t}, z_{1:t})\widetilde{\pi}_t(\widehat{z}_{1:t})d\widehat{z}_{1:t}.$$

3.1.2. SMC Samplers

Although very general, the SMC algorithm presented above, in principle, requires the sequence of p.d.f.'s to have an increasing support. However it has been shown in Peters (2005) and Del Moral et al. (2006) that these algorithms can be applied to sequences of p.d.f.'s defined on the same support, leading to the so-called SMC sampler algorithm discussed below. This development is central for the insurance applications explored in this paper.

Given the sequence of densities $\{\pi_t\}_{t\geq 1}$ (and its unnormalized version, $\{\gamma_t\}_{t\geq 1}$), where each element is defined over the same support, say $\mathbb{R}^d$, we create another sequence, defined on $\mathbb{R}^{d\times t}$, the *path space*

$$\widetilde{\pi}_t(z_{1:t}) \propto \widetilde{\gamma}_t(z_{1:t}) = \gamma_t(z_t)\prod_{s=1}^{t-1} L_s(z_{s+1}, z_s), \tag{9}$$

which, for any Markov kernel $L_s(z_{s+1}, z_s)$ is a density with $\pi_t(z_t)$ as marginal (which can be seen by integrating out $z_{1:t-1}$). Note that, in Equation (9) time runs backwards, from t to 1. For completeness we define $\widetilde{\pi}_1(z_{1:1}) = \pi_1(z_1)$ and $\widetilde{\gamma}_1(z_{1:1}) = \gamma_1(z_1)$.

If $q_1 \equiv \widetilde{q}_1$ is an IS density targeting $\pi_1 \equiv \widetilde{\pi}_1$ then, see Equation (6),

$$\widetilde{q}_t(z_{1:t}) = q_1(z_1)\prod_{j=2}^{t} K_j(z_{j-1}, z_j),$$

is defined, for Markov kernels $K_j(z_{j-1}, z_j)$, as an IS density targeting $\widetilde{\pi}_t(z_{1:t})$. For $t = 1$ we define $K_1 \equiv 1$.

As in the SMC algorithm, to generate a set of weighted samples $\{z_t^{(j)}, W_t^{(j)}\}_{j=1}^M$ from $\pi_t(z_t)$ one can use a sequence of IS steps on the path space where the unnormalized importance weights are, at each time step $t \geq 1$, given by, see Equation (7),

$$w_t^{(j)} = \frac{\widetilde{\gamma}_t(z_{1:t}^{(j)})}{\widetilde{q}_t(z_{1:t}^{(j)})} = w_{t-1}^{(j)}\frac{\gamma_t(z_t^{(j)})L_{t-1}(z_t^{(j)}, z_{t-1}^{(j)})}{\gamma_{t-1}(z_{t-1}^{(j)})K_t(z_{t-1}^{(j)}, z_t^{(j)})} = w_{t-1}^{(j)}\alpha_t^{(j)}, \tag{10}$$

where $w_0^{(j)} \equiv 1$, for all $j = 1, \ldots, N$. The normalized weights are then computed as

$$W_t^{(j)} = \frac{w_t^{(j)}}{\sum_{k=1}^N w_t^{(k)}}.$$

The pseudo-code of the SMC sampler procedure just described is found in Algorithm 1.

Algorithm 1: SMC sampler algorithm.

Inputs: (Forward) mutation kernels $\{K_t(z_{t-1}, z_t)\}_{t=2}^{T}$, (artificial) backward kernels $\{L_{t-1}(z_t, z_{t-1})\}_{t=2}^{T}$, MCMC move kernel $\{M_t(\widehat{z}_t, z_t)\}_{t=1}^{T}$;

for $j = 1, \ldots, N$ **do**

  Sample i.i.d. $z_1^{(j)} \sim \pi_1(\cdot)$;

  Set $w_1^{(j)} = 1$;

  Set $W_1^{(j)} = \frac{1}{N}$;

end

for $t = 2, \ldots, T$ **do**

  for $j = 1, \ldots, N$ **do**

    Sample $z_t^{(j)} \sim K_t(z_{t-1}^{(j)}, \cdot)$;

    Calculate the weights $w_t^{(j)} = w_{t-1}^{(j)} \dfrac{\gamma_t(z_t^{(j)}) L_{t-1}(z_t^{(j)}, z_{t-1}^{(j)})}{\gamma_{t-1}(z_{t-1}^{(j)}) K_t(z_{t-1}^{(j)}, z_t^{(j)})} = w_{t-1}^{(j)} \alpha_t^{(j)}$;

  end

  Calculate the normalized weights $W_t^{(j)} = \dfrac{w_t^{(j)}}{\sum_{j=1}^{N} w_t^{(j)}}$;

  if $\mathrm{ESS}_t < N/2$ **then**

    for $j = 1, \ldots, N$ **do**

      Resample $\widehat{z}_t^{(j)}$, i.i.d from $\{z_t^{(k)}, W_t^{(k)}\}_{k=1}^{N}$;

      Sample $z_t^{(j)} \sim M_t(\widehat{z}_t^{(j)}, \cdot)$;

      Set $W_t^{(j)} = 1/N$;

    end

  end

end

Result: Weighted random samples $\{z_t^{(j)}, W_t^{(j)}\}_{j=1}^{N}$ approximating π_t, for all $t = 1, \ldots, T$.

The introduction of the sequence of kernels $\{L_{t-1}\}_{t=2}^{T}$ creates a new degree of freedom in the design of SMC samplers compared with the usual SMC algorithms, where only the forward mutation kernels $\{K_t\}_{t=2}^{T}$ should be designed. As discussed in Peters (2005) and Del Moral et al. (2006) if one wants to minimize the variance of the importance weights one strategy is to use the following approximation to the optimal backward kernel that minimizes the variance of the incremental weights (which cannot be computed in practice and must be approximated)

$$L_t(z_{t+1}, z_t) = \frac{\gamma_t(z_t) K_{t+1}(z_t, z_{t+1})}{\frac{1}{N} \sum_{j=1}^{N} w_t^{(j)} K_{t+1}(z_t^{(j)}, z_{t+1})}, \tag{11}$$

which leads to incremental weights

$$\alpha_t^{(j)} = \frac{\gamma_t(z_t^{(j)})}{\frac{1}{N} \sum_{k=1}^{N} w_{t-1}^{(k)} K_t(z_{t-1}^{(k)}, z_t^{(j)})}. \tag{12}$$

With the methodological tools provided by the SMC samplers we now proceed on how to adapt these methods to the allocation of risks under our generic marginalized and conditional models.

3.2. Allocations for the Marginalized Model

For a generic random vector $\mathbf{Z} = (Z_1, \ldots, Z_d)$ with known marginal densities and distribution functions, respectively $f_{Z_i}(z_i)$ and $F_{Z_i}(z_i)$, and copula density $c(u_1, \ldots, u_d)$ on $[0,1]^d$, due to Sklar's theorem (see Sklar (1959) and (McNeil et al. 2010, chp. 5)) the joint density of $\mathbf{Z}$ can be written as

$$f_{\mathbf{Z}}(\mathbf{z}) = c(\mathbf{u}) \prod_{i=1}^{d} f_{Z_i}(z_i),$$

where $\mathbf{u} = (u_1, \ldots, u_d) \in [0,1]^d$ and $u_i = F_{Z_i}(z_i)$. In order to approximate the marginal risk contributions ρ_i from Equation (4) we can use samples from the distribution

$$\pi(\mathbf{z}) = f_{\mathbf{Z}}(\mathbf{z} \,|\, \mathbf{z} \in \mathcal{G}_{\mathbf{Z}}) = \frac{f_{\mathbf{Z}}(\mathbf{z}) \mathbb{1}_{\mathcal{G}_{\mathbf{Z}}}(\mathbf{z})}{\mathbb{P}[\mathbf{Z} \in \mathcal{G}_{\mathbf{Z}}]}, \tag{13}$$

where the set $\mathcal{G}_{\mathbf{Z}} = \mathcal{G}_{\mathbf{Z}}(B)$ is defined, for $B = \mathrm{VaR}_{99\%}(S)$, as

$$\mathcal{G}_{\mathbf{Z}} = \left\{ \mathbf{z} \in \mathbb{R}^d \, : \, \sum_{i=1}^{d} z_i \geq B \right\}, \tag{14}$$

and the indicator function $\mathbb{1}_{\mathcal{G}_{\mathbf{Z}}}(\mathbf{z})$ is one when $\mathbf{z} \in \mathcal{G}_{\mathbf{Z}}$ and zero otherwise. It should be noted that since the boundary B in Equation (14) is given by $\mathrm{VaR}_{99\%}(S)$ with $S = \sum_{i=1}^{d} Z_i$ we have $\mathbb{P}[\mathbf{Z} \in \mathcal{G}_{\mathbf{Z}}] = 0.01$, see discussion on this point in Targino et al. (2015).

3.2.1. Reaching a Rare Event Using Intermediate Steps

Instead of directly targeting the conditional distribution $(Z_1, \ldots, Z_d) \,|\, \{S \geq \mathrm{VaR}_{99\%}(S)\}$ the idea of the SMC sampler of Algorithm 1 is to sequentially sample from intermediate distributions with conditioning events that become rarer until the point we reach the distribution of interest (see Equation (14)). The benefit of such an approach is that the samples (particles) from a previous step (with a less rare conditioning event) are "guided" to the next algorithmic step (when targeting a rarer conditioning set) and, if carefully designed, no samples are wasted on the way to the target distribution, in the sense that no samples are incrementally weighted with a strictly zero weight. This "herds" the samples into the target sampling region of interest.

In order to sample from the target distribution defined in Equation (13) we use a sequence of intermediate distributions $\{\pi_t\}_{t=1}^{T}$, such that $\pi_T \equiv \pi$ and

$$\pi_t(\mathbf{z}) = f_{\mathbf{Z}}(\mathbf{z} \,|\, \mathbf{z} \in \mathcal{G}_{\mathbf{Z}_t}), \tag{15}$$

with $\mathcal{G}_{\mathbf{Z}_t} = \mathcal{G}_{\mathbf{Z}_t}(B_t)$ given by

$$\mathcal{G}_{\mathbf{Z}_t} = \left\{ \mathbf{z} \in \mathbb{R}^d \, : \, \sum_{i=1}^{d} z_i \geq B_t \right\}.$$

Remark 4. *Differently from Targino et al. (2015), in order to make the algorithm more easily comparable with the one used for the conditional model, we do not transform the original random variable* $\mathbf{Z}$ *through its marginal distribution functions. Therefore, instead of sampling from the conditional copula we sample from the conditional joint distribution of* $\mathbf{Z}$*.*

The thresholds $B_1, \ldots, B_{T-1}$ are chosen in order to have increasingly rarer conditioning events as a function of t, starting from the unconditional joint density. In other words, $\{B_t\}_{t=1}^{T}$ needs to satisfy $0 = B_1 < \ldots < B_{T-1} < B_T = B = \mathrm{VaR}_{99\%}(S)$. Note that the choice $B_1 = 0$ assumes $S > 0$, $\mathbb{P}$-a.s., otherwise $B_1 = -\infty$. Depending on the choice of the thresholds $\{B_t\}_{t=1}^{T-1}$ it may be the case that the densities defined in Equation (15) are only known up to a normalizing constant so, from now on, we work with γ_t, the unnormalized version of π_t:

$$\pi_t(z) \propto \gamma_t(z) = f_Z(z)\mathbb{1}_{\mathcal{G}_{Z_t}}(z). \tag{16}$$

If, at algorithmic time t, we have a set of N weighted samples $\{W_t^{(j)}, z_t^{(j)}\}_{j=1}^N$ from π_t, with $z_t^{(j)} = (z_{1,t}^{(j)}, \dots, z_{d,t}^{(j)})$ then we construct the following empirical approximation:

$$\mathbb{E}[Z_i \mid S \geq B_t] \approx \sum_{j=1}^{N} W_t^{(j)} z_{i,t}^{(j)}. \tag{17}$$

It should be noticed, though, that in our application the final threshold $B_T = B = \text{VaR}_{99\%}(S)$ is not previously known. In these cases, an adaptive strategy, similar to the one studied in Cérou et al. (2012) can be implemented, where neither $B_1, \dots, B_{T-1}$ nor B_T needs to be previously known. More details on this aspect of the algorithm are provided in Section 9.1.

3.3. *Allocations for The Conditional Model*

From the discussion in Section 2 we see that the main difference between the marginalized and conditional models is the fact that the former density is analytically known (in fact, it its approximated by an analytically known density) whilst the latter is defined through an integral of a known density, see Equations (1) and (2). In this section we discuss how to adapt the algorithm presented in Section 3.2 for situations where the target density cannot be analytically computed but a positive and unbiased estimator for it can be calculated.

Following the recent developments on *pseudo-marginal* methods (see Andrieu and Roberts (2009) and Finke (2015) for a survey in the topic) we substitute the unknown density $f_{\overline{Z}}$ in Equation (2) by a positive and unbiased estimate $\widehat{f}_{\overline{Z}}$ and show the SMC procedure still targets the correct distribution—a strategy similar to the ones proposed in Everitt et al. (2016) and McGree et al. (2015). In the context of rare event simulations a similar idea has been independently developed in Vergé et al. (2016) where the authors study the impact of the parameter uncertainty in the probability of the rare event, whilst we analyse the impact in expectations conditional to the rare event (as in Equation (5)).

The idea of replacing an unknown density by a positive and unbiased estimate is in the core of many recently proposed algorithms, such as the Particle Markov Chain Monte Carlo (PMCMC) of Andrieu et al. (2010), the Sequential Monte Carlo Squared (SMC^2) of Chopin et al. (2013) and Fulop and Li (2013) (see also the island particle filter of Vergé et al. (2015)) and the Importance Sampling Squared (IS^2) of Tran et al. (2014). In the context of Sequential Monte Carlo algorithms this argument first appeared as a brief note in Rousset and Doucet's comments of Beskos et al. (2006), where it reads that "(...) a straightforward argument shows that it is not necessary to know $w_k(X_{t_0:t_k}^{(i)})$ [*the weights*] exactly. Only an unbiased positive estimate $\hat{w}_k(X_{t_0:t_k}^{(i)})$ of $w_k(X_{t_0:t_k}^{(i)})$ is necessary to obtain asymptotically consistent SMC estimates under weak assumptions".

To introduce the concept we first estimate $f_{\overline{Z}}$ by $f_{\overline{Z}}(\cdot \mid \boldsymbol{\theta})$, which can be seen as a "one sample" approximation to the integral in Equation (2); then we show how to use an estimator based on $M \geq 1$ samples from $f_{\boldsymbol{\theta}}$. These two approaches have been named in the literature (see Everitt et al. (2016) and references therein) as, respectively, the single auxiliary variable (SAV) and the multiple auxiliary variable (MAV) methods.

3.3.1. Single Auxiliary Variable Method

To avoid direct use of $f_{\overline{Z}}$ on the SMC sampler algorithm we provide a procedure on the joint space of $\overline{\mathbf{Z}}$ and the parameter $\boldsymbol{\theta}$, defined as $\mathcal{Y} = \mathbb{R}^d \times \boldsymbol{\Theta}$. The reader is referred to Finke (2015) for an extensive list of known algorithms which can also be interpreted in a *extended space* way. The target distribution on this new space is defined as the joint distribution of $\overline{\mathbf{Z}}$ and $\boldsymbol{\theta}$ and its marginal with respect to $\overline{\mathbf{Z}}$ is precisely the density of the conditional model.

Formally, for $\boldsymbol{y} = (\overline{z}, \boldsymbol{\theta})$, $\mathcal{G}_{\overline{Z}}(\overline{B}) = \mathcal{G}_{\overline{Z}} = \left\{\overline{z} \in \mathbb{R}^d \,:\, \sum_{i=1}^d \overline{z}_i \geq \overline{B}\right\}$ and $\overline{B} = \text{VaR}_{99\%}(\overline{S})$ we define

$$\pi^{y}(y) \propto \gamma^{y}(y) = f_{\overline{Z}}(\overline{z} \mid \theta) f_{\theta}(\theta) \mathbb{1}_{\mathcal{G}_{\overline{Z}}}(\overline{z}),$$

which has the desired marginal target distribution of interest:

$$\overline{\pi}(\overline{z}) \propto \overline{\gamma}(\overline{z}) = \int_{\Theta} f_{\overline{Z}}(\overline{z} \mid \theta) f_{\theta}(\theta) d\theta \mathbb{1}_{\mathcal{G}_{\overline{Z}}}(\overline{z}). \tag{18}$$

Similarly to the densities defined in Equations (9) and (16) we define a sequence of target distributions both in $\mathcal{Y}$ and $\mathcal{Y}^t$, respectively, as

$$\pi_t^{y}(y_t) \propto \gamma_t^{y}(y_t) = f_{\overline{Z}}(\overline{z}_t \mid \theta_t) f_{\theta}(\theta_t) \mathbb{1}_{\mathcal{G}_{\overline{Z}_t}}(\overline{z}_t),$$

and

$$\begin{aligned}\widetilde{\pi}_t^{y}(y_{1:t}) \propto \widetilde{\gamma}_t^{y}(y_{1:t}) &= \gamma_t^{y}(y_t) \prod_{s=1}^{t-1} L_s^{y}(y_{s+1}, y_s) \\ &= f_{\overline{Z}}(\overline{z}_t \mid \theta_t) f_{\theta}(\theta_t) \mathbb{1}_{\mathcal{G}_{\overline{Z}_t}}(\overline{z}_t) \prod_{s=1}^{t-1} \overline{L}_s(\overline{z}_{s+1}, \overline{z}_s \mid \theta_s) f_{\theta}(\theta_s),\end{aligned}$$

where the second identity specifies the choices of L_s^{y}, in terms of $\overline{L}_s$ and f_{θ}.

Assuming we can perfectly sample from the distribution of θ (in our application this distribution is a posterior, from which samples are generated via simulation algorithms), to move y samples backwards from time $s+1$ to s we split this process into sampling θ_s from f_{θ} (ignoring θ_{s+1}) and then, conditional on θ_s, moving $\overline{z}_{s+1}$ to $\overline{z}_s$. In other words, to sample

$$y_s = (\overline{z}_s, \theta_s) \,\Big|\, \{y_{s+1} = (\overline{z}_{s+1}, \theta_{s+1})\} \sim L_s^{y}(y_{s+1}, y_s),$$

we split the process in two stages,

1. $\theta_s \sim f_{\theta}(\theta_s)$;
2. $\overline{z}_s \mid \overline{z}_{s+1} \sim \overline{L}_s(\overline{z}_{s+1}, \overline{z}_s \mid \theta_s)$.

The importance distribution on the path space of y can be expressed as

$$\widetilde{q}_t^{y}(y_{1:t}) = q_1^{y}(y_1) \prod_{s=2}^{t} K_s^{y}(y_{s-1}, y_s) = \overline{q}_1(\overline{z}_1) f_{\theta}(\theta_1) \prod_{s=2}^{t} \overline{K}_s(\overline{z}_{s-1}, \overline{z}_s \mid \theta_s) f_{\theta}(\theta_s),$$

and, once again, the second identity provides the choices of q_1^{y} and K_s^{y}, i.e.,

$$q_1^{y}(y_1) = \overline{q}_1(\overline{z}_1) f_{\theta}(\theta_1) \quad \text{and} \quad K_s^{y}(y_{s-1}, y_s) = \overline{K}_s(\overline{z}_{s-1}, \overline{z}_s \mid \theta_s) f_{\theta}(\theta_s).$$

Therefore, a SMC procedure targeting the sequence $\{\pi_t^{y}(y_t)\}_{t=1}^{T}$ produces unnormalized weights

$$\begin{aligned}w_t^{y} &= \frac{\widetilde{\gamma}_t^{y}(y_{1:t})}{\widetilde{q}_t^{y}(y_{1:t})} \\ &= w_{t-1}^{y} \frac{\gamma_t^{y}(y_t) L_{t-1}^{y}(y_t, y_{t-1})}{\gamma_{t-1}^{y}(y_{t-1}) K_t^{y}(y_{t-1}, y_t)} \\ &= w_{t-1}^{y} \frac{f_{\overline{Z}}(\overline{z}_t \mid \theta_t) f_{\theta}(\theta_t) \mathbb{1}_{\mathcal{G}_{\overline{Z}_t}}(\overline{z}_t) \overline{L}_{t-1}(\overline{z}_t, \overline{z}_{t-1} \mid \theta_{t-1}) f_{\theta}(\theta_{t-1})}{f_{\overline{Z}}(\overline{z}_{t-1} \mid \theta_{t-1}) f_{\theta}(\theta_{t-1}) \mathbb{1}_{\mathcal{G}_{\overline{Z}_{t-1}}}(\overline{z}_{t-1}) \overline{K}_t(\overline{z}_{t-1}, \overline{z}_t \mid \theta_t) f_{\theta}(\theta_t)} \\ &= w_{t-1}^{y} \frac{f_{\overline{Z}}(\overline{z}_t \mid \theta_t) \mathbb{1}_{\mathcal{G}_{\overline{Z}_t}}(\overline{z}_t) \overline{L}_{t-1}(\overline{z}_t, \overline{z}_{t-1} \mid \theta_{t-1})}{f_{\overline{Z}}(\overline{z}_{t-1} \mid \theta_{t-1}) \mathbb{1}_{\mathcal{G}_{\overline{Z}_{t-1}}}(\overline{z}_{t-1}) \overline{K}_t(\overline{z}_{t-1}, \overline{z}_t \mid \theta_t)},\end{aligned}$$

that can be used to create weighted samples from $\overline{\pi}_t(\overline{z}_t)$, which is the desired marginal of $\pi_t^{y}(y_t)$, the density required for the capital allocation.

Remark 5. *From the structure of the mutation kernels* K_t^y *it should be noticed that at each iteration* t *a new value of* $\boldsymbol{\theta}_t$ *needs to be generated and used to sample* $\overline{\mathbf{z}}_t \mid \boldsymbol{\theta}_t$. *In other words, for each particle* $j = 1, \ldots, N$ *a different* $\boldsymbol{\theta}_t^{(j)}$ *is to be used for each* $\overline{\mathbf{z}}_t^{(j)} \mid \boldsymbol{\theta}_t^{(j)}$.

3.3.2. Multiple Auxiliary Variable

In the previous algorithm we, indirectly, estimate the density $f_{\overline{\mathbf{Z}}}(\overline{\mathbf{z}})$ by $f_{\overline{\mathbf{Z}}}(\overline{\mathbf{z}} \mid \boldsymbol{\theta})$. In this section we discuss how to use a different and more robust estimator, using $M \geq 1$ samples from $\boldsymbol{\theta}$. In the context of pseudo-marginal Monte Carlo Markov Chain (MCMC) Andrieu and Vihola (2015) show that reducing the variance of the estimate of the unknown density $f_{\overline{\mathbf{Z}}}(\overline{\mathbf{z}})$ leads to reduced asymptotic variance of estimators from the MCMC. For SMC algorithms this strategy has been used, for example, in McGree et al. (2015) and Everitt et al. (2016).

Before proceeding, we note that even in the case that $M = 1$ the algorithm still produces asymptotic and unbiased estimators (when the number of particles $N \to \infty$). However, the rate of variance reduction in the asymptotic estimates is directly affected by the choice of M (in a non-trivial manner). Furthermore, the asymptotic variance of Central Limit Theorem (CLT) estimators under the class of such pseudo-marginal Monte Carlo approaches is strictly ordered in M, with M increasing reducing the the asymptotic variance.

For any $M \geq 1$, a positive and unbiased estimate for $f_{\overline{\mathbf{Z}}}(\overline{\mathbf{z}})$ can be constructed as

$$\widehat{f}_{\overline{\mathbf{Z}}}(\overline{\mathbf{z}};\, \boldsymbol{\vartheta}) = \frac{1}{M} \sum_{i=1}^{M} f_{\overline{\mathbf{Z}}}(\overline{\mathbf{z}} \mid \boldsymbol{\theta}^{(i)}), \tag{19}$$

where $\boldsymbol{\vartheta} = (\boldsymbol{\theta}^{(1)}, \ldots, \boldsymbol{\theta}^{(M)}) \in \Theta^M$ and each $\boldsymbol{\theta}^{(m)}$ is sampled independently from $f_{\boldsymbol{\theta}}(\boldsymbol{\theta})$. Note that when only one sample of $\boldsymbol{\theta}$ is used to estimate $f_{\overline{\mathbf{Z}}}(\overline{\mathbf{z}})$ the estimator is reduced to $\widehat{f}_{\overline{\mathbf{Z}}}(\overline{\mathbf{z}};\, \boldsymbol{\vartheta}) = f_{\overline{\mathbf{Z}}}(\overline{\mathbf{z}} \mid \boldsymbol{\theta})$. Also, note that $\widehat{f}_{\overline{\mathbf{Z}}}(\overline{\mathbf{z}};\, \boldsymbol{\vartheta}) \to f_{\overline{\mathbf{Z}}}(\overline{\mathbf{z}})$ point-wise when $M \to \infty$, by the law of large numbers. Indeed, since the random variable $\boldsymbol{\vartheta}$ has density $f_{\boldsymbol{\vartheta}}(\boldsymbol{\vartheta}) = \prod_{i=1}^{M} f_{\boldsymbol{\theta}}(\boldsymbol{\theta}^{(i)})$ we obtain

$$\begin{aligned}
\int_{\boldsymbol{\Theta}^M} \widehat{f}_{\overline{\mathbf{Z}}}(\overline{\mathbf{z}};\, \boldsymbol{\vartheta}) f_{\boldsymbol{\vartheta}}(\boldsymbol{\vartheta}) d\boldsymbol{\vartheta} &= \int_{\boldsymbol{\Theta}^M} \frac{1}{M} \sum_{i=1}^{M} f_{\overline{\mathbf{Z}}}(\overline{\mathbf{z}} \mid \boldsymbol{\theta}^{(i)}) \prod_{i=1}^{M} f_{\boldsymbol{\theta}}(\boldsymbol{\theta}^{(i)}) d\boldsymbol{\theta}^{(1)} \cdots d\boldsymbol{\theta}^{(M)} \\
&= \int_{\boldsymbol{\Theta}} f_{\overline{\mathbf{Z}}}(\overline{\mathbf{z}} \mid \boldsymbol{\theta}) f_{\boldsymbol{\theta}}(\boldsymbol{\theta}) d\boldsymbol{\theta} = f_{\overline{\mathbf{Z}}}(\overline{\mathbf{z}}).
\end{aligned}$$

Therefore the density $\overline{\pi}(\overline{\mathbf{z}})$ constructed in Equation (18) is the marginal of the new target density defined on $\mathcal{Y}_M = \mathbb{R}^d \times \boldsymbol{\Theta}^M$

$$\pi^{y}(y;\, \boldsymbol{\vartheta}) \propto \gamma^{y}(y;\, \boldsymbol{\vartheta}) = \widehat{f}_{\overline{\mathbf{Z}}}(\overline{\mathbf{z}};\, \boldsymbol{\vartheta}) f_{\boldsymbol{\vartheta}}(\boldsymbol{\vartheta}) \mathbb{1}_{\mathcal{G}_{\overline{\mathbf{Z}}}}(\overline{\mathbf{z}}).$$

Apart from the cumbersome notation, the same argument from the previous section can be used to show that a SMC procedure with estimated density $\widehat{f}_{\overline{\mathbf{Z}}}(\overline{\mathbf{z}};\, \boldsymbol{\vartheta})$ replacing $f_{\overline{\mathbf{Z}}}(\overline{\mathbf{z}})$ has unnormalized weights given by

$$w_t^{y} = w_{t-1}^{y} \frac{\widehat{f}_{\overline{\mathbf{Z}}}(\overline{\mathbf{z}}_t;\, \boldsymbol{\vartheta}_t) \mathbb{1}_{\mathcal{G}_{\overline{\mathbf{Z}}_t}}(\overline{\mathbf{z}}_t) \overline{L}_{t-1}(\overline{\mathbf{z}}_t, \overline{\mathbf{z}}_{t-1} \mid \boldsymbol{\vartheta}_{t-1})}{\widehat{f}_{\overline{\mathbf{Z}}}(\overline{\mathbf{z}}_{t-1};\, \boldsymbol{\vartheta}_{t-1}) \mathbb{1}_{\mathcal{G}_{\overline{\mathbf{Z}}_{t-1}}}(\overline{\mathbf{z}}_{t-1}) \overline{K}_t(\overline{\mathbf{z}}_{t-1}, \overline{\mathbf{z}}_t \mid \boldsymbol{\vartheta}_t)},$$

when targeting a sequence $\{\overline{\pi}_t(\overline{\mathbf{z}}_t)\}_{t=1}^{T}$ with $\overline{\pi}_T(\overline{\mathbf{z}}_T) = \overline{\pi}(\overline{\mathbf{z}})$.

The algorithms described in this section contain several degrees of freedom, whose choices are discussed in detail in Section 9. In the next section we formally define the elements necessary for constructing the statistical models underlying the risk drivers $\overline{\mathbf{Z}}$ and $\mathbf{Z}$. We also present the formulas for the Solvency Capital Requirements (SCRs) under both the conditional and marginalized models.

After this brief introduction to SMC algorithms, in the following section we introduce the random variables used in the risk allocation process. In particular, we formally define the random vectors $\mathbf{Z}$ and $\overline{\mathbf{Z}}$ discussed in Section 2, and identify its components with the one-year reserve risk and the one-year premium risk.

4. Swiss Solvency Test and Claims Development

For the rest of this work we assume all random variables are defined in the filtered probability space $(\Omega, \mathcal{F}, \mathbb{P}, \{\mathcal{F}(t)\}_{t\geq 0})$. We denote cumulative payments for accident year $i = 1, \ldots, t$ until development year $j = 0, \ldots, J$ (with $t > J$) on the $\ell = 1, \ldots, L$ LoB by $C_{i,j}^{(\ell)}$. Moreover, in the ℓ-th LoB incremental payments for claims with accident year i and development year j are denoted by $X_{i,j}^{(\ell)} = C_{i,j}^{(\ell)} - C_{i,j-1}^{(\ell)}$. Remark that these payments are made in accounting year $i + j$.

The information (regarding claims payments) available at time $t = 0, \ldots, I + J$ for the ℓ-th LoB is assumed to be given by

$$\mathcal{D}^{(\ell)}(t) = \{X_{i,j}^{(\ell)} : 1 \leq i \leq t,\ 0 \leq j \leq J,\ 1 \leq i + j \leq t\},$$

and, similarly, the total information (regarding claims payments) available at time t is denoted as

$$\mathcal{D}(t) = \bigcup_{1\leq \ell \leq L} \mathcal{D}^{(\ell)}(t). \tag{20}$$

Remark 6. *By a slight abuse of notation we also use $\mathcal{D}^{(\ell)}(t)$ and $\mathcal{D}(t)$ for the sigma-field generated by the corresponding sets. Note that $\mathcal{D}(t) \subset \mathcal{F}(t)$ for all $t \geq 0$, as we assume that $\mathcal{F}(t)$ contains not only information about claims payments, but also about premium and administrative costs.*

The general aim now is to predict the future cumulative payments $C_{i,j}^{(\ell)}$ for $i + j > t$ at time t, given the information $\mathcal{F}(t)$, in particular, the so-called ultimate claim $C_{i,J}^{(\ell)}$. For more information we refer to Wüthrich (2015).

4.1. Conditional Predictive Model

As noted previously, we generically denote parameters in the Bayesian model for the ℓ LoB by $\boldsymbol{\theta}^{(\ell)}$. For the ease of exposition, whenever a quantity is defined conditional on $\boldsymbol{\theta}^{(\ell)}$ it is going to be denoted with a bar on top of it.

At time $t \geq I$, LoB ℓ and accident year $i > t - J$ predictors for the ultimate claim $C_{i,J}^{(\ell)}$ and the corresponding claims reserves are defined, respectively, as

$$\overline{\mathscr{C}}_{i,J}^{(\ell)}(t) = \mathbb{E}[C_{i,J}^{(\ell)} \mid \boldsymbol{\theta}^{(\ell)}, \mathcal{F}(t)] \quad \text{and} \quad \overline{\mathcal{R}}_{i}^{(\ell)}(t) = \overline{\mathscr{C}}_{i,J}^{(\ell)}(t) - C_{i,t-i}^{(\ell)}. \tag{21}$$

Under modern solvency regulations, such as Solvency II European Comission (2009) and the Swiss Solvency Test FINMA (2007) an important variable to be analysed is the claims development result (CDR). For accident year $i = 1, \ldots, I$, accounting year $t + 1 > I$ and LoB ℓ, the CDR is defined as

$$\begin{aligned}\overline{\mathrm{CDR}}_{i}^{(\ell)}(t+1) &= \overline{\mathcal{R}}_{i}^{(\ell)}(t) - (X_{i,t-i+1}^{(\ell)} + \overline{\mathcal{R}}_{i}^{(\ell)}(t+1)) \\ &= \overline{\mathscr{C}}_{i,J}^{(\ell)}(t) - \overline{\mathscr{C}}_{i,J}^{(\ell)}(t+1),\end{aligned} \tag{22}$$

and an application of the tower property of the expectation shows that (subject to integrability)

$$\mathbb{E}[\overline{\mathrm{CDR}}_{i}^{(\ell)}(t+1) \mid \boldsymbol{\theta}^{(\ell)}, \mathcal{F}(t)] = 0. \tag{23}$$

Thus, the prediction process in Equation (21) is a martingale in t and we aim to study the volatility of these martingale innovations.

Equation (23) justifies the prediction of the CDR by zero and the uncertainty of this prediction can be assessed by the conditional mean squared error of prediction (msep):

$$\text{msep}_{\overline{\text{CDR}}_i^{(\ell)}(t+1)\,|\,\boldsymbol{\theta}^{(\ell)},\mathcal{F}(t)}(0) = \mathbb{E}[(\overline{\text{CDR}}_i^{(\ell)}(t+1) - 0)^2 \,|\, \boldsymbol{\theta}^{(\ell)}, \mathcal{F}(t)] \tag{24}$$

$$= \text{Var}(\overline{\text{CDR}}_i^{(\ell)}(t+1) \,|\, \boldsymbol{\theta}^{(\ell)}, \mathcal{F}(t))$$

$$= \text{Var}(\overline{\mathscr{C}}_{i,J}^{(\ell)}(t+1) \,|\, \boldsymbol{\theta}^{(\ell)}, \mathcal{F}(t)). \tag{25}$$

Moreover, we denote the aggregated (over all accident years) CDR and the reserves, conditional on the knowledge of the parameter $\boldsymbol{\theta}^{(\ell)}$, respectively, by

$$\overline{\text{CDR}}^{(\ell)}(t+1) = \sum_{i=t-J+1}^{t} \overline{\text{CDR}}_i^{(\ell)}(t+1) \quad \text{and} \quad \overline{\mathcal{R}}^{(\ell)}(t) = \sum_{i=t-J+1}^{t} \overline{\mathcal{R}}_i^{(\ell)}(t). \tag{26}$$

Using this notation we also define the total prediction uncertainty incurred when predicting $\overline{\text{CDR}}^{(\ell)}(t+1)$ by zero as

$$\text{msep}_{\overline{\text{CDR}}^{(\ell)}(t+1)\,|\,\boldsymbol{\theta}^{(\ell)},\mathcal{F}(t)}(0) = \text{Var}\left(\sum_{i=t-J+1}^{t} \overline{\mathscr{C}}_{i,J}^{(\ell)}(t+1) \,\middle|\, \boldsymbol{\theta}^{(\ell)}, \mathcal{F}(t) \right).$$

Remark 7. *It should be remarked that, in general, as the parameter vector $\boldsymbol{\theta}^{(\ell)}$ is unknown none of the quantities presented in this section can be directly calculated unless an explicit estimate for the parameter is used.*

4.2. Marginalized Predictive Model

Even though cumulative claims models are defined conditional on unobserved parameter values, any quantity that has to be calculated based on these models should only depend on observable variables. Under the Bayesian paradigm, unknown quantities are modelled using a prior probability distribution reflecting prior beliefs about these parameters.

Analogously to Section 4.1 we define the marginalized (Bayesian) ultimate claim predictor and its reserves, respectively, as

$$\mathscr{C}_{i,J}^{(\ell)}(t) = \mathbb{E}[C_{i,J}^{(\ell)} \,|\, \mathcal{F}(t)] = \mathbb{E}[\overline{\mathscr{C}}_{i,J}^{(\ell)}(t) \,|\, \mathcal{F}(t)] \quad \text{and} \quad \mathcal{R}_i^{(\ell)}(t) = \mathscr{C}i,J^{(\ell)}(t) - C_{i,t-i}^{(\ell)}. \tag{27}$$

We also define the marginalized CDR and notice, again using the tower property, that its mean is equal to zero

$$\text{CDR}_i^{(\ell)}(t+1) = \mathscr{C}i,J^{(\ell)}(t) - \mathscr{C}i,J^{(\ell)}(t+1) \quad \text{with} \quad \mathbb{E}[\text{CDR}_i^{(\ell)}(t+1) \,|\, \mathcal{F}(t)] = 0.$$

Furthermore, summing over all accident years i we follow Equation (26) and denote by $\mathcal{R}^{(\ell)}(t)$ and $\text{CDR}^{(\ell)}(t+1)$ the aggregated version of the marginalized reserves and CDR, where the uncertainty in the later is measured via

$$\text{msep}_{\text{CDR}^{(\ell)}(t+1)\,|\,\mathcal{F}(t)}(0) = \text{Var}\left(\sum_{i=t-J+1}^{t} \mathscr{C}i,J^{(\ell)}(t+1) \,\middle|\, \mathcal{F}(t) \right). \tag{28}$$

4.3. Solvency Capital Requirement (SCR)

In this section we discuss how two important concepts in actuarial risk management, namely the technical result (TR) and the solvency capital requirement (SCR), can be defined for both the conditional and the marginalized models.

In this context the TR is calculated netting all income and expenses arising from the LoBs, while the SCR denotes the minimum capital required by the regulatory authorities in order to cover the company's business risks. More precisely, the SCR for accounting year $t+1$ quantifies the risk of having a substantially distressed result at time $t+1$, evaluated in light of the available information at time t.

As an important shorthand notation, we introduce three sets of random variables, representing the total claim amounts of the current year (CY) claims and of prior year (PY) claims, the later for both the conditional and marginalized models. These random variables are defined, respectively, as

$$Z_{CY}^{(\ell)} = \mathscr{C}t+1, J^{(\ell)}(t+1), \quad \overline{Z}_{PY}^{(\ell)} = \sum_{i=t-J+1}^{t} \left(\overline{\mathscr{C}}_{i,J}^{(\ell)}(t+1) - C_{i,t-i}^{(\ell)} \right) \text{ and}$$

$$Z_{PY}^{(\ell)} = \sum_{i=t-J+1}^{t} \left(\mathscr{C}i, J^{(\ell)}(t+1) - C_{i,t-i}^{(\ell)} \right). \tag{29}$$

In the standard SST model, CY claims do not depend on any unknown parameters and are split into small claims $Z_{CY,s}^{(\ell)}$ for the LoBs $\ell = 1, \ldots, L$ and into large events $Z_{CY,l}^{(p)}$ for the perils $p = 1, \ldots, P$. Small claims are also called attritional claims and large claims can be individual large claims or catastrophic events, like earthquakes. In this context the company can choose thresholds $\beta^{(\ell)}$ such that claims larger than these amounts are classified as large claims in its respective LoBs.

To further simplify the notation we also group all the random variables related to the conditional and the marginalized models in two random vectors, defined as follows

$$\overline{\mathbf{Z}} = (\overline{Z}_1, \ldots, \overline{Z}_{2L+P}) = (\overline{Z}_{PY}^{(1)}, \ldots, \overline{Z}_{PY}^{(L)}, Z_{CY,s}^{(1)}, \ldots, Z_{CY,s}^{(L)}, Z_{CY,l}^{(1)}, \ldots, Z_{CY,l}^{(P)}), \tag{30}$$

$$\mathbf{Z} = (Z_1, \ldots, Z_{2L+P}) = (Z_{PY}^{(1)}, \ldots, Z_{PY}^{(L)}, Z_{CY,s}^{(1)}, \ldots, Z_{CY,s}^{(L)}, Z_{CY,l}^{(1)}, \ldots, Z_{CY,l}^{(P)}). \tag{31}$$

Next we give more details on how the TR and the SCR are calculated in the generic structure of the conditional and the marginalized models.

4.3.1. SCR for the Conditional Model

At time $t+1$ the technical result (TR) of the ℓ-th LoB in accounting year $(t, t+1]$ based on the conditional model is defined as the following $\mathcal{F}(t+1)$–measurable random variable:

$$\overline{\mathrm{TR}}^{(\ell)}(t+1) = \Pi^{(\ell)}(t+1) - K^{(\ell)}(t+1) - \mathscr{C}_{t+1,J}^{(\ell)}(t+1) + \overline{\mathrm{CDR}}^{(\ell)}(t+1),$$

where $\Pi^{(\ell)}(t+1)$ and $K^{(\ell)}(t+1)$ are, respectively, the earned premium and the administrative costs of accounting year $(t, t+1]$. For simplicity, we assume that these two quantities are known at time t, i.e., the premium and administrative costs of accounting year $(t, t+1]$ are assumed to be previsible and, hence, $\mathcal{F}(t)$-measurable. Moreover, it should be noticed that in this context $\mathcal{F}(t)$ not only includes the claims payment information defined in Equation (20). The general sigma-field $\mathcal{F}(t)$ should be seen as a sigma-field generated by the inclusion in $\mathcal{D}(t)$ of the information about $\Pi^{(\ell)}(t+1)$ and $K^{(\ell)}(t+1)$, for $\ell = 1, \ldots, L$.

Given the technical result for all the LoBs, the company's overall TR based on the conditional model, and aggregated cost and premium are denoted, respectively, by

$$\overline{\mathrm{TR}}(t+1) = \sum_{\ell=1}^{L} \overline{\mathrm{TR}}^{(\ell)}(t+1), \quad \Pi(t+1) = \sum_{\ell=1}^{L} \Pi^{(\ell)}(t+1) \quad \text{and} \quad K(t+1) = \sum_{\ell=1}^{L} K^{(\ell)}(t+1).$$

In order to cover the company's risks over an horizon of one year, the Swiss Solvency Test is concerned with the 99% ES (in light of all the data up to time t):

$$\overline{\mathrm{SCR}}(t+1) = \mathrm{ES}_{99\%}[-\overline{\mathrm{TR}}(t+1) \mid \mathcal{F}(t)],$$

where $\overline{\mathrm{SCR}}$ denotes the solvency capital requirement.

It is important to notice that even though the ES operator is being applied to a "conditional random variable", namely $\overline{\mathrm{TR}}$, the operator is *not* being taken conditional on the knowledge of $\boldsymbol{\theta} = (\boldsymbol{\theta}^{(1)}, \ldots, \boldsymbol{\theta}^{(L)})$, otherwise this quantity would not be computable (as discussed in Remark 7). Instead, the SCR is calculated based on the marginalized version of the conditional model, where the parameter uncertainty is integrated out. More precisely, the expected shortfall is based on the following (usually intractable) distribution

$$f_{\overline{Z}}(\overline{z} \mid \mathcal{F}(t)) = \int f_{\overline{Z}}(\overline{z} \mid \boldsymbol{\theta}, \mathcal{F}(t)) \pi(\boldsymbol{\theta} \mid \mathcal{F}(t)) d\boldsymbol{\theta}.$$

In order to compute the SCR based on the conditional model we first discuss the measurablity of the terms in the conditional TR, which can be rewritten as

$$\overline{\mathrm{TR}}(t+1) = -K(t+1) + \Pi(t+1) + \sum_{\ell=1}^{L} \sum_{i=t-J+1}^{t} \left(\overline{\mathscr{C}}_{i,J}^{(\ell)}(t) - C_{i,t-i}^{(\ell)} \right) - \sum_{\ell=1}^{L} \left(\overline{Z}_{PY}^{(\ell)} + Z_{CY}^{(\ell)} \right).$$

From the above equation we see the first two terms are, by assumption, $\mathcal{F}(t)$ measurable and so are all the terms of the form $C_{i,t-i}^{(\ell)}$ (payments already completed by time t), while the last summation is $\mathcal{F}(t+1)$ measurable and, therefore, a random variable at time t. Due to the dependence on the unknown parameter $\boldsymbol{\theta}$ the conditional ultimate claim predictor $\overline{\mathscr{C}}_{i,J}^{(\ell)}(t)$ is usually *not* $\mathcal{F}(t)$ measurable. However, under the special models introduced in Section 5 we have that $\overline{\mathscr{C}}_{i,J}^{(\ell)}(t)$ depends only on the claims data up to time t and not on the unknown parameter vector, making it $\mathcal{F}(t)$ measurable. In this case one has

$$\overline{\mathrm{SCR}}(t+1) = K(t+1) - \Pi(t+1) - \sum_{\ell=1}^{L} \overline{\mathcal{R}}^{(\ell)}(t) + \mathrm{ES}_{99\%}\left[\sum_{\ell=1}^{L} \overline{Z}_{PY}^{(\ell)} + Z_{CY}^{(\ell)} \,\middle|\, \mathcal{F}(t) \right], \tag{32}$$

where, by assumption, $\sum_{\ell=1}^{L} \overline{\mathcal{R}}^{(\ell)}(t) = \sum_{\ell=1}^{L} \sum_{i=t-J+1}^{t} \left(\overline{\mathscr{C}}_{i,J}^{(\ell)}(t) - C_{i,t-i}^{(\ell)} \right)$ is $\mathcal{F}(t)$-measurable.

4.3.2. SCR for the Marginalized Model

As the parameter uncertainty is dealt with in a previous step, the calculation of the SCR for the marginalized model is simpler than its conditional counterpart.

Similarly to the conditional case, we define the TR for the marginalized model as

$$\mathrm{TR}^{(\ell)}(t+1) = \Pi^{(\ell)}(t+1) - K^{(\ell)}(t+1) - \mathscr{C}_{t+1,J}^{(\ell)}(t+1) + \mathrm{CDR}^{(\ell)}(t+1),$$

and its aggregated version as

$$\mathrm{TR}(t+1) = \sum_{\ell=1}^{L} \mathrm{TR}^{(\ell)}(t+1).$$

Furthermore, the SCR for the marginalized model is given by

$$\mathrm{SCR}(t+1) = \mathrm{ES}_{99\%}[-\mathrm{TR}(t+1) \mid \mathcal{F}(t)] \tag{33}$$

$$= K(t+1) - \Pi(t+1) - \sum_{\ell=1}^{L} \mathcal{R}^{(\ell)}(t) + \mathrm{ES}_{99\%}\left[\sum_{\ell=1}^{L} Z_{PY}^{(\ell)} + Z_{CY}^{(\ell)} \,\middle|\, \mathcal{F}(t) \right], \tag{34}$$

where in this case the expected shortfall is calculated with respect to the density $f_Z(z \mid \mathcal{F}(t))$.

Remark 8. *For the models discussed in Section 5, as $\overline{\mathscr{C}}_{i,J}^{(\ell)}(t)$ does not depend on the parameter vector $\boldsymbol{\theta}$ and we also have that $\overline{\mathcal{R}}^{(\ell)}(t) = \mathcal{R}^{(\ell)}(t)$.*

Remark 9. *As we assume the cost of claims processing and assessment $K(t+1)$ and premium $\Pi(t+1)$ are known at time t they do not differ from the conditional to the marginalized model.*

5. Modelling of Individual LoBs PY Claims

For the modelling of the PY claims reserving risk we need to model $\overline{Z}_{PY}$ or Z_{PY} as given in Equation (29). The uncertainty in these random variables will be assessed by the conditional and marginalized mean square error of prediction (msep), introduced in Equations (25) and (28). In order to calculate the msep we must first expand our analysis to the study of the claims reserving uncertainty. To do so, in this section we present a fully Bayesian version of the gamma-gamma chain-ladder (CL) model, which has been studied in Peters et al. (2017).

Since in this section we present the model for individual LoBs, for notational simplicity we omit the upper index (ℓ) from all random variables and parameters.

Model Assumptions 1. *[Gamma-gamma Bayesian chain ladder model] We make the following assumptions:*

(a) Conditionally, given $\boldsymbol{\phi} = (\phi_0, \dots, \phi_{J-1})$ and $\boldsymbol{\sigma} = (\sigma_0, \dots, \sigma_{J-1})$, cumulative claims $(C_{i,j})_{j=0,\dots,J}$ are independent (in accident year i) Markov processes (in development year j) with

$$C_{i,j+1} \mid \{\mathcal{F}(i+j),\ \boldsymbol{\phi},\ \boldsymbol{\sigma}\} \sim \Gamma\big(C_{i,j}\sigma_j^{-2},\ \phi_j\sigma_j^{-2}\big),$$

for all $1 \le i \le t$ and $0 \le j \le J-1$.

(b) The parameter vectors $\boldsymbol{\phi}$ and $\boldsymbol{\sigma}$ are independent.

(c) For given hyper-parameters $f_j > 0$ the components of $\boldsymbol{\phi}$ are independent such that

$$\phi_j \sim \lim_{\gamma_j \to 1} \Gamma\big(\gamma_j,\ f_j(\gamma_j - 1)\big),$$

for $0 \le j \le J-1$, where the limit infers that they are eventually distributed from an improper uninfomative prior.

(d) The components σ_j of $\boldsymbol{\sigma}$ are independent and F_{σ_j}-distributed, having support in $(0, d_j)$ for given constants $0 < d_j < \infty$ for all $0 \le j \le J-1$.

(e) $\boldsymbol{\phi}$, $\boldsymbol{\sigma}$ and $C_{1,0}, \dots, C_{t,0}$ are independent and $\mathbb{P}[C_{i,0} > 0] = 1$, for all $1 \le i \le t$.

In Model Assumptions 1 (c) the (improper) prior distribution for $\boldsymbol{\phi}$ should be seen as a non-informative limit when $\boldsymbol{\gamma} = (\gamma_0, \dots, \gamma_{J-1}) \to \mathbf{1} = (1, \dots, 1)$ of the (proper) prior assumption

$$\phi_j \sim \Gamma\big(\gamma_j,\ f_j(\gamma_j - 1)\big).$$

The limit in (c) does not lead to a proper probabilistic model for the prior distribution, however, based on "reasonable" observations $\{C_{i,j}\}_{i,j}$ the posterior model can be shown to be well defined (see Equation (38)), a result that has been proved using the dominated convergence theorem in Peters et al. (2017).

From Model Assumptions 1 (a), conditional on a specific value of the parameter vectors $\boldsymbol{\phi}$ and $\boldsymbol{\sigma}$, we have that

$$\begin{aligned} \mathbb{E}[C_{i,j+1} \mid \mathcal{F}(i+j),\ \boldsymbol{\phi},\ \boldsymbol{\sigma}] &= \phi_j^{-1} C_{i,j}, \\ \mathrm{Var}(C_{i,j+1} \mid \mathcal{F}(i+j),\ \boldsymbol{\phi},\ \boldsymbol{\sigma}) &= \phi_j^{-2}\sigma_j^2 C_{i,j}, \end{aligned} \tag{35}$$

which provides a stochastic formulation of the classical CL model of Mack (1993).

Even though the prior is assumed improper and does not integrate to one, the conditional posterior for $\phi_j \mid \sigma_j, \mathcal{F}(t)$ is proper and, in addition, also gamma distributed (see Appendix A and (Merz and Wüthrich 2015, Lemma 3.2)). More precisely, we have that

$$\phi_j \mid \boldsymbol{\sigma}, \mathcal{F}(t) \sim \Gamma(a_j, b_j), \tag{36}$$

with the following parameters

$$a_j = 1 + \sum_{i=1}^{t-j-1} C_{i,j}\sigma_j^{-2} \quad \text{and} \quad b_j = \sum_{i=1}^{t-j-1} C_{i,j+1}\sigma_j^{-2}. \tag{37}$$

Therefore, given σ this model belongs to the family of Bayesian models with conjugate priors that allows for closed form (conditional) posteriors – for details see Wüthrich (2015).

The marginal posterior distribution of the elements of the vector σ is given by

$$\pi(\sigma_j \mid \mathcal{F}(t)) \propto h_j(\sigma_j \mid \mathcal{F}(t)) = \Gamma(a_j) b_j^{-a_j} f_{\sigma_j}(\sigma_j) \prod_{i=1}^{t-j-1} \frac{(C_{i,j+1}\sigma_j^{-2})^{C_{i,j}\sigma_j^{-2}}}{\Gamma(C_{i,j}\sigma_j^{-2})}, \tag{38}$$

with a_j and b_j defined in Equation (37). We note that as long as Model Assumptions 1 (d) and the conditions in Lemma A1 are satisfied, then one can ensure the posterior distribution of σ is proper.

Therefore, under Model Assumptions 1 inference for all the unknown parameters can be performed. It should be noticed, though, that differently from the (conditional) posteriors for ϕ_j Equation (36), the posterior for σ_j Equation (38) is not recognized as a known distribution. Thus, whenever expectations with respect to the distribution of $\sigma_j \mid \mathcal{F}(t)$ need to be calculated one needs to make use of numerical procedures, such as numerical integration or Markov Chain Monte Carlo (MCMC) methods.

5.1. MSEP Results Conditional on σ

Following Model Assumptions 1 we now discuss how to explicitly calculate the quantities introduced in Section 4. We start with the equivalent of the classic CL factor. From the model structure in Equation (35) we define the posterior Bayesian CL factors, given σ, as

$$\widehat{f}_j(t) = \mathbb{E}[\phi_j^{-1} \mid \sigma_j, \mathcal{F}(t)], \tag{39}$$

which, using the gamma distribution from Equation (36), takes the form

$$\widehat{f}_j(t) = \frac{\sum_{k=1}^{t-j-1} C_{k,j+1}}{\sum_{k=1}^{t-j-1} C_{k,j}},$$

i.e., $\widehat{f}_j(t)$ is identical to the classic CL factor estimate.

Following Equation (21) we define the conditional ultimate claim predictor

$$\overline{\mathscr{C}}_{i,J}(t) = \mathbb{E}[C_{i,J} \mid \sigma, \mathcal{F}(t)] = \mathbb{E}_{\phi}\Big[\mathbb{E}[C_{i,J} \mid \phi, \sigma, \mathcal{F}(t)] \,\Big|\, \sigma, \mathcal{F}(t)\Big],$$

which can be shown (see (Wüthrich 2015, Theorem 9.5)) to be equal to

$$\overline{\mathscr{C}}_{i,J}(t) = C_{i,t-i} \prod_{j=t-i}^{J-1} \widehat{f}_j(t), \tag{40}$$

where this is exactly the classic chain ladder predictor of Mack (1993). For this reason we may take Model Assumptions 1 as a distributional model for the classical CL method. Additionally, the conditional reserves defined in Equation (21) and Equation (26) are also the same as the classic CL ones, that is,

$$\overline{\mathcal{R}}(t) = \sum_{i=1}^{t} \overline{\mathscr{C}}_{i,J}(t) - C_{i,t-i}. \tag{41}$$

The importance of Equation (40) relies on the fact that it does not depend on the parameter vector σ. In other words, the ultimate claim predictor based on the Bayesian model from Model Assumptions 1 conditional on σ – which is, in general, a random variable – is a real number (independent of σ). This justifies the argument used on the calculation of Equation (32).

Remark 10. *Using the notation from the previous sections the parameter vector* $\boldsymbol{\sigma}$ *plays the role of* $\boldsymbol{\theta}$ *as the only unknown, since, due to conjugacy properties,* $\boldsymbol{\phi}$ *can be marginalized analytically.*

For the Bayesian model from Model Assumptions 1 the msep conditional on σ has been derived in (Wüthrich 2015, Theorem 9.16) as follows, for $i + J > t$

$$\text{msep}_{\overline{\text{CDR}}_i(t+1)\,|\,\sigma,\mathcal{F}(t)}(0) = (\overline{\mathscr{C}}_{i,J}(t))^2 \left[\left(1 + \frac{\overline{\Psi}_{t-i}(t)}{\overline{\beta}_{t-i}(t)}\right) \prod_{j=t-i+1}^{J-1} \left(1 + \overline{\beta}_j(t)\overline{\Psi}_j(t)\right) - 1 \right], \quad (42)$$

where

$$\overline{\beta}_j(t) = \frac{C_{t-j,j}}{\sum_{i=1}^{t-j} C_{i,j}} \quad \text{and} \quad \overline{\Psi}_j(t) = \frac{\sigma_j^2}{\sum_{k=1}^{t-j-1} C_{k,j} - \sigma_j^2}. \quad (43)$$

Moreover, the conditional msep has been shown to be finite if, and only if, $\sigma_j^2 < \sum_{k=1}^{t-j-1} C_{k,j}$. We also refer to Remark 12, below.

The aggregated conditional msep for $\overline{\text{CDR}}(t+1) = \sum_{i=1}^{t} \overline{\text{CDR}}_i(t+1)$ is also derived in (Wüthrich 2015, Theorem 9.16), and given by

$$\text{msep}_{\overline{\text{CDR}}(t+1)\,|\,\sigma,\mathcal{F}(t)}(0) = \sum_{i=t-J+1}^{t} \text{msep}_{\overline{\text{CDR}}_i(t+1)\,|\,\sigma,\mathcal{F}(t)}(0)$$
$$+2 \sum\sum_{t-J+1 \le i < k \le t} \overline{\mathscr{C}}_{i,J}(t)\overline{\mathscr{C}}_{k,J}(t) \left[(1 + \overline{\Psi}_{t-i}(t)) \prod_{j=t-i+1}^{J-1} \left(1 + \overline{\beta}_j(t)\overline{\Psi}_j(t)\right) - 1 \right]. \quad (44)$$

Remark 11. *The assumption that* $\sigma_j^2 < \sum_{k=1}^{t-j-1} C_{k,j}$ *is made in order to guarantee the conditional msep is finite and we enforce this assumption to hold for all the examples presented in this work. See also Remark 12, below.*

5.2. Marginalized MSEP Results

The results in the previous section are based on derivations presented in Merz and Wüthrich (2015) and Wüthrich (2015) where the parameter vector σ is assumed to be known. In this section we study the impact of the uncertainty in σ over the mean and variance of $\mathscr{C}i, J(t+1) \mid \mathcal{F}(t)$ in light of Model Assumptions 1, which can be seen as a fully Bayesian version of the models previously mentioned.

In order to have well defined posterior distributions for σ, through this section we follow Lemma A1 and assume that, for all development years $0 \le j \le J-1$ and $t \ge I$, we have $(t-j-1) \wedge I = 1$ or at least one accident year $1 \le i \le (t-j-1) \wedge I$ is such that $\frac{C_{i,j+1}}{C_{i,j}} \neq \widehat{f}_j(t)$. For all the numerical results presented this assumption is satisfied.

Lemma 1. *The ultimate claim estimator under the marginalized model is equal to the classic chain ladder predictor, i.e.,* $\mathscr{C}i, J(t) = \mathbb{E}[C_{i,J} \mid \mathcal{F}(t)] = \overline{\mathscr{C}}_{i,J}(t)$.

Proof. Due to the posterior independence of the elements of $\boldsymbol{\phi}$ (also used in Equations (39) and (40)) and the fact that $\overline{\mathscr{C}}_{i,J}(t)$ does not depend on σ we have

$$\begin{aligned}
\mathscr{C}i, J(t) &= \mathbb{E}[C_{i,J} \mid \mathcal{F}(t)] \\
&= \mathbb{E}\big[\mathbb{E}[C_{i,J} \mid \boldsymbol{\phi}, \sigma, \mathcal{F}(t)] \mid \mathcal{F}(t)\big] \\
&= \mathbb{E}\Big[\mathbb{E}\big[\mathbb{E}[C_{i,J} \mid \boldsymbol{\phi}, \sigma, \mathcal{F}(t)] \mid \sigma, \mathcal{F}(t)\big] \mid \mathcal{F}(t)\Big] \\
&= \mathbb{E}\Big[\mathbb{E}\big[C_{i,t-i} \prod_{j=t-i}^{J-1} \phi_j^{-1} \mid \sigma, \mathcal{F}(t)\big] \mid \mathcal{F}(t)\Big] \\
&= \mathbb{E}\Big[\overline{\mathscr{C}}_{i,J}(t) \mid \mathcal{F}(t)\Big] = \overline{\mathscr{C}}_{i,J}(t).
\end{aligned}$$

□

Proposition 1. *The msep in the marginalized model is equal to the posterior expectation of the msep in the conditional model, i.e.,*

$$\begin{aligned}
msep_{CDR(t+1) \mid \mathcal{F}(t)}(0) &= Var\Big(\sum_{i=1}^{I} \mathscr{C}i, J(t+1) \mid \mathcal{F}(t)\Big) \\
&= \mathbb{E}[msep_{\overline{CDR}(t+1) \mid \sigma, \mathcal{F}(t)}(0) \mid \mathcal{F}(t)].
\end{aligned} \tag{45}$$

Proof. From the law of total variance we have that

$$\begin{aligned}
\mathrm{Var}\Big(\sum_{i=1}^{I} \mathscr{C}i, J(t+1) \mid \mathcal{F}(t)\Big) &= \mathrm{Var}\Big(\mathbb{E}\big[\sum_{i=1}^{I} \mathscr{C}i, J(t+1) \mid \mathcal{F}(t), \sigma\big] \mid \mathcal{F}(t)\Big) \\
&\quad + \mathbb{E}\Big[\mathrm{Var}\big(\sum_{i=1}^{I} \mathscr{C}i, J(t+1) \mid \mathcal{F}(t), \sigma\big) \mid \mathcal{F}(t)\Big] \\
&= \mathbb{E}\Big[\mathrm{Var}\big(\sum_{i=1}^{I} \mathscr{C}i, J(t+1) \mid \mathcal{F}(t), \sigma\big) \mid \mathcal{F}(t)\Big],
\end{aligned}$$

and the last equality follows from Lemma 1 and the fact that $\mathbb{E}[\overline{\mathscr{C}}_{i,J}(t+1) \mid \mathcal{F}(t), \sigma] = \overline{\mathscr{C}}_{i,J}(t)$ is independent of σ. □

Remark 12. *Following the conditions required for finiteness of the conditional msep, in the unconditional case, one can see that $msep_{CDR(t+1) \mid \mathcal{F}(t)}(0) < \infty$ whenever $\sum_{k=1}^{t-j-1} C_{k,j} > d_j^2$. Furthermore, we note that this condition can be controlled during the model specification, i.e., the range of the σ_j^2 is chosen such that all posteriors are well-defined.*

5.3. Statistical Model of PY Risk in the SST

Note that the distributional models derived in Sections 5.1 and 5.2 are rather complex. To maintain some degree of tractability, the overall PY uncertainty distribution is usually approximated by a log-normal distribution via a moment matching procedure.

5.3.1. Conditional PY Model

As discussed in Section 4.3, when modelling the risk of PY claims we work with the random variables $\overline{Z}_{PY}$, defined in Equation (29). Due to their relationship with the conditional CDR, see Equations (22) and (23) and the results discussed in Section 5.1, we can use the derived properties of these random variables to construct the model being used for $\overline{Z}_{PY}$.

The conditional mean (see Equations (22), (23) and (41)) and variance (see Equations (25) and (44)) of the random variable $\overline{Z}_{PY}$ are as follows

$$\mathbb{E}[\overline{Z}_{PY} \mid \sigma, \mathcal{F}(t)] = \overline{\mathcal{R}}(t), \tag{46}$$

$$\text{Var}(\overline{Z}_{PY} \mid \sigma, \mathcal{F}(t)) = \text{msep}_{\overline{\text{CDR}}(t+1) \mid \sigma, \mathcal{F}(t)}(0). \tag{47}$$

Given mean and variance, we make the following approximation, also proposed in the Swiss Solvency Test (see (FINMA 2007, sct. 4.4.10)).

Model Assumptions 2 [Conditional log-normal approximation.] *We assume that*

$$\overline{Z}_{PY} \mid \sigma, \mathcal{F}(t) \sim \text{LN}\left(\overline{\mu}_{PY}, \overline{\sigma}^2_{PY}\right),$$

with $\overline{\sigma}^2_{PY} = \log\left(\frac{\text{msep}_{\overline{\text{CDR}}(t+1) \mid \sigma, \mathcal{F}(t)}(0)}{\overline{\mathcal{R}}(t)^2} + 1\right)$ and $\overline{\mu}_{PY} = \log\left(\overline{\mathcal{R}}(t)\right) - \frac{\overline{\sigma}^2_{PY}}{2}$.

Although the distribution of $\overline{Z}_{PY} \mid \sigma, \mathcal{F}(t)$ under Model Assumptions 1 can not be described analytically it is simple to simulate from it. To test the approximation of Model Assumptions 2 we simulate its distribution under the gamma-gamma Bayesian CL model (with fixed σ) and compare it against the log-normal approximation proposed. For the hyper-parameters presented in Table 2 (and calculated in Section 8) the quantile-quantile plot of the approximation is presented in Figure 1. For all the LoBs we see that the log-normal distribution is a sensible approximation to the original model assumptions. Note that although the parameters used for the comparison are based on the marginalized model Figures 5 and 6 show that they are "representative" values for the distributions of $\overline{\mu}_{PY}$ and $\overline{\sigma}_{PY}$.

5.3.2. Marginalized PY Model

As an alternative to the conditional Model Assumptions 2 we use the moments of $Z_{PY} \mid \mathcal{F}(t)$ calculated in Lemma 1 and Proposition 1 and then approximate its distribution. Note that due to the intractability of the distribution of $\sigma \mid \mathcal{F}(t)$ the variance term defined in Equation (45) can only be calculated numerically, for example, via MCMC.

Model Assumptions 3 [Marginalized log-normal approximation.] *We assume that*

$$Z_{PY} \mid \mathcal{F}(t) \sim \text{LN}\left(\mu_{PY}, \sigma^2_{PY}\right)$$

with $\sigma^2_{PY} = \log\left(\frac{\text{msep}_{\text{CDR}(t+1) \mid \mathcal{F}(t)}(0)}{\overline{\mathcal{R}}(t)^2} + 1\right)$ and $\mu_{PY} = \log\left(\overline{\mathcal{R}}(t)\right) - \frac{\sigma^2_{PY}}{2}$.

The same comparison based on the quantile-quantile plot of Figure 1 can be performed for the marginalized model and the results are presented in Figure 2. Once again, the log-normal model presents a viable alternative to the originally postulated gamma-gamma Bayesian CL model, even though for Motor Hull, Property and Others the right tail of the log-normal distribution is slightly heavier.

Table 2. Parameters and capital calculations for the marginalized and conditional models.

LoB	Reserve/ Premium	σ	μ	CoVa	Expectation	Standalone		Marginalized			Conditional		
						$ES_{99\%}$	SCR	$ES_{99\%}$	SCR	Div. Benefit	$ES_{99\%}$	SCR	Div. Benefit
1	2365.44	0.0287	7.7659	2.87%	2365.44	2546.31	180.87	2489.85	124.41	31.22%	2492.05	126.61	30.00%
2	99.37	0.2164	4.5755	21.90%	99.37	173.23	73.86	131.73	32.36	56.19%	132.59	33.21	55.03%
3	405.99	0.1142	5.9998	11.46%	405.99	547.25	141.26	479.11	73.12	48.24%	485.27	79.28	43.88%
4	870.19	0.0315	6.7682	3.15%	870.19	946.06	75.87	905.48	35.29	53.49%	905.29	35.10	53.73%
5	1105.95	0.0193	7.0083	1.93%	1105.95	1,164.04	58.09	1137.06	31.11	46.44%	1136.88	30.93	46.76%
6	274.91	0.0410	5.6156	4.10%	274.91	306.43	31.52	287.33	12.42	60.59%	286.97	12.06	61.74%
7	7.150	0.0547	1.9657	5.48%	7.15	8.26	1.11	7.45	0.30	73.27%	7.43	0.28	74.50%
8	48.18	0.0493	3.8738	4.93%	48.18	54.89	6.71	50.51	2.32	65.36%	50.43	2.25	66.44%
9	72.20	0.1332	4.2706	13.38%	72.2	102.16	29.96	85.32	13.12	56.21%	85.15	12.95	56.77%
Total PY	5249.38				5249.38	5848.63	599.25	5573.84	324.45	45.86%	5582.06	332.67	44.49%
1	503.14	0.0685	6.0958	6.86%	448.94	533.07	84.13	499.16	50.21	40.32%	498.37	49.43	41.25%
2	573.26	0.0702	6.0356	7.03%	402.87	504.20	101.33	472.25	69.38	31.53%	471.66	68.79	32.11%
3	748.76	0.0683	6.3013	6.84%	547.23	654.38	107.15	603.36	56.13	47.62%	602.61	55.38	48.31%
4	299.73	0.0923	5.3596	9.25%	216.70	272.05	55.35	239.69	22.99	58.47%	239.57	22.87	58.69%
5	338.63	0.0648	5.6841	6.49%	303.77	349.69	45.92	319.17	15.40	66.47%	318.71	14.94	67.45%
6	254.21	0.0804	5.4296	8.05%	228.79	282.62	53.83	249.63	20.85	61.28%	249.31	20.52	61.88%
7	7.20	0.1047	1.8628	10.5%	6.48	8.52	2.04	7.01	0.53	73.84%	7.01	0.53	74.06%
8	34.64	0.0981	3.3172	9.84%	27.72	35.84	8.13	30.32	2.60	67.95%	30.28	2.57	68.44%
9	46.28	0.1004	3.6066	10.06%	37.03	48.16	11.14	41.83	4.81	56.83%	41.79	4.77	57.19%
Total CY,s	2805.85				2219.53	2688.53	469.02	2462.42	242.9	48.21%	2459.31	239.8	48.87%
Peril	$\beta^{(5)}$	γ	α	CoVa	Expectation	Standalone		Marginalized			Conditional		
						$ES_{99\%}$	SCR	$ES_{99\%}$	SCR	Div. benefit	$ES_{99\%}$	SCR	Div. benefit
1	2.50		2.80		3.89	20.14	16.25	4.03	0.15	99.1%	4.01	0.12	99.27%
2	13.35	300	1.85		27.08	191.21	164.13	39.96	12.88	92.15%	39.61	12.53	92.36%
3	6.28	100	1.50		14.34	84.31	69.97	16.5	2.16	96.91%	16.45	2.11	96.98%
4	3.88	100	1.80		8.10	61.34	53.24	8.94	0.84	98.42%	8.91	0.81	98.48%
5	0.50		2.00		1.00	10.00	9.00	1.07	0.07	99.19%	1.12	0.12	98.69%
Total CY,l					54.41	367	312.59	70.5	16.1	94.85%	70.1	15.69	94.98%
Total	8055.26				7523.32	8904.18	1380.86	8106.77	583.45	57.75%	8111.5	588.18	57.40%

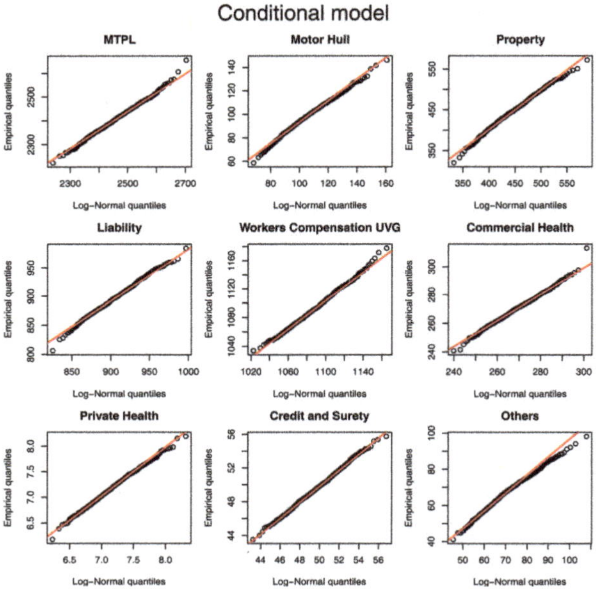

Figure 1. Quantile-Quantile plots for the different lines of business (LoBs) comparing (vertical axis) the empirical distribution of $\overline{Z}_{PY} \mid \sigma, \mathcal{F}(t)$ based on Model Assumptions 1 and (horizontal axis) the log-normal approximation from Model Assumptions 2. Based on 1000 samples.

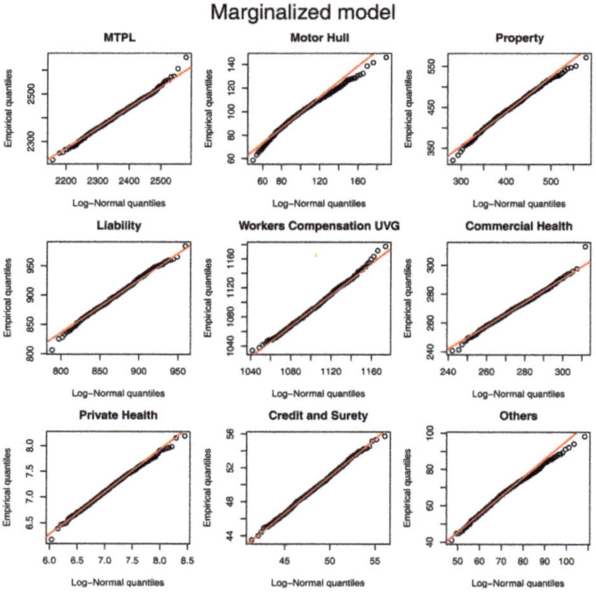

Figure 2. Quantile-Quantile plots for the different LoBs comparing (vertical axis) the empirical distribution of $Z_{PY} \mid \mathcal{F}(t)$ based on Model Assumptions 1 and (horizontal axis) the log-normal approximation from Model Assumptions 3 and using posterior samples as in Figures 5 and 6. Based on 1000 samples.

6. Modelling of Individual LoBs CY Claims

Model Assumptions 1 do not assume any specific distribution for $\mathbb{E}[C_{t+1,J} \mid \mathcal{F}(t+1)]$, the CY claims. These claims are treated differently in the Swiss Solvency Test from PY claims and the models used for these claims are explained in Sections 6.1 and 6.2, below. Throughout this section, we denote by $\lambda_{CY} = \lambda_{CY,s} + \lambda_{CY,l}$ the expected number of CY claims over the next year, which is the sum of the expected CY small claims $\lambda_{CY,s}$ and the expected CY large claims $\lambda_{CY,l}$.

6.1. Modelling of Small CY Claims

As mentioned in the SST Technical Document (FINMA 2007, sct. 4.4.7), *the SST does not make any explicit assumption about the distribution of individual claims; instead, the annual claims expenses are only represented with their expected value and variance*. More precisely, in (FINMA 2007, sct. 8.4.5.2) the distribution of the premium risk, $Z_{CY,s}$ is assumed to be such that

$$\mathrm{CoVa}^2(Z_{CY,s} \mid \mathcal{F}(t)) = a_1 + \frac{a_2+1}{\lambda_{CY,s}}, \tag{48}$$

where the constants a_1 and a_2 are provided by the regulatory authority (under the names of *parameter uncertainty* and *random fluctuation*, respectively). Their values for the 2015 solvency test are found in FINMA (2016). In order to fully specify the model for CY small claims one also needs to decide on the mean of the variable $Z_{CY,s} \mid \mathcal{F}(t)$, but we postpone a detailed discussion on this point until Section 8.2, where we also present the value of $\lambda_{CY,s}$.

Model Assumptions 4 [Distribution of CY small claims] *For known constants v, $r_s > 0$ and $\mathbb{E}[Z_{CY,s} \mid \mathcal{F}(t)]$ we set*

$$Z_{CY,s} \mid \mathcal{F}(t) \sim \mathrm{LN}\Big(\mu_{CY,s}, \sigma^2_{CY,s}\Big),$$

with $\sigma^2_{CY,s} = \log\left(a_1 + \frac{a_2+1}{\lambda_{CY,s}} + 1\right)$ and $\mu_{CY,s} = \log(\mathbb{E}[Z_{CY,s} \mid \mathcal{F}(t)]) - \frac{\sigma^2_{CY,s}}{2}$.

6.2. Modelling of Large CY Claims

In the SST (see (FINMA 2007, sct. 4.4.8)), large CY claims are split into two groups. The first group of large claims are those triggered by the same market-wide event (a hailstorm, for example) and with many simultaneous (small) claims. These types of claims are likely to affect all market participants and are called "cumulated claims". The second group encompasses individual claims with a large claim amount, which includes, as exemplified in (FINMA 2007, sct. 4.4.8), fire in a factory building.

For each risk trigger, CY large claims are required to be modelled as a compound Poisson random variable with i.i.d. Pareto severities, i.e.,

$$Z_{CY,l} = \sum_{k=1}^{N} Y_k, \tag{49}$$

where $N \sim Pois(\lambda)$ is the number of large claims in LoB under consideration and $Y_k \overset{i.i.d.}{\sim} Pareto(\beta, \alpha_\beta)$ model the intensity of large claims. Here we denote by $X \sim Pareto(\beta, \alpha_\beta)$ a random variable with density $f(x) = \frac{\alpha\beta^\alpha}{x^{\alpha+1}}$, for $x \geq \beta$. It is assumed in the SST that large claims are i.i.d. within the same risk trigger and also between different risk triggers, and independent of all Z_{PY} and $Z_{CY,s}$.

As a notational remark, if Z follows a Compound Poisson – Pareto model as a shorthand notation we write $Z \sim$ CP-P(λ, β, α), with the same parameter interpretation as in Equation (49).

6.2.1. SST Model for Cumulated Claims

In this section we discuss the modelling of cumulated claims (those triggered by a market-wide event) which are modelled as an event that impacts the whole market and then scales down to an individual insurance company through its market share. In particular, we present the modelling approach used in (1) Motor Hull LoB due to hail events and (2) Workers Compensation (UVG) LoB due to a market-wide large accident.

In both cases market-wide parameters for a compound Poisson model with Pareto intensities have been determined by the regulator, (based on a large claims data set). The aggregated market-wide loss is given by

$$Z_{mkt} = \sum_{k=1}^{N_{mkt}} Y_{k,mkt} \sim \text{CP-P}(\lambda_{mkt}, \beta_{mkt}, \alpha_{mkt}),$$

where CP-P$(\lambda_{mkt}, \beta_{mkt}, \alpha_{mkt})$ denotes a compound distribution with frequency given by $Pois(\lambda_{mkt})$ and severity given by $Pareto(\beta_{mkt}, \alpha_{mkt})$. The corresponding market-wide parameter values are found in FINMA (2016).

Denoting by β the company's threshold after which losses are classified as large and m its market share in the ℓ-th LoB, to be consistent with its assumption the company should model market-wide large events as events above the threshold of

$$\beta^* = \frac{\beta}{m}.$$

Then, the market-wide total loss (viewed from the specific company in consideration) is defined as

$$Z^* = \sum_{k=1}^{N^*} Y_k^* \sim \text{CP-P}(\lambda^*, \beta^*, \alpha_{mkt}),$$

from which it is easy to see that the only unknown parameter is λ^*, since in the SST the Pareto parameter α_{mkt} is kept the same. This frequency parameter is chosen such that the company's view of the market-wide events is equivalent to the suggested market-wide process. In other words, $\lambda_{mkt} = \mathbb{P}[Y_k^* > \beta_{mkt}]\lambda^*$ hence

$$\lambda^* = \lambda_{mkt} \left(\frac{\beta/m}{\beta_{mkt}}\right)^{-\alpha_{mkt}}. \tag{50}$$

Therefore, from the company's point of view, its own large claims are modelled as

$$Z_{comp} \sim \text{CP-P}(\lambda^*, \beta, \alpha_{mkt}).$$

Following the SST Technical Document FINMA (2007), an upper bound γ (provided by the regulator) is included in each Pareto random variable within the random sum. In other words, the final distribution of the company's large cumulated claims is given by

$$\widetilde{Z} = \sum_{k=1}^{N^*} \widetilde{Y}_k \sim \text{CP-P}(\lambda^*, \beta, \alpha_{mkt}, \gamma),$$

where $\widetilde{Y}_k \sim \text{Pareto}(\beta, \alpha_{mkt}, \gamma)$, a Pareto distribution defined in $[\beta, \gamma]$ with tail index α_{mkt}.

For efficiency purposes, this distribution is approximated by a single Pareto, with the same mean. This leads us to the following model assumptions.

Model Assumptions 5 [Marginal distribution of cumulated claims]. *For α_{mkt}, β_{mkt} and γ provided by the regulator in FINMA (2016), $\beta \in \{1, 5\}$, $m \in (0,1)$,*

$$Z_{CY,l} \sim \text{Pareto}\left(\lambda^* \frac{\beta^{\alpha_{mkt}}}{1-(\beta/\gamma)^{\alpha_{mkt}}} \left(\frac{1}{\beta^{\alpha_{mkt}-1}} - \frac{1}{\gamma^{\alpha_{mkt}-1}}\right), \alpha_{mkt}\right)$$

where λ^* is defined in Equation (50).

Remark 13. *The reader should note that for large CY claims no parameter uncertainty is considered, since both λ_{mkt}, α_{mkt} and γ are given by the regulator, the market share, m can be perfectly calculated and β is chosen by the company.*

6.2.2. SST Model for Individual Claims

For individual large events, the SST provides p_1, the probability of observing losses larger than CHF 1 million and standard values for α_β, for $\beta = 1$ and $\beta = 5$ (see Table FINMA (2016)). Since the probability of large claims provided by the SST is based on a lower threshold of CHF 1 million, a thinning process of the CP-P has to be done if the company decides to use $\beta = 5$.

Following the same procedure presented in Section 6.2.1 we can see that the company's large individual claims are modelled as

$$Z_{comp} \sim \text{CP-P}(\lambda_\beta, \beta, \alpha_\beta),$$

with an expected number of claims larger than β equal to

$$\lambda_\beta = \lambda_{CY,l} = p_1 \lambda_{CY} \left(\frac{\beta}{1}\right)^{-\alpha_\beta}, \tag{51}$$

where λ_{CY} denotes the expected total number of CY claims in the ℓ-th LoB. Similarly, the regulator also requires a upper bound in the Pareto random variables, leading to the following distribution of large losses

$$\widetilde{Z} \sim \text{CP-P}(\lambda_\beta, \beta, \alpha_{mkt}, \gamma).$$

As in Section 6.2.1, the distribution of $Z_{CY,l} \mid \mathcal{F}(t)$ is approximated by a single Pareto, with the same mean and Pareto index α_β.

Model Assumptions 6 [Marginal distribution of large individual claims.] *For α_β, p_1 and γ provided by the regulator in FINMA (2016), $\beta \in \{1, 5\}$ and $\lambda_{CY} > 0$,*

$$Z_{CY,l} \mid \mathcal{F}(t) \sim \text{Pareto}\left(\lambda_\beta \frac{\beta^{\alpha_{mkt}}}{1 - (\beta/\gamma)^{\alpha_{mkt}}} \left(\frac{1}{\beta^{\alpha_{mkt}-1}} - \frac{1}{\gamma^{\alpha_{mkt}-1}}\right), \alpha_{mkt}\right),$$

with λ_β defined in Equation (51).

7. Joint Distribution of PY and CY Claims

Although the SST does not assume any parametric form for the joint distribution of $\mathbf{Z} \mid \mathcal{F}(t)$ or $\overline{\mathbf{Z}} \mid \mathcal{F}(t)$ (defined in Equations (30) and (31), respectively) it is required that a pre-specified *correlation matrix* Λ is used (see FINMA (2016)). In this section we discuss how to use the conditional and marginalized models to define a joint distribution satisfying this correlation assumption.

It is important to notice, though, that the SST correlation matrix may not be attainable for some joint distributions, as discussed in Appendix B in the case of log-normal marginals (in Devroye and Letac (2015) the authors discuss a similar problem). Let us denote by $\mathcal{S}_n$ the set of all $n \times n$, symmetric, positive semi-definite matrices with diagonal terms equal to 1; and by $S(C) = \text{Corr}(\mathbf{U})$ the correlation matrix of a random vector $\mathbf{U} \sim C$, with elements $U_i \sim [0, 1]$. The question asked in Devroye and Letac (2015) is: given $S \in \mathcal{S}_n$, does there exist a copula C such that $S(C) = S$? The answer is *yes*, if $n \leq 9$ and the authors postulate that for $n \geq 10$ there exists $S \in \mathcal{S}_n$ such that there is no copula C such that $S(C) = S$.

It should be noted that, since in the SST the CY large claims are assumed to be independent from all the other risks, the correlation matrix of $(\mathbf{Z}_{PY}, \mathbf{Z}_{CY,s}, \mathbf{Z}_{CY,l}) \mid \mathcal{F}(t)$ is essentially a correlation matrix between $(\mathbf{Z}_{PY}, \mathbf{Z}_{CY,s}) \mid \mathcal{F}(t)$ and the same is true also for the conditional model.

Regardless of assuming a conditional or a marginalized model, SST's correlation matrix Λ should be such that, for $i, j = 1, \ldots, 2L + P$ (recall that L are the number of LoBs and P the number of perils),

$$\Lambda_{i,j} = \text{Corr}(Z_i, Z_j \mid \mathcal{F}(t)) = \text{Corr}(\overline{Z}_i, \overline{Z}_j \mid \mathcal{F}(t)).$$

Remark 14. *In the conditional model we need to "integrate out" the parameter uncertainty, otherwise the (conditional) correlation would be dependent on an unknown parameter and could not be matched with the numbers provided by the SST.*

7.1. Conditional Joint Model

Under Model Assumptions 2, 4, 5 and 6our interest lies on modelling the joint behaviour of the vector $\overline{\mathbf{Z}} \mid \sigma, \mathcal{F}(t)$. Under Model Assumptions 1 it can be shown that the required conditional independence between $\mathbf{Z}_{CY,l}$ and $(\mathbf{Z}_{PY}, \mathbf{Z}_{CY,s})$ given $\mathcal{F}(t)$ is equivalent to the conditional independence between $\mathbf{Z}_{CY,l}$ and $(\mathbf{Z}_{PY}, \mathbf{Z}_{CY,s})$ given $\mathcal{F}(t)$ and $\boldsymbol{\sigma}$.

Moreover, since all the marginal conditional distributions of the prior year claims and small current year claims are assumed to be log-normal, following Equations (30) and (31), the notation can be further simplified to

$$\overline{Z}_i \mid \sigma, \mathcal{F}(t) \sim \mathrm{LN}(\overline{m}_i(\sigma), \overline{V}_i(\sigma)), \text{ for } i = 1, \ldots, 2L, \tag{52}$$

with $\overline{m}_i(\sigma)$, and $\overline{V}_i(\sigma)$ defined in Model Assumptions 2 and 4. For example, for $i = L+1$, $\overline{m}_i(\sigma) = \mu^{(1)}_{CY,s}$, defined in Model Assumptions 4.

We are now ready to define the joint conditional model to be used.

Model Assumptions 7 [Conditional joint model.] *Based on Model Assumptions 2 and 4 we link the marginals of the conditional model through a Gaussian copula with correlation matrix $\overline{\Omega}$, with elements $(\overline{\Omega})_{i,j} = \overline{\omega}_{i,j}$. More formally, given $\mathcal{F}(t)$ and σ, the joint distribution of $\overline{\mathbf{Z}}$ is given by*

$$F_{\overline{\mathbf{Z}}}(\overline{z}_1, \ldots, \overline{z}_{2L}; \overline{\Omega} \mid \mathcal{F}(t), \sigma) = C\Big(F_{\overline{Z}_1}(\overline{z}_1 \mid \mathcal{F}(t), \sigma), \ldots, F_{\overline{Z}_{2L}}(\overline{z}_{2L} \mid \mathcal{F}(t), \sigma); \overline{\Omega}\Big),$$

where $F_{\overline{Z}_i}(\,\cdot \mid \mathcal{F}(t), \sigma)$ denotes the conditional distribution of $\overline{Z}_i \mid \mathcal{F}(t), \sigma$ defined in Equation (52) and $C(\,\cdot\,; \overline{\Omega})$ is the Gaussian copula with correlation matrix denoted by $\overline{\Omega}$.

Remark 15. *In this section the parameter matrix $\overline{\Omega}$ should be understood as a deterministic variable, differently from σ and $\boldsymbol{\phi}$. For this reason we do not include it on the right hand side of the conditioning bar. Instead, whenever $\overline{\Omega}$ needs to be explicitly written, we include it on the left hand side of the bar, separated by the function (or functional, for expectations) arguments by a semicolon.*

In order to match SST's correlation matrix Λ, under Model Assumptions 2 and 4, the following equation needs to be solved with respect to $\overline{\Omega}$:

$$\Lambda_{i,j} = \mathrm{Corr}(\overline{Z}_i, \overline{Z}_j; \overline{\Omega} \mid \mathcal{F}(t)). \tag{53}$$

To compute the right hand side of the equation above we first notice that

$$\mathrm{Cov}(\overline{Z}_i, \overline{Z}_j; \overline{\Omega} \mid \mathcal{F}(t)) = \mathbb{E}[\overline{Z}_i \overline{Z}_j; \overline{\Omega} \mid \mathcal{F}(t)] - \mathbb{E}[\overline{Z}_i \mid \mathcal{F}(t)]\mathbb{E}[\overline{Z}_j \mid \mathcal{F}(t)],$$

where, from Equation (46) and the discussion in Section 6.1,

$$\begin{aligned} \mathbb{E}[\overline{Z}_i \mid \mathcal{F}(t)] &= \mathbb{E}[\mathbb{E}[\overline{Z}_i \mid \mathcal{F}(t), \sigma] \mid \mathcal{F}(t)] \\ &= \mathbb{E}[\overline{m}_i \mid \mathcal{F}(t)] = \begin{cases} \overline{\mathcal{R}}^{(i)}(t), \text{ if } 1 \le i \le L, \\ \mathbb{E}[Z^{(i-L)}_{CY,s} \mid \mathcal{F}(t)], \text{ if } L+1 \le i \le 2L, \end{cases} \end{aligned}$$

and from Equation (A3), Appendix B,

$$\begin{aligned} \mathbb{E}[\overline{Z}_i \overline{Z}_j; \overline{\Omega} \mid \mathcal{F}(t)] &= \mathbb{E}[\mathbb{E}[\overline{Z}_i \overline{Z}_j; \overline{\Omega} \mid \mathcal{F}(t), \sigma] \mid \mathcal{F}(t)] \\ &= \mathbb{E}\left[\exp\left\{\overline{m}_i + \frac{\overline{V}_i^2 + 2\overline{V}_i \overline{\omega}_{i,j} \overline{V}_j + \overline{V}_j^2}{2} + \overline{m}_j\right\} \,\Big|\, \mathcal{F}(t)\right]. \end{aligned}$$

Therefore, to satisfy Equation (53) $\overline{\Omega}_{i,j}$ needs to be chosen such that the following implicit relationship (which can be solved through any univariate root search algorithm) holds:

$$\Lambda_{i,j}\sqrt{\mathrm{Var}(\overline{Z}_i \mid \mathcal{F}(t))\mathrm{Var}(\overline{Z}_j \mid \mathcal{F}(t))} + \mathbb{E}[\overline{Z}_i \mid \mathcal{F}(t)]\mathbb{E}[\overline{Z}_j \mid \mathcal{F}(t)] - \mathbb{E}[\overline{Z}_i\overline{Z}_j;\, \overline{\Omega} \mid \mathcal{F}(t)] = 0.$$

7.2. Marginalized Joint Model

Similarly to Section 7.1, in this section we will fully characterize the joint distribution of $\mathbf{Z} \mid \mathcal{F}(t)$ under Model Assumptions 3, 4, 5 and 6.

From these assumptions we define the following notation:

$$Z_i \mid \mathcal{F}(t) \sim \mathrm{LN}(m_i,\, V_i), \text{ for } i = 1, \ldots, 2L. \tag{54}$$

Model Assumptions 8 [Marginalized joint model.] *Based on Model Assumptions 3 and 4 we link the marginal distributions of the marginalized model through a Gaussian copula with correlation matrix Ω, with elements $(\Omega)_{i,j} = \omega_{i,j}$. More formally, given $\mathcal{F}(t)$, the joint distribution of $\mathbf{Z}$ is given by*

$$F_{\mathbf{Z}}(z_1, \ldots, z_{2L};\, \Omega \mid \mathcal{F}(t)) = C\Big(F_{Z_1}(z_1 \mid \mathcal{F}(t)), \ldots, F_{Z_{2L}}(z_{2L} \mid \mathcal{F}(t));\, \Omega\Big),$$

where F_{Z_i} denotes the conditional distribution of $Z_i \mid \mathcal{F}(t)$ defined in (Equation 54) and $C(\,\cdot\,; \Omega)$ is the Gaussian copula with correlation matrix Ω.

In order to match SST's correlation matrix, in the joint marginalized model the Gaussian copula correlation Ω is chosen such that (see Equation (A4), Appendix B) it satisfies

$$\Lambda_{i,j} = \frac{\exp\{V_i \omega_{i,j} V_j\} - 1}{\left[(e^{V_i^2} - 1)(e^{V_j^2} - 1)\right]^{1/2}}.$$

8. Data Description and Parameter Estimation

In this section we discuss how we set up the parameters in the models discussed so far, starting from the balance sheet of a fictitious insurance company. Using this balance sheet and the information contained in the SST we generate realistic claims triangles (see Appendix C) and, based on them, we show how to perform Bayesian inference for the unknown parameters. Our starting point is the fictitious balance sheet shown in Table 1, which is intended to represent a large insurance company in Switzerland (for this reason all monetary units should be understood as millions of Swiss Francs (CHF)).

8.1. Hyperparameters for ϕ_j

Based on SST's standard runoff pattern (see Table 3) we first compute the implied CL factors $f_j^{(\ell)}$ as follows (once again we suppress the index ℓ of the LoB). If F_j is the deterministic *cumulative* claims payment pattern for development year j we define

$$f_j = \frac{F_{j+1}}{F_j}, \text{ for } j = 0, \ldots, J-1.$$

These values can, then, be used as a hyperparameter in the prior for ϕ_j (see Model Assumptions 1, item (c)).

To generate data from the model (see Section C) we fix $\phi_j = 1/f_j$ and $\sigma_j = s_j/f_j$, where s_j is Mack's standard deviation estimate calculated from exogenous triangles. The values of s_j are presented in Table 4. That is, $\{F_j\}_j$ should be understood as a (deterministic) prior payment pattern.

Table 3. Swiss Solvency Test (SST)'s (2015) standard development patterns for claims provision (normalized to have at most 30 development years and rounded to 2 digits).

LoB	Year 0	Year 1	Year 2	Year 3	Year 4	Year 5	Year 6	Year 7	Year 8	Year 9	Year 10	Year 11	Year 12	Year 13	Year 14	Year 15
1	30.18%	15.63%	5.78%	4.94%	4.43%	4.34%	4.09%	3.92%	3.66%	3.50%	3.08%	2.64%	2.16%	1.86%	1.50%	1.30%
2	81.08%	18.67%	0.24%	0%	0%	0%	0%	0%	0%	0%	0%	0%	0%	0%	0%	0%
3	58.24%	35.06%	4.36%	1.37%	0.64%	0.33%	0%	0%	0%	0%	0%	0%	0%	0%	0%	0%
4	26.55%	23.53%	8.33%	6.18%	4.79%	4.15%	3.63%	3.14%	2.55%	2.11%	1.80%	1.59%	1.35%	1.20%	1.12%	1.02%
5	40.62%	24.92%	7.14%	4.86%	4.43%	3.13%	2.57%	1.67%	1.31%	1.22%	1.05%	0.69%	0.60%	0.56%	0.51%	0.47%
6	36.83%	47.68%	14.20%	0.88%	0.28%	0.14%	0%	0%	0%	0%	0%	0%	0%	0%	0%	0%
7	46.26%	38.05%	10.78%	2.94%	1.27%	0.69%	0%	0%	0%	0%	0%	0%	0%	0%	0%	0%
8	45.85%	35.28%	11.35%	3.72%	1.62%	0.91%	0.52%	0.32%	0.20%	0.13%	0.10%	0%	0%	0%	0%	0%
9	58.24%	35.06%	4.36%	1.37%	0.64%	0.33%	0%	0%	0%	0%	0%	0%	0%	0%	0%	0%

LoB	Year 16	Year 17	Year 18	Year 19	Year 20	Year 21	Year 22	Year 23	Year 24	Year 25	Year 26	Year 27	Year 28	Year 29	Year 30
1	1.06%	0.88%	0.73%	0.64%	0.60%	0.53%	0.47%	0.44%	0.41%	0.37%	0.29%	0.21%	0.15%	0.12%	0.10%
2	0%	0%	0%	0%	0%	0%	0%	0%	0%	0%	0%	0%	0%	0%	0%
3	0%	0%	0%	0%	0%	0%	0%	0%	0%	0%	0%	0%	0%	0%	0%
4	0.88%	0.77%	0.72%	0.66%	0.60%	0.55%	0.52%	0.49%	0.45%	0.4%	0.31%	0.22%	0.16%	0.13%	0.11%
5	0.43%	0.40%	0.37%	0.35%	0.33%	0.31%	0.29%	0.27%	0.26%	0.24%	0.23%	0.22%	0.20%	0.19%	0.18%
6	0%	0%	0%	0%	0%	0%	0%	0%	0%	0%	0%	0%	0%	0%	0%
7	0%	0%	0%	0%	0%	0%	0%	0%	0%	0%	0%	0%	0%	0%	0%
8	0%	0%	0%	0%	0%	0%	0%	0%	0%	0%	0%	0%	0%	0%	0%
9	0%	0%	0%	0%	0%	0%	0%	0%	0%	0%	0%	0%	0%	0%	0%

Table 4. Mack's standard deviation parameter estimates, s_j, based on exogenous triangles and for the development lengths given in Table 3.

LoB	Year 0	Year 1	Year 2	Year 3	Year 4	Year 5	Year 6	Year 7	Year 8	Year 9	Year 10	Year 11	Year 12	Year 13	Year 14
1	0.5673	0.2280	0.1922	0.2681	0.2683	0.3949	0.2652	0.2641	0.2789	0.3055	0.1458	0.1577	0.2140	0.1001	0.1016
2	0.6640	0.0659													
3	1.3614	0.4921	0.3215	0.0875	0.0666										
4	0.8248	0.4328	0.4021	0.3644	0.3772	0.2729	0.5268	0.244	0.2786	0.1559	0.2660	0.0776	0.0757	0.1220	0.0418
5	0.9914	0.3317	0.1807	0.1072	0.0740	0.0444	0.0359	0.0255	0.0190	0.0106	0.0166	0.0094	0.0040	0.0105	0.0040
6	0.6069	0.2405	0.0597	0.0371	0.0172										
7	0.1053	0.0450	0.0157	0.0113	0.0091										
8	0.3098	0.0737	0.0310	0.0203	0.0137	0.0051	0.0020	0.0026	0.0020	0.0014	0.0011				
9	0.9163	0.1910	0.1248	0.0340	0.0258										
LoB	**Year 15**	**Year 16**	**Year 17**	**Year 18**	**Year 19**	**Year 20**	**Year 21**	**Year 22**	**Year 23**	**Year 24**	**Year 25**	**Year 26**	**Year 27**	**Year 28**	**Year 29**
1	0.0466	0.1097	0.1081	0.0583	0.1353	0.0916	0.0916	0.0916	0.0916	0.0916	0.0916	0.0916	0.0916	0.0916	0.0916
2															
3															
4	0.0272	0.0886	0.0422	0.0190	0.0238	0.0190	0.0152	0.0122	0.0097	0.0078	0.0062	0.0050	0.0040	0.0032	0.0025
5	0.0040	0.0040	0.0040	0.0040	0.0040	0.0040	0.0040	0.0040	0.0040	0.0040	0.0040	0.0040	0.0040	0.0040	0.0040
6															
7															
8															
9															

8.2. Current Year Small and Large Claims

To calculate the expected number of CY claims, λ_{CY}, defined in Section 6, we first set our prior belief for the *claims ratio* for each LoB, i.e., how much of the premium in that LoB is used to cover incoming claims (all the rest covers business' costs). This information is available in Table 5, along with the *average claim amount*. Based on these values the expected number of claims is defined as

$$\lambda_{CY} = \frac{\text{Claims ratio} \times \text{Premium}}{\text{Average claim amount}}.$$

Table 5. Claims ratio, average claim amount (in millions of CHF) and market share.

LoB	Claims Ratio	Average Claim Amount	Market Share
1	90%	0.005	
2	75%	0.003	20%
3	75%	0.004	
4	75%	0.004	
5	90%	0.004	10%
6	90%	0.003	
7	90%	0.002	
8	80%	0.003	
9	80%	0.003	

Given the expected number of CY claims, λ_{CY}, this value is used to compute the expected number of individual large claims, $\lambda_{CY,l}$, as in Equation (51). Using the fact that $\lambda_{CY,s} = \lambda_{CY} - \lambda_{CY,l}$ we calculate the coefficient of variation for small CY claims as given in Equation (48).

The last ingredient in Model Assumptions 4 is $\mathbb{E}[Z_{CY,s} \mid \mathcal{F}(t)]$ which is given by

$$\mathbb{E}[Z_{CY,s} \mid \mathcal{F}(t)] = \text{Claims ratio} \times \text{Premium} - \mathbb{E}[Z_{CY,l} \mid \mathcal{F}(t)],$$

and the expectation on the right hand side is given either in Model Assumptions 5 or Model Assumptions 6, depending on the LoB.

For the large claims from Model Assumptions 5 and 6 we assume the threshold for large claims β to be equal to 5 (millions of CHF). For the large cumulated claims we use LoBs market share as given in Table 5. The resulting parameters can be found in Table 2. Note these parameters are the same both for the marginalized and conditional models.

8.3. Parameter Estimation

In this section we discuss how to compute the posterior distributions of the variance parameters σ_j in Model Assumptions 1, which are used to compute quantities such as the marginalized msep from Section 5.2.

In order to compute the posteriors of σ_j, we assume priors centred at Mack's Mack (1993) CL standard deviation estimator normalized by the CL factor f, both implied by the data. Formally,

$$\widehat{\sigma}_j(t) = \frac{\sqrt{\widehat{s}_j^2(t)}}{\widehat{f}_j(t)}, \ \forall 0 \leq j \leq J-1, \tag{55}$$

where $\widehat{s}^2_{J-1}(t) = \min\{\widehat{s}^2_{J-3}(t), \widehat{s}^2_{J-2}(t), \widehat{s}^4_{J-2}(t)/\widehat{s}^2_{J-3}(t)\} = \min\{\widehat{s}^2_{J-3}(t), \widehat{s}^4_{J-2}(t)/\widehat{s}^2_{J-3}(t)\}$.

To generate samples from the posteriors we use a Metropolis-Hastings algorithm, with proposals given by a truncated Normal centred at the current point and standard deviation equal to $10 \times d_j$. All the chains are started at the CL variance estimate and the upper limit for the prior, $d_j = k \times \widehat{\sigma}_j(t)$ is set as $k = 5$ times the CL variance estimate. To be left with $N_{MCMC} = 1000$ samples from the posterior we ran the Markov chains for 12,500 iterations, discarding the first 20% as a burn-in and keeping every 10th iteration of the remaining simulations.

Some of the results are presented in Figure 3 where one finds the unnormalized posteriors, the histogram of the MCMC outputs and a red dashed line indicating the CL variance estimate for three different LoBs: (a) MTPL, (b) Motor Hull and (c) Property. As expected, for unidimensional and unimodal densities the resulting estimates are highly accurate. It is also worth noticing that the larger the development year j the more diffuse the posterior is, due to the diminishing amount of data available. In the limit, when $j = J - 1$ the information available is not enough to estimate the variance parameter and, therefore, as can be seen from the posterior distribution derived in Equation (38), the posterior is the same as the prior.

Using the sample of size $N_{MCMC} = 1000$ mentioned above, the calculated parameters for the marginalized model are presented in Table 2. For the conditional model we use the same sample from the posterior and calculate the one value of σ_{PY} and μ_{PY} for each sampled value σ. The resulting (transformed) samples are presented as histograms in Figures 5 and 6 and, for comparison only, the relevant marginalized parameters are included as a red dashed line.

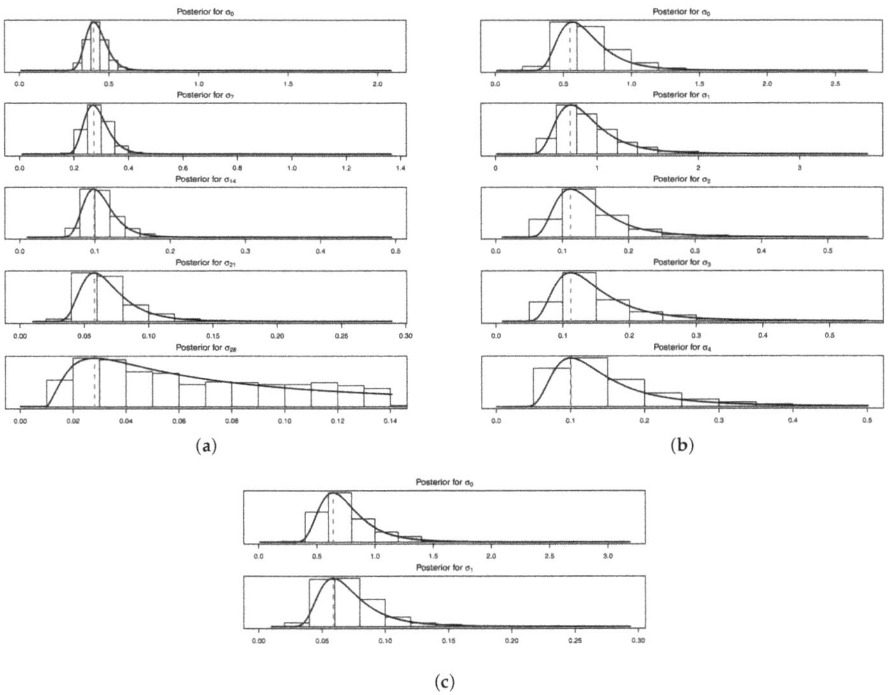

Figure 3. Posterior distributions for σ_j for the (**a**) Motor Third Part Liability (MTPL) (**b**) Property and (**c**) Motor Hull lines of business. One sees solid lines representing the unnormalized posteriors, the histogram of the Markov Chain Monte Carlo (MCMC) outputs and a red dashed line indicating the CL standard deviation estimate. Note that for LoB MTPL we only plot selected development periods: $j \in \{0, 7, 14, 21, 28\}$.

8.4. The Correlation Matrices

For the copula correlation matrices we follow the procedures outlined in Sections 7.1 and 7.2. The resulting matrix for the marginalized model is found in Table 6. From FINMA (2016) it can be seen the values in $\boldsymbol{\Omega}_{PY,CY,s}$ are very similar to ones in the standard $\boldsymbol{\Lambda}_{PY,CY,s}$. Also, it worth noticing that differently from SST's original correlation matrix, the block $\boldsymbol{\Omega}_{PY,CY,s}$ is no longer symmetric, i.e., in order to have $\mathrm{Corr}(Z_{PY}^{(1)}, Z_{CY}^{(2)} \mid \mathcal{F}(t)) = \mathrm{Corr}(Z_{PY}^{(2)}, Z_{CY}^{(1)} \mid \mathcal{F}(t))$ the term $(1,2)$ of the matrix $\boldsymbol{\Omega}_{PY,CY,s}$ is not equal to the term $(2,1)$ of the same matrix.

The results for the copula correlation $\overline{\boldsymbol{\Omega}}_{PY,CY,s}$ follow the same patterns as $\boldsymbol{\Omega}_{PY,CY,s}$ and for this reason its values are omitted.

Table 6. Copula correlation matrix from the marginalized model. Correlation block for the marginalized model: $\boldsymbol{\Omega}_{PY}$ (Table 7); $\boldsymbol{\Omega}_{PY,CY,s}$ (Table 8); $\boldsymbol{\Omega}_{CY,s}$ (Table 9).

$$\boldsymbol{\Omega} = \left[\begin{array}{c|c|c} \boldsymbol{\Omega}_{PY} & \boldsymbol{\Omega}_{PY,CY,s} & \mathbf{0}_{L\times P} \\ \hline & \boldsymbol{\Omega}_{CY,s} & \mathbf{0}_{L\times P} \\ \hline & & \mathbf{I}_{P\times P} \end{array}\right]$$

Table 7. Correlation block for the marginalized model: $\boldsymbol{\Omega}_{PY}$.

LoB	1	2	3	4	5	6	7	8	9
1	1	0.1517	0.1505	0.2501	0.5001	0.2501	0.1501	0.2502	0.2511
2		1	0.1520	0.1517	0.1517	0.1517	0.1517	0.1517	0.2532
3			1	0.1505	0.1505	0.1505	0.1505	0.1505	0.2515
4				1	0.2501	0.1501	0.1501	0.1501	0.2511
5					1	0.2501	0.1501	0.2501	0.2511
6						1	0.1501	0.2502	0.2511
7							1	0.1502	0.2511
8								1	0.2511
9									1

Table 8. Correlation block for the marginalized model: $\boldsymbol{\Omega}_{PY,CY,s}$.

LoB	1	2	3	4	5	6	7	8	9
1	0.5004	0.5005	0.1502	0.2505	0.2503	0.2504	0.1504	0.2506	0.2506
2	0.5046	0.5046	0.2528	0.1519	0.2528	0.1518	0.1519	0.1519	0.2529
3	0.1506	0.2509	0.5013	0.2510	0.1506	0.1506	0.1508	0.1507	0.2511
4	0.2503	0.1502	0.2503	0.5008	0.1502	0.1503	0.1504	0.1504	0.2506
5	0.2503	0.2503	0.1502	0.1503	0.5004	0.2504	0.1504	0.2506	0.2506
6	0.2503	0.1502	0.1502	0.1503	0.2503	0.5006	0.2507	0.2506	0.2506
7	0.1502	0.1503	0.1502	0.1504	0.1502	0.2505	0.5010	0.1504	0.2506
8	0.2503	0.1502	0.1502	0.1504	0.2503	0.2504	0.1504	0.5009	0.2506
9	0.2511	0.2511	0.2511	0.2513	0.2511	0.2512	0.2514	0.2513	0.5018

Table 9. Correlation block for the marginalized model: $\boldsymbol{\Omega}_{CY,s}$.

LoB	1	2	3	4	5	6	7	8	9
1	1	0.5006	0.1503	0.2506	0.2504	0.1504	0.1505	0.1505	0.2507
2		1	0.2505	0.1504	0.2504	0.1504	0.1505	0.1505	0.2507
3			1	0.2506	0.1503	0.1504	0.1505	0.1505	0.2507
4				1	0.1504	0.1505	0.1506	0.1506	0.2509
5					1	0.2505	0.1505	0.2507	0.2507
6						1	0.2508	0.2508	0.2508
7							1	0.1507	0.2510
8								1	0.2509
9									1

9. Details of the SMC Algorithm

9.1. Selection of Intermediate Sets

Recall that a key component of the proposed SMC Sampler solution is to create a relaxation of the rare-conditional events that constrain the target posterior into a sequence of increasingly difficult constraints. In this section we discuss how one can select the sequence of constraint relaxations in an adaptive manner.

For both the marginalized and the conditional models we use an adaptive strategy similar to Cérou et al. (2012) in order to select adaptively online (as the algorithm runs) the levels $B_1, \ldots, B_T$, as well as the total number of intermediate sets T. When levels are being chosen adaptively one of the main advantages of the proposed SMC algorithm is the ability to estimate, in one run, the company-wide value at risk, the expected shortfall as well as the risk allocations.

Starting from $B_0 = 0$ (or $\overline{B}_0 = 0$ if the conditional model is being used) the idea consists of, at each algorithmic iteration $t-1$, choosing the next level, B_t, such that a percentage $p_0 \in (0,1)$ of the $(t-1)$–particles is above this set. More formally, we set B_t to be the $1-p_0$ empirical quantile of the weighted sample $\{s_{t-1}^{(j)}, W_{t-1}^{(j)}\}_{j=1}^N$ or $\{\overline{s}_{t-1}^{(j)}, W_{t-1}^{(j)}\}_{j=1}^N$, where s_{t-1} and $\overline{s}_{t-1}$ denote, respectively, the sum of the components of z_t and $\overline{z}_t$. Therefore, at algorithmic time t the level B_t corresponds to an estimate of the $(1-p_0^t)$-th quantile of the target distribution. In our examples we set $p_0 = 0.4, 0.5$ and 0.7 which induces intermediate quantiles seen in Table 10 for the algorithm. Note that, given a value of p_0 the number of levels in the algorithm is deterministic. For example, for $p_0 = 0.5$ there are 7 levels until the estimated quantile is above 99%.

Table 10. Intermediate quantiles for different values of p_0.

p_0	1	2	3	4	5	6	7
0.4	0.6	0.84	0.936	0.9744	0.9898	0.9959	
0.5	0.5	0.75	0.875	0.9375	0.9688	0.9844	0.9922
0.7	0.3	0.51	0.657	0.7599	0.8319	0.8824	0.9176
p_0	8	9	10	11	12	13	
0.4							
0.5							
0.7	0.9424	0.9596	0.9718	0.9802	0.9862	0.9903	

An alternative approach to choosing the level sets is to use the classic normalizing constant estimator derived from the SMC sampler algorithm (see (Del Moral et al. 2006, sct. 3.2.1)). Using the notation from Section 3 we have that the normalizing constant $\mathcal{Z}_t = \mathbb{P}[S > B_t]$ can be estimated as

$$\widehat{\mathcal{Z}}_t = \widehat{\mathcal{Z}}_{t-1} \sum_{j=1}^{N} W_{t-1}^{(j)} \widetilde{\alpha}_t^{(j)}, \tag{56}$$

where W_{t-1} and $\widetilde{\alpha}_t$ are, respectively the normalized and the incremental weights at time $t-1$.

Similarly to our proposed estimate, in this alternative route one would choose B_t such that $p_0 \times 100\%$ of the time $t-1$ particles are above this level. Using the estimator in Equation (56) one could stop the algorithm as soon as $\widehat{\mathcal{Z}}_t < \alpha$. The main disadvantage of this approach is that although $\widehat{\mathcal{Z}}_t$ can be proven to be unbiased and asymptotically normally distributed when the number of particles $N \to \infty$ (see (Del Moral 2004, Propositions 7.4.1 and 9.4.1) and Pitt et al. (2012) for a proof in the special case of state-space models) one can not guarantee $\widehat{\mathcal{Z}}_t \in [0,1]$. In our experiments the results based on this classic estimate were deemed unsatisfactory, as we observed estimates of the normalizing constant as large as 15, as finite sample realizations.

9.2. Marginalized Model

9.2.1. The Forward Kernel

Similarly to (Targino et al. 2015, sct. 6.1) we propose a mutation kernel $K_t(z_{t-1}, z_t)$ such that the condition $\sum_{i=1}^{d} z_{i,t} > B_t$ is always satisfied. Due to the independence assumption of the CY large claims (the P Pareto variables) we first independently mutate the Pareto coordinates, following their true (unconditional) marginal and then mutate the other $2L$ variables.

First we split the vector into its log-normal and Pareto components, $z_t = (z'_t, z''_t)$, where $z'_t = (z_{t,1}, \ldots, z_{t,2L})$ and $z''_t = (z_{t,2L+1}, \ldots, z_{t,2L+P})$. Using this notation and denoting $z_{t,-m}$ the vector z_t without its m-th component, we use

$$\begin{aligned} K_t(z_{t-1}, z_t) &= K'_t(z'_{t-1}, z'_t \mid z''_t)\, K''_t(z''_{t-1}, z''_t) \\ &= \left\{ \frac{1}{2L} \sum_{m=1}^{2L} \left[K_t'^{(-m)}(z'_{t-1}, z'_{t,-m}) K_t'^{(m)}(z'_{t-1}, z'_{t,m} \mid z'_{t,-m}, z''_t) \right] \right\} \\ &\times \prod_{i=2L+1}^{2L+P} Pareto(z''_t; \alpha_i, \beta_i), \end{aligned}$$

where the kernel $K_t'^{(-m)}(z'_{t-1}, \cdot\,)$, which mutates all but the m-th dimension of z'_{t-1}, consists of independent moves in each dimension, i.e.,

$$K_t'^{(-m)}(z'_{t-1}, z'_{t,-m}) = \prod_{\substack{i=1 \\ i \neq m}}^{2L} K_t'^{(-m,i)}(z'_{t-1,i}, z'_{t,i}).$$

Note that these moves are also independent of the P Pareto mutations.

Let us denote $\{z_{t-1}^{(j)}, W_{t-1}^{(j)}\}_{j=1}^{N}$ the weighted sample approximating

$$\pi_t(z_{t-1}) = f_Z(z_{t-1} \mid z_{t-1} \in \mathcal{G}_{Z_{t-1}}),$$

as defined in Equation (15). The components of the mutation kernel are then defined as

$$K_t'^{(-m,i)}(z'_{t-1}, z'_{t,i}) = LN(z'_{t,i}; \widehat{\mu}_i, \widehat{\sigma}_i), \quad \text{for } i = 1, \ldots, 2L,\ i \neq m, \tag{57}$$

where $\widehat{\mu}_i$ and $\widehat{\sigma}_i$ are the empirical mean and variance of $\{z_{t-1}^{(j)}, W_{t-1}^{(j)}\}_{j=1}^{N}$ when $i = 1, \ldots, 2L$

$$\begin{aligned} \widehat{\mu}_{t-1,i} &= \sum_{j=1}^{N} W_{t-1}^{(j)} z_{t-1,i}^{(j)}, \\ \widehat{\sigma}_{t-1,i}^2 &= \widehat{\mu}_{t-1,i}^2 - \sum_{j=1}^{N} W_{t-1} \left(z_{t-1,i}^{(j)} \right)^2. \end{aligned}$$

For the mutation of the remaining dimension, m, to ensure all the samples satisfy the condition $\sum_{i=1}^{d} z_{i,t} > B_t$ we proceed as follows. First we define

$$B_t^z(m) = \max \left\{ 0,\, B_t - \sum_{\substack{i=1 \\ i \neq m}}^{d} z_{t,i} \right\},$$

and then sample the last component $z_{m,t} \in [B_t^z(m), +\infty)$ according to

$$K_t^{(m)}(z_{t-1}, z_{t,m} \mid z_{t,-m}) = TN(z_{t,m}; \widehat{\mu}_m, \widehat{\sigma}_m, B_t^z(m), +\infty), \quad \text{for } m = 1, \ldots, 2L, \tag{58}$$

where $TN(\cdot\,;\mu,\sigma,a,b)$ denotes the density of a Normal distribution with mean μ and variance σ^2 truncated on support $[a,b]$.

9.2.2. The Backward Kernel

For the backward kernel we follow the discussion in Section 3.1.2 and use the (approximation to the) optimum kernel of Del Moral et al. (2006), given by equation Equation (11)

$$L_t(z_{t+1},z_t)=\frac{\gamma_t(z_t)K_{t+1}(z_t,z_{t+1})}{\frac{1}{N}\sum_{j=1}^{N}w_t^{(j)}K_{t+1}(z_t^{(j)},z_{t+1})},$$

where $w_t^{(j)}$ denotes the *unnormalized* weights at time t and the weighted sample $\{z_t^{(j)},\,w_t^{(j)}\}_{j=1}^{N}$ targets the unnormalized density $\gamma_t(z_t)$. Proceeding in this way the unnormalized weights for the SMC sampler algorithm (see Algorithm 1) satisfy the following recursion

$$w_t^{(j)}=w_{t-1}^{(j)}\frac{\gamma_t(z_t)}{\frac{1}{N}\sum_{k=1}^{N}w_t^{(k)}K_t(z_{t-1},\,z_t)}.$$

9.2.3. The MCMC Move Kernel

To improve particle diversity after a resampling step (which is performed whenever the effective sample size drops bellow $N/2$) the following MCMC move kernel is applied to the particles.

As in (Targino et al. 2015, sct. 6.2) we propose a Gibbs-type update combined with a slice sampler (see Neal (2003)). For notational simplicity we suppress the dependence in t in the vector z_t and denote $v^*(m)=(z_1^*,\ldots,z_m^*,z_{m+1},\ldots,z_d)$ the vector where the first m components have already been updated in the Gibbs scan. The full conditional for the m-th component of z_t is given by

$$\pi_t(z_m^*\,|\,z_1^*,\ldots,z_{m-1}^*,z_{m+1},\ldots,z_d)\propto\pi_t(v^*(m))\propto f_Z(v^*(m))\mathbb{1}_{\mathcal{G}_{Z_t}}(v^*(m)),$$

which is can be sampled from using an unidimensional slice sampler (see Neal (2003)).

9.3. Conditional Model

Following the discussion in Section 3.3.2 we use equation Equation (19) as an approximation to the unknown density $f_{\overline{Z}}(\overline{z})$. For our simulations $M=5$ samples of the unknown parameter $\boldsymbol{\theta}$ are used, where

$$\boldsymbol{\theta}=(\boldsymbol{\sigma}^{(1)},\ldots,\boldsymbol{\sigma}^{(L)}),$$

and each vector $\boldsymbol{\sigma}^{(\ell)}=(\sigma_1^{(\ell)},\ldots,\sigma_J^{(\ell)})$ contains all the unknown variance parameters for the ℓ-th LoB. Therefore, $\boldsymbol{\vartheta}=(\boldsymbol{\theta}^{(1)},\ldots,\boldsymbol{\theta}^{(M)})$ and it should be noticed the superscript have a different interpretation from those in $\sigma_j^{(\ell)}$.

As the parameter estimation step described in Section 8.3 is independent of the allocation process we assume N_{MCMC} samples for each unknown parameter vector $\boldsymbol{\sigma}$ have already been created. Therefore, to sample $\overline{z}\sim f_{\overline{Z}}(\overline{z})$ we first sample an index $n\sim U(\{1,\ldots,N_{MCMC}\})$ and then $\overline{z}\sim f_{\overline{Z}}(\overline{z}\,|\,\boldsymbol{\theta}^{(n)})$.

9.3.1. The Forward Kernel

The forward kernel used for the conditional model follows the same structure as the one used in the marginalized model and described in Section 9.2.1: first we sample the P independent Pareto variables (with the same distribution as in the marginalized case) and then the remaining $2L$ variables. More precisely,

$$\overline{K}_t^{\prime(-m,i)}(\overline{z}_{t-1}^{\prime},\,\overline{z}_{t,i}^{\prime}\,|\,\boldsymbol{\vartheta}_t)=\overline{K}_t^{\prime(-m,i)}(\overline{z}_{t-1}^{\prime},\,\overline{z}_{t,i}^{\prime})=K_t^{\prime(-m,i)}(\overline{z}_{t-1}^{\prime},\overline{z}_{t,i}^{\prime}),$$

where the last term is defined in equation Equation (57) and $\widehat{\mu}_i$ and $\widehat{\sigma}_i$ are now the empirical mean and variance of $\{\overline{\mathbf{z}}_{t-1}^{(j)}, W_{t-1}^{(j)}\}_{j=1}^{N}$. Likewise,

$$\overline{K}_t^{\prime(m)}(\overline{\mathbf{z}}_{t-1}', \overline{z}_{t,m}' \mid \overline{\mathbf{z}}_{t,-m}', \boldsymbol{\vartheta}_t) = \overline{K}_t^{\prime(m)}(\overline{\mathbf{z}}_{t-1}', \overline{z}_{t,m}' \mid \overline{\mathbf{z}}_{t,-m}') = K_t^{\prime(m)}(\overline{\mathbf{z}}_{t-1}', \overline{z}_{t,m}' \mid \overline{\mathbf{z}}_{t,-m}'),$$

with the last term defined in equation Equation (58). As samples from $f_{\boldsymbol{\vartheta}}(\boldsymbol{\vartheta})$ have already been generated through MCMC then the mutation kernel in the extended space, $K_t^{\boldsymbol{y}}(\boldsymbol{y}_{t-1}, \boldsymbol{y}_t)$, is completely characterized.

9.3.2. The Backward Kernel

As in Section 9.2.2 we use the optimum backward kernel in the extended space $\mathcal{Y} = \mathbb{R}^d \times \Theta^M$, which for the conditional model leads to the following incremental weights (see Equation (12))

$$\begin{aligned}\alpha_t &= \frac{\gamma_t^{\boldsymbol{y}}(\boldsymbol{y}_t)}{\frac{1}{N}\sum_{j=1}^{N} w_{t-1}^{(j)} K_t^{\boldsymbol{y}}(\boldsymbol{y}_{t-1}, \boldsymbol{y}_t)} \\ &= \frac{\widehat{f}_{\overline{\mathbf{Z}}}(\overline{\mathbf{z}}_t;\, \boldsymbol{\vartheta}_t) f_{\boldsymbol{\vartheta}}(\boldsymbol{\vartheta}_t) \mathbb{1}_{\mathcal{G}_{\overline{\mathbf{Z}}_t}}(\overline{\mathbf{z}}_t)}{\frac{1}{N}\sum_{j=1}^{N} w_{t-1}^{(j)} K_t(\mathbf{z}_{t-1}, \mathbf{z}_t) f_{\boldsymbol{\vartheta}}(\boldsymbol{\vartheta}_t)} \\ &= \frac{\widehat{f}_{\overline{\mathbf{Z}}}(\overline{\mathbf{z}}_t;\, \boldsymbol{\vartheta}_t) \mathbb{1}_{\mathcal{G}_{\overline{\mathbf{Z}}_t}}(\overline{\mathbf{z}}_t)}{\frac{1}{N}\sum_{j=1}^{N} w_{t-1}^{(j)} K_t(\mathbf{z}_{t-1}, \mathbf{z}_t)}.\end{aligned}$$

9.3.3. The MCMC Move Kernel

The MCMC move kernel used for the conditional model needs to keep the target distribution in the extended space, $\pi_t^{\boldsymbol{y}}(\boldsymbol{y}_t)$, invariant. The strategy adopted is to first sample $\boldsymbol{\vartheta}^* \sim f_{\boldsymbol{\vartheta}}(\vartheta)$ and then $\mathbf{z}_t \mid \boldsymbol{\vartheta}^* \sim \widehat{f}_{\overline{\mathbf{Z}}}(\overline{\mathbf{z}}_t;\, \boldsymbol{\vartheta}_t^*) \mathbb{1}_{\mathcal{G}_{\overline{\mathbf{Z}}_t}}(\overline{\mathbf{z}}_t)$.

For the second step above we use exactly the same Gibbs-sampler update as in Section 9.2.3, with $f_{\mathbf{Z}}(\,\cdot\,)$ replaced by $\widehat{f}_{\overline{\mathbf{Z}}}(\,\cdot\,;\, \boldsymbol{\vartheta}_t)$.

10. Results

In this section we present the results of the SMC procedure when used to calculate the expected shortfall allocations from Equations (4) and (5) of the solvency capital requirement.

Before proceeding to the results calculated via the SMC algorithm, in order to understand the simulated data presented in Figure 4, in Table 2 we present some results based on a "brute force" Monte Carlo (rejection-sampling) simulation, which is taken as the base line for comparisons with the SMC algorithm. The table is divided in three blocks of rows, with PY claims, CY small (CY,s) claims and CY large (CY,l) claims.

First of all, it should be noticed that the reserves presented on the first block of Table 2 are the ones implied by the data, which we then assume to be the true ones (ignoring, from now on, the initial synthetic data from Table 1). That is, based on initial parameters we have generated synthetic claims development triangles, which naturally deviate slightly from their expected values. The parameters σ and μ for PY claims are related to the marginalized model (for the parameters of the conditional model see Figures 5 and 6). It is also important to note that only the PY parameters are different between the conditional and marginalized models.

For each LoB the standalone expected shortfall (ES) is calculated analytically and its value is, then, combined with the LoB's expectation to calculate the solvency capital requirement (SCR). These values are added up, both within risk type (i.e., PY, CY,s and CY,l) and globally, in order to calculate the overall standalone capital. For the marginalized and conditional models the columns "ES" and "SCR" denote, respectively, the expected shortfall and capital allocations to each LoB. These values are compared to their standalone counterparts to generate the diversification benefit, which is around 45% for PY and CY,s claims (regardless of the model used) and ranges between 30% and 70% within the PY and CY,s groups. Due to the independence assumptions the largest diversification benefit comes from the CY,l claims, where the capital is reduced by around 95%.

The data presented in Table 2 is calculated as follows. For the marginalized model (and conditional model in brackets), 5×10^9 (2.5×10^7) independent samples of the model are generated in order to calculate the overall $\text{VaR}_{99\%}$. Conditional on this value, for each LoB we then generate 5×10^7 (5×10^5) samples above the VaR and use the average of these samples as the true ES allocation (presented in Table 2). In order to asses the variance of the estimators, we divide these samples into $N_{rep} = 500$ groups of $N_{MC} = 10^5$ ($N_{MC} = 10^3$ for the conditional model) simulations. More formally, we approximate the ES allocations ρ_i, defined in Equation (4), by

$$\widehat{\mathbb{E}}[\widehat{\rho}_{i,MC}] = \frac{1}{N_{rep}} \sum_{k=1}^{N_{rep}} \widehat{\rho}_{i,MC}^{(k)}, \tag{59}$$

where $\widehat{\rho}_{i,MC}^{(k)}$ stands for the estimate (using N_{MC} particles) from the k-th run (out of N_{rep}), which is defined according to

$$\widehat{\rho}_{i,MC} = \frac{1}{N_{MC}} \sum_{j=1}^{N_{MC}} Z_i^{(j)}.$$

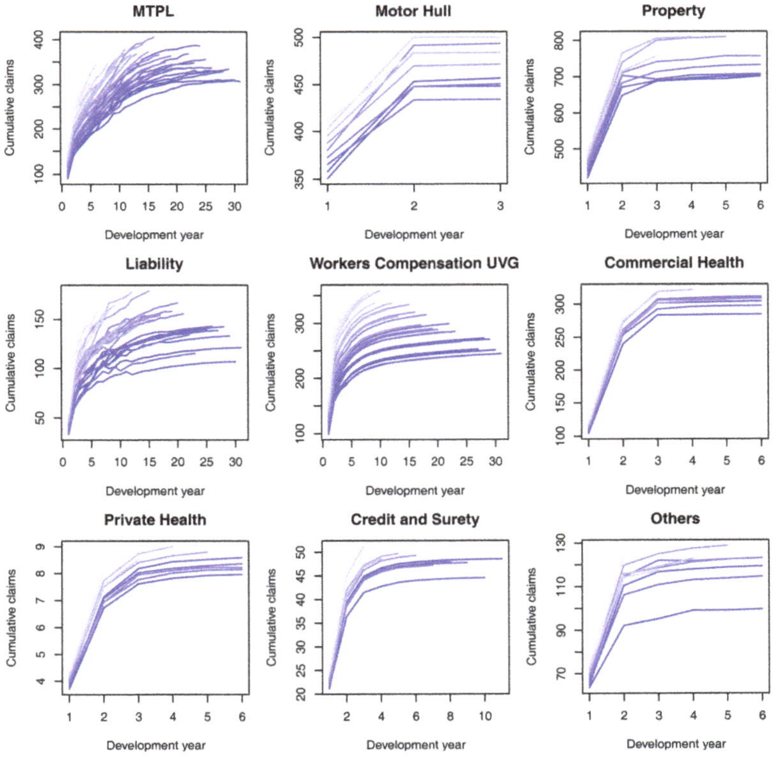

Figure 4. Cumulative claims payment (in millions of CHF). Lighter colours represent more recent accident years.

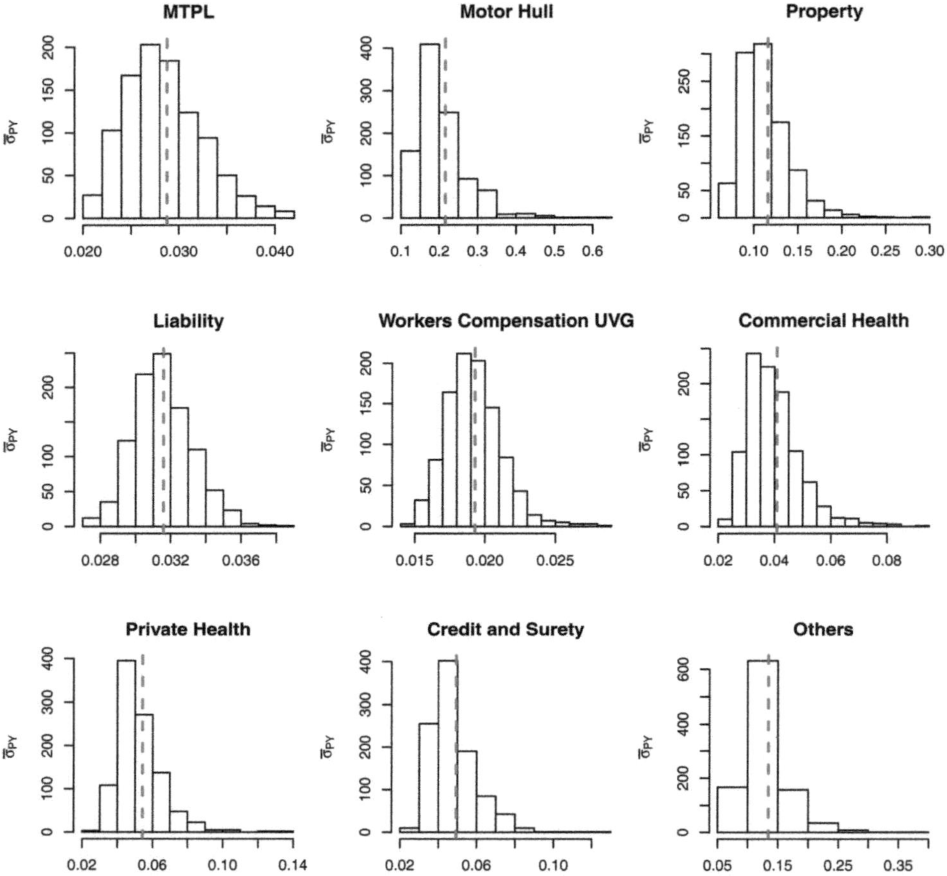

Figure 5. Histogram of the parameter $\overline{\sigma}_{PY}$ for the conditional model. Red dashed line: σ_{PY}.

Similarly to the analysis performed in Peters et al. (2017) the impact of the prior density can be assessed by comparing the sum of the SCR allocations with the SCR from the "empirical Bayes model", i.e., the model where the prior for σ is set as a Dirac mass on $\widehat{\sigma}_j(t)$, see Equation (55). In this case we have that the total capital is equal to SCR = 505.48 and the fully Bayesian model with prior defined with $k = 5$ (see Section 8.3) requires 15% more capital (both in the marginalized and conditional cases).

To check the accuracy of the SMC procedure we first analyse the estimate of the level sets (intermediate VaRs). For $p_0 = 0.5$, Figures 7 and 8 show, respectively, the histogram of the levels $B_1, \ldots, B_7$ (as per Table 10) for the marginalized and conditional models. The red dashed bars represent the true value of the quantiles (based on the "brute force" MC simulations), which is very close to the mode of the empirical distribution of the SMC estimates. It should be noticed, though, that the SMC estimates seem to be negatively biased and the bias appears to become more pronounced for extreme quantiles. Apart from this negligible bias we assume the levels are being sensibly estimated and proceed, as in Targino et al. (2015), to calculate the relative bias and the variance reduction of the SMC method when compared to a MC procedure.

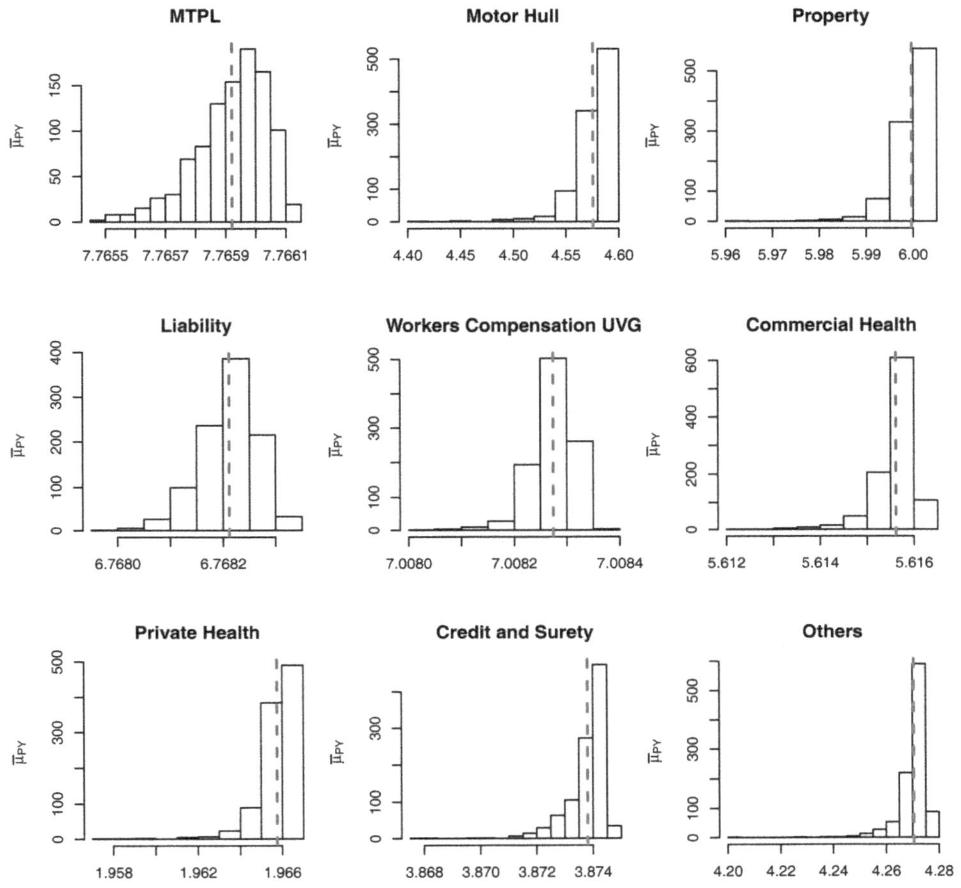

Figure 6. Histogram of the parameter $\overline{\mu}_{PY}$ for the conditional model. Red dashed line: μ_{PY}.

For each of the LoBs the plots on the Figures 9 and 10 show the relative bias, defined as

$$\text{Relative Bias} = \frac{\widehat{\mathbb{E}}[\widehat{\rho}_{i,SMC}] - \widehat{\mathbb{E}}[\widehat{\rho}_{i,MC}]}{\widehat{\mathbb{E}}[\widehat{\rho}_{i,MC}]},$$

where $\widehat{\mathbb{E}}[\widehat{\rho}_{i,SMC}]$ is computed analogously to the MC estimate but, instead, using the SMC method, with $N_{SMC} = 100$. The behaviour of the two models is very similar, and we observe that the bias in the PY and CY,s allocations are negligible (less than 5%) while for some of the large CY risks a higher bias (of more than 10%) may be observed. Apart from the difficulty of performing the estimation based on Pareto distributions we stress the fact that although these errors may look large, as we can see from Table 2, their impact in the overall capital are almost imperceptible, due to the small capital charge due to these risks.

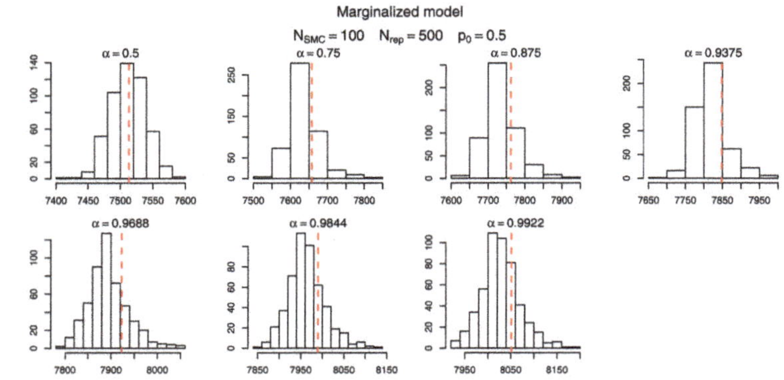

Figure 7. Histograms levels used in the SMC sampler algorithm with $p_0 = 0.5$ in the marginalized model. The red dashed bar represents the true value of the α quantile.

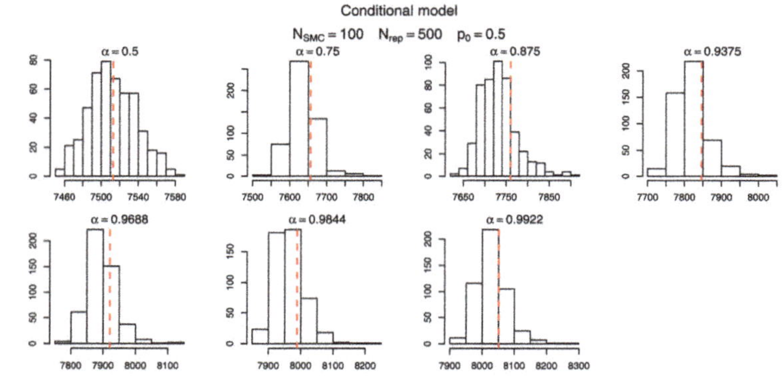

Figure 8. Histograms levels used in the Sequential Monte Carlo (SMC) sampler algorithm with $p_0 = 0.5$ in the conditional model. The red dashed bar represents the true value of the α quantile.

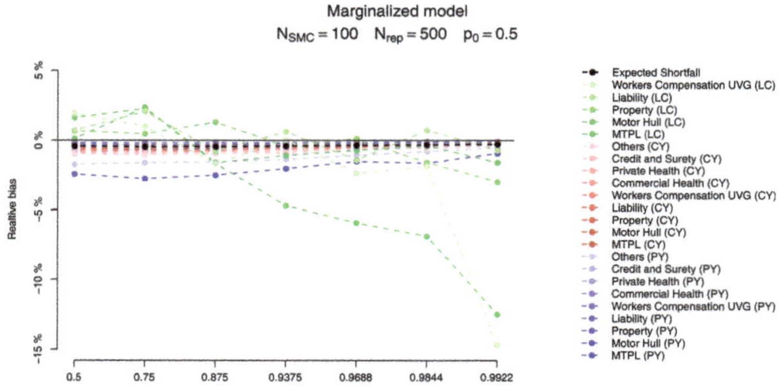

Figure 9. Bias for the marginalized model. Note that although the bias for some of the CY large claims is around 10% their allocated capital is rather small, as seen in Figure 11 (a).

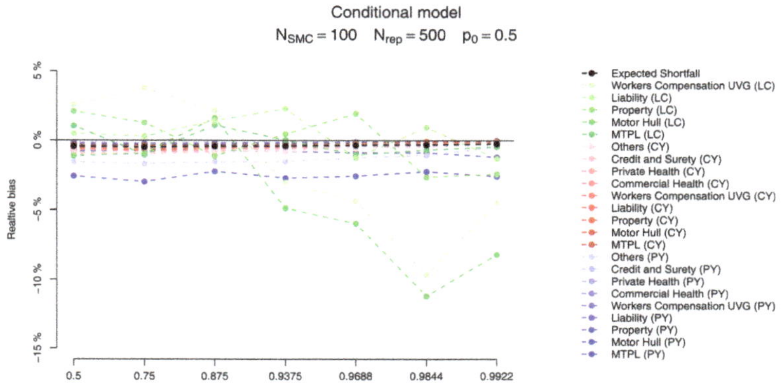

Figure 10. Bias for the conditional model. Note that although the bias for some of the current year (CY) large claims is around 10% their allocated capital is rather small, as seen in Figure 11 (b).

Another way to compare the SMC calculations is through the actual capital charges, as seen in Figure 11. In this figure we compare the 99% SCR calculated via the MC scheme discussed above with the SMC results for the quantile level right before 99% (which, for $p_0 = 0.5$ is 98.44%) and the one right after it (99.22%). From this figure we see the SMC calculation based on the 99.22% quantile is very precise, for both the marginalized and conditional models. Visually, the only perceivable difference comes from the CY,l claims, which accounts (in total) for less than 2% of the overall capital.

To calculate the improvement generated by the SMC algorithm compared to the MC procedure we need to analyse the variance of the estimates generated by both methods, under similar computational budgets.

We start by noticing that the expected number of samples in the Monte Carlo scheme in order to have N_{MC} samples satisfying the α condition is equal to $M_{MC} = N_{MC}/(1-\alpha)$, which can be prohibitive if α is very close to 1. Then, similarly to Equation (59) we define the empirical variance of the MC and the SMC algorithms which are, then, compared as follows

$$\text{Variance Reduction} = M_{MC} \times \widehat{\text{Var}}(\widehat{\rho}_{i,MC}) \Big/ T \times N_{SMC} \times \widehat{\text{Var}}(\widehat{\rho}_{i,SMC}). \tag{60}$$

The variance reduction statistics defined in Equation (60) takes into account how many samples one needs to use in order to generate N_{MC} samples via rejection sampling or N_{SMC} using the SMC algorithm. The later also takes into account the fact that T levels are being used and in each one N_{SMC} samples need to be generated. For the conditional model we further multiply the denominator by the number of samples used to estimate the unknown density, which in our examples is set to $M = 5$.

The results follow on Figures 12 and 13. As in Targino et al. (2015) we observe that the variance of the SMC estimates become smaller (compared to the MC results) for larger quantiles. In particular, for the quantiles of interest the variance of the marginal ES allocation estimates are around $10^{0.5} \approx 3$ times smaller than its MC counterparts, while the overall ES estimate is slightly less variable for the MC scheme.

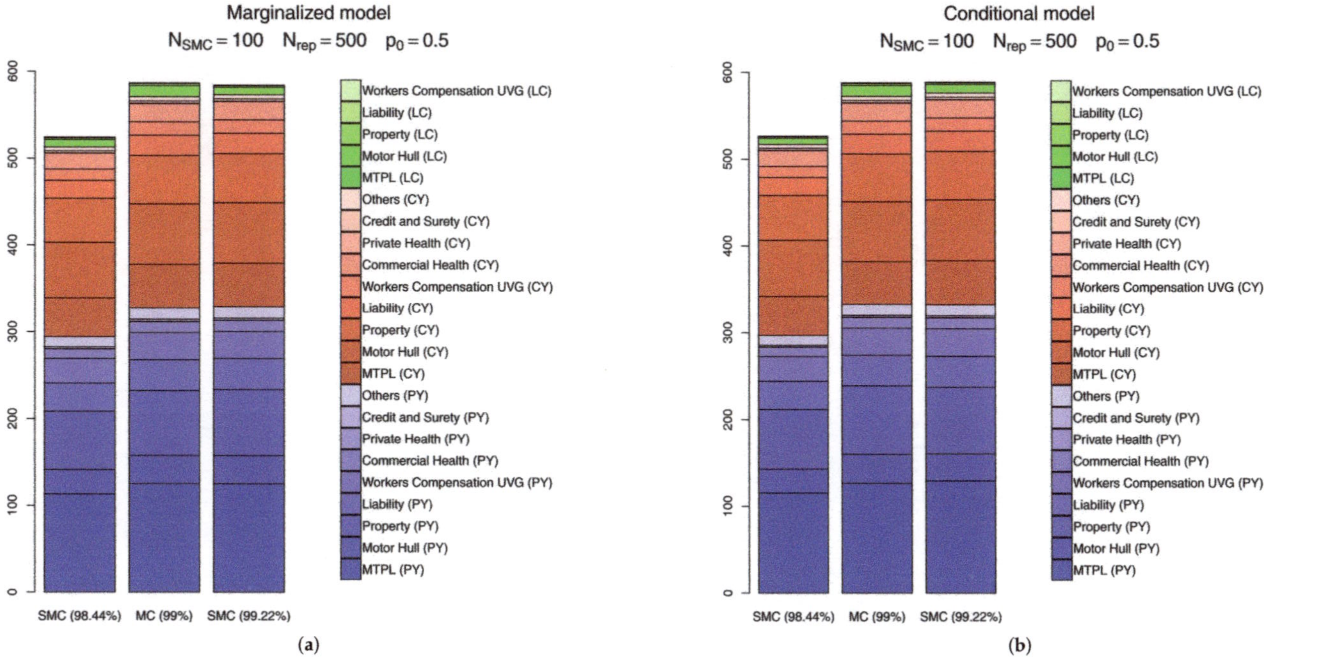

Figure 11. Comparison between the "true" allocations (calculated via a large Monte Carlo procedure) and the SMC sampler solution for the (**a**) marginalized and (**b**) conditional models.

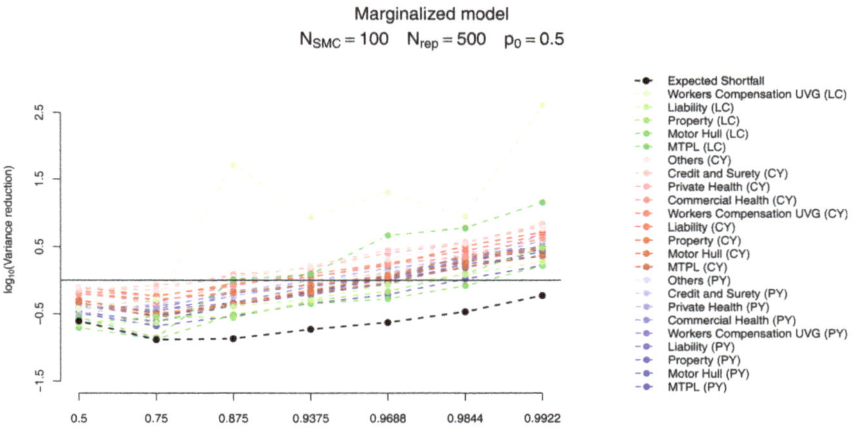

Figure 12. Variance reduction for the marginalized model.

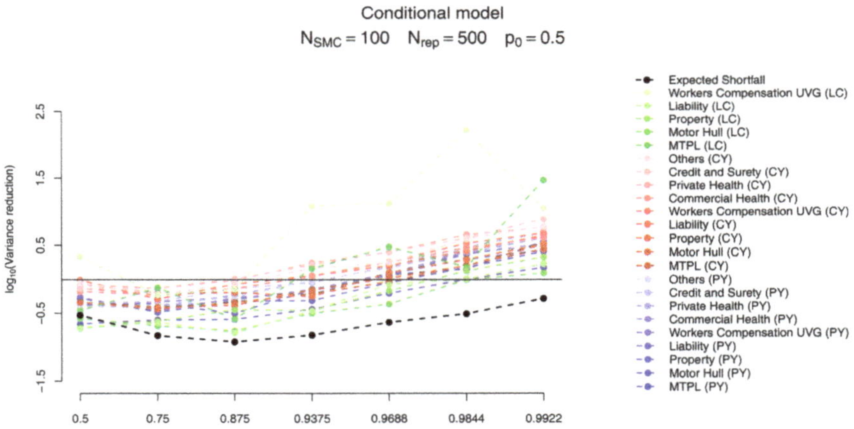

Figure 13. Variance reduction for the conditional model.

For the marginalized model we also present two plots in Figure 14, related, respectively, to the sensitivity to (a) the parameter p_0 and (b) the number of samples, N_{SMC}. In Figure 14a, for the same number of samples, $N_{SMC} = 100$ we analyse the bias relative to the 99% ES allocations of the first quantile larger than 99% (top plot) and the previous one (bottom plot) for $p_0 \in \{0.4, 0.5, 0.7\}$. The quantiles used in these different setups are presented in Table 10. Although the results may look slightly different, the main message is the same: the "higher" quantile is effectively unbiased for PY and CY,s risks but presents a negative bias of around 10% for some of the CY,l risks.

Regarding the sensitivity to the number of particles in the SMC algorithm, as expected, the absolute bias decreases when the number of samples increases, as seen in Figure 14b. Although the SMC algorithm is generically guaranteed to be unbiased when $N_{SMC} \to +\infty$ the trade-off between bias and the variance reduction in the allocation problem may lead us to accept a small bias in order to have a smaller variance.

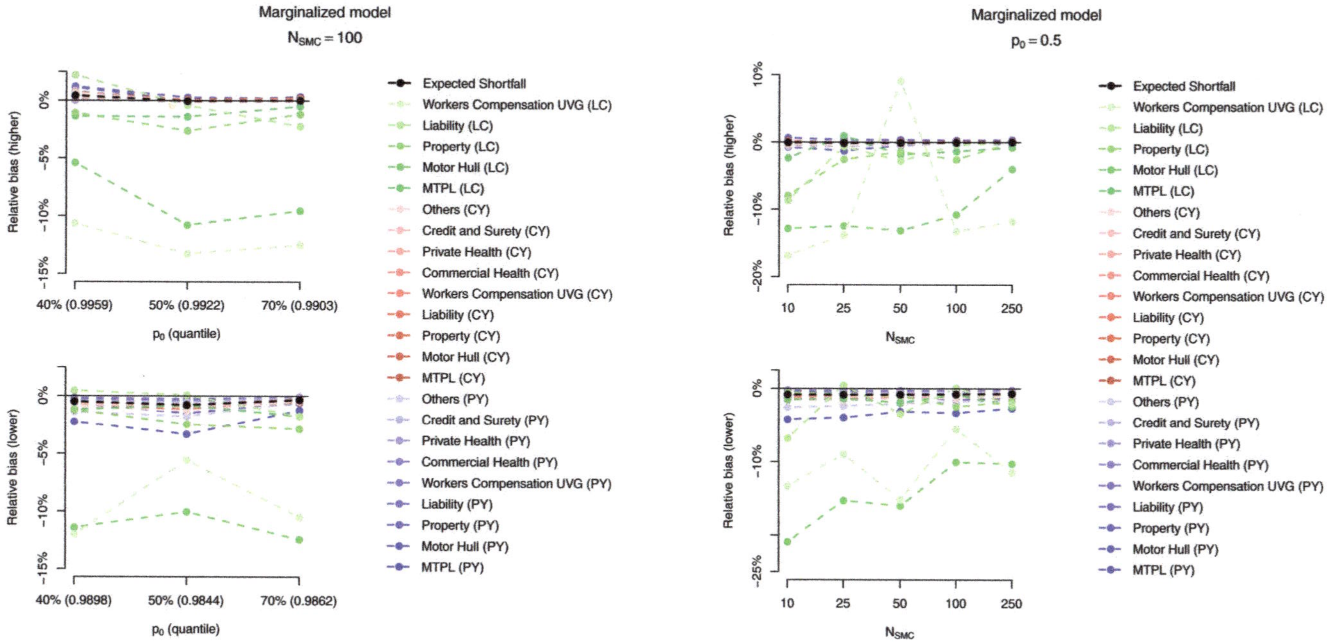

(a)

(b)

Figure 14. Relative bias in the marginalized model as a function of (**a**) the parameter p_0 and (**b**) the sample size in the SMC sampler, N_{SMC}.

11. Conclusions

In this paper we provide a complete and self-contained view of the capital allocation process for general insurance companies. As prescribed by the Swiss Solvency Test we break down the company's overall Solvency Capital Requirement (SCR) into the one-year reserve risk, due to claims from previous years (PY) and the one-year premium risk due to claims' payments in the current year (CY). The later is further split into the risk of normal/small claims (CY,s) and large claims (CY,l). For the premium risk in each line of business we assume a log-normal distribution for CY,s risks with mean and variance as per the SST, which also describe a distribution for CY,l risks, in this case Pareto. For the reserve risk, as in Peters et al. (2017), we postulate a Bayesian gamma-gamma model which, for allocation purposes, is approximated by log-normal distributions leading to what we name the conditional (when the log-normal approximation is performed conditional on the unknown parameters) and the marginalized (when the log-normal approximation is performed after the parameter uncertainty has been integrated out) models.

As seen in Figures 1 and 2, when assuming a Bayesian gamma-gamma model these two approximations do not deviate considerably from the actual model assumptions. Regarding the allocations, Figure 11 shows the results for both models are, once again, very close to each other (and to the "true" allocations, calculated via a large Monte Carlo exercise). Therefore, the decision on which approximation to use should not interfere with the allocation or reserving results, and is left to the reader.

The allocation process is performed using state-of-the-art (pseudo-marginal) Sequential Monte Carlo (SMC) algorithms, which are presented in a self-contained and accessible format. Although the algorithms described form an extremely flexible class, we provide an off-the-shelf version, where minimal or no tuning is needed. The algorithms are also shown to be computationally efficient in a series of numerical experiments.

One of the advantages of our proposed methodology is that it is able to compute in one single *loop* (1) the value at risk (VaR) and (2) the Expected Shortfall (ES), both at the company level and (3) the capital allocations for the risk drivers. This procedure should be compared with routinely applied methodologies, where one simulation is performed to compute the VaR, which is used in a different simulation to compute the allocations, in a process that accumulate different errors.

Moreover, even ignoring the computational cost of calculating a precise estimate for the required VaR in a "brute force" Monte Carlo scheme, the proposed SMC algorithm is numerically shown to provide estimates that are less volatile than comparable "brute force" implementations.

Author Contributions: All authors contributed equally to the paper.

Conflicts of Interest: The authors declare no conflict of interest.

Appendix A. Posterior Distributions

For ease of exposition we omit the LoB index ℓ. Under Model Assumptions 1 the posterior distribution of the parameter vectors $\boldsymbol{\phi}$ and $\boldsymbol{\sigma}$, for $t \geq I$, is given by

$$
\begin{aligned}
\pi(\boldsymbol{\phi},\boldsymbol{\sigma}\,|\,\mathcal{F}(t)) &\propto g(\mathcal{F}(t)\,|\,\boldsymbol{\phi},\,\boldsymbol{\sigma})f_{\boldsymbol{\phi}}(\boldsymbol{\phi})f_{\boldsymbol{\sigma}}(\boldsymbol{\sigma}) \\
&= \left[g(C_{1,0},\ldots,C_{t,0})\prod_{j=0}^{J-1}\prod_{i=1}^{t-j-1}\frac{(\phi_j\sigma_j^{-2})^{C_{i,j}\sigma_j^{-2}}}{\Gamma(C_{i,j}\sigma_j^{-2})}C_{i,j+1}^{C_{i,j}\sigma_j^{-2}-1}\exp\left\{-\phi_j\sigma_j^{-2}C_{i,j+1}\right\}\right] \\
&\times\left[\prod_{j=0}^{J-1}\lim_{\gamma_j\to 1}\frac{(f_j(\gamma_j-1))^{\gamma_j}}{\Gamma(\gamma_j)}\phi_j^{\gamma_j-1}\exp\left\{-\phi_j f_j(\gamma_j-1)\right\}\right]\times\left[\prod_{j=0}^{J-1}f_{\sigma_j^2}(\sigma_j^2)\right] \\
&\propto\left[\prod_{j=0}^{J-1}\lim_{\gamma_j\to 1}\phi_j^{\gamma_j-1+\sum_{i=1}^{t-j-1}C_{i,j}\sigma_j^{-2}}\exp\left\{-\phi_j\left(f_j(\gamma_j-1)+\sum_{i=1}^{t-j-1}C_{i,j+1}\sigma_j^{-2}\right)\right\}\right] \\
&\times\left[\prod_{j=0}^{J-1}f_{\sigma_j^2}(\sigma_j^2)\prod_{i=1}^{t-j-1}\frac{(C_{i,j+1}\sigma_j^{-2})^{C_{i,j}\sigma_j^{-2}}}{\Gamma(C_{i,j}\sigma_j^{-2})}\right] \\
&\propto\left[\prod_{j=0}^{J-1}\phi_j^{\sum_{i=1}^{t-j-1}C_{i,j}\sigma_j^{-2}}\exp\left\{-\phi_j\left(\sum_{i=1}^{t-j-1}C_{i,j+1}\sigma_j^{-2}\right)\right\}\right] \\
&\times\left[\prod_{j=0}^{J-1}f_{\sigma_j}(\sigma_j)\prod_{i=1}^{t-j-1}\frac{(C_{i,j+1}\sigma_j^{-2})^{C_{i,j}\sigma_j^{-2}}}{\Gamma(C_{i,j}\sigma_j^{-2})}\right].
\end{aligned}
$$

From the functional form of $\pi(\boldsymbol{\phi},\,\boldsymbol{\sigma}\,|\,\mathcal{F}(t))$ it can be seen that the components ϕ_j of $\boldsymbol{\phi}$ and σ_j of $\boldsymbol{\sigma}$ are independent *a posteriori*, which is a direct consequence of the prior independence. Moreover, since $\pi(\boldsymbol{\phi}\,|\,\boldsymbol{\sigma},\,\mathcal{F}(t))\propto\pi(\boldsymbol{\phi},\,\boldsymbol{\sigma}\,|\,\mathcal{F}(t))$, we have that

$$
\phi_j\,|\,\boldsymbol{\sigma},\,\mathcal{F}(t)\sim\Gamma(a_j,\,b_j), \tag{A1}
$$

with $a_j=1+\sum_{i=1}^{t-j-1}C_{i,j}\sigma_j^{-2}$ and $b_j=\sum_{i=1}^{t-j-1}C_{i,j+1}\sigma_j^{-2}$.

The marginal posterior $\pi(\boldsymbol{\sigma}\,|\,\mathcal{F}(t))$ and its unnormalized version $h(\boldsymbol{\sigma}\,|\,\mathcal{F}(t))$ are calculated as

$$
\begin{aligned}
\pi(\boldsymbol{\sigma}\,|\,\mathcal{F}(t)) &= \int\pi(\boldsymbol{\phi},\,\boldsymbol{\sigma}\,|\,\mathcal{F}(t))d\boldsymbol{\phi} \\
&\propto\prod_{j=0}^{J-1}\frac{\Gamma(a_j)}{b_j^{a_j}}f_{\sigma_j}(\sigma_j)\prod_{i=1}^{t-j-1}\frac{(C_{i,j+1}\sigma_j^{-2})^{C_{i,j}\sigma_j^{-2}}}{\Gamma(C_{i,j}\sigma_j^{-2})}=h(\boldsymbol{\sigma}\,|\,\mathcal{F}(t)).
\end{aligned}
$$

Lemma A1. *(from Peters et al. (2017)) For $0\le j\le J-1$ and $t\ge 1$ if either $t-j-1=1$ or at least one accident year $1\le i\le t-j-1$ is such that $\frac{C_{i,j+1}}{C_{i,j}}\neq\widehat{f}_j(t)$ then the marginal posterior $\pi(\boldsymbol{\sigma}\,|\,\mathcal{F}(t))$ is integrable, i.e.,*

$$
\int_0^{d_j}h_j(\sigma_j\,|\,\mathcal{F}(t))d\sigma_j<\infty.
$$

Appendix B. Correlation Bounds in the Log-Normal–Gaussian Copula Model

As mentioned in Section 7 and discussed, for example in (Embrechts et al. 2002, Fallacy 2), for given marginal distributions not all linear correlations between -1 and 1 can be achieved. This can also be seen in the following Lemma (see (Denuit and Dhaene 2003, sct. 2)).

Lemma A2 (Correlation bounds). *Let (X_1, X_2) be a bivariate random variable with marginal distributions F_1 and F_2. Then the correlation between X_1 and X_2 is bounded by*

$$\frac{Cov(F_1^{-1}(U),\, F_2^{-1}(1-U))}{\sqrt{Var(X_1)Var(X_2)}} \leq Corr(X_1,\, X_2) \leq \frac{Cov(F_1^{-1}(U),\, F_2^{-1}(U))}{\sqrt{Var(X_1)Var(X_2)}},$$

for U uniformly distributed in $[0,1]$.

Although theoretically interesting, Lemma A2 may provide bounds that are too wide and, in some cases just state that the correlation lies between -1 and 1. In the sequel we show that in the particular case of a random vector with log-normal marginals and Gaussian copula it is possible to calculate precisely the intended correlation and numerically check its limits.

Let us assume a random vector $\boldsymbol{X} = (X_1, \ldots, X_{2L})$ is normally distributed with $\boldsymbol{X} \sim \mathrm{N}(\boldsymbol{m},\, \boldsymbol{V})$, where a general term of the covariance matrix $\boldsymbol{V}$ is given by $(\boldsymbol{V})_{i,j} = V_{i,j}$ and $V_{i,i} = V_i^2$. Moreover, we denote by $\boldsymbol{\Omega} = \mathrm{Corr}(\boldsymbol{X})$ the correlation matrix of the random vector $\boldsymbol{X}$, i.e.,

$$\boldsymbol{V} = \mathrm{diag}(V_1, \ldots, V_{2L})\, \boldsymbol{\Omega}\, \mathrm{diag}(V_1, \ldots, V_{2L}),$$

with $(\boldsymbol{\Omega})_{i,j} = (\boldsymbol{\Omega})_{j,i} = \omega_{i,j}$.

If we define $Z_i = e^{X_i}$, for $i = 1, \ldots, 2L$ then $Z_i \sim \mathrm{LN}(m_i,\, V_i)$ with

$$\mathbb{E}[Z_i] = \exp\left\{m_i + \frac{V_i^2}{2}\right\},$$
$$\mathrm{Var}(Z_i) = (\mathbb{E}[Z_i])^2\left(e^{V_i^2} - 1\right). \tag{A2}$$

On the other hand, since $X_i + X_j \sim N(m_i + m_j,\, V_i^2 + V_j^2 + 2V_i\omega_{i,j}V_j)$ we have that

$$\mathbb{E}[Z_iZ_j] = \mathbb{E}[e^{X_i + X_j}] = \exp\left\{m_i + m_j + \frac{V_i^2 + V_j^2 + 2V_i\omega_{i,j}V_j}{2}\right\}. \tag{A3}$$

Therefore, using Equations (A2) and (A3) the correlation between Z_i and Z_j can be written as

$$\mathrm{Corr}(Z_i,\, Z_j) = \frac{\exp\{V_i\omega_{i,j}V_j\} - 1}{\left[(e^{V_i^2} - 1)(e^{V_j^2} - 1)\right]^{1/2}}. \tag{A4}$$

Since $\exp(\cdot)$ is a strictly increasing function and the marginal distributions of $(X_1, \ldots, X_{2L})$ are continuous, from (McNeil et al. 2010, Proposition 5.6) we can conclude that $(Z_1, \ldots, Z_{2L})$ has the same copula as $(X_1, \ldots, X_{2L})$: a Gaussian copula with correlation matrix $\boldsymbol{\Omega}$.

From equation Equation (A4) it is easy to see the correlation between Z_i and Z_j is a monotone function of $\omega_{i,j}$ which implies that $\mathrm{Corr}(Z_i,\, Z_j)$ will be minimal when $\omega_{i,j} = -1$ and maximal when $\omega_{i,j} = 1$. Therefore, for a given pair of standard deviations it is possible to compute the interval of admissible correlations for the pair $(Z_i,\, Z_j)$. In Figure A1 the lower (left plot) and upper (right plot) present bounds for the correlations.

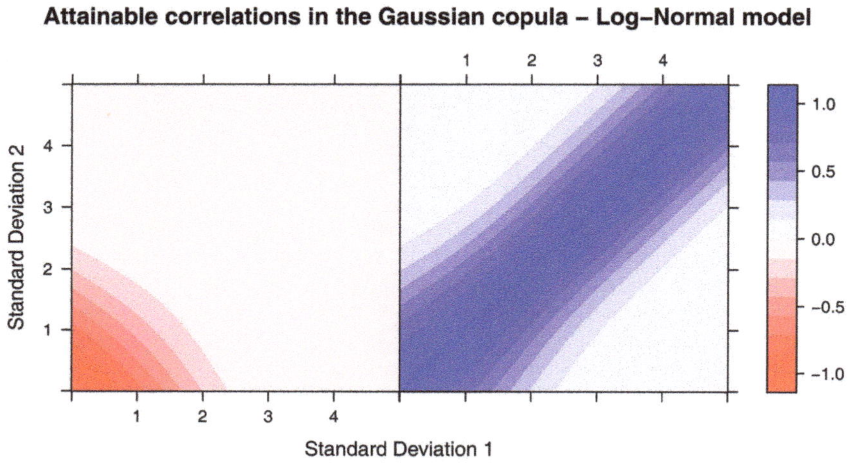

Figure A1. Lower (**left**) and upper (**right**) bound for correlations in a Gaussian-copula model with Log-Normal marginal distributions, as a function of the scale parameters σ_1 and σ_2.

Figure A1 shows that even when the copula correlation is set to -1 if at least one of the standard deviation parameters is "large" then minimum possible correlation between the log-normal variables is close to zero. For example, if $\sigma_1 = \sigma_2 = 2$ then the lower bound for the correlations is approximately -2%. As actuarial risks are usually positively correlated this may not be a problem from the modelling point of view. The upper limit for the correlations have a different behaviour. If both standard deviations are the same then the range of attainable correlations is upper bounded by 1, meaning that any positive correlation can be achieved. Problems arrive when the standard deviations are sufficiently different from each other. If $\sigma_1 = 1$ then the correlation is upper bounded by 66% if $\sigma_2 = 2$, 16% if $\sigma_2 = 3$ and about 1% if $\sigma_2 = 4$.

Appendix C. Data Generating Process

In this appendix we describe the process used to generate claims triangles using the balance sheet data from Table 1 in a way that the estimated reserves from the data match closely the reserves from Table 1.

First of all, for each LoB we set the maximum number of development years as the number of years it takes until $F_j = 1$, where F_j denotes the *cumulative* payment pattern for development year j (see Section 8.1). As claims in the "Motor Third Part Liability (MTPL)" and "Workers Compensation (UVG)" LoBs should take between 20 and 30 years to settle, we make a simplifying assumption that $I = \max(J+1, 10)$.

For different accident years we calculate the present value of the runoff pattern, using a constant claim inflation $r = 2\%$ for all years and LoBs. More precisely, we have that

$$PV_i(F_j) = (1+r)^{-i} F_j \text{ for } j = 1, \dots, J \text{ and } j + i > I.$$

For the most recent accident year, $i = I$, we define the expected ultimate claim by

$$C^*_{I,J} = R \times \frac{\sum_{j=1}^{J} P_{I,j}}{\sum_{j=1}^{J} F_j},$$

where R denotes the reserves from Table 1 and

$$P_{I,j} = \frac{PV_I(F_j)}{\sum_{i=1}^{I}\sum_{j=1}^{J} PV_i(F_j)}.$$

Note that $C^*_{I,J}$ is neither the ultimate claim predictor for the conditional model defined in Equation (21) nor the marginalized one from Equation (27). In this context $C^*_{I,J}$ is just an auxiliary variable being used in order to simulate triangles which have estimated reserves similar to the original ones in Table 1.

For the remaining accident years the expected ultimate claim is taken as the present value of $C^*_{I,J}$. In other words,

$$C^*_{i,J} = PV_{i-I}(C^*_{I,J}) = (1+r)^{I-i} C^*_{I,J}.$$

Given all the values of $C^*_{i,J}$, we compute $E^*_i = F_0 \times C^*_{i,J}$, the expected initial payment for each accident year. These values are, then, combined with the coefficients of variation for CY small claims and used to simulate the first column of our triangles as

$$C_{i,0} \sim LN(m^*_i, V^*_i),$$

with the auxiliary parameters $m^*_i = \log(E^*_i) - V^*_i/2$, $V^*_i = \log(1 + \text{CoVa}^2_{CY})$ and CoVa_{CY} the coefficient of variation of CY small claims, based on Model Assumptions 4. For the remaining development years we follow Model Assumptions 1 (a) with $\phi_j = 1/f_j$ and $\sigma_j = s_j/f_j$, as discussed in Section 8.1.

Figure 4 presents the generated cumulative claims payments for all LoBs, where each line represents the cumulative claims payment. In each plot the lighter colours represent more recent accident years which are not yet fully developed. The reserves calculated based on this dataset are presented in Table 2 and given these values the original reserves from Table 1 are ignored.

References

Andrieu, Christophe, Arnaud Doucet, and Roman Holenstein. 2010. Particle Markov chain Monte Carlo methods. *Journal of the Royal Statistical Society: Series B (Statistical Methodology)* 72: 269–342.

Andrieu, Christophe, and Gareth O. Roberts. 2009. The pseudo-marginal approach for efficient Monte Carlo computations. *The Annals of Statistics* 37: 697–725.

Andrieu, Christophe, and Matti Vihola. 2015. Convergence properties of pseudo-marginal Markov chain Monte Carlo algorithms. *The Annals of Applied Probability* 25: 1030–77.

Asimit, Alexandru V., Raluca Vernic, and Ričardas Zitikis. 2013. Evaluating risk measures and capital allocations based on multi-losses driven by a heavy-tailed background risk: The multivariate Pareto-II model. *Risks* 1: 14–33.

Bargès, Mathieu, Hélène Cossette, and Etienne Marceau. 2009. TVaR-based capital allocation with copulas. *Insurance: Mathematics and Economics* 45: 348–61.

Beskos, Alexandros, Omiros Papaspiliopoulos, Gareth O. Roberts, and Paul Fearnhead. 2006. Exact and computationally efficient likelihood-based estimation for discretely observed diffusion processes (with discussion). *Journal of the Royal Statistical Society: Series B (Statistical Methodology)* 68: 333–82.

Cérou, Frédéric, Pierre Del Moral, Teddy Furon, and Arnaud Guyader. 2012. Sequential Monte Carlo for rare event estimation. *Statistics and Computing* 22: 795–808.

Chopin, Nicolas, Pierre E Jacob, and Omiros Papaspiliopoulos. 2013. SMC^2: An efficient algorithm for sequential analysis of state space models. *Journal of the Royal Statistical Society: Series B (Statistical Methodology)* 75: 397–426.

European Comission. 2009. *Directive 2009/138/EC of the European Parliament and of the Council of 25 November 2009 on the taking-up and pursuit of the business of Insurance and Reinsurance (Solvency II)*. Technical Report. Available Online: http://eur-lex.europa.eu/legal-content/EN/ALL/?uri=CELEX:32009L0138 (accessed on 3 May 2017).

Cossette, Hélène, Marie-Pier Côté, Etienne Marceau, and Khouzeima Moutanabbir. 2013. Multivariate distribution defined with Farlie–Gumbel–Morgenstern copula and mixed Erlang marginals: Aggregation and capital allocation. *Insurance: Mathematics and Economics* 52: 560–72.

Creal, Drew. 2012. A survey of sequential Monte Carlo methods for economics and finance. *Econometric Reviews* 31: 245–96.

De Jong, Piet, and Ben Zehnwirth. 1983. Claims reserving, state-space models and the Kalman filter. *Journal of the Institute of Actuaries* 110: 157–81.

Del Moral, Pierre. 1996. Non-linear filtering: interacting particle resolution. *Markov Processes and Related Fields* 2: 555–81.

Del Moral, Pierre. 2004. *Feynman-Kac Formulae*. Berlin: Springer.

Del Moral, Pierre, Arnaud Doucet, and Ajay Jasra. 2006. Sequential Monte Carlo samplers. *Journal of the Royal Statistical Society: Series B (Statistical Methodology)* 68: 411–36.

Del Moral, Pierre, Gareth W Peters, and Christelle Vergé. 2013. An introduction to stochastic particle integration methods: With applications to risk and insurance. In *Monte Carlo and Quasi-Monte Carlo Methods 2012*. Berlin: Springer, pp. 39–81.

Denuit, Michel, and Jan Dhaene. 2003. Simple characterizations of comonotonicity and countermonotonicity by extremal correlations. *Belgian Actuarial Bulletin* 3: 22–27.

Devroye, Luc, and Gérard Letac. 2015. Copulas with prescribed correlation matrix. In *In Memoriam Marc Yor-Séminaire de Probabilités XLVII*. Berlin: Springer, pp. 585–601.

Dhaene, Jan, Luc Henrard, Zinoviy Landsman, Antoine Vandendorpe, and Steven Vanduffel. 2008. Some results on the CTE-based capital allocation rule. *Insurance: Mathematics and Economics* 42: 855–63.

Dhaene, Jan, Andreas Tsanakas, Emiliano A. Valdez, and Steven Vanduffel. 2012. Optimal capital allocation principles. *Journal of Risk and Insurance* 79: 1–28.

Douc, Randal, and Olivier Cappé. 2005. Comparison of resampling schemes for particle filtering. Paper presented the 4th International Symposium on Image and Signal Processing and Analysis (ISPA 2005), Zagreb, Croatia, September 15–17, pp. 64–69.

Doucet, Arnaud, and Adam M. Johansen. 2009. A tutorial on particle filtering and smoothing: Fifteen years later. *Handbook of Nonlinear Filtering* 12: 656–704.

Embrechts, Paul, Alexander McNeil, and Daniel Straumann. 2002. Correlation and dependence in risk management: Properties and pitfalls. In *Risk Management: Value at Risk and Beyond*. Cambridge: Cambridge University Press, pp. 176–223.

Embrechts, Paul, Giovanni Puccetti, Ludger Rüschendorf, Ruodu Wang, and Antonela Beleraj. 2014. An academic response to Basel 3.5. *Risks* 2: 25–48.

Everitt, Richard G., Adam M. Johansen, Ellen Rowing, and Melina Evdemon-Hogan. 2016. Bayesian model comparison with un-normalised likelihoods. *Statistics and Computing* 27: 403–22.

Finke, Axel. 2015. On Extended State-Space Constructions for Monte Carlo Methods. Ph.D. dissertation, University of Warwick, Coventry, UK.

FINMA. 2007. *Technical Document on the Swiss Solvency Test*. Technical Report. Bern: FINMA.

FINMA. 2016. Standardmodell Schadenversicherung. Available Online: https://www.finma.ch/de/~/media/finma/dokumente/dokumentencenter/myfinma/2ueberwachung/sst/standard-model-nonlife-2016.zip?la=de (accessed on 13 July 2016).

Fulop, Andras, and Junye Li. 2013. Efficient learning via simulation: A marginalized resample-move approach. *Journal of Econometrics* 176: 146–61.

Furman, Edward, and Zinoviy Landsman. 2005. Risk capital decomposition for a multivariate dependent gamma portfolio. *Insurance: Mathematics and Economics* 37: 635–49.

Gandy, Axel, and F. Din-Houn Lau. 2015. The chopthin algorithm for resampling. *arXiv*, preprint arXiv:1502.07532.

Geweke, John. 1989. Bayesian inference in econometric models using Monte Carlo integration. *Econometrica: Journal of the Econometric Society*: 1317–39. doi:0012-9682(198911)57:6<1317:BIIEMU>2.0.CO;2-5.

Gilks, Walter R., and Carlo Berzuini. 2001. Following a moving target Monte Carlo inference for dynamic Bayesian models. *Journal of the Royal Statistical Society: Series B (Statistical Methodology)* 63: 127–46.

Gordon, Neil J., David J. Salmond, and Adrian F.M. Smith. 1993. Novel approach to nonlinear/non-Gaussian Bayesian state estimation. *IEEE Proceedings F-Radar and Signal Processing* 140: 107–13.

Landsman, Zinoviy M., and Emiliano A. Valdez. 2003. Tail conditional expectations for elliptical distributions. *North American Actuarial Journal* 7: 55–71.

Liu, Jun S., and Rong Chen. 1995. Blind deconvolution via sequential imputations. *Journal of the American Statistical Association* 90: 567–76.

Liu, Jun S., and Rong Chen. 1998. Sequential Monte Carlo methods for dynamic systems. *Journal of the American Statistical Association* 93: 1032–44.

Mack, Thomas. 1993. Distribution-free calculation of the standard error of chain ladder reserve estimates. *Astin Bulletin* 23: 213–25.

Martino, Luca, Víctor Elvira, and Francisco Louzada. 2017. Effective sample size for importance sampling based on discrepancy measures. *Signal Processing* 131: 386–401.

McGree, James M., Christopher C. Drovandi, Gentry White, and Anthony N. Pettitt. 2015. A pseudo-marginal sequential Monte Carlo algorithm for random effects models in Bayesian sequential design. *Statistics and Computing* 26: 1–16.

McNeil, Alexander J., Rüdiger Frey, and Paul Embrechts. 2010. *Quantitative Risk Management: Concepts, Techniques, and Tools*. Princeton: Princeton University Press.

Merz, Michael, and Mario V. Wüthrich. 2015. Claims run-off uncertainty: The full picture. Available at SSRN 2524352, version of 3/Jul/2015. Available Online: https://papers.ssrn.com/sol3/papers.cfm?abstract_id=2524352 (accessed on 3 May 2017).

Neal, Radford M. 2003. Slice sampling. *Annals of Statistics* 31: 705–41.

Panjer, Harry H. 2001. *Measureement of Risk, Solvency Requirements and Allocation of Capital within Financial Conglomerates*. Waterloo: University of Waterloo, Institute of Insurance and Pension Research.

Peters, Gareth W. 2005. Topics in Sequential Monte Carlo Samplers. Master's thesis, University of Cambridge, Cambridge, UK.

Peters, Gareth W., Rodrigo S. Targino, and Mario V. Wüthrich. 2017. Full bayesian analysis of claims reserving uncertainty. *Insurance: Mathematics and Economics* 73: 41–53.

Pitt, Michael K., Ralph dos Santos Silva, Paolo Giordani, and Robert Kohn. 2012. On some properties of Markov chain Monte Carlo simulation methods based on the particle filter. *Journal of Econometrics* 171: 134–51.

Sklar, Abe. 1959. Fonctions de répartition à n dimensions et leurs marges. *Fonctions de Repartition à n Dimensions et Leurs Marges* 8: 229–31.

Targino, Rodrigo S., Gareth W. Peters, and Pavel V. Shevchenko. 2015. Sequential Monte Carlo samplers for capital allocation under copula-dependent risk models. *Insurance: Mathematics and Economics* 61: 206–26.

Tasche, Dirk. 1999. Risk contributions and performance measurement. *Report of the Lehrstuhl für mathematische Statistik, TU München*. Available Online: https://pdfs.semanticscholar.org/2659/60513755b26ada0b4fb688460e8334a409dd.pdf (accessed on 3 May 2017).

Tran, Minh-Ngoc, Marcel Scharth, Michael K. Pitt, and Robert Kohn. 2014. Importance sampling squared for bayesian inference in latent variable models. Available at SSRN 2386371. Available Online: https://ssrn.com/abstract=2386371 (accessed on 3 May 2017).

Vergé, Christelle, Cyrille Dubarry, Pierre Del Moral, and Eric Moulines. 2015. On parallel implementation of sequential Monte Carlo methods: The island particle model. *Statistics and Computing* 25: 243–60.

Vergé, Christelle, Jérôme Morio, and Pierre Del Moral. 2016. An island particle algorithm for rare event analysis. *Reliability Engineering & System Safety* 149: 63–75.

Verrall, Richard J. 1989. A state space representation of the chain ladder linear model. *Journal of the Institute of Actuaries* 116: 589–609.

Wüthrich, Mario V. 2015. Non-Life Insurance: Mathematics & Statistics. Available at SSRN 2319328, version of 29/Jun/2015. Available at SSRN 2386371. Available Online: https://papers.ssrn.com/sol3/papers.cfm?abstract_id=2319328 (accessed on 3 May 2017).

risks

MDPI

Article

An Integrated Approach to Pricing Catastrophe Reinsurance

Carolyn W. Chang [1,*] and Jack S. K. Chang [2]

1 Department of Finance, California State University, Fullerton, CA 92831, USA
2 Department of Finance & Law, California State University, Los Angeles, CA 90032, USA; jchang@calstatela.edu
* Correspondence: cchang@fullerton.edu; Tel.: +1-657-278-3074

Received: 3 July 2017; Accepted: 14 September 2017; Published: 19 September 2017

Abstract: We propose an integrated approach straddling the actuarial science and the mathematical finance approaches to pricing a default-risky catastrophe reinsurance contract. We first apply an incomplete-market version of the no-arbitrage martingale pricing paradigm to price the reinsurance contract as a martingale by a measure change, then we apply risk loading to price in—as in the traditional actuarial practice—market imperfections, the underwriting cycle, and other idiosyncratic factors identified in the practice and empirical literatures. This integrated approach is theoretically appealing for its merit of factoring risk premiums into the probability measure, and yet practical for being applicable to price a contract not traded on financial markets. We numerically study the catastrophe pricing effects and find that the reinsurance contract is more valuable when the catastrophe is more severe and the reinsurer's default risk is lower because of a stronger balance sheet. We also find that the price is more sensitive to the severity of catastrophes than to the arrival frequency; implying (re)insurers should focus more on hedging the severity than the arrival frequency in their risk management programs.

Keywords: mathematical finance; actuarial science; catastrophe arrivals; catastrophe reinsurance; default risk; Monte Carlo simulation

---

1. Introduction

Catastrophe (cat hereafter) reinsurance contracts are not traded on financial markets, instead they are one-shot deals made between reinsurers and insurers. In actuarial science, catastrophe reinsurance is conventionally priced according to a two-stage process where in the first stage, catastrophe modelers like RMS (Risk Management Solutions), AIR (AIR Worldwide) and EQE (EQECAT) produce loss distributions through catastrophe modeling and calibration, and in the second stage insurers and reinsurers negotiate prices based on the given loss distributions with additional consideration of non-modeled market factors. This two-stage process is complex as many elements, including input data quality, catastrophe modeling output, and non-modeled market factors, can affect premiums, and some of these elements cannot be quantified but require subjective judgements. It is therefore fair to say that cat reinsurance pricing, as summarized in the following pricing norm, is a mix of art and science:

Layer premium = Expected layer loss + Risk load factor × Standard Deviation,

where the expected layer loss and standard deviation are obtained from catastrophe models inclusive of the consideration of the modeled factors of input quality, model errors and output uncertainty, while the risk load factor is a subjective entry that depends on risk preference, reinsurers' capital position, and (re)insurance market conditions, among other considerations.

Reinsurers may also load non-modeled market factors on top of the modeled factors to increase the premium. In the academic literature, Froot (2001) and Froot and O'Connell (2008) have shown that reinsurers' monopolistic power and the high costs of capital resulted from inefficient corporate forms[1] have led to unusually high risk loadings with spreads at around 5–8 times the expected loss. Moreover, these multiples tend to jump even higher in the aftermath of a major cat event due to reinsurers' "reloading" of balance sheets. In practice, reinsurers may also load geographic concentration, data quality in capturing exposure characteristics, a cedant's loss experience, and reinsurance relationship.

The merit of the traditional actuarial pricing approach is that it works in the imperfect global reinsurance market, where many reinsurers also ensemble multiple pricing models to reign in model errors. The drawback is that the pricing norm is ad hoc but not derived from prevailing financial valuation theories.

In mathematical finance, theoreticians have attempted to price cat reinsurance as if it were traded on financial markets by using option pricing theory, non-arbitrage martingale pricing theory, and utility optimization theory. They also take cat losses as exogenously given with a common assumption that loss arrivals follow a compound Poisson process or its variations as in Bowers et al. (1986), in lieu of using the loss output from a cat modeler. For example, Chang et al. (1989) value reinsurance in an option theoretical framework, Dassios and Jang (2003) value cat reinsurance using the Cox process with shot noise intensity under a no-arbitrage martingale probability measure, and Lee and Yu (2007) value default-risky cat reinsurance with catastrophe bonds under a no-arbitrage martingale probability measure. However, the unrealistic perfect-market assumptions, the overly-simplified specification of the loss arrival process, and the lack of data to calibrate the process have made direct implementation of these theories in the global reinsurance market impractical.

In this paper, we propose an integrated approach to pricing a default-risky cat reinsurance contract. First, we apply an incomplete-market version of the no-arbitrage martingale pricing paradigm of Harrison and Kreps (1979) and Harrison and Pliska (1981)[2], which is internally consistent with option pricing theory, to factor in the modeled risk premiums by means of a measure change. We then add risk loading/markup (used interchangeably hereafter) to price in the non-modeled market factors identified in practice and the empirical literature. This integrated approach is theoretically appealing in being able to factor the risk premiums into the probability measure, and yet applicable to pricing a contract traded on the global reinsurance market by taking into consideration non-modeled risk loading. We could have used the equilibrium approach by imposing a preference assumption, however applying utility functions to resolve problems incurred in incomplete markets is often impractical as the results become overly complicated to be fully specified by practitioners (see Carr et al. (2001)). Another problem with the equilibrium approach as documented by many empirical studies is that

1 Traditional reinsurers tend to invest in illiquid and information-intensive financial activities, and so they charge premiums based on correlations with their own pre-existing portfolios and U.S. nationwide cat risks, rather than with any market portfolio, resulting in significantly higher cost of capital.

2 A martingale is a stochastic variable with no drift such that the current expectation of the future value of the variable is always equal to the current value of the variable. The above authors show that the absence of arbitrage is equivalent to the existence of an equivalent martingale pricing measure Q (or risk-neutral/risk-neutralized pricing measure as used by some authors) such that all normalized (with respect to a chosen numeraire) security prices are martingales and as such they can be priced by taking expectations under the measure Q. The beauty of martingale pricing is that it applies to both complete and incomplete markets as "absence of arbitrage" is the only required assumption. When markets are complete with the absence of arbitrage, martingale pricing theory guarantees that the equivalent martingale measure is unique, thus the market price of risk does not explicitly enter into the valuation process. In this context, options can be priced preference-free *as if* agents were risk-neutral as in the Black–Scholes model. When markets are incomplete, however, the absence of arbitrage no longer guarantees a unique martingale measure. In this case, information related to the market prices of risk that embeds the risk-aversion behavior of agents is needed to uniquely identify the equivalent martingale measure (see Geman (2005) for a review). The procedure of embedding the market price of risk to obtain such a unique measure is often called *risk-neutralization*.

for a CRRA (Constant Relative Risk Aversion) utility to work, the risk-aversion parameter must be unreasonably small (e.g., Bollerslev et al. (2011)).

Our integrated approach proceeds as follows:

(1) We first model a default-risky reinsurer by employing Merton (1974) structural approach to endogenize default.

- On the asset side, since the reinsurer holds a large proportion of fixed-income assets in the asset portfolio, we model the asset dynamics taking into account explicitly the impact of stochastic interest rates. We make a measure change from the physical pricing measure to the equivalent martingale pricing measure Q by embedding the market price of interest rate risk.
- On the liability side, since the reinsurer's non-catastrophic liability shocks are idiosyncratic and small, we apply the law of large numbers to assume away this risk premium. We also make a measure change from the physical pricing measure to the equivalent martingale pricing measure Q by embedding the market price of interest rate risk.

(2) We model catastrophe arrivals. We make use of the empirical finding that catastrophe derivatives are zero-beta assets, and thus both the loss number and the amount of losses have zero risk premiums.

(3) We proceed to price a default-risky reinsurance contract under the equivalent martingale pricing measure Q as a martingale.

(4) Finally, we extend the pricing formula to incorporate risk load/markup to account for the observed empirical characteristics of the (re)insurance market. The interpretation of the markup is the same as in the traditional actuarial pricing approach except that (1) our expectation is taken with respect to the risk-neutralized martingale pricing measure, but in the traditional approach the expectation is taken with respect to the physical pricing measure; and (2) our markup only needs to account for market imperfections and other idiosyncratic factors, while the markup in the traditional actuarial approach accounts for both modeled and non-modeled factors.

To load non-modeled market factors, we suggest calibrating the markup using empirical cat reinsurance data as it has become increasingly available because of the growth of the market. Although endogenizing the markup could further enrich the analysis and provide more intuition, it constitutes a major undertaking in an incomplete-market general equilibrium setting encompassing two heterogeneous agents. Besides considering market imperfections such as "taxes, agency costs, issuance costs", risk aversions, and costs of capital associated with bearing the catastrophe risk of the two counterparties, one may also need to consider the insurance underwriting cycle, optimum total catastrophe financing, the tradeoff between capital reserve and hedging, reinsurers' monopolistic/oligopolistic positions in the reinsurance markets, and other idiosyncratic factors identified in the empirical literature. We will leave this task to a future project.

2. Modeling Reinsurer Default with Asset, Interest Rate, Liability, and Catastrophe Loss

Dynamics

Since the reinsurer's asset-liability structure and catastrophe loss specification are important factors in modeling the reinsurer's default, we begin by employing Merton (1974) structural approach to model the balance sheet of the reinsurer in a continuous-time no-arbitrage martingale framework. The Merton approach has the advantage of linking the valuation of financial claims to the firm's assets and capital structure. Thus unlike the more recent approach to incorporate jumps and to integrate with the capital asset pricing model (CAPM) in order to analyze corporate bond spreads (e.g., Collin-Dufresne et al. (2012) and Coval et al. (2009)), our structural model builds upon the work of Duan et al. (1995), Duan and Yu (2005), and Lee and Yu (2007) to properly allow for the asset, liability, interest rate, and cat loss dynamics.

We employ a one-factor interest rate model assuming the asset price and the instantaneous interest rate processes are governed by the following correlated general Wiener process with drifts:

$$\frac{dV_t}{V_t} = \mu(V_t,t)dt + \sigma(V_t,t)dZ_{V,t}, \quad (1)$$

$$dr_t = \mu(r_t,t)dt + \sigma(r_t,t)dZ_{r,t}, \quad (2)$$

where $Z_{v,t}$ and $Z_{r,t}$ are correlated Wiener processes.

Typically, reinsurers hold a large proportion of fixed-income assets in the asset portfolio and issue catastrophe bonds to lay off catastrophe risk (see Lee and Yu (2007)). To explicitly examine the interest rate exposure, a further decomposition of the asset process is required to provide a direct interpretation of interest rate risk. Projecting $dZ_{V,t}$ onto $dZ_{r,t}$ yields

$$dZ_{V,t} = \varphi dZ_{r,t} + \sqrt{1-\varphi^2}dW_{V,t}, \quad (3)$$

where $\varphi = \frac{Cov(dZ_{V,t},dZ_{r,t})}{dt}$. As a result of this projection, $W_{V,t}$, denoting the credit risk on the assets of the reinsurance company, is orthogonal to Z_t by construction. As explained in footnote 7 of Duan et al. (1995), the term credit risk here is used to designate all risks other than the interest rate risk. To the extent that defaults on fixed income assets are related to interest rates, the credit risk is considered as part of the interest rate risk, thus $W_{V,t}$ may not strictly correspond to the conventional definition of credit risk.

Theorem 1. *In the one-factor interest rate model, Equation (1) can be risk-neutralized to the following risk-neutralized asset price process with a measure change,* $dZ_t^* = dZ_t + \frac{\lambda_r\sqrt{r_t}}{v}dt$ *and* $dW_{V,t}^* = dW_{V,t}$, *from the physical measure to the equivalent martingale measure Q:*

$$\frac{dV_t}{V_t} = r_t dt + \phi_V v\sqrt{r_t}dZ_t^* + \sigma_V dW^*_{V,t}. \quad (4)$$

Proof.

As shown in Appendix A of Lee and Yu (2007), substituting Equation (3) into Equation (1) yields

$$\frac{dV_t}{V_t} = \mu(V_t,t)dt + \sigma(V_t,t)\varphi dZ_{r,t} + \sigma(V_t,t)\sqrt{1-\varphi^2}dW_{V,t}, \quad (5)$$

and further substituting Equation (2) into Equation (5) yields

$$\frac{dV_t}{V_t} = \mu_V dt + \phi_V dr_t + \sigma_V dW_{V,t}, \quad (6)$$

where $\mu_V = [\mu(V_t,t) - \frac{\sigma(V_t,t)\varphi\mu(r_t,t)}{\sigma(r_t,t)}]$, $\phi_V = \sigma(V_t,t)\varphi/\sigma(r_t,t)$ is the instantaneous interest rate elasticity of the assets of the reinsurance company, and $\sigma_V = \sigma(V_t,t)\sqrt{1-\varphi^2}$ is the volatility of the credit risk.

Next, we assume the general instantaneous interest rate process, Equation (2), is specified by the squared-root process of Cox et al. (1985 and CIR hereafter) to avoid negative interest rates:

$$dr_t = \kappa(m - r_t)dt + v\sqrt{r_t}dZ_t, \quad (7)$$

where r_t denotes the instantaneous interest rate at time t; κ is the mean-reverting force measurement; m is the long-run mean of the interest rate; and v is the volatility parameter for the interest rate.

Substituting Equation (7) into Equation (6), the reinsurance company's asset dynamics can be described as:

$$\frac{dV_t}{V_t} = (\mu_V + \phi_V \kappa m - \phi_V \kappa r_t)dt + \phi_V v\sqrt{r_t} dZ_t + \sigma_V dW_{V,t}. \tag{8}$$

The dynamics for the interest rate process under the risk-neutralized pricing measure, denoted by Q, can be written as

$$dr_t = \kappa^*(m^* - r_t)dt + v\sqrt{r_t}\, dZ_t^*, \tag{9}$$

where $\kappa^* = \kappa + \lambda_r$; $m^* = \frac{\kappa m}{\kappa + \lambda_r}$; $dZ_t^* = dZ_t + \frac{\lambda_r \sqrt{r_t}}{v} dt$; λ_r, the market price of interest rate risk, is constant under the assumptions of Cox et al. (1985); and Z_t^* is a Wiener process under Q.

As $W_{V,t}$ is orthogonal to Z_t by construction and is considered as part of the interest rate risk, we can risk-neutralize Equation (8) by making use of the market price of the interest rate risk alone so that $\mu_V + \phi_V \kappa m - \phi_V \kappa r_t = r_t + \phi_V r_t$, and a measure change from the physical measure to the equivalent martingale measure Q that $dZ_t^* = dZ_t + \frac{\lambda_r \sqrt{r_t}}{v} dt$ and $d = dW_{V,t}$. Upon rearrangement we derive the risk-neutralized asset price process. □

On the liability side, the reinsurer faces the liability of providing reinsurance coverage to other lines of business, plus the liability of providing reinsurance coverage for catastrophes. Since the former liability represents the present value of future claims related to non-catastrophic policies, its value, denoted as L_t, can be modeled like Equation (6) as follows:

$$dL_t = \mu_L L_t dt + \phi_L L_t dr_t + \sigma_L L_t dW_{L,t}, \tag{10}$$

where $\mu_L = [\mu(L_t, t) - \frac{\sigma(L_t,t)\varphi\mu(r_t,t)}{\sigma(r_t,t)}]$ and $\phi_L = \sigma(L_t, t)\varphi/\sigma(r_t, t)$ denote respectively the instantaneous expected return for the non-catastrophic policies and the interest rate elasticity of the liability of the reinsurance company; $\varphi = \frac{Cov(dZ_{L,t}, dZ_{r,t})}{dt}$; and $\sigma_V = \sigma(L_t, t)\sqrt{1 - \varphi^2}$ is the volatility of the credit risk. This continuous diffusion process reflects the effects of interest rate changes and other small day-to-day shocks. Since the small day-to-day shocks, denoted as $W_{L,t}$, pertain to idiosyncratic shocks to the capital market, we assume a zero risk premium for this risk.

Lemma 1. *The liability process, Equation (10), can be risk-neutralized under Q using the market price of interest rate risk as:*

$$dL_t = r_t L_t dt + \phi_L v\sqrt{r_t} L_t dZ_t^* + \sigma_L L_t dW_{L,t}^*. \tag{11}$$

Proof.

Substituting Equation (7) into Equation (10), the reinsurance company's liability dynamics can be described as:

$$\frac{dL_t}{L_t} = (\mu_L + \phi_L \kappa m - \phi_L \kappa r_t)dt + \phi_L v\sqrt{r_t} dZ_t + \sigma_L dW_{L,t}. \tag{12}$$

Next the dynamics for the interest rate process under the risk-neutralized pricing measure Q is given in Equation (9) as

$$dr_t = \kappa^*(m^* - r_t)dt + v\sqrt{r_t}\, dZ_t^*,$$

where $\kappa^* = \kappa + \lambda_r$; $m^* = \frac{\kappa m}{\kappa + \lambda_r}$; $dZ_t^* = dZ_t + \frac{\lambda_r \sqrt{r_t}}{v} dt$; λ_r, the market price of interest rate risk, is constant, and Z_t^* is a Wiener process under Q.

As $W_{L,t}$ is orthogonal to Z_t by construction and is considered as part of the interest rate risk, we can risk-neutralize Equation (12) by making use of the market price of interest rate risk alone so that $\mu_L + \phi_L \kappa m - \phi_L \kappa r_t = r_t + \lambda_r \phi_L r_t$, and a measure change from the physical measure to the equivalent martingale measure Q that $dZ_t^* = dZ_t + \frac{\lambda_r \sqrt{r_t}}{v} dt$ and $dW_{L,t}^* = dW_{L,t}$. Upon rearrangement we derive the risk-neutralized liability price process. □

To model the catastrophic component of the liability, we first model the aggregate catastrophe loss as a compound Poisson process as in Bowers et al. (1986). The cumulative catastrophe loss at time t, denoted as C_t, is described as follows:

$$C_t = \sum_{j=1}^{N(t)} c_j, \tag{13}$$

where the loss number process $\{N(t),\ t \geq 0\}$ is assumed to be driven by a Poisson process with intensity λ. Term c_j denotes the amount of loss caused by the jth catastrophe covered by the reinsurance contract during the specific period, where $j = 1, 2, \ldots, N(t)$, and is assumed to be mutually independent, identical, and lognormally-distributed, and independent of the loss number process; its logarithmic means and standard deviations are denoted as μ_c and σ_c, respectively. We assume the loss process is exogenously calibrated by a catastrophe modeler, e.g., AIR Worldwide for hurricanes and windstorms and RMS for earthquakes. We also make the common assumption that catastrophe derivatives are zero-beta assets, and thus both the loss number process $\{N(t)\}$ and the amount of losses $(c_t$ have a zero-risk premium[3]. The loss process, Equation (13), thus retains its original distributional characteristics after changing from the physical probability measure to the risk-neutralized measure.

3. Pricing a Cat Reinsurance Contract and the Monte Carlo Simulation Results

The reinsurer's future payoff to the insurer can be specified as:

$$PO_{R,T} = \begin{cases} M - A & \text{if } C_T \geq M \text{ and } V_T \geq L_T + M - A, \\ C_T - A & \text{if } M > C_T \geqq A \text{ and } V_T \geq L_T + C_T - A, \\ \left(\frac{V_T}{L_T+M-A}\right)(M - A) & \text{if } C_T \geq M \text{ and } V_T < L_T + M - A, \\ \left(\frac{V_T}{L_T+C_T-A}\right)(C_T - A) & \text{if } M > C_T \geqq A \text{ and } V_T < L_T + C_T - A, \\ 0 & \text{otherwise,} \end{cases} \tag{14}$$

where V_T is the value of the reinsurer's assets at T; L_T is the value of the reinsurer's liabilities at T; C_T is the catastrophe loss covered by the reinsurance contract; and M and A are respectively the cap and attachment points arranged in the reinsurance contract. For example, when C_T is larger than the reinsurance cap M and the reinsurer's total assets are larger than total liability inclusive of the reinsurance obligation $M - A$, the payoff is $M - A$. When the reinsurer's total assets are smaller than total liability inclusive of the reinsurance obligation $M - A$, the reinsurer will default, and the payoff to the insurer then is only $(\frac{V_T}{L_T+M-A})(M - A)$. The present value of this future payoff determines the value of the reinsurance contract, computed as a martingale under the risk-neutralized pricing measure Q as:

$$PV_{R,0} = E_0^Q[e^{-\int_0^T r_s\,ds} \times PO_{R,T}], \tag{15}$$

where E_0^Q denotes the expectation taken on the issuing date under the risk-neutralized pricing measure Q. In Appendix A, we demonstrate how to compute $PV_{R,0}$ via Monte Carlo simulation.

To incorporate the observed empirical characteristics of the (re)insurance market, we let the sell-side reinsurance pricing be $(1 + u)PV_{R,0}$, where u denotes the risk loading/price markup that is higher in a hard market, but lower in a soft market.

To demonstrate the implementation using Monte Carlo simulation, we consider a base case in which all of the parameter values in the asset, liability, interest rate, and catastrophe loss dynamics are

[3] Gürtler et al. (2012) show that this premium can be significant when a mega catastrophe strikes, but we assume this scenario away in this paper.

consistent with previous literature[4], as summarized in Table 1 below. We also assume the reinsurance market is still hard with a markup of 40%[5]. Simulations were run on a monthly basis with 20,000 paths.

Table 1. Parameter Definitions and Base Values.

Asset Parameters		
V	Reinsurer's assets	$V/L = 1.3$
μ_V	Drift due to credit risk	Irreverent
ϕ_V	Interest rate elasticity of asset	−3
σ_v	Volatility of credit risk	5%
$W_{V,t}$	Wiener process for credit shocks	
Liability Parameters		
L	Reinsurer's liabilities	100
μ_L	Drift due to idiosyncratic risk	0
ϕ_L	Interest rate elasticity of liability	−3
σ_L	Volatility of idiosyncratic risk	2%
$W_{L,t}$	Wiener process for idiosyncratic shocks	
Interest Rate Parameters		
r	Initial instantaneous interest rate	2%
κ	Magnitude of mean-reverting force	0.2
m	Long-run mean of interest rate	5%
v	Volatility of interest rate	10%
λ_r	Market price of interest rate risk	−0.01
Z	Wiener process for interest rate shocks	
Catastrophe loss Parameters for C_t		
$N(t)$	Poisson process for the arrival of catastrophes	
λ	Catastrophe arrival intensity	0.5
μ_C	Mean of the logarithm of the losses per arrival	2
σ_C	Standard deviation of the logarithm of the losses per arrival	0.5
Other Parameters		
A	Attachment level of a reinsurance contract	10~30
M	Cap level of loss paid by a reinsurance contract	60~90
T	Maturity	3 years
u	Reinsurance markup	0.4

Table 2 below summarizes the corresponding reinsurance values across all coverage layers to form the reinsurer's sell-side pricing schedule. As expected, as the attachment point increases, the reinsurance value decreases, while as the cap/detachment point increases, the reinsurance value increases. We also observe that lower layer coverage is more expensive than higher layer coverage, e.g., the price for layer (20, 60) is 2.73468 while the price for layer (25, 65) is 1.59048, reflecting that the lower the layer the higher the probability of penetration.

4 See Lee and Yu (2007) and Duan and Simonato (1999).

5 The size of the markup is an empirical issue, and here we assume a plausible scenario to demonstrate pricing. Zanjani (2002) states that the marginal capital requirement for catastrophe reinsurance is about five times the premium with a price impact of about 30%.

Table 2. Reinsurance Pricing across All Coverage Layers.

Coverage	$M = 60$	$M = 65$	$M = 70$	$M = 75$	$M = 80$	$M = 85$	$M = 90$
$A = 10$	7.26957	7.28648	7.29306	7.30003	7.30261	7.30284	7.30634
$A = 15$	4.45191	4.46950	4.47824	4.48331	4.48579	4.48792	4.99274
$A = 20$	2.73468	2.75143	2.76143	2.76739	2.16897	2.17120	2.17444
$A = 25$	1.57234	1.59048	1.59951	1.60448	1.60706	1.60929	1.61162
$A = 30$	0.93787	0.98590	1.05583	1.06080	1.06338	1.06561	1.06740

Next we examine the catastrophe effects by extending the base value scenario in Table 1 to consider three levels of catastrophe arrival intensity $\lambda = (0.5, 1, 2)$; three levels of loss volatility: $\sigma_c = (0.5, 1, 2)$; and three leverage scenarios: $V/L = (1.1, 1.3, 1.5)$, with decreasing leverage. Table 3 below shows that, as expected, as the leverage decreases the default risk decreases such that the reinsurance contract becomes more valuable. It also shows that increases in both catastrophe arrival intensity and loss volatility raise the reinsurance value as hedging becomes more desirable. As catastrophe arrival intensifies and the loss becomes more unpredictable, insurers should increasingly purchase reinsurances as the expected losses accentuate. We further observe that the loss volatility effect is more acute than the arrival intensity effect. For example, when V/L is 1.1, doubling the arrival intensity from 0.5 to 1 increases the reinsurance value from 7.30634 to 13.24426, but doubling the loss volatility from 0.5 to 1 increases the reinsurance value from 7.30634 to 20.75633. This finding suggests that insurers should be more concerned with hedging the severity of a catastrophe than with the intensity of the arrival. Finally, as expected, the reinsurance contract is more valuable when the catastrophe is more severe and the default risk is lower.

Table 3. Impacts of Catastrophe Intensity and Loss Volatility on Pricing.

(λ, σ_C)	Reinsurance Price $(1+u)PV_{R,0}$ for Coverage Payer (90, 10)		
	$V/L = 1.1$	$V/L = 1.3$	$V/L = 1.5$
(0.5, 0.5)	7.30634	7.40443	7.58688
(1, 0.5)	13.24426	13.78995	14.12347
(2, 0.5)	19.56788	19.98765	20.31452
(0.5, 1)	20.75633	21.24536	21.76542
(1, 1)	24.18776	24.35473	24.87682
(2, 1)	27.78653	28.89672	29.45328
(0.5, 2)	40.28763	41.69782	43.13476
(1, 2)	43.21675	43.87862	44.34724
(2, 2)	48.8976	49.90163	51.27658

4. Concluding Remarks

We have proposed an integrated approach to price a default-risky cat reinsurance contract by straddling the traditional actuarial science and the mathematical finance approaches. We first embedded modeled risk premiums by applying an incomplete-market version of the no-arbitrage martingale pricing paradigm in mathematical finance to price the contract as a martingale by a measure change, we then added on risk loading as commonly practiced by actuaries to price in non-modeled market factors such as market imperfections, the underwriting cycle, and other idiosyncratic factors identified in the empirical reinsurance pricing literature. This integrated approach is theoretically appealing in being able to factor model risk premiums into the probability measure, and yet applicable to a contract not traded on financial markets. We demonstrated the catastrophe arrival effects using simulation and found that the price is more sensitive to catastrophe severity than to arrival frequency; implying (re)insurers should focus more on hedging the severity than the arrival frequency in their risk management programs. Finally, as expected, the reinsurance contract is more valuable when the catastrophe is more severe and the reinsurer's default risk is lower with a stronger balance sheet.

Author Contributions: Carolyn W. Chang and Jack S. K. Chang jointly work on the whole paper from conceiving the idea to the implementation of the simulation.

Conflicts of Interest: The authors declare no conflict of interest.

Appendix A. Procedures of the Monte Carlo Simulation Method

In this section, we numerically assess the reinsurance value $PV_{R,0}$ using Equation (15). Because the premium depends on the values of the reinsurer's assets and liabilities, we have to specify the stochastic processes for these variables (Equations (9) and (11)). Applying Ito's lemma to the logarithm of the value of a reinsurer's assets, Equation (9) becomes the following system:

$$d\ln(V_t) = (r_t - \frac{1}{2}\varphi_V v^2 r_t - \frac{1}{2}\sigma_V{}^2)dt + \varphi_V v\sqrt{r_t}dZ_t{}^* + \sigma_V dW_{V,t}{}^*. \quad \text{(A1)}$$

We can solve the above equation. Its solution, for any $0 \leq q < 1$, is:

$$V_{t+q} = V_t \exp(\sigma_V(W_{V,t+q}{}^* - W_{V,t}{}^*)) * \exp[(1 - \frac{1}{2}\varphi_V{}^2 v^2)\int_t^{t+q} r_s ds + \varphi_V v \int_t^{t+q} \sqrt{r_s}dZ_s{}^*] \quad \text{(A2)}$$

Similarly, by Ito's lemma, Equation (11) gives rise to:

$$d\ln(L_t) = (r_t - \frac{1}{2}\varphi_L v^2 r_t - \frac{1}{2}\sigma_L{}^2)dt + \varphi_L v\sqrt{r_t}dZ_t{}^* + \sigma_L dW_{L,t}{}^*. \quad \text{(A3)}$$

Its solution is:

$$L_{t+q} = L_t \exp(\sigma_L(W_{L,t+q}{}^* - W_{L,t}{}^*)) * \exp[(1 - \frac{1}{2}\varphi_L{}^2 v^2)\int_t^{t+q} r_s ds + \varphi_L v \int_t^{t+q} \sqrt{r_s}dZ_s{}^*] \quad \text{(A4)}$$

We set $q = \frac{1}{52}$, say, on a weekly basis, and simulate the risk-neutralized interest rate process per Equation (8) in order to approximate the whole sample path for the term of reinsurance coverage. This in turn allows us to compute two quantities of interest: $\int_t^{t+1} r_s ds$ and $\int_t^{t+1} \sqrt{r_s}dZ_s{}^*$. Second, we simulate $(W_{V,t+q}{}^* - W_{V,t}{}^*)$ and $(W_{L,t+q}{}^* - W_{L,t}{}^*)$ using the fact that they are independent of the path of r_t, and the coefficient of correlation between them is chosen to be zero to reflect that the credit risk shock and the idiosyncratic day-to-day liability shock are likely to be uncorrelated. Combining $(W_{V,t+q}{}^* - W_{V,t}{}^*)$ with $\int_t^{t+1} r_s ds$ and $\int_t^{t+1} \sqrt{r_s}dZ_s{}^*$ yields a simulated value of V_{t+1} as described in Equation (A2). Similarly, combining $(W_{L,t+q}{}^* - W_{L,t}{}^*)$ with $\int_t^{t+1} r_s ds$ and $\int_t^{t+1} \sqrt{r_s}dZ_s{}^*$ yields a simulated value of L_{t+1} as described in Equation (A4). Third, we generate $(N_{t+1} - N_t)$, $(c_{t+1} - c_t)$ and $(c_{index,t+1} - c_{index,t})$. Since $(N_{t+1} - N_t)$ has a Poisson distribution with intensity parameter λ, it can be simulated easily. For a given value of $(N_{t+1} - N_t)$, we then simulate $\sum_{j=N_t}^{N_{t+1}} \ln c_j$ and $\sum_{j=N_t}^{N_{t+1}} \ln c_{index,j}$, knowing that $\ln c_j$ and $\ln c_{index,j}$ are normal random variables and the coefficient of correlation between them is ρ_c. After simulating these processes, $PV_{R,0}$ can be easily calculated via averaging over the contingent payoffs corresponding to the simulated values.

We implemented the simulation using MATLAB and below are two snapshots of the code, where in Figure A1 we display the asset, liability, and interest rate processes, and in Figure A2 the Poisson catastrophe arrival process.

Editor – /Users/changd/Documents/Miscellaneous/CatOpMix140928.m

0928.m | CatOpMix140928.m | poissrndd.m | +

```
/Users/changd/Documents/Miscellaneous/0928.m 31209(A,M,F,K,phiv,phil,V0,Wu,Wd,Crow,Clamda,Csigma)

%clearvars -except rMaxValue rK rF

%tic

close all

%V0=130;%´Aªì Asset

L0=100;%´Aªì Liability

r=0.02;%Interest rate 5% = 0.05

T=3;%3 year=3

dt=1/12;%Monthy

Period=T/dt;%´À¼Æ

k=0.2;%ªø´A§i¼Æ¦^Åk³t²v

m=0.05;%ªø´A§i¼Æ

%phiv=-3*(100/V0);%Interest rate elasticity of asset

%phil=-3;%Interest rate elasticity of liability

v=0.10;%Volatility parameter for the Interest rate

St=20000;%simulation times


lamr=0;%Interest rate intensity

Sigmav=0.05;%Volatility of credit risk

Sigmal=0.02;%Volatility of credit risk

k_s=k+lamr;%k-star

m_s=k*m/(k+lamr);%m-star


%Clamda=0.5;%Catastrophe interesity

Cmu=2;% mean of logarithm of CAT losses for the insurer

%Csigma=0.5;% mean of logarithm of CAT losses for the insurer

%Crow=0.8;%Corration of INDEX CATLOSS and com CATLOSS : 0.3 or 0.5 or 0.8

%Wu=0.4;%Åv¼Æ0.4=40%

%Wd=0.05;%Åv¼Æ0.05

R=80;
```

Figure A1. MATLAB code for the asset, liability, and interest rate processes.

Editor - /Users/changd/Documents/Miscellaneous/poissrndd.m

0928.m | CatOpMix140928.m | poissrndd.m | +

```
function r = poissrndd(lambda,m,n,state,method)
%POISSRND Random matrices from Poisson distribution.
%   R = POISSRND(LAMBDA) returns a matrix of random numbers chosen
%   from the Poisson distribution with parameter LAMBDA.
%
%   The size of R is the size of LAMBDA. Alternatively,
%   R = POISSRND(LAMBDA,M,N) returns an M by N matrix.
%
%   Use R = POISSRND(LAMBDA,M,N,STATE) to initialise the random
%   number generator with STATE. Use R = POISSRND(LAMBDA,[],[],STATE)
%   when M and N are not given and POISSRND([],[],[],STATE) when
%   only the random number generator needs to be initialised.
%   POISSRND([],[],[],0) resets the generator to its initial state.
%   POISSRND([],[],[],J), for integer J, resets the generator to its J-th state.
%   POISSRND([],[],[],sum(100*clock)) resets it to a different state each time.
%   Note: POISSRND actually initialises RAND and RANDN.
%
%   Use R = POISSRND(LAMBDA,M,N,STATE,METHOD) to determine the method.
%   METHOD='normal' (default) uses a waiting time method.
%   METHOD='fast' uses a waiting time method at lambda<1000 and
%           normal distribution with mean and variance equal to lambda
%           at labda>=1000.
%   METHOD=value equal to 'fast' but with the border set at value
%       instead of 1000.
%   Use R = POISSRND(LAMBDA,[],[],[],METHOD) when M, N and STATE are
%   not given.
%
%   For more information see the M-file.

% Addition 1 (12-3-1999):
```

Figure A2. MATLAB code for the Poisson catastrophe arrival process.

References

Bollerslev, Tim, Michael Gibson, and Hao Zhou. 2011. Dynamic estimation of volatility risk premia and investor risk aversion from option-implied and realized volatilities. *Journal of Econometrics* 160: 235–45. [CrossRef]

Bowers, Newton L., Hans U. Gerber, James C. Hickman, Donald A. Jones, and Cecil J. Nesbitt. 1986. *Actuarial Mathematics*. Itasca: Society of Actuaries.

Carr, Peter, Helyette Geman, and Dilip B. Madan. 2001. Pricing and hedging in incomplete markets. *Journal of Financial Economics* 62: 131–67. [CrossRef]

Chang, Jack S. K., C. Sherman Cheung, and Itzhak Krinsky. 1989. On the derivation of reinsurance premiums. *Insurance: Mathematic and Economics* 8: 137–44. [CrossRef]

Collin-Dufresne, Pierre, Robert S. Goldstein, and Fan Yang. 2012. On the relative pricing of long-maturity index options and collateralized debt obligations. *The Journal of Finance* 68: 1983–2014. [CrossRef]

Coval, Joshua D., Jakub W. Jurek, and Erik Stafford. 2009. Economic catastrophe bonds. *American Economic Review* 99: 628–66. [CrossRef]

Cox, John, Jonathan Ingersoll, and Stephen Ross. 1985. The term structure of interest rates. *Econometrica* 53: 385–407. [CrossRef]

Dassios, Angelos, and Ji-Wook Jang. 2003. Pricing of catastrophe reinsurance and derivatives using the cox process with shot noise intensity. *Finance and Stochastics* 7: 73–95. [CrossRef]

Duan, Jin Chuan, and Min-Teh Yu. 2005. Fair insurance guaranty premia in the presence of risk-based capital regulations, stochastic interest rates and catastrophe risk. *Journal of Banking and Finance* 29: 2435–54. [CrossRef]

Duan, Jin Chuan, Arthur F. Moreau, and C. W. Sealey. 1995. Deposit insurance and bank interest rate risk: Pricing and regulatory implications. *Journal of Banking and Finance* 19: 1091–108. [CrossRef]

Duan, Jin-Chuan, and Jean-Guy Simonato. 1999. Estimating and Testing Exponential-Affine Term Structure Models by Kalman Filter. *Review of Quantitative Finance and Accounting* 13: 111–135.

Froot, Kenneth A. 2001. The market for catastrophe risk: A clinical examination. *Journal of Financial Economics* 60: 529–71. [CrossRef]

Froot, Kenneth A., and Paul G. J. O'Connell. 2008. On the pricing of intermediated risks: Theory and application to catastrophe reinsurance. *Journal of Banking and Finance* 32: 69–85. [CrossRef]

Geman, Hélyette. 2005. From measure changes to time changes in asset pricing. *Journal of Banking and Finance* 29: 2701–22. [CrossRef]

Gürtler, Marc, Martin Hibbelin, and Christine Winkelvos. 2012. The impact of the financial crisis and natural catastrophes on cat bonds. Working paper IF40V1, Technische Universität Braunschweig, Braunschweig, Germany.

Harrison, John Michael, and David M. Kreps. 1979. Martingales and arbitrage in multiperiod securities markets. *Journal of Economic Theory* 20: 381–408. [CrossRef]

Harrison, John Michael, and Stanley R. Pliska. 1981. Martingales and stochastic integrals in the theory of continuous trading. *Stochastic Processes and their Applications* 11: 215–60. [CrossRef]

Lee, Jin Ping, and Min-The Yu. 2007. Valuation of catastrophe reinsurance with cat bonds. *Insurance: Mathematics and Economics* 41: 264–78.

Merton, Robert. 1974. On the pricing of corporate debt: The risk structure of interest rates. *The Journal of Finance* 29: 449–70.

Zanjani, George. 2002. Pricing and capital allocation in catastrophe insurance. *Journal of Financial Economics* 65: 283–305. [CrossRef]

risks

MDPI

Article

Bond and CDS Pricing via the Stochastic Recovery Black-Cox Model

Albert Cohen [1,]* and Nick Costanzino [2,]*

[1] Department of Mathematics, Michigan State University, East Lansing, MI 48824, USA
[2] Quantitative Analytics, Barclays Capital, 745 7th Ave, New York, NY 10019, USA
* Correspondence: albert@math.msu.edu (A.C.); Nick.Costanzino@barclayscapital.com (N.C.)

Academic Editor: Mogens Steffensen
Received: 18 January 2017; Accepted: 10 April 2017; Published: 19 April 2017

Abstract: Building on recent work incorporating recovery risk into structural models by Cohen & Costanzino (2015), we consider the Black-Cox model with an added recovery risk driver. The recovery risk driver arises naturally in the context of imperfect information implicit in the structural framework. This leads to a two-factor structural model we call the Stochastic Recovery Black-Cox model, whereby the asset risk driver A_t defines the default trigger and the recovery risk driver R_t defines the amount recovered in the event of default. We then price zero-coupon bonds and credit default swaps under the Stochastic Recovery Black-Cox model. Finally, we compare our results with the classic Black-Cox model, give explicit expressions for the recovery risk premium in the Stochastic Recovery Black-Cox model, and detail how the introduction of separate but correlated risk drivers leads to a decoupling of the default and recovery risk premiums in the credit spread. We conclude this work by computing the effect of adding coupons that are paid continuously until default, and price perpetual (consol bonds) in our two-factor firm value model, extending calculations in the seminal paper by Leland (1994).

1. Background and Motivation

Most legacy credit models assume that recovery is a constant. It is well known, however, that recovery rates are not constant and indeed are correlated to a variety of risk drivers, including default and interest rates. For example, in their study on real-world recovery rates, Altman et al. [1] show that realized recovery rates are inversely proportional to realized default rates. This phenomena has been successfully incorporated into recent economic capital models (c.f. [2–7]) but still hasn't enjoyed mainstream adoption in pricing models. One notable exception has been in CDO pricing, where stochastic recovery has been added to many legacy models. This was necessary after the most recent credit-liquidity crisis, whereby for a period of time it was not possible to calibrate standard CDO models to the complete set of CDX.IG and ITRAXX.IG tranche quotes. The inability to calibrate the standard CDO models has been attributed to the assumption that recovery at default is deterministic, and does not depend on time or state variables. This has led to adding stochastic recovery to CDO models (c.f. [8–13]), which is now standard practice in industry.

However, stochastic recovery has not yet received equally widespread interest and acceptance for other credit products such as defaultable bonds, credit default swaps and credit linked notes. In fact, there are a dearth of pricing formulas for credit products where recovery is modeled explicitly. This has become commonplace even though recovery is clearly a key component in the determination of credit spreads [14]. One recent approach to stochastic recovery modeling can be found in [15]. Take for example bond pricing, where the price of a zero-coupon defaultable bond is given by the risk-neutral expected present value of the payoff Π_τ (where τ is the default time):

$$\Pi_\tau := N\mathbb{1}_{\{\tau>T\}} + R_\tau \mathbb{1}_{\{\tau\le T\}}. \tag{1}$$

The first term describes receiving the full repayment of the notional N at maturity T in the event of no default (i.e., $\tau > T$), while the second term describes receiving a recovery R_τ in the event of default before maturity (i.e., $\tau \leq T$). The price of a zero-coupon defaultable bond is therefore given by

$$\begin{aligned} B_{t,T} &= \widetilde{\mathbb{E}}_t[D(t, \tau \wedge T)\Pi_\tau] \\ &= N D(t,T)\widetilde{\mathbb{P}}_t[\tau > T] + \widetilde{\mathbb{E}}_t[D(t,\tau)R_\tau \mathbb{1}_{\{\tau \leq T\}}] \end{aligned} \tag{2}$$

where $\wedge$ is the min operator $a \wedge b := \min\{a, b\}$, $\widetilde{\mathbb{P}}_t$ (resp. $\widetilde{\mathbb{E}}_t$) is the risk-neutral probability of default (resp. risk-neutral expectation) conditioned on information about the default and recovery process known at t, and $D(t,s)$ is the present value of a dollar at time t received at time s. To evaluate (2) one needs a model for D, default time τ, and recovery at default R_τ. As noted in [15], it is common in structural models such as the Merton and Black-Cox models to make the simplifying assumption that a single risk factor A_t representing the evolution of the underlying firm assets determines both the default time τ and recovery at default R_τ. Symbolically, for a fixed $f \in [0,1]$ and a filtered probability space $\left(\Omega, \{\mathcal{F}_t^A\}_{t \geq 0}, \mathcal{F}, \widetilde{\mathbb{P}}\right)$,

$$\begin{aligned} \{\tau \leq t\} &\in \mathcal{F}_t^A, \quad \forall t \geq 0 \\ R_\tau &:= f A_\tau \end{aligned} \tag{3}$$

where the natural filtration $\mathcal{F}_t^A$ is the minimal $\sigma-$algebra containing $\sigma(A_u)$ for all $u \in [0,t]$. Under this assumption, the price of a defaultable zero-coupon bond simplifies to

$$B_{t,T} = N D(t,T)\widetilde{\mathbb{P}}_t[\tau > T] + f\widetilde{\mathbb{E}}_t[D(t,\tau)A_\tau \mathbb{1}_{\{\tau \leq T\}}] \tag{4}$$

which can be computed using only the single risk factor A_t.

The lack of recovery modeling is even more explicit in the case of pricing Credit Default Swaps. For instance, the value of the default protection leg of a CDS per unit notional is given by

$$V_{t,T}^{\text{Protection}} = \widetilde{\mathbb{E}}_t\left[D(t,\tau)(1 - R_\tau)\mathbb{1}_{\{\tau \leq T\}}\right] \tag{5}$$

which is the expected risk-neutral discounted recovery amount given default. However, it is common to make the simplifying assumption that recovery is a constant so that $R_\tau \equiv R$ in (5) and the recovery term can be taken out of the expectation to obtain the simplified expression

$$V_{t,T}^{\text{Protection}} = (1 - R)\widetilde{\mathbb{E}}_t\left[D(t,\tau)\mathbb{1}_{\{\tau \leq T\}}\right]. \tag{6}$$

Under this simplifying assumption, which is standard in typical CDS pricing (c.f. [16–18] etc.), one simply needs a model for default τ and need not concern themselves with modeling recovery in the event of default. In this paper, we explicitly model recovery and remove the constant recovery assumption in CDS pricing thereby valuing the protection leg of the CDS using (5) directly rather than (6).

As described by the above examples of bond and CDS pricing, lack of recovery modeling inherent in classical structural models such as Merton and Black-Cox stems from the fact that default and recovery are driven by the same process. This feature makes it impossible to disentangle the effects of default and recovery. For instance, in the Merton model [19], the default time is defined as

$$\tau_{\text{Merton}} := T\mathbb{1}_{\{A_T < N\}} + \infty\mathbb{1}_{\{A_T \geq N\}}. \tag{7}$$

This default time has the benefit that recovery at default is random in the sense that it is defined through the random variable A_T. However, a deficiency in the model is that default is only possible at the maturity T of the bond (i.e., $\tau_{\text{Merton}} \in \{T, \infty\}$). This is in direct violation of empirical evidence showing that firms default on their bonds at times before maturity as well. Black & Cox introduced their model [20] in order to remove this deficiency by allowing default to occur at times up to and including maturity (i.e., $\tau_{BC} \in \{[0,T], \infty\}$). The authors are able to achieve this by introducing an additional first passage default time τ_K, defined as the first time the assets A_t are less than the barrier K:

$$\tau_K := \arg\inf\{t \in [0,\infty) : A_t \leq K\} \tag{8}$$

with the usual convention that $\inf\{\emptyset\} = +\infty$. The full Black-Cox default time τ_{BC} is then

$$\tau_{BC} \quad = \tau_K \mathbb{1}_{\{\tau_K \leq T\}} + T\mathbb{1}_{\{\tau_K > T, A_T < N\}} + \infty \mathbb{1}_{\{\tau_K > T, A_T \geq N\}}. \tag{9}$$

However, the very same default mechanism in the Black-Cox model that allows for default before maturity forces recovery at default to be a constant. That is, (9) implies that for default before maturity, the asset value at default is equal to the predetermined constant barrier K (i.e., $A_{\tau_{BC}} = K$). Hence Black-Cox improves the default modeling of Merton at the expense of constraining recovery to a predetermined known constant K when $\tau_{BC} < T$.[1] The main reason for this is that the Black-Cox model (as in all one-factor structural models) intertwines default and recovery risks. In one-factor structural models, the same process that determines default, namely A_t, also determines recovery. This structure results in default and recovery rates being multiplicatively linked through the credit spread, which in turn makes the separation of default risk from recovery risk impossible. To disentangle the default risk from the recovery risk in a structural model, one needs to introduce a separate recovery risk driver. This leads us to the Stochastic Recovery Black-Cox model considered herein.

This paper is organized as follows. In Section 2, we review the classic Black-Cox (BC) model as a benchmark for our later results in Section 4 where we include recovery risk. In Section 3, we motivate the need for adding a recovery risk driver into the BC model and present our correlated asset-recovery model (49), which we compare with Moody's PD-LGD model presented in [4]. In Section 4, we define the Stochastic Recovery Black-Cox (SRBC) model and use it to price instruments based on credit quality. Specifically, in Sections 4.1 and 4.4, we price bonds and CDS with the SRBC model. The SRBC setting is essentially a two-factor Black-Cox model where the extra factor is recovery risk. We then compare the prices obtained from the two-factor SRBC model with the original Black-Cox model. In Section 5, we provide an algorithm to compute the market implied recovery rate as well as analytical formulas for the recovery risk premium. Finally, in Section 6, we investigate the addition of coupon payments to bond prices in the stochastic recovery structural model.

2. Review of Credit Risk and Pricing in the Black-Cox Model

In this section, we briefly review bond and CDS pricing in the classical Black-Cox framework. In the original Black-Cox model [20], the default boundary K was taken to be exponential in time, i.e., $K(t) = Ke^{-\beta(T-t)}$. However to simplify the exposition and results, we consider the case of a flat-boundary corresponding to $\beta = 0$, i.e., $K(t) \equiv K$, although the results can be trivially extended to the exponential boundary case as well. The results of this section will mainly serve as a benchmark for which to compare the results in Sections 4.1 and 4.4, where recovery risk is incorporated into Bond and CDS pricing via the Stochastic Recovery Black-Cox model described in Section 3.

We begin by listing the assumptions that form the Black-Cox model.

---

1 This constraint can be improved upon slightly by introducing a curved (time-dependent) boundary $\tau_K := \arg\inf\{t \in [0,T] : A_t \leq K(t)\}$ for a suitably chosen $K(t)$. However, the fact remains there is still a single driver for both recovery and default.

Assumption 1. (Constant Rates) *The short rate is assumed to be a constant r so that the discount factor is given by*

$$D(t,s) = e^{-r(s-t)}. \tag{10}$$

Assumption 2. (Asset Dynamics) *The* $\widetilde{\mathbb{P}}_t$*-dynamics of the firms asset value* A_t *at time t are assumed to follow*

$$dA_t = rA_t dt + \sigma_A A_t dW_t^A. \tag{11}$$

where r, σ_A *are constant and* W_t^A *is a standard Brownian process.*

Assumption 3. (Default Time) *Default is defined as*

$$\tau_{\mathrm{BC}} = \tau_{\mathrm{K}} \mathbb{1}_{\{\tau_{\mathrm{K}} \leq T\}} + T \mathbb{1}_{\{\tau_{\mathrm{K}} > T, A_T < N\}} + \infty \mathbb{1}_{\{\tau_{\mathrm{K}} > T, A_T \geq N\}}. \tag{12}$$

where τ_{BC} *is explicitly given in* (9).

Assumption 4. (Recovery Dynamics) *Recovery at default is given by the asset value at default,*

$$R_{\tau_{\mathrm{BC}}} = A_{\tau_{\mathrm{BC}}}. \tag{13}$$

The collection of Assumptions 1–4 form the Black-Cox model, and can be used to price defaultable bonds as well as other products such as CDS which we do in Sections 2.1 and 2.2 below.

Assumption 4 isn't often thought of as an explicit assumption of the Black-Cox model, since, as a one-factor model, this assumption is embedded in the default time. This is another example of the intertwining of default and recovery. Furthermore, notice in Assumption 4 that if $\tau_{\mathrm{BC}} < T$ then by definition $A_{\tau_{\mathrm{BC}}} \equiv K$ so recovery given default is constant and deterministic. The main focus of this paper is to remove Assumption 4 and allow for stochastic recovery at default by decoupling the asset risk driver from the recovery risk driver. This should not be confused with adding stochasticity to the default boundary (c.f. [21,22]) since single-factor models with stochastic boundary still cannot disentangle the credit puzzle, as again, the asset value determines both default and recovery amount at default.

The Black-Cox model can be used to price credit products and compute related credit risk measures. For instance, in the case of a zero-coupon bond the price of such a defaultable zero-coupon bond is then given by the risk-neutral pricing formula

$$\begin{aligned} B_{t,T} &= N\widetilde{\mathbb{E}}_t[D(t,T)\,\mathbb{1}_{\{\tau > T\}}] + \widetilde{\mathbb{E}}_t[D(t,\tau)R_\tau\,\mathbb{1}_{\{\tau \leq T\}}] \\ &= ND(t,T)\,\widetilde{\mathbb{P}}_t[\tau > T] + \widetilde{\mathbb{E}}_t[D(t,\tau)R_\tau\,\mathbb{1}_{\{\tau \leq T\}}]. \end{aligned} \tag{14}$$

Given the price of a defaultable zero-coupon bond via (14), we define the credit spread of the bond $B_{t,T}$ as the spread $S_{t,T}$ over the risk-free rate r which reprices the bond. Thus $S_{t,T}$ is defined implicitly by the solution to

$$B_{t,T} = Ne^{-(r+S_{t,T})(T-t)} \tag{15}$$

which returns the formula

$$S_{t,T} = \frac{1}{T-t}\ln\left(\frac{N}{B_{t,T}}\right) - r. \tag{16}$$

The risk-neutral probability of default $\widetilde{\mathrm{PD}}_{t,T}$ at time t is defined as the probability under the risk-neutral measure $\widetilde{\mathbb{P}}$ that the default event τ occurs at or before maturity T,

$$\widetilde{\mathrm{PD}}_{t,T} = \widetilde{\mathbb{P}}_t\left[\tau \leq T\right]. \tag{17}$$

The risk-neutral expected loss given default $\widetilde{\mathrm{LGD}}_{t,T}$ at time t is defined as

$$\widetilde{\mathrm{LGD}}_{t,T} = 1 - \frac{\widetilde{\mathbb{E}}_t[D(t,\tau)R_\tau \mid \tau \leq T]}{D(t,T)N} \tag{18}$$

The term structure of expected Recovery Given Default $\widetilde{R}_{t,T}$ can easily be inferred from the term structure of Loss Given Default (18) via the relation $\widetilde{\mathrm{LGD}}_{t,T} = 1 - \widetilde{\mathrm{R}}_{t,T}$.

The other credit product we consider is a Credit Default Swap (CDS). In a CDS, one party (the buyer) pays premiums to another party (the seller) to insure against default on a bond (c.f. [16–18]). Pricing consists of separately modeling the present value of the fixed premiums paid by the protection buyer, and the present value of the contingent default payment leg received by the buyer. The difference between the two is then the value of the CDS. If there is no upfront fee at initiation of the contract, then the premium P is given as the value that makes the contract worthless at initiation.

To be more precise, let T be the expiry of the CDS contract and let $\mathbb{T}_n := \{t = t_0, t_1, t_2, ...t_n = T\}$ be the premium payment dates. For $i = 1...n$ we define $\Delta t_i = t_i - t_{i-1}$ to be the time between payments. The premium leg of the transaction is then given by the expected present value of the premium payments $P_{t,T}$ that the buyer pays (and seller receives), namely

$$V^{\text{Premium}}_{t,T} = P_{t,T}N \times \left(\sum_{i=1}^{n} D(t,t_i)\widetilde{\mathbb{P}}_t[\tau > t_i]\Delta t_i + \mathcal{A}_p\right) \tag{19}$$

where $\mathcal{A}_p$ is the accrual payment in case default occurs between two payment dates. Instead of considering premiums paid at discrete dates, we pass to the continuous limit (see [23]) and consider the continuous premium formulation

$$\begin{aligned} V^{\text{Premium}}_{t,T} &= P_{t,T}N \times \left(\widetilde{\mathbb{E}}_t\left[\int_t^T D(t,s)\mathbb{1}_{\{\tau>s\}}ds\right] + \frac{1}{2}\cdot\widetilde{\mathbb{E}}_t\left[D(t,\tau)\mathbb{1}_{\{\tau\leq T\}}\right]\right) \\ &= P_{t,T}N \times \left(\int_t^T e^{-r(s-t)}\widetilde{\mathbb{P}}_t[\tau > s]ds + \frac{1}{2}\cdot\int_t^T e^{-r(s-t)}\widetilde{\mathbb{P}}_t[\tau \in ds]\right) \end{aligned} \tag{20}$$

where the second term is the value of the accrual, i.e.,

$$\mathcal{A}_p := \frac{1}{2}\int_t^T D(t,s)\widetilde{\mathbb{P}}_t\left[\tau \in ds\right]. \tag{21}$$

Under the same continuous premium formulation, the value of the protection (default) leg can then be written as

$$\begin{aligned} V^{\text{Protection}}_{t,T} &= N \times \left(\widetilde{\mathbb{E}}_t\left[D(t,\tau)\left(1 - \frac{R_\tau}{N}\right)\mathbb{1}_{\{\tau\leq T\}}\right]\right) \\ &= N\widetilde{\mathbb{E}}_t\left[D(t,\tau\wedge T)\right] - B_{t,T} \\ &= N\left(D(t,T)\widetilde{\mathbb{P}}_t\left[\tau > T\right] + \widetilde{\mathbb{E}}_t\left[D(t,\tau)\mathbb{1}_{\{\tau\leq T\}}\right]\right) - B_{t,T}. \end{aligned} \tag{22}$$

Using usual no arbitrage principles, the CDS premium $P_{t,T}$ is given as the value that balances these two equations, namely

$$\begin{aligned}
P_{t,T} &= \frac{\widetilde{\mathbb{E}}_t\left[D(t,\tau)\left(1-\frac{R_\tau}{N}\right)\mathbb{1}_{\{\tau\leq T\}}\right]}{\int_t^T D(t,s)\widetilde{\mathbb{P}}_t[\tau>s]ds+\frac{1}{2}\int_t^T D(t,s)\widetilde{\mathbb{P}}_t\left[\tau\in ds\right]} \\
&= \frac{1}{N}\frac{N\left(D(t,T)\widetilde{\mathbb{P}}_t\left[\tau>T\right]+\widetilde{\mathbb{E}}_t\left[D(t,\tau)\mathbb{1}_{\{\tau\leq T\}}\right]\right)-B_{t,T}}{\int_t^T D(t,s)\widetilde{\mathbb{P}}_t[\tau>s]ds+\frac{1}{2}\int_t^T D(t,s)\widetilde{\mathbb{P}}_t\left[\tau\in ds\right]} \\
&= \frac{D(t,T)\widetilde{\mathbb{P}}_t\left[\tau>T\right]+\widetilde{\mathbb{E}}_t\left[D(t,\tau)\mathbb{1}_{\{\tau\leq T\}}\right]-\frac{B_{t,T}}{N}}{\widetilde{\mathbb{E}}_t\left[\int_t^T D(t,s)\mathbb{1}_{\{\tau>s\}}ds\right]+\frac{1}{2}\cdot\widetilde{\mathbb{E}}_t\left[D(t,\tau)\mathbb{1}_{\{\tau\leq T\}}\right]} \\
&= \frac{e^{-r(T-t)}\widetilde{\mathbb{P}}_t\left[\tau>T\right]+\widetilde{\mathbb{E}}_t\left[e^{-r(\tau-t)}\mathbb{1}_{\{\tau\leq T\}}\right]-\frac{B_{t,T}}{N}}{\widetilde{\mathbb{E}}_t\left[\int_t^{\tau\wedge T} e^{-r(s-t)}ds\right]+\frac{1}{2}\cdot\widetilde{\mathbb{E}}_t\left[e^{-r(\tau-t)}\mathbb{1}_{\{\tau\leq T\}}\right]}.
\end{aligned} \tag{23}$$

To evaluate (23), we need a model for recovery R_t and default τ. A standard assumption [17] in a hazard rate framework is that recovery is a constant, under which our CDS premium (23) reduces to the classical result

$$P_{t,T} = (1-\bar{R})\frac{\widetilde{\mathbb{E}}_t\left[D(t,\tau)\mathbb{1}_{\{\tau\leq T\}}\right]}{\widetilde{\mathbb{E}}_t\left[\int_t^T D(t,s)\mathbb{1}_{\{\tau>s\}}ds\right]+\frac{1}{2}\cdot\widetilde{\mathbb{E}}_t\left[D(t,\tau)\mathbb{1}_{\{\tau\leq T\}}\right]} \tag{24}$$

where $\bar{R} = R_\tau/N$.

In Sections 2.1 and 2.2 we present Bond and CDS prices, respectively, for the Black-Cox model which does not account for recovery risk. In Sections 4.1 and 4.4, respectively, we present bond and CDS prices under the Stochastic Recovery Black-Cox model which does take into account recovery risk.

2.1. Bond Pricing with the Black-Cox Model

In this section we price a zero coupon bond with default risk using the Black-Cox model. The structure of the price depends on whether the boundary K is larger or smaller than the notional N.

Definition 1. (Weak and Strong Covenants in Black-Cox Model) *Let K be the default barrier and N be the notional of the zero-coupon bond in the Black-Cox framework. We say the bond has a weak (resp. strong) covenant if $K \leq N$ (resp. $K \geq N$).*

Definition 2. (Distances to Default) *Define the following distance to default, which we will use in bond and CDS pricing under both weak and strong covenants.*

• *Weak Covenant* $(K \leq N)$

$$
\begin{aligned}
d_0^w &= \frac{\ln\left(\frac{A_t}{N}\right) + (r - \frac{1}{2}\sigma_A^2)(T-t)}{\sigma_A\sqrt{T-t}} \\
d_1^w &= \frac{\ln\left(\frac{A_t}{N}\right) + (r + \frac{1}{2}\sigma_A^2)(T-t)}{\sigma_A\sqrt{T-t}} \\
x_0^w &= \frac{\ln\left(\frac{K^2}{NA_t}\right) + (r - \frac{1}{2}\sigma_A^2)(T-t)}{\sigma_A\sqrt{T-t}} \\
x_1^w &= \frac{\ln\left(\frac{K^2}{NA_t}\right) + (r + \frac{1}{2}\sigma_A^2)(T-t)}{\sigma_A\sqrt{T-t}}
\end{aligned} \tag{25}
$$

• *Strong Covenant* $(K \geq N)$

$$
\begin{aligned}
d_0^s &= \frac{\ln\left(\frac{A_t}{K}\right) + (r - \frac{1}{2}\sigma_A^2)(T-t)}{\sigma_A\sqrt{T-t}} \\
d_1^s &= \frac{\ln\left(\frac{A_t}{K}\right) + (r + \frac{1}{2}\sigma_A^2)(T-t)}{\sigma_A\sqrt{T-t}} \\
x_0^s &= \frac{\ln\left(\frac{K}{A_t}\right) + (r - \frac{1}{2}\sigma_A^2)(T-t)}{\sigma_A\sqrt{T-t}} \\
x_1^s &= \frac{\ln\left(\frac{K}{A_t}\right) + (r + \frac{1}{2}\sigma_A^2)(T-t)}{\sigma_A\sqrt{T-t}}
\end{aligned} \tag{26}
$$

Notice that the weak covenant distances to default d_0^w, d_1^w are the usual Merton distances to default (c.f. [15]).

Lemma 1. (Probability of Hitting the Barrier) *Let τ_K be the first passage time* (8). *Then for any constant default barrier $K > 0$ and $A_t \geq K$*

$$
\widetilde{\mathbb{P}}_t\left[\tau_K \leq T\right] = \Phi(-d_0^s) + \left(\frac{K}{A}\right)^{\frac{2r}{\sigma_A^2}-1} \Phi(x_0^s) \tag{27}
$$

where Φ is the cumulative normal distribution function and d_0^s, x_0^s are given by (26).

Proof. We begin this proof by noting that the value of a bond in the Black-Cox model requires a barrier at covenant value K. One can therefore calculate directly the probability of no-default using barrier option theory. To carry out this computation, we define the function W corresponding to a digital option: t

$$
W(A,t) := \widetilde{\mathbb{P}}_t\left[A_T > N\right] = \Phi\left(d_0^w\right) = 1 - \widetilde{\mathrm{PD}}_{t,T}^{\mathrm{Merton}}. \tag{28}
$$

From this definition (28) of W, if we add a lower barrier at K (See for example Ch.10 in [24]) then the value $\bar{W}$ of a digital option with a lower barrier at K is

$$\begin{aligned}\bar{W}(A,t) &:= \widetilde{\mathbb{P}}_0[A_T > N, \tau_K > T] = W(A,t) - \left(\frac{K}{A}\right)^{\frac{2r}{\sigma_A^2}-1} W\left(\frac{K^2}{A},t\right) \\ &= \Phi\left(d_0^w\right) - \left(\frac{K}{A}\right)^{\frac{2r}{\sigma_A^2}-1} \Phi\left(x_0^w\right).\end{aligned} \tag{29}$$

Therefore, by setting $N = K$ in (25) and (29), we obtain the result

$$\widetilde{\mathbb{P}}_t[\tau_K > T] = \widetilde{\mathbb{P}}_t[A_T > K, \tau_K > T] = \Phi\left(d_0^s\right) - \left(\frac{K}{A}\right)^{\frac{2r}{\sigma_A^2}-1} \Phi\left(x_0^s\right) \tag{30}$$

and (27) above follows.

□

Note: The result (27) can also be found in, for instance, Appendix B of [25]. We provide another direct proof within the constructive proof of Theorem 3 below, by computing $\int_K^\infty \widetilde{\mathbb{P}}_t\left[A_T \in da, \tau_K > T\right]$ in the strong covenant case.

Theorem 1. (Bond Pricing under the Black-Cox Model) *Suppose that Assumptions 1–4 are satisfied. Then the price of a defaultable zero-coupon bond* (14) *is given by:*

I. Weak Covenant Case. *If $K \leq N$ the price of a zero-coupon bond is given by*

$$\begin{aligned}B_{t,T}^{\mathrm{BC}}(w) &= e^{-r(T-t)} N \left[\Phi(d_0^w) - \left(\frac{K}{A_t}\right)^{\frac{2r}{\sigma_A^2}-1} \Phi(x_0^w)\right] \\ &+ A_t \left[\Phi(-d_1^w) + \left(\frac{K}{A_t}\right)^{\frac{2r}{\sigma_A^2}+1} \Phi(x_1^w)\right]\end{aligned} \tag{31}$$

and the risk-neutral PD and LGD in the case of a weak covenant are

$$\widetilde{\mathrm{PD}}_{t,T}^{\mathrm{BC}}(w) = \Phi\left(-d_0^w\right) + \left(\frac{K}{A_t}\right)^{\frac{2r}{\sigma_A^2}-1} \Phi(x_0^w) \tag{32}$$

and

$$\widetilde{\mathrm{LGD}}_{t,T}^{BC}(w) = 1 - e^{r(T-t)} \frac{A_t}{N} \frac{\Phi\left(-d_1^w\right) + \left(\frac{K}{A_t}\right)^{\frac{2r}{\sigma_A^2}+1} \Phi\left(x_1^w\right)}{\Phi\left(-d_0^w\right) + \left(\frac{K}{A_t}\right)^{\frac{2r}{\sigma_A^2}-1} \Phi\left(x_0^w\right)}. \tag{33}$$

II. Strong Covenant Case. *If $K \geq N$ the price of a zero-coupon bond is given by*

$$\begin{aligned}B_{t,T}^{\mathrm{BC}}(s) &= e^{-r(T-t)} N \left[\Phi(d_0^s) - \left(\frac{K}{A_t}\right)^{\frac{2r}{\sigma_A^2}-1} \Phi(x_0^s)\right] \\ &+ A_t \left[\Phi(-d_1^s) + \left(\frac{K}{A_t}\right)^{\frac{2r}{\sigma_A^2}+1} \Phi(x_1^s)\right]\end{aligned} \tag{34}$$

and the risk-neutral PD and LGD in the case of a strong covenant are

$$\widetilde{\mathrm{PD}}^{\mathrm{BC}}_{t,T}(s) = \Phi\left(-d_0^s\right) + \left(\frac{K}{A_t}\right)^{\frac{2r}{\sigma_A^2}-1} \Phi(x_0^s) \tag{35}$$

and

$$\widetilde{\mathrm{LGD}}^{\mathrm{BC}}_{t,T}(s) = 1 - e^{r(T-t)} \frac{A_t}{N} \frac{\Phi\left(-d_1^s\right) + \left(\frac{K}{A_t}\right)^{\frac{2r}{\sigma_A^2}+1} \Phi\left(x_1^s\right)}{\Phi\left(-d_0^s\right) + \left(\frac{K}{A_t}\right)^{\frac{2r}{\sigma_A^2}-1} \Phi\left(x_0^s\right)}. \tag{36}$$

Proof. The proof uses the same integral techniques employed in Theorem 3 below. Using the barrier option characterization of the addition of a covenant, the price of a bond is expressed as

$$\begin{aligned} B^{\mathrm{BC}}_{t,T} &= Ne^{-r(T-t)} \cdot \widetilde{\mathbb{P}}_t[A_T \geq N, \tau_K > T] + \widetilde{\mathbb{E}}_t[e^{-r(T-t)} A_T \mathbb{1}_{\{A_T \geq N, \tau_K > T\}^c}] \\ &= Ne^{-r(T-t)} \cdot \widetilde{\mathbb{P}}_t[A_T \geq N, \tau_K > T] + A_t - \widetilde{\mathbb{E}}_t[e^{-r(T-t)} A_T \mathbb{1}_{\{A_T \geq N, \tau_K > T\}}]. \end{aligned} \tag{37}$$

This computation requires the joint density $\tilde{\mathbb{P}}_t[A_T \in da, \tau_K > T]$, which is found in [26]. We compute the associated integrals explicitly in our constructive proof of Theorem 3 for the case of stochastic recovery in the Black-Cox framework.

To carry out these integrals for the standard Black-Cox model, we set $\gamma = \rho_{A,R} = \frac{A_0}{R_0} = 1$ in the integrals constructed for the proof of Theorem 3. The difference between the weak and strong covenant cases (with or without stochastic recovery) is that in the strong covenant case,

$$\{A_T \geq N, \tau_K > T\} = \{A_T \geq K, \tau_K > T\} = \{\tau_K > T\}. \tag{38}$$

This fact is reflected in the appropriate substitution in the lower limits of the integrals against the joint density $\tilde{\mathbb{P}}_t[A_T \in da, \tau_K > T]$.

□

Remark 1. (Special Case where $K = N$) *Note that the special case where $K = N$ is included in both the strong and weak covenant formulas in that*

$$\begin{aligned} &\lim_{K \to N+} B^{\mathrm{BC}}_{t,T}(s) = \lim_{K \to N-} B^{\mathrm{BC}}_{t,T}(w) \\ &= e^{-r(T-t)} \left[N\Phi(-d_0) - \left(\frac{N}{A_t}\right)^{\frac{2r}{\sigma_A^2}-1} \Phi(x_0) \right] + A_t \left[\Phi(-d_1) + \left(\frac{N}{A_t}\right)^{\frac{2r}{\sigma_A^2}+1} \Phi(x_1) \right]. \end{aligned} \tag{39}$$

2.2. CDS Pricing with the Black-Cox Model

We now price CDS premiums using the Black-Cox model. In keeping with the continuous CDS pricing model, we extend the premium rate defined in [23] to include recovery at τ_{BC} while protection is paid as long as τ_K has not occurred.

Theorem 2. (CDS Premium under Black-Cox Model) *Suppose that Assumptions 1–4 are satisfied. Then the CDS premium* (23) *is given by*

$$P^{\mathrm{BC}}_{t,T} = \frac{e^{-r(T-t)} \widetilde{\mathbb{P}}_t\left[\tau_{\mathrm{BC}} > T\right] + \widetilde{\mathbb{E}}_t\left[e^{-r(\tau_{\mathrm{BC}}-t)} \mathbb{1}_{\{\tau_{\mathrm{BC}} \leq T\}}\right] - \frac{B^{\mathrm{BC}}_{t,T}}{N}}{\frac{1 - \widetilde{\mathbb{E}}_t[e^{-r(\tau_{\mathrm{BC}}-t)} \mathbb{1}_{\{\tau_{\mathrm{BC}} \leq T\}}] - e^{-r(T-t)} \widetilde{\mathbb{P}}_t[\tau_{\mathrm{BC}} > T]}{r} + \frac{1}{2} \cdot \widetilde{\mathbb{E}}_t\left[e^{-r(\tau_{\mathrm{BC}}-t)} \mathbb{1}_{\{\tau_{\mathrm{BC}} \leq T\}}\right]}. \tag{40}$$

In the strong covenant case, where $K \geq N$, this reduces to the closed formula

$$P^{\mathrm{BC}}_{t,T}(s) = \frac{e^{-r(T-t)}\widetilde{\mathbb{P}}_t\left[\tau_{\mathrm{K}} > T\right] + \widetilde{\mathbb{E}}_t\left[e^{-r(\tau_{\mathrm{K}}-t)}\mathbb{1}_{\{\tau_{\mathrm{K}} \leq T\}}\right] - \frac{B^{\mathrm{BC}}_{t,T}(s)}{N}}{\frac{1-\widetilde{\mathbb{E}}_t[e^{-r(\tau_{\mathrm{K}}-t)}\mathbb{1}_{\{\tau_{\mathrm{K}}\leq T\}}]-e^{-r(T-t)}\widetilde{\mathbb{P}}_t[\tau_{\mathrm{K}}>T]}{r} + \frac{1}{2}\cdot\widetilde{\mathbb{E}}_t\left[e^{-r(\tau_{\mathrm{K}}-t)}\mathbb{1}_{\{\tau_{\mathrm{K}}\leq T\}}\right]}$$

$$\widetilde{\mathbb{P}}_t\left[\tau_{\mathrm{K}} > T\right] = \Phi\left(d_0^s\right) - \left(\frac{K}{A_t}\right)^{\frac{2r}{\sigma_A^2}-1}\Phi\left(x_0^s\right) = 1 - \widetilde{\mathrm{PD}}^{\mathrm{BC}}_{t,T}(s) \tag{41}$$

$$\widetilde{\mathbb{E}}_t[e^{-r(\tau_{\mathrm{K}}-t)}\mathbb{1}_{\{\tau_{\mathrm{K}}\leq T\}}] = A_t\left[\Phi(-d_1^s) + \left(\frac{K}{A_t}\right)^{\frac{2r}{\sigma_A^2}+1}\Phi(x_1^s)\right].$$

In the weak covenant case, where $K \geq N$, this reduces to the closed formula

$$P^{\mathrm{BC}}_{t,T}(w) = \frac{e^{-r(T-t)}\widetilde{\mathbb{P}}_t\left[\tau_{\mathrm{BC}} > T\right] + \widetilde{\mathbb{E}}_t\left[e^{-r(\tau_{\mathrm{BC}}-t)}\mathbb{1}_{\{\tau_{\mathrm{BC}} \leq T\}}\right] - \frac{B^{\mathrm{BC}}_{t,T}(w)}{N}}{\frac{1-\widetilde{\mathbb{E}}_t[e^{-r(\tau_{\mathrm{BC}}-t)}\mathbb{1}_{\{\tau_{\mathrm{BC}}\leq T\}}]-e^{-r(T-t)}\widetilde{\mathbb{P}}_t[\tau_{\mathrm{BC}}>T]}{r} + \frac{1}{2}\cdot\widetilde{\mathbb{E}}_t\left[e^{-r(\tau_{\mathrm{BC}}-t)}\mathbb{1}_{\{\tau_{\mathrm{BC}}\leq T\}}\right]}$$

$$\widetilde{\mathbb{P}}_t\left[\tau_{\mathrm{BC}} > T\right] = \widetilde{\mathbb{P}}_t\left[\tau_{\mathrm{K}} > T, A_T \geq N\right] = 1 - \widetilde{\mathrm{PD}}^{\mathrm{BC}}_{t,T}(w)$$

$$\widetilde{\mathbb{P}}_t\left[\tau_{\mathrm{K}} > T\right] = \Phi\left(d_0^s\right) - \left(\frac{K}{A_t}\right)^{\frac{2r}{\sigma_A^2}-1}\Phi\left(x_0^s\right) = 1 - \widetilde{\mathrm{PD}}^{\mathrm{BC}}_{t,T}(s) \tag{42}$$

$$\widetilde{\mathbb{E}}_t\left[e^{-r(\tau_{\mathrm{BC}}-t)}\mathbb{1}_{\{\tau_{\mathrm{BC}}\leq T\}}\right] = \widetilde{\mathbb{E}}_t[e^{-r(\tau_{\mathrm{K}}-t)}\mathbb{1}_{\{\tau_{\mathrm{K}}\leq T\}}] + e^{-r(T-t)}\left(\widetilde{\mathbb{P}}_t[\tau_{\mathrm{K}} > T] - \widetilde{\mathbb{P}}_t[\tau_{\mathrm{K}} > T, A_T \geq N]\right)$$

$$\widetilde{\mathbb{E}}_t[e^{-r(\tau_{\mathrm{K}}-t)}\mathbb{1}_{\{\tau_{\mathrm{K}}\leq T\}}] = A_t\left[\Phi(-d_1^s) + \left(\frac{K}{A_t}\right)^{\frac{2r}{\sigma_A^2}+1}\Phi(x_1^s)\right].$$

Note

- The numerator in (40) follows from direct substitution of the bond price calculated in Theorem 1 into the numerator in the general CDS formula (23). This direct substitution of the risky bond price also reflects the flexibility in assigning a weak or strong covenant, and will in fact be the only change observed when stochastic recovery is included in Section 5.
- To complete the proof of Theorem 2, we will need to compute the denominator in (23). In the BC, and SRBC model forthcoming, this reduces to computing

$$\widetilde{\mathbb{E}}_t[e^{-r(\tau_{\mathrm{K}}-t)}\mathbb{1}_{\{\tau_{\mathrm{K}}\leq T\}}]. \tag{43}$$

We are able to compute (43) by reducing to something more manageable via the fact that the discounted asset price is a local martingale. The reduced form follows from the optional sampling theorem:

$$\widetilde{\mathbb{E}}_t[e^{-r(\tau_{\mathrm{K}}-t)}\mathbb{1}_{\{\tau_{\mathrm{K}}\leq T\}}] = \frac{A_t - \widetilde{\mathbb{E}}_t[e^{-r(T-t)}A_T\mathbb{1}_{\{\tau_{\mathrm{K}}>T\}}]}{K}. \tag{44}$$

Proof. From Assumption 4, the general CDS premium (23) reduces to

$$
\begin{aligned}
P_{t,T}^{\mathrm{BC}} &= \frac{e^{-r(T-t)}\widetilde{\mathbb{P}}_t\left[\tau_{\mathrm{BC}} > T\right] + \widetilde{\mathbb{E}}_t\left[e^{-r(\tau_{\mathrm{BC}}-t)}\mathbb{1}_{\{\tau_{\mathrm{BC}}\leq T\}}\right] - \frac{B_{t,T}^{\mathrm{BC}}}{N}}{\widetilde{\mathbb{E}}_t\left[\int_t^T e^{-r(T-t)}\mathbb{1}_{\{\tau_{\mathrm{BC}}>s\}}ds\right] + \frac{1}{2}\cdot\widetilde{\mathbb{E}}_t\left[e^{-r(\tau_{\mathrm{BC}}-t)}\mathbb{1}_{\{\tau_{\mathrm{BC}}\leq T\}}\right]} \\
&= \frac{e^{-r(T-t)}\widetilde{\mathbb{P}}_t\left[\tau_{\mathrm{BC}} > T\right] + \widetilde{\mathbb{E}}_t\left[e^{-r(\tau_{\mathrm{BC}}-t)}\mathbb{1}_{\{\tau_{\mathrm{BC}}\leq T\}}\right] - \frac{B_{t,T}^{\mathrm{BC}}}{N}}{\widetilde{\mathbb{E}}_t\left[\int_t^{\tau_{\mathrm{BC}}\wedge T} e^{-r(s-t)}ds\right] + \frac{1}{2}\cdot\widetilde{\mathbb{E}}_t\left[e^{-r(\tau_{\mathrm{BC}}-t)}\mathbb{1}_{\{\tau_{\mathrm{BC}}\leq T\}}\right]} \\
&= \frac{e^{-r(T-t)}\widetilde{\mathbb{P}}_t\left[\tau_{\mathrm{BC}} > T\right] + \widetilde{\mathbb{E}}_t\left[e^{-r(\tau_{\mathrm{BC}}-t)}\mathbb{1}_{\{\tau_{\mathrm{BC}}\leq T\}}\right] - \frac{B_{t,T}^{\mathrm{BC}}}{N}}{\frac{1-\widetilde{\mathbb{E}}_t[e^{-r(\tau_{\mathrm{BC}}-t)}\mathbb{1}_{\{\tau_{\mathrm{BC}}\leq T\}}]-e^{-r(T-t)}\widetilde{\mathbb{P}}_t[\tau_{\mathrm{BC}}>T]}{r} + \frac{1}{2}\cdot\widetilde{\mathbb{E}}_t\left[e^{-r(\tau_{\mathrm{BC}}-t)}\mathbb{1}_{\{\tau_{\mathrm{BC}}\leq T\}}\right]}.
\end{aligned}
\tag{45}
$$

The main quantity to solve for now is $\widetilde{\mathbb{E}}_t\left[e^{-r(\tau_{\mathrm{BC}}-t)}\mathbb{1}_{\{\tau_{\mathrm{BC}}\leq T\}}\right]$, and upon it's computation and insertion into (45), we have the formula for the premium. By the structural definition of τ_{BC}, it follows that

$$
\{\tau_{\mathrm{BC}} \leq T\} = \{\tau_{\mathrm{K}} \leq T\} \cup \{\tau_{\mathrm{K}} > T, K < A_T < N\} \tag{46}
$$

and so

$$
\begin{aligned}
\widetilde{\mathbb{P}}_t\left[\tau_{\mathrm{BC}} > T\right] &= \widetilde{\mathbb{P}}_t\left[\tau_{\mathrm{K}} > T, A_T \geq N\right] \\
\widetilde{\mathbb{E}}_t\left[e^{-r(\tau_{\mathrm{BC}}-t)}\mathbb{1}_{\{\tau_{\mathrm{BC}}\leq T\}}\right] &= \widetilde{\mathbb{E}}_t[e^{-r(\tau_{\mathrm{K}}-t)}\mathbb{1}_{\{\tau_{\mathrm{K}}\leq T\}}] + e^{-r(T-t)}\widetilde{\mathbb{P}}_t[\tau_{\mathrm{K}} > T, K < A_T < N] \\
&= \widetilde{\mathbb{E}}_t[e^{-r(\tau_{\mathrm{K}}-t)}\mathbb{1}_{\{\tau_{\mathrm{K}}\leq T\}}] \\
&\quad + e^{-r(T-t)}\left(\widetilde{\mathbb{P}}_t[\tau_{\mathrm{K}} > T] - \widetilde{\mathbb{P}}_t[\tau_{\mathrm{K}} > T, A_T \geq N]\right).
\end{aligned}
\tag{47}
$$

In the case $K \geq N$, the event $\{\tau_{\mathrm{BC}} > T\}$ reduces to the event $\{\tau_{\mathrm{K}} > T\}$. Consequently, we utilize (44), (45), and the integral in (81) below to return the value (41). In the case that $K \leq N$, similar calculations lead to (42).

□

3. Modeling Recovery Risk within a Structural Framework

The original Merton and Black-Cox structural models have been extended in several directions by many different authors, including stochastic interest rates, bankruptcy costs, taxes, debt subordination, strategic default, time dependent and stochastic default barrier, jumps in the asset value process, etc. While these extensions are by no means exhaustive (c.f. [16] for a more thorough discussion), they relax several of the main assumptions in the original models. However, none consider recovery as a risk factor, and assume the only risk driver is the asset value itself, or perhaps interest rates if stochastic rates are modeled. Empirical research, however, has shown that recoveries need not be constant in time and that typically the time-series of default probabilities and recoveries are inversely correlated [1,27]. To make matters even more complicated, Hillebrand [28] shows that this correlation does not necessarily have to vary co-monotonously over the whole economic cycle. The correlation between PD and LGD has been investigated by several researchers in the context of credit capital. For instance, Giese [3] incorporates PG-LGD correlations into a single-factor Vasicek framework and finds that capital increases by up to 35% at the 99.9% confidence interval for high-yield credit portfolios. While investigating stressed LGDs, Miu and Ozdemir [6] find that in order to compensate for neglecting the PD-LGD correlation in credit capital modeling, the mean LGD must be increased by about 37% from its unbiased estimate in order to compensate for the lack of correlations.

We incorporate recovery risk into the Black-Cox model for three main reasons. First, as discussed in Section 2, the Black-Cox model has a constant recovery K in the event of default before redemption time. However, there is a large body of empirical evidence showing that recovery rates are inversely correlated with probabilities of default [1,14,27,29–34] and so recovery risk is a real financial phenomena that should be modeled. Second, this correlation can have a very large effect on credit capital [5,6]. Ignoring this effect in a pricing model could potentially lead to large mispricings or significant misestimation of risk. Finally, we show that including recovery risk in a structural framework is a mechanism which allows for larger spreads. This is important because empirical literature suggests that structural models tend to underestimate observed credit spreads by 10–15% on average (c.f. [35–38]). In [39], Gemmill argues that the extra observed spread is explained by other factors such as liquidity risk. However, just as in the Merton case [15], we show in Lemma 9 that adding recovery risk can lead to an increase in the credit spread over constant recovery models, and suggest that recovery risk is another possible mechanism to explain the additional observed spread.

3.1. The Correlated Asset-Recovery Model

Let A_t denote the asset price at time $t > 0$ and let R_t denote the recovery amount at time $t > 0$. The unobservable process R_t is interpreted as the amount that would be recovered if default were to occur at t. The asset and recovery processes are modeled as two correlated geometric Brownian motions on $(\Omega, \mathcal{F}, \mathbb{P})$ given by

$$\begin{aligned} dA_t &= \mu_A A_t dt + \sigma_A A_t dW_t^A \\ dR_t &= \mu_R R_t dt + \sigma_R R_t dW_t^R \\ \rho_{A,R} dt &= dW_t^A dW_t^R \end{aligned} \tag{48}$$

where (W_t^A, W_t^R) are correlated, standard Brownian motions on our probability space.

3.2. Some Preliminary Results

Lemma 2. *(Existence of Risk Neutral Measure) Let (A_t, R_t) be the coupled measurable stochastic processes on $(\Omega, \mathcal{F}, \mathbb{P})$ given by (48). Then there exists a risk-neutral measure $\widetilde{\mathbb{P}}_t$ such that $(X_t, \mathcal{F}_t^X)$ is martingale under $\widetilde{\mathbb{P}}_t$, where X is the coupled process $X_t := e^{-rt}(A_t, R_t)$. Furthermore, (A_t, R_t) satisfy*

$$\begin{aligned} dA_t &= rA_t dt + \sigma_A A_t dW_t^A \\ dR_t &= rR_t dt + \sigma_R R_t dW_t^R. \end{aligned} \tag{49}$$

Proof. The proof follows from the results in [40] as the pair (A_t, R_t) is a two-dimensional diffusion. □

Lemma 3. *(Solution to the PD-LGD Equations) Let (A_t, R_t) be given by (48). Then, under the physical measure, (A_t, R_t) is given by*

$$\begin{aligned} A_t &= A_0 \exp\left((\mu_A - \frac{1}{2}\sigma_A^2)t + \sigma_A W_t^A\right) \\ R_t &= R_0 \exp\left((\mu_R - \frac{1}{2}\sigma_R^2)t + \sigma_R W_t^R\right) \end{aligned} \tag{50}$$

and under the risk-neutral measure,

$$\begin{aligned} A_t &= A_0 \exp\left((r - \frac{1}{2}\sigma_A^2)t + \sigma_A W_t^A\right) \\ R_t &= R_0 \exp\left((r - \frac{1}{2}\sigma_R^2)t + \sigma_R W_t^R\right). \end{aligned} \tag{51}$$

As an application of Lemma 3, we give a simple proof of Theorems 1–3 in [4]. This result is the first comparison of recovery to asset values when the underlying asset is in state K.

Lemma 4. *(Expected Recovery at Default) Consider the Asset-Recovery model (48) and define*

$$\gamma := \rho_{A,R}\frac{\sigma_R}{\sigma_A} \tag{52}$$

$$\delta^{\mathbb{P}} := (\mu_R - \frac{1}{2}\sigma_R^2) - \gamma(\mu_A - \frac{1}{2}\sigma_A^2) \tag{53}$$

$$\delta^{\widetilde{\mathbb{P}}} := \delta = (r - \frac{1}{2}\sigma_R^2) - \gamma(r - \frac{1}{2}\sigma_A^2). \tag{54}$$

Then

$$\widetilde{\mathbb{E}}[R_s|A_s = K] = \mathbb{E}[R_s|A_s = K]e^{(\delta^{\widetilde{\mathbb{P}}} - \delta^{\mathbb{P}})s} \tag{55}$$

where

$$\mathbb{E}[R_s|A_s = K] = R_0\left(\frac{K}{A_0}\right)^{\gamma} e^{\delta^{\mathbb{P}}s + \frac{1}{2}\sigma_R^2(1-\rho_{A,R}^2)s} \tag{56}$$

$$\widetilde{\mathbb{E}}[R_s|A_s = K] = R_0\left(\frac{K}{A_0}\right)^{\gamma} e^{\delta^{\widetilde{\mathbb{P}}}s + \frac{1}{2}\sigma_R^2(1-\rho_{A,R}^2)s}. \tag{57}$$

Proof. We consider first the behavior of X under the physical measure, and prove (56). By Lemmas 2 and 3, and by (48), we can consider now the solution form under two standard Brownian motions W_A and W on the probability space $(\Omega, \mathcal{F}, \widetilde{\mathbb{P}})$ where

$$\begin{aligned} A_t &= A_0 \exp\left((\mu_A - \frac{1}{2}\sigma_A^2)t + \sigma_A W_t^A\right) \\ R_t &= R_0 \exp\left((\mu_R - \frac{1}{2}\sigma_R^2)t + \sigma_R W_t^R\right) \\ W_t^R &= \rho_{A,R} W_t^A + \sqrt{1 - \rho_{A,R}^2} W_t \\ \mathbb{P}[dW_t^A dW_t &= 0] = 1. \end{aligned} \tag{58}$$

Using (58) the recovery process R_t under the physical measure can be explicitly written as

$$R_t = R_0\Big(\frac{A_t}{A_0}\Big)^{\gamma} \exp\left(\delta^{\mathbb{P}}t + \sigma_R\sqrt{1 - \rho_{A,R}^2}W_t\right) \tag{59}$$

where γ and $\delta^{\mathbb{P}}$ are defined by (52) and (53) respectively. Then, using (59) we have

$$\mathbb{E}[R_s|A_s = K] = \mathbb{E}\left[R_0\Big(\frac{A_s}{A_0}\Big)^{\gamma} \exp\left(\delta^{\mathbb{P}}s + \sigma_R\sqrt{1 - \rho_{A,R}^2}W_s\right)|A_s = K\right] \tag{60}$$

$$= R_0\Big(\frac{K}{A_0}\Big)^{\gamma}\mathbb{E}_s\left[\exp\left(\delta^{\mathbb{P}}s + \sigma_R\sqrt{1 - \rho_{A,R}^2}W_s\right)\right] \tag{61}$$

$$= R_0\left(\frac{K}{A_0}\right)^{\gamma} e^{\delta^{\mathbb{P}}s + \frac{1}{2}\sigma_R^2(1-\rho_{A,R}^2)s}. \tag{62}$$

To prove (57) we simply set $\mu_A = \mu_R = r$ in (59) to recognize R under the risk-neutral measure as a shift from $\delta^{\mathbb{P}}$ to $\delta^{\widetilde{\mathbb{P}}}$, and (55) follows directly by dividing the closed form solution (57) by (56). □

Under this framework, the price of a zero-coupon bond with face N is

$$B_{t,T} = \widetilde{\mathbb{E}}_t[Ne^{-r(T-t)}\mathbb{1}_{\{\tau>T\}}] + \widetilde{\mathbb{E}}_t[e^{-r(\tau-t)}R_\tau\mathbb{1}_{\{\tau\leq T\}}]. \tag{63}$$

where default τ depends on A_t and recovery upon default R_τ depends on R_t through (49), thus correlating default and recovery.

In Sections 4.1 and 4.4 we compute the bond and CDS prices (and related credit measures such as probability of default, loss-given-default and credit spreads) in the Stochastic Recovery Black-Cox default model where default time is defined via (9), but recovery is stochastic and correlated to asset value via (48).

3.3. Comparison of Recovery to Asset Upon Default

One of the features of the stochastic recovery model (48) we work with is that it is possible for the recovery value modeled, R_t, to surpass the asset value A_t at some time $t \leq T$. This is due to the fact that A is the manager's estimated asset value instead of the actual asset value upon recovery. Upon default, it may come to pass that the actual value is higher than the estimated asset value A. Hence, it is possible that when default occurs, the debt holders are paid in full, and there is still some remaining capital. So, $R_t > N > A_t$ is possible, for example. In fact, this is entirely possible when default occurs due to liquidity issues. In this context, A_t is the default driving process, and R_t the actual firm value. Hence, this model we work with proposes that there is less information about the asset than in the classic single-name models of Merton and Black and Cox. We also note here that in the end, it is the firm manager that decides firm default. Whether due to capital structure reasons or more pressingly due to day-to-day operational costs, it is the manager who has final say in this matter. This reinforces the fact that A is used to determine default, but R determines post-default recovery. We note that this allows for the possibility that credit spreads can be negative, at times. Given the correlated asset-recovery process (48), it is natural to estimate the probability that assets priced in recovery exceed the barrier K or notional N. The following Lemma provides such an estimate.

Lemma 5. *At the first passage time τ_K, we have the estimates*

$$\begin{aligned}
\widetilde{\mathbb{P}}_t[R_{\tau_K}\mathbb{1}_{\{\tau_K<T\}} > K] &\leq \min\left\{\frac{R_t}{Ke^{-r(T-t)}}\left[\Phi(-d^s_\gamma) + \left(\frac{K}{A_t}\right)^{\frac{2r}{\sigma_A^2}+(2\gamma-1)}\Phi(x^s_\gamma)\right], 1\right\} \\
\widetilde{\mathbb{P}}_t[R_{\tau_K\wedge T} > N] &\leq \min\left\{\frac{R_t}{Ne^{-r(T-t)}}, 1\right\}.
\end{aligned} \tag{64}$$

Proof. By the Markov Inequality and Optional Sampling Theorem, it follows that after once again setting (wlog) $t = 0$,

$$\begin{aligned}
\widetilde{\mathbb{P}}_0[R_{\tau_K}1_{\{\tau_K<T\}} > K] &= \widetilde{\mathbb{P}}_0[e^{-r(\tau_K\wedge T)}R_{\tau_K\wedge T}\mathbb{1}_{\{\tau_K<T\}} > Ke^{-r(\tau_K\wedge T)}] \\
&\leq \widetilde{\mathbb{P}}_0[e^{-r(\tau_K\wedge T)}R_{\tau_K\wedge T}\mathbb{1}_{\{\tau_K<T\}} > Ke^{-rT}] \\
&= \widetilde{\mathbb{P}}_0[e^{-r\tau_K}R_{\tau_K}\mathbb{1}_{\{\tau_K<T\}} > Ke^{-rT}] \\
&\leq \frac{\widetilde{\mathbb{E}}_0[e^{-r\tau_K}R_{\tau_K}\mathbb{1}_{\{\tau_K<T\}}]}{Ke^{-rT}} \\
&= \frac{R_0 - \widetilde{\mathbb{E}}_0[e^{-rT}R_T\mathbb{1}_{\{\tau_K\geq T\}}]}{Ke^{-rT}}.
\end{aligned} \tag{65}$$

The numerator in (65) is computed using the same integral techniques employed in the proof of Theorem 3, except with a lower limit of K instead of N (i.e., strong covenant.) The second inequality, for the probability that recovered value is above notional, is proved in the same fashion:

$$\begin{aligned}\widetilde{\mathbb{P}}_0[R_{\tau_K \wedge T} > N] &= \widetilde{\mathbb{P}}_0[e^{-r(\tau_K \wedge T)} R_{\tau_K \wedge T} > Ne^{-r(\tau_K \wedge T)}] \\ &\le \widetilde{\mathbb{P}}_0[e^{-r(\tau_K \wedge T)} R_{\tau_K \wedge T} > Ne^{-rT}] \\ &\le \frac{\widetilde{\mathbb{E}}_0[e^{-r(\tau_K \wedge T)} R_{\tau_K \wedge T}]}{Ne^{-rT}} \\ &= \frac{R_0}{Ne^{-rT}}.\end{aligned} \tag{66}$$

□

3.4. *Connection between Recovery Risk and PD-LGD Correlation*

In related work, Moody's KMV has recently proposed a PD-LGD Correlation model in the context of credit capital [4]. While the structural model they propose is the same two-factor structural model in (49), the motivation for the model is different. The motivation for Moody's model is the empirically observed PD-LGD correlation presented in Altman et.al. [1], which is justified economically in [27,34,41] among other works. However, the study in [1] was conducted in the physical measure (realized-post-ante default rates) rather than in the risk neutral measure used in pricing, and the economic considerations are different. Nevertheless, in [4], the authors attempt to price a bond with this model by integration. Indeed, we are able price bonds and CDS's in this model via a martingale analysis, completing the analysis initially suggested in [4] by integrating against a joint density for process and first passage time. In particular, in Sections 4.1 and 4.4 below, we explicitly compute the bond price using stochastic calculus and the Optional Sampling Theorem, returning closed form solutions.

4. The Black-Cox Model with Recovery Risk

In this section we introduce the assumptions that define the Stochastic Recovery Black-Cox model (SRBC) and use it to price bonds and CDS in Sections 4.1 and 4.4 respectively. The SRBC model essentially relaxes the recovery assumption, Assumption 2, by replacing it with a weaker assumption on the dynamics of the recovery value, Assumption 4, allowing for randomness in recovery. In particular, the SRBC Model assumes the following:

Assumption 5. (Constant Rates) *The short rate is assumed to be a constant r so that the discount factor is given by*

$$D(t,s) = e^{-r(s-t)}. \tag{67}$$

Assumption 6. (Correlated Asset-Recovery Dynamics) *The $\widetilde{\mathbb{P}}_t$-dynamics of the firms asset value A_t and recovery value R_t at time t are assumed to follow*

$$\begin{aligned}dA_t &= rA_t dt + \sigma_A A_t dW_t^A \\ dR_t &= rR_t dt + \sigma_R R_t dW_t^R \\ \rho_{A,R} dt &= \langle dW_t^A, dW_t^R \rangle\end{aligned} \tag{68}$$

where $r, \sigma_A, \sigma_R, \rho_{A,R}$ are constants and W_t^A, W_t^R are standard Brownian processes.

Assumption 7. (Default Time) *Default is given by the standard Black-Cox (BC) default time:*

$$\tau_{BC} = \tau_K \mathbb{1}_{\{\tau_K \le T\}} + T \mathbb{1}_{\{\tau_K > T, A_T < N\}} + \infty \mathbb{1}_{\{\tau_K > T, A_T \ge N\}}. \tag{69}$$

where τ_{BC} is also explicitly given in (9).

The collection of Assumptions 5–7 form the Stochastic Recovery Black-Cox model, and can be used to price defaultable bonds as well as other products such as CDS. which we do in Sections 4.1 and 4.4 below. Note that, just as in the original Black-Cox model, the constant interest-rate assumption can be relaxed to include time varying deterministic rates $r = r(t)$ with little effort.

4.1. Bond Pricing with Recovery Risk

If default can occur before the maturity T, say if the bond issuer is forced into default if assets A ever fall below a default point K, then the bond price must reflect this extra possibility. Our main result in this section is the computation of a closed formula for such a price, where a recovery that is correlated to the asset is substituted at default. This incorporates the model first presented by the authors in [4].

Theorem 3. (Bond Price under Stochastic Recovery Black Cox Model) *Suppose Assumptions 5, 6, 7 hold. Then the general price of a zero-coupon bond and related risk metrics are:*

$$\begin{aligned} B_{t,T}^{\mathrm{SRBC}} &= e^{-r(T-t)} \widetilde{\mathbb{E}}_t \left[B_{T,T}^{\mathrm{SRBC}} \right] \\ &= e^{-r(T-t)} \widetilde{\mathbb{E}}_t \left[N \mathbb{1}_{\{A_T \ge N, \tau_K > T\}} + R_T \mathbb{1}_{\{A_T \ge N, \tau_K > T\}^c} \right] \\ &= N e^{-r(T-t)} \cdot \widetilde{\mathbb{P}}_t[A_T \ge N, \tau_K > T] + \left[R_t - \widetilde{\mathbb{E}}_t[e^{-r(T-t)} R_T \mathbb{1}_{\{A_T \ge N, \tau_K > T\}}] \right] \\ S_{t,T}^{\mathrm{SRBC}} &= \frac{1}{T-t} \ln \left(\frac{1}{1 - \widetilde{\mathrm{PD}}_{t,T}^{\mathrm{BC}} \cdot \widetilde{\mathrm{LGD}}_{t,T}^{\mathrm{SRBC}}} \right). \end{aligned} \tag{70}$$

For sake of consistency, we point out that the SRBC *bond prices reduce to the Stochastic Recovery Merton (SRM) bond prices computed in [15] as $K \to 0$. To enable comparison with the BC model, we once again present the result for both weak and strong covenants:*

I. Weak Covenant Case. *If $K \le N$ the price of a zero-coupon bond is given by*

$$B_{t,T}^{\mathrm{SRBC}}(w) = N e^{-r(T-t)} \left[\Phi(d_0^w) - \left(\frac{K}{A_t} \right)^{\frac{2r}{\sigma_A^2} - 1} \Phi(x_0^w) \right] + R_t \left[\Phi(-d_\gamma^w) + \left(\frac{K}{A_t} \right)^{\frac{2r}{\sigma_A^2} + 2\gamma - 1} \Phi(x_\gamma^w) \right]. \tag{71}$$

The risk-neutral PD and LGD in the case of a weak covenant are

$$\begin{aligned} \widetilde{\mathrm{LGD}}_{t,T}^{\mathrm{SRBC}}(w) &= 1 - e^{r(T-t)} \frac{R_t}{N} \frac{\Phi\left(-d_\gamma^w\right) + \left(\frac{K}{A_t}\right)^{\frac{2r}{\sigma_A^2} + 2\gamma - 1} \Phi\left(x_\gamma^w\right)}{\Phi\left(-d_0^w\right) + \left(\frac{K}{A_t}\right)^{\frac{2r}{\sigma_A^2} - 1} \Phi\left(x_0^w\right)} \\ \widetilde{\mathrm{PD}}_{t,T}^{\mathrm{SRBC}}(w) &= \Phi\left(-d_0^w\right) + \left(\frac{K}{A_t} \right)^{\frac{2r}{\sigma_A^2} - 1} \Phi(x_0^w) = \widetilde{\mathrm{PD}}_{t,T}^{\mathrm{BC}}(w). \end{aligned} \tag{72}$$

II. Strong Covenant Case. *If $K \ge N$ the price of a zero-coupon bond is given by*

$$B_{t,T}^{\mathrm{SRBC}}(s) = N e^{-r(T-t)} \left[\Phi(d_0^s) - \left(\frac{K}{A_t} \right)^{\frac{2r}{\sigma_A^2} - 1} \Phi(x_0^s) \right] + R_t \left[\Phi(-d_\gamma^s) + \left(\frac{K}{A_t} \right)^{\frac{2r}{\sigma_A^2} + 2\gamma - 1} \Phi(x_\gamma^s) \right]. \tag{73}$$

The risk-neutral PD and LGD in the case of a strong covenant are

$$\begin{aligned} \widetilde{\mathrm{LGD}}^{\mathrm{SRBC}}_{t,T}(s) &= 1 - e^{r(T-t)} \frac{R_t}{N} \frac{\Phi\left(-d^s_\gamma\right) + \left(\frac{K}{A_t}\right)^{\frac{2r}{\sigma_A^2}+2\gamma-1} \Phi\left(x^s_\gamma\right)}{\Phi\left(-d^s_0\right) + \left(\frac{K}{A_t}\right)^{\frac{2r}{\sigma_A^2}-1} \Phi\left(x^s_0\right)} \\ \widetilde{\mathrm{PD}}^{\mathrm{SRBC}}_{t,T}(s) &= \Phi\left(-d^s_0\right) + \left(\frac{K}{A_t}\right)^{\frac{2r}{\sigma_A^2}-1} \Phi(x^s_0) = \widetilde{\mathrm{PD}}^{\mathrm{BC}}_{t,T}(s) \end{aligned} \tag{74}$$

where

$$\begin{aligned} d^w_\gamma &= d^w_0 + \gamma\sigma_A\sqrt{T-t} \\ d^s_\gamma &= d^s_0 + \gamma\sigma_A\sqrt{T-t} \\ x^w_\gamma &= x^w_0 + \gamma\sigma_A\sqrt{T-t} \\ x^s_\gamma &= x^s_0 + \gamma\sigma_A\sqrt{T-t}. \end{aligned} \tag{75}$$

Remark 2. *We remark that the* risk-adjusted *SRBC distances-to-default d_γ, x_γ in* (75) *reduce to the standard distances-to-default (d_0, x_0) and (d_1, x_1) of the BC model if $\gamma = 0$ or $\gamma = 1$, respectively. This adjustment for gamma reflects the uncertainty of the firm manager in the partial information setting of what the recoverable value of the firm's assets truly are, and affects only the recovery term. It should be noted that the probability of default is the same as in the case of no stochastic recovery. It is only the Loss-Given-Default that is affected by adding R as a recovery driver.*

The price for the zero-coupon bond under the SRBC setting is computed by employing the optional sampling theorem to the local martingale $e^{-rt}R_t$. We use $\tau := \min\{\tau_K, T\}$, a bounded stopping time adapted to the filtration generated by the joint process (A, R). The same technique is also used in the proof of the strong covenant case.

Proof. Without loss of generality, set $t = 0$. Under the risk-neutral measure, the corresponding bond price at issue is

$$\begin{aligned} B^{\mathrm{SRBC}}_{0,T} &= R_0 - \widetilde{\mathbb{E}}_0[e^{-rT}R_T \mathbb{1}_{\{A_T \geq N, \tau_K > T\}}] + Ne^{-rT} \cdot \widetilde{\mathbb{P}}_0[A_T \geq N, \tau_K > T] \\ &= R_0 - \widetilde{\mathbb{E}}_0\left[\exp\left(\delta T + \sigma_R\sqrt{1-\rho^2_{A,R}}W_T\right)\right] \widetilde{\mathbb{E}}_0\left[e^{-rT}R_0\left(\frac{A_T}{A_0}\right)^\gamma \mathbb{1}_{\{A_T \geq N, \tau_K > T\}}\right] \\ &\quad + Ne^{-rT} \cdot \widetilde{\mathbb{P}}_0[A_T \geq N, \tau_K > T] \\ &= R_0 - \frac{R_0}{A_0^\gamma} e^{-(r-\delta-\frac{1}{2}\sigma_R^2(1-\rho^2_{A,R}))T} \cdot \widetilde{\mathbb{E}}_0\left[A_T^\gamma \mathbb{1}_{\{A_T \geq N, \tau_K > T\}}\right] + Ne^{-rT} \cdot \widetilde{\mathbb{P}}_0[A_T \geq N, \tau_K > T] \\ &= R_0 - \frac{R_0}{A_0^\gamma} e^{[-\gamma r + \frac{1}{2}(\gamma-\gamma^2)\sigma_A^2]T} \int_N^\infty a^\gamma \widetilde{\mathbb{P}}_0\left[A_T \in da, \tau_K > T\right] + Ne^{-rT} \int_N^\infty \widetilde{\mathbb{P}}_0[A_T \in da, \tau_K > T]. \end{aligned} \tag{76}$$

We are able to calculate these two integrals using a result found in [26]:

Theorem 4. (Joint Density for Location and Maximum)

Begin with a standard Brownian motion W on a probability space and define

$$\begin{aligned}
X_t &= \mu t + \sigma W_t \\
\tau_a &= \min\{t : X_t = a\} \\
\underline{X}_t &= \min_{0\le s\le t} X_s \\
g(x,y,t,\mu) &:= \frac{1}{\sigma\sqrt{t}}\phi\Big(\frac{x-\mu t}{\sigma\sqrt{t}}\Big)\Big(1-\exp\Big(-\frac{4y^2-4xy}{2\sigma^2 t}\Big)\Big) \\
\phi(x) &:= \frac{1}{\sqrt{2\pi}}e^{-\frac{x^2}{2}} = \Phi'(x).
\end{aligned} \tag{77}$$

Then

$$\widetilde{\mathbb{P}}_0\left[X_t \in dx, \underline{X}_t \ge y\right] = g(-x,-y,t,-\mu)dx = g(x,y,t,\mu)dx. \tag{78}$$

Proof. See the proof of Theorem 2.1(i) in [26]. □

We employ the notation of Theorem 2.1(i) in [26] and focus on standard Brownian motions by setting

$$\begin{aligned}
\mu &:= r - \frac{1}{2}\sigma_A^2 \\
\sigma &:= \sigma_A \\
y &:= \ln\frac{K}{A_0} \le 0 \\
w &:= \ln\frac{N}{A_0} \le 0 \\
X_t &:= \ln\frac{A_t}{A_0} \\
\underline{X}_t &:= \min_{0\le s\le t}\ln\frac{A_s}{A_0}.
\end{aligned} \tag{79}$$

From these definitions, it follows that

$$\begin{aligned}
A_t &= A_0 e^{X_t} \\
\{\tau_K > T\} &= \Big\{\underline{X}_T > \ln\Big(\frac{K}{A_0}\Big)\Big\} := \big\{\tau_y^X > T\big\}.
\end{aligned} \tag{80}$$

Using this notation, we now compute the remaining integrals in (76):

$$\begin{aligned}
&\int_N^\infty a^\gamma \cdot \widetilde{\mathbb{P}}_0\Big[A_T \in da, \tau_K > T\Big] = \widetilde{\mathbb{E}}_0\Big[A_T^\gamma \mathbb{1}_{\{A_T > N, \tau_K > T\}}\Big] \\
&= \widetilde{\mathbb{E}}_0\Big[e^{\gamma\left(\ln(A_0)+X_T\right)}\mathbb{1}_{\{X_T > w, \tau_y^X > T\}}\Big] = \int_w^\infty e^{\gamma(x+\ln A_0)}\widetilde{\mathbb{P}}_0\Big[X_T \in dx, \tau_y^X > T\Big] \\
&= \int_w^\infty e^{\gamma(x+\ln A_0)}\frac{1}{\sigma_A\sqrt{T}}\phi\Big(-\frac{(x-\mu T)}{\sigma_A\sqrt{T}}\Big)\Big(1-\exp\Big(-\frac{4y(y-x)}{2\sigma_A^2 T}\Big)\Big)dx \\
&= (A_0)^\gamma\int_w^\infty \frac{1}{\sqrt{2\pi\sigma_A^2 T}}\exp\Big(-\frac{(x-\mu T)^2 - 2\sigma_A^2\gamma T x}{2\sigma_A^2 T}\Big)dx \\
&- (A_0)^\gamma\int_w^\infty \frac{1}{\sqrt{2\pi\sigma_A^2 T}}\exp\Big(-\frac{(x-\mu T)^2 + 4y(y-x) - 2\sigma_A^2\gamma T x}{2\sigma_A^2 T}\Big)dx.
\end{aligned} \tag{81}$$

It follows from completing the square in the exponent of the normal density that

$$
\begin{aligned}
&\int_w^\infty \frac{1}{\sqrt{2\pi\sigma_A^2 T}} \exp\Big(-\frac{(x-\mu T)^2 - 2\sigma_A^2\gamma T x}{2\sigma_A^2 T}\Big)dx \\
&= e^{(\gamma\mu + \frac{1}{2}\gamma^2\sigma_A^2)T}\Phi\left(-\frac{w-(\mu+\gamma\sigma_A^2)T}{\sqrt{\sigma_A^2 T}}\right) \\
&\int_w^\infty \frac{1}{\sqrt{2\pi\sigma_A^2 T}} \exp\Big(-\frac{(x-\mu T)^2 + 4y(y-x) - 2\sigma_A^2\gamma T x}{2\sigma_A^2 T}\Big)dx \\
&= e^{\frac{2\mu y}{\sigma_A^2}+2\gamma y} e^{[\gamma\mu + \frac{1}{2}\gamma^2\sigma_A^2]T}\Phi\left(-\frac{w-2y-(\mu+\gamma\sigma_A^2)T}{\sqrt{\sigma_A^2 T}}\right).
\end{aligned}
\tag{82}
$$

Substitution of the results of (82) into (81) and leads to

$$
\begin{aligned}
&R_0 - \frac{R_0}{A_0^\gamma} e^{-(\gamma(r-\frac{1}{2}\sigma_A^2)+\frac{1}{2}\gamma^2\sigma_A^2)T}\int_N^\infty a^\gamma \widetilde{\mathbb{P}}_0\Big[A_T \in da, \tau_K > T\Big] \\
&= R_0 - R_0\left(\Phi\left(-\frac{w-(\mu+\gamma\sigma_A^2)T}{\sqrt{\sigma_A^2 T}}\right) - e^{2\gamma y+\frac{2\mu y}{\sigma_A^2}}\Phi\left(-\frac{w-2y-(\mu+\gamma\sigma_A^2)T}{\sqrt{\sigma_A^2 T}}\right)\right) \\
&= R_0\left[\Phi\left(\frac{w-(\mu+\gamma\sigma_A^2)T}{\sqrt{\sigma_A^2 T}}\right) + e^{2\gamma y+\frac{2\mu y}{\sigma_A^2}}\Phi\left(-\frac{w-2y-(\mu+\gamma\sigma_A^2)T}{\sqrt{\sigma_A^2 T}}\right)\right].
\end{aligned}
\tag{83}
$$

Similiarily, substituting $\gamma = 0$ into (81) results in

$$
\int_w^\infty \widetilde{\mathbb{P}}_0\Big[X_T \in dx, \tau_y^X > T\Big] = \Phi\left(-\frac{w-\mu T}{\sqrt{\sigma_A^2 T}}\right) - e^{\frac{2\mu y}{\sigma_A^2}}\Phi\left(-\frac{w-2y-\mu T}{\sqrt{\sigma_A^2 T}}\right). \tag{84}
$$

Assembling the computations in (83) and (84), along with substitution of w, y in terms of K, N and A_0, and using the form (76) leads to the closed-form solution for the weak covenant case. Note that we have $w = \ln\frac{N}{A_0}$ as our lower limit of integration in the weak covenant case. To switch to the strong covenant case, we substitute $y = \ln\frac{K}{A_0}$ for our lower limit and the result for bond price and associated spreads and loss given default follows.

□

4.2. Consistency and Reduction to Black-Cox Model

As a result of the closed form above for $B_{t,T}^{\text{SRBC}}$, the consistency of the model as $T \to t$ follows quickly for both weak and strong covenants:

Lemma 6. *If $A_t > N$ in the weak covenant case, or if $A_t > K$ in the strong covenant case, then*

$$
\begin{aligned}
\lim_{T\to t^+} B_{t,T}^{\text{SRBC}}(\cdot) &= N \\
\lim_{(\gamma,R_t)\to(1,A_t)} B_{t,T}^{\text{SRBC}}(\cdot) &= B_{t,T}^{\text{BC}}(\cdot).
\end{aligned}
\tag{85}
$$

Proof. Consider that for both weak and strong covenants, the explicit formulae for distances-to-default lead to

$$\begin{aligned} \lim_{T\to t^+}\left[\Phi(d_0^{(\cdot)}) - \left(\frac{K}{A_t}\right)^{\frac{2r}{\sigma_A^2}-1}\Phi(x_0^{(\cdot)})\right] &= 1 \\ \lim_{T\to t^+}\left[\Phi(-d_\gamma^{(\cdot)}) + \left(\frac{K}{A_t}\right)^{\frac{2r}{\sigma_A^2}+(2\gamma-1)}\Phi(x_\gamma^{(\cdot)})\right] &= 0. \end{aligned} \tag{86}$$

Hence, $\lim_{T\to t^+} B_{t,T}^{\text{SRBC}}(\cdot) = N$ follows from the closed-formula given in Theorem 3, as does the reduction to the Black-Cox price when $\gamma \to 1$ and $R_t \to A_t$.

□

4.3. Greeks and Comparison with Standard Black-Cox model

Using our closed formula for bond price, we also compute the Greeks assuming stochastic recovery:

Lemma 7. (Greeks for SRBC). *Let $B_{t,T}^{\text{SRBC}}$ be the zero-coupon bond price from the Black-Cox model with stochastic recovery* (70) *under a weak covenant. Then the* ***Recovery Greeks*** *are given by*

$$\begin{aligned} \frac{\partial}{\partial R} B_{t,T}^{\text{SRBC}}(\cdot) &= \Phi(-d_\gamma^{(\cdot)}) + \left(\frac{K}{A}\right)^{\kappa_\gamma}\Phi(x_\gamma^{(\cdot)}) \\ \frac{\partial}{\partial \gamma} B_{t,T}^{\text{SRBC}}(\cdot) &= R\cdot\left[\sigma_A\sqrt{T-t}\left(-\phi(-d_\gamma^{(\cdot)}) + \left(\frac{K}{A}\right)^{\kappa_\gamma}\phi(x_\gamma^{(\cdot)})\right)\right] \\ &\quad + R\cdot\left[2\ln\left(\frac{K}{A}\right)\left(\frac{K}{A}\right)^{\kappa_\gamma}\Phi(x_\gamma^{(\cdot)})\right] \\ \kappa_\alpha &:= \frac{2r}{\sigma_A^2} + (2\alpha-1)\,,\ \forall\alpha\in\mathbb{R}. \end{aligned} \tag{87}$$

4.4. CDS Pricing with Recovery Risk

In this section, we price CDS using the SRBC model. We again consider both the weak and strong-covenant cases, and the results below depend on the bond prices in both covenant settings. Because of the general definition of a CDS premium under a structural model in Section 2, the premium here is the same as that computed for the BC model, with the exception that recovery is now defined by the correlated process R:

Theorem 5. (CDS Premium under Stochastic Recovery Black-Cox Model) *Suppose Assumptions 5–7 hold. Then the CDS premium* (23) *is given by:*

$$P_{t,T}^{\text{SRBC}} = \frac{e^{-r(T-t)}\widetilde{\mathbb{P}}_t\left[\tau_{\text{BC}} > T\right] + \widetilde{\mathbb{E}}_t\left[e^{-r(\tau_{\text{BC}}-t)}\mathbb{1}_{\{\tau_{\text{BC}}\le T\}}\right] - \frac{B_{t,T}^{\text{SRBC}}}{N}}{\frac{1-\widetilde{\mathbb{E}}_t\left[e^{-r(\tau_{\text{BC}}-t)}\mathbb{1}_{\{\tau_{\text{BC}}\le T\}}\right]-e^{-r(T-t)}\widetilde{\mathbb{P}}_t\left[\tau_{\text{BC}}>T\right]}{r} + \frac{1}{2}\cdot\widetilde{\mathbb{E}}_t\left[e^{-r(\tau_{\text{BC}}-t)}\mathbb{1}_{\{\tau_{\text{BC}}\le T\}}\right]}. \tag{88}$$

In the strong covenant case, where $K \geq N$, this reduces to the closed formula

$$
\begin{aligned}
P^{\mathrm{SRBC}}_{t,T}(s) &= \frac{e^{-r(T-t)}\widetilde{\mathbb{P}}_t\left[\tau_K > T\right] + \widetilde{\mathbb{E}}_t\left[e^{-r(\tau_K - t)}\mathbb{1}_{\{\tau_K \leq T\}}\right] - \frac{B^{\mathrm{SRBC}}_{t,T}(s)}{N}}{\frac{1-\widetilde{\mathbb{E}}_t[e^{-r(\tau_K-t)}\mathbb{1}_{\{\tau_K\leq T\}}]-e^{-r(T-t)}\widetilde{\mathbb{P}}_t[\tau_K>T]}{r} + \frac{1}{2}\cdot\widetilde{\mathbb{E}}_t\left[e^{-r(\tau_K-t)}\mathbb{1}_{\{\tau_K\leq T\}}\right]} \\
\widetilde{\mathbb{P}}_t\left[\tau_K > T\right] &= \Phi\left(d^s_0\right) - \left(\frac{K}{A_t}\right)^{\frac{2r}{\sigma_A^2}-1}\Phi\left(x^s_0\right) = 1 - \widetilde{\mathrm{PD}}^{\mathrm{BC}}_{t,T}(s) \\
\widetilde{\mathbb{E}}_t[e^{-r(\tau_K-t)}\mathbb{1}_{\{\tau_K\leq T\}}] &= A_t\left[\Phi(-d^s_1) + \left(\frac{K}{A_t}\right)^{\frac{2r}{\sigma_A^2}+1}\Phi(x^s_1)\right].
\end{aligned}
\tag{89}
$$

In the weak covenant case, where $K \geq N$, this reduces to the closed formula

$$
\begin{aligned}
P^{\mathrm{SRBC}}_{t,T}(w) &= \frac{e^{-r(T-t)}\widetilde{\mathbb{P}}_t\left[\tau_{\mathrm{BC}} > T\right] + \widetilde{\mathbb{E}}_t\left[e^{-r(\tau_{\mathrm{BC}} - t)}\mathbb{1}_{\{\tau_{\mathrm{BC}} \leq T\}}\right] - \frac{B^{\mathrm{SRBC}}_{t,T}(w)}{N}}{\frac{1-\widetilde{\mathbb{E}}_t[e^{-r(\tau_{\mathrm{BC}}-t)}\mathbb{1}_{\{\tau_{\mathrm{BC}}\leq T\}}]-e^{-r(T-t)}\widetilde{\mathbb{P}}_t[\tau_{\mathrm{BC}}>T]}{r} + \frac{1}{2}\cdot\widetilde{\mathbb{E}}_t\left[e^{-r(\tau_{\mathrm{BC}}-t)}\mathbb{1}_{\{\tau_{\mathrm{BC}}\leq T\}}\right]} \\
\widetilde{\mathbb{P}}_t\left[\tau_{\mathrm{BC}} > T\right] &= \widetilde{\mathbb{P}}_t\left[\tau_K > T, A_T \geq N\right] = 1 - \widetilde{\mathrm{PD}}^{\mathrm{BC}}_{t,T}(w) \\
\widetilde{\mathbb{P}}_t\left[\tau_K > T\right] &= \Phi\left(d^s_0\right) - \left(\frac{K}{A_t}\right)^{\frac{2r}{\sigma_A^2}-1}\Phi\left(x^s_0\right) = 1 - \widetilde{\mathrm{PD}}^{\mathrm{BC}}_{t,T}(s) \\
\widetilde{\mathbb{E}}_t\left[e^{-r(\tau_{\mathrm{BC}}-t)}\mathbb{1}_{\{\tau_{\mathrm{BC}}\leq T\}}\right] &= \widetilde{\mathbb{E}}_t[e^{-r(\tau_K-t)}\mathbb{1}_{\{\tau_K\leq T\}}] + e^{-r(T-t)}\left(\widetilde{\mathbb{P}}_t[\tau_K > T] - \widetilde{\mathbb{P}}_t[\tau_K > T, A_T \geq N]\right) \\
\widetilde{\mathbb{E}}_t[e^{-r(\tau_K-t)}\mathbb{1}_{\{\tau_K\leq T\}}] &= A_t\left[\Phi(-d^s_1) + \left(\frac{K}{A_t}\right)^{\frac{2r}{\sigma_A^2}+1}\Phi(x^s_1)\right].
\end{aligned}
\tag{90}
$$

Proof. Changing to the SRBC model requires only a change to the corresponding bond price in (23), as the default trigger (time) remains τ_{BC}.

□

Because of this closed form, we have consistency in our model as our parameters return to the standard Black-Cox model without stochastic recovery:

Lemma 8. (Premiums Are Model-Consistent) *The SRBC CDS premiums* (88) *are consistent with the BC CDS premiums* (40), *in that*

$$\lim_{(\gamma,R_t)\to(1,A_t)} P^{\mathrm{SRBC}}_{t,T}(\cdot) = P^{\mathrm{BC}}_{t,T}(\cdot). \tag{91}$$

Proof. This result follows directly from the closed form for CDS premiums in Theorems 2 and 5, and the result

$$\lim_{(\gamma,R_t)\to(1,A_t)} B^{\mathrm{SRBC}}_{t,T}(\cdot) = B^{\mathrm{BC}}_{t,T}(\cdot) \tag{92}$$

in Lemma 6.

□

5. The Implied Recovery and Recovery Risk Premium

5.1. Implied Recovery Rates From Observed CDS Premia

We introduce notation in this section only for the function of A and t that defines the probability of default. Specifically, define for any $\alpha \in \mathbb{R}$:

$$
\begin{aligned}
F_{\alpha}^{(w)}(A,t) &:= \Phi(-d_{\alpha}^{w}) + \left(\frac{K}{A}\right)^{\kappa_\alpha} \Phi(x_{\alpha}^{w}) \\
F_{\alpha}^{(s)}(A,t) &:= \Phi(-d_{\alpha}^{s}) + \left(\frac{K}{A}\right)^{\kappa_\alpha} \Phi(x_{\alpha}^{s}).
\end{aligned}
\tag{93}
$$

Here, κ_α is the quantity defined in (87). Furthermore, define

$$
\begin{aligned}
\mathrm{MGF}(A_t,t;w) &:= \widetilde{\mathbb{E}}_t[e^{-r(\tau_{\mathrm{BC}}-t)}\mathbb{1}_{\{\tau_{\mathrm{BC}}\le T\}}] \\
\mathrm{MGF}(A_t,t;s) &:= \widetilde{\mathbb{E}}_t[e^{-r(\tau_{\mathrm{K}}-t)}\mathbb{1}_{\{\tau_{\mathrm{K}}\le T\}}] \\
\mathrm{Pay}(A_t,t;w) &:= \frac{1-\mathrm{MGF}(A_t,t;w) - e^{-r(T-t)}\left(1-\widetilde{\mathrm{PD}}_{t,T}^{\mathrm{BC}}(w)\right)}{r} + \frac{1}{2}\mathrm{MGF}(A_t,t;w) \\
\mathrm{Pay}(A_t,t;s) &:= \frac{1-\mathrm{MGF}(A_t,t;s) - e^{-r(T-t)}\left(1-\widetilde{\mathrm{PD}}_{t,T}^{\mathrm{BC}}(s)\right)}{r} + \frac{1}{2}\mathrm{MGF}(A_t,t;s) \\
\mathrm{Pro}(A_t,R_t,\gamma,t;w) &:= \mathrm{MGF}(A_t,t;w) - \frac{R_t}{N}F_{\gamma}^{(w)}(A,t) \\
\mathrm{Pro}(A_t,R_t,\gamma,t;s) &:= \mathrm{MGF}(A_t,t;s) - \frac{R_t}{N}F_{\gamma}^{(s)}(A,t).
\end{aligned}
\tag{94}
$$

Using the results of Theorem 3 to calculate the quantity $\widetilde{\mathbb{E}}_t\left[D(t,\tau)\frac{R_{\tau_{\mathrm{BC}}}}{N}\mathbb{1}_{\{\tau_{\mathrm{BC}}\le T\}}\right]$ of the protection leg (22) in terms of recovery R_t, we obtain the result

$$
\begin{aligned}
P_{t,T}^{\mathrm{SRBC}}(w) &= \frac{\mathrm{Pro}(A_t,R_t,\gamma,t;w)}{\mathrm{Pay}(A_t,t;w)} \\
P_{t,T}^{\mathrm{SRBC}}(s) &= \frac{\mathrm{Pro}(A_t,R_t,\gamma,t;s)}{\mathrm{Pay}(A_t,t;s)}.
\end{aligned}
\tag{95}
$$

We also define the recovery rate $\bar{R}_{t,T} = \bar{R}(t,T) := \frac{R_t}{N}$, and solve the Stochastic Recovery Black-Cox CDS premium $P_{t,T}^{\mathrm{SRBC}}$ in (95) for the recovery rate to yield the *Implied Recovery Rate*

$$
\begin{aligned}
\bar{R}_{t,T}^{\mathrm{Imp}}(w) &= \frac{\mathrm{MGF}(A_t,t;w) - \mathrm{Pay}(A_t,t;w)\bar{P}_{t,T}^{\mathrm{Mkt}}(w)}{F_{\gamma}^{(w)}(A,t)} \\
\bar{R}_{t,T}^{\mathrm{Imp}}(s) &= \frac{\mathrm{MGF}(A_t,t;s) - \mathrm{Pay}(A_t,t;s)\bar{P}_{t,T}^{\mathrm{Mkt}}(s)}{F_{\gamma}^{(s)}(A,t)}.
\end{aligned}
\tag{96}
$$

Suppose now there are two CDS on the same obligor, except one references a senior issue with maturity $T_{\mathrm{Sr}} = T$ while the other references a junior issue with maturity $T_{\mathrm{Jr}} = T$. Denote the premiums associated to these two CDS as $P^{\mathrm{Mkt}}_{\mathrm{Sr}}$ and $P^{\mathrm{Mkt}}_{\mathrm{Jr}}$ respectively. Then the market implied recovery ratio is

$$\begin{aligned} \frac{\bar{R}^{\mathrm{Imp}}_{\mathrm{Jr}}(t,T)(w)}{\bar{R}^{\mathrm{Imp}}_{\mathrm{Sr}}(t,T)(w)} &= \frac{1-\frac{\mathrm{Pay}(A_t,t;w)}{\mathrm{MGF}(A_t,t;w)}P^{\mathrm{Mkt}}_{\mathrm{Jr}}(t,T)}{1-\frac{\mathrm{Pay}(A_t,t;w)}{\mathrm{MGF}(A_t,t;w)}P^{\mathrm{Mkt}}_{\mathrm{Sr}}(t,T)} \\ \frac{\bar{R}^{\mathrm{Imp}}_{\mathrm{Jr}}(t,T)(s)}{\bar{R}^{\mathrm{Imp}}_{\mathrm{Sr}}(t,T)(s)} &= \frac{1-\frac{\mathrm{Pay}(A_t,t;s)}{\mathrm{MGF}(A_t,t;s)}P^{\mathrm{Mkt}}_{\mathrm{Jr}}(t,T)}{1-\frac{\mathrm{Pay}(A_t,t;s)}{\mathrm{MGF}(A_t,t;s)}P^{\mathrm{Mkt}}_{\mathrm{Sr}}(t,T)} \end{aligned} \tag{97}$$

where as before $\bar{R}^{\mathrm{Imp}}_{\mathrm{Sr}}(t,T)$ and $\bar{R}^{\mathrm{Imp}}_{\mathrm{Jr}}(t,T)$ are the market implied term structures for recovery rates at time t. Notice that the right hand side of (97) requires the observed CDS premiums as well as the calibrated parameters of the original Black-Cox model, but is independent of the partial information parameter γ. Inverting recovery to obtain implied premiums for junior and senior issues with the same maturity leads to

$$\begin{aligned} \frac{P^{\mathrm{Imp}}_{\mathrm{Jr}}(t,T)(w)}{P^{\mathrm{Imp}}_{\mathrm{Sr}}(t,T)(w)} &= \frac{1-\bar{R}^{\mathrm{Jr}}_{t,T}\frac{F^{(w)}_{\gamma}(A_t,t)}{\mathrm{MGF}(A_t,t;w)}}{1-\bar{R}^{\mathrm{Sr}}_{t,T}\frac{F^{(w)}_{\gamma}(A_t,t)}{\mathrm{MGF}(A_t,t;w)}} \\ \frac{P^{\mathrm{Imp}}_{\mathrm{Jr}}(t,T)(w)}{P^{\mathrm{Imp}}_{\mathrm{Sr}}(t,T)(s)} &= \frac{1-\bar{R}^{\mathrm{Jr}}_{t,T}\frac{F^{(s)}_{\gamma}(A_t,t)}{\mathrm{MGF}(A_t,t;s)}}{1-\bar{R}^{\mathrm{Sr}}_{t,T}\frac{F^{(s)}_{\gamma}(A_t,t)}{\mathrm{MGF}(A_t,t;s)}} \end{aligned} \tag{98}$$

which also requires knowledge of the recovery process, as well as γ.

Remark 3. *The spread-ratio* (98) *is the Stochastic Recovery Black-Cox model implementation of Equation (6) in [14] used to extract recovery risk premiums from empirical data.*

5.2. The Price of Recovery Risk

Lemma 9. (Comparison of the Black-Cox and 2d Black-Cox Model). *Using our notation for F_α defined in* (93) *above, we can write our zero-coupon bond prices as*

$$\begin{aligned} B^{\mathrm{BC}}_{t,T}(w) &= Ne^{-r(T-t)}\cdot[1-F^{(w)}_0(A_t,t)] + A_tF^{(w)}_1(A_t,t) \\ B^{\mathrm{BC}}_{t,T}(s) &= Ne^{-r(T-t)}\cdot[1-F^{(s)}_0(A_t,t)] + A_tF^{(s)}_1(A_t,t) \\ B^{\mathrm{SRBC}}_{t,T}(w) &= Ne^{-r(T-t)}\cdot[1-F^{(w)}_0(A_t,t)] + R_tF^{(w)}_{\gamma}(A_t,t) \\ B^{\mathrm{SRBC}}_{t,T}(s) &= Ne^{-r(T-t)}\cdot[1-F^{(s)}_0(A_t,t)] + R_tF^{(s)}_{\gamma}(A_t,t). \end{aligned} \tag{99}$$

Suppressing the (w/s) superscript, we are able to compute the price of Recovery Risk *in our zero coupon bond and associated credit spread:*

$$\begin{aligned} B^{\mathrm{SRBC}}_{t,T} &= B^{\mathrm{BC}}_{t,T} + RR(B_{t,T}) \\ &= B^{\mathrm{BC}}_{t,T} + [R_tF_{\gamma}(A_t,t) - A_tF_1(A_t,t)] \\ S^{\mathrm{SRBC}}_{t,T} &= S^{\mathrm{BC}}_{t,T} + RR(S_{t,T}) \\ &= S^{\mathrm{BC}}_{t,T} + \frac{1}{T-t}\ln\left(\frac{1+e^{r(T-t)}\frac{A_t}{N}\frac{F_1(A_t,t)}{1-F_0(A_t,t)}}{1+e^{r(T-t)}\frac{R_t}{N}\frac{F_{\gamma}(A_t,t)}{1-F_0(A_t,t)}}\right). \end{aligned} \tag{100}$$

6. The Effect of Coupons

If coupons are paid at rate C per unit time, in addition to notional N, then (conditioned on the information $(A_t, R_t) = (A, R)$) the total value of a coupon bond in our model is now derived from the expected present value of coupons paid *until* $\tau_K \wedge T$:

$$\begin{aligned} B_{t,T}^{\mathrm{SRBC},c} &:= B_{t,T}^{\mathrm{SRBC}} + \widetilde{\mathbb{E}}_t[\mathrm{PV}_{t,T}\,[\mathrm{Cpns}]] \\ \widetilde{\mathbb{E}}_t[\mathrm{PV}_{t,T}\,[\mathrm{Cpns}]] &:= \widetilde{\mathbb{E}}_t\left[\int_t^T Ce^{-r(s-t)}\mathbb{1}_{\{\tau_K > s\}}ds\right]. \end{aligned} \tag{101}$$

By using moment-generating functions similar to those employed in calculating the premium-leg of our CDS, we compute the expected present value of coupon income to be

$$\begin{aligned} &\widetilde{\mathbb{E}}_t[\mathrm{PV}_{t,T}\,[\mathrm{Cpns}]] = \widetilde{\mathbb{E}}_t\left[\int_t^{\tau_K \wedge T} Ce^{-r(s-t)}ds\right] \\ &= \frac{C}{r}\left[1 - \widetilde{\mathbb{E}}_t\left[e^{-r(\tau_K - t)}\mathbb{1}_{\{\tau_K \le T\}}\right] - e^{-r(T-t)}\widetilde{\mathbb{P}}_t\left[\tau_K > T\right]\right] \\ &= \frac{C}{r}\left[1 - \frac{A}{K}\left[\Phi(-d_1^s) + \left(\frac{K}{A}\right)^{\frac{2r}{\sigma_A^2}+1}\Phi(x_1^s)\right] - e^{-r(T-t)}\left(\Phi\left(d_0^s\right) - \left(\frac{K}{A}\right)^{\frac{2r}{\sigma_A^2}-1}\Phi\left(x_0^s\right)\right)\right]. \end{aligned} \tag{102}$$

An interesting limit in these calculation is the passage to an infinite horizon for redemption time. In the next section, we calculate the value of perpetual bonds and show consistency with the value (102) computed for coupon bonds under finite horizon.

6.1. Perpetual Bonds

For bondholders interested in long-term bonds, say of the 100-year variety [42,43], an approximation of this long-term bond as a perpetual bond with stochastic recovery is a useful measure of the risk involved with such an instrument. The addition of stochastic recovery, even when the firm-value level that triggers default is known, reflects the uncertainty of what the true value of a firm's assets may be worth upon default when bankruptcy occurs far off into the future.

We begin with some modeling assumptions:

- Managers set a bankruptcy level K and accordingly we recall the definition (8) of τ_K as the first passage time of assets A to level K.
- Coupons are paid continuously at rate C, there is a risk-free interest rate r, and recovery at bankruptcy is R_{τ_K}.

Based on the above assumptions, and conditioned on the information $(A_0, R_0) = (A, R)$, the value of debt at time 0 (wlog) is

$$B_0 = \widetilde{\mathbb{E}}_0\left[\int_0^{\tau_K} Ce^{-rs}ds + e^{-r\tau_K}R_{\tau_K}\mathbb{1}_{\{\tau_K < \infty\}}\right]. \tag{103}$$

Lemma 10. *For market parameters (γ, r, σ_A) such that*

$$\min\left\{\gamma r - \frac{1}{2}\gamma(1-\gamma)\sigma_A^2, \frac{2r}{\sigma_A^2} + 2\gamma - 1\right\} > 0, \tag{104}$$

the value of a perpetual bond under stochastic recovery is

$$B_0 = \frac{C}{r}\left(1 - \left(\frac{K}{A}\right)^{\frac{2r}{\sigma_A^2}}\right) + R\left(\frac{K}{A}\right)^{\frac{2r}{\sigma_A^2}+2\gamma-1} \tag{105}$$

and

$$B_0 = \lim_{T\to\infty}\left(B^{\mathrm{SRBC}}_{0,T} + \widetilde{\mathbb{E}}_0[PV_{0,T}\,[\mathrm{Cpns}]]\right). \tag{106}$$

Remark 4. *In the Leland model [44] of perpetual bond issuance under a structural model for firm value, the recovery upon default is modeled as*

$$R_{\tau_K} = (1-\alpha)A_{\tau_K} = (1-\alpha)K \tag{107}$$

for fractional bankruptcy cost ratio α. If we substitute $R = (1-\alpha)A$ and $\gamma = 1$ into (105), then we retain the classical Leland [44] formula

$$B_0 = \frac{C}{r}\left(1 - \left(\frac{K}{A}\right)^{\frac{2r}{\sigma_A^2}}\right) + (1-\alpha)K\left(\frac{K}{A}\right)^{\frac{2r}{\sigma_A^2}}. \tag{108}$$

Proof. We begin by rewriting (103) as

$$\begin{aligned} B_0 &= \widetilde{\mathbb{E}}_0\left[\frac{C}{r}(1-e^{-r\tau_K}) + e^{-r\tau_K}R_{\tau_K}\mathbb{1}_{\{\tau_K<\infty\}}\right] \\ &= \frac{C}{r} + \widetilde{\mathbb{E}}_0\left[e^{-r\tau_K}\left(R_{\tau_K} - \frac{C}{r}\right)\mathbb{1}_{\{\tau_K<\infty\}}\right]. \end{aligned} \tag{109}$$

For $\gamma = \rho_{A,R}\frac{\sigma_R}{\sigma_A}$ and orthogonal decomposition

$$W^R_t = \rho_{A,R}W^R_t + \sqrt{1-\rho^2_{A,R}}W_t, \tag{110}$$

Ito-Calculus leads to, $\forall t \le s$,

$$\frac{R_s}{R_t} = \left(\frac{A_s}{A_t}\right)^{\gamma} e^{[(r-\frac{1}{2}\sigma_R^2)-\gamma(r-\frac{1}{2}\sigma_A^2)](s-t)+\sigma_R\sqrt{1-\rho^2_{A,R}}(W_s-W_t)}. \tag{111}$$

Substituting $t = 0$ and $s = \tau_K$ returns

$$R_{\tau_K} = R_0\left(\frac{K}{A_0}\right)^{\gamma} e^{[(r-\frac{1}{2}\sigma_R^2)-\gamma(r-\frac{1}{2}\sigma_A^2)]\tau_K+\sigma_R\sqrt{1-\rho^2_{A,R}}W_{\tau_K}}. \tag{112}$$

If we define $f_K(t)$ as the density of our first passage time to level K, then we see that

$$\begin{aligned} B_0 &= \frac{C}{r} + \widetilde{\mathbb{E}}_0\left[e^{-r\tau_K}\left(R_{\tau_K} - \frac{C}{r}\right)\mathbb{1}_{\{\tau_K<\infty\}}\right] \\ &= \frac{C}{r} + \int_0^\infty e^{-rt}\left(\widetilde{\mathbb{E}}_0\left[R_{\tau_K} \mid \tau_K = t\right] - \frac{C}{r}\right) f_K(t)dt. \end{aligned} \tag{113}$$

Assuming that at default, the bondholder receives instead the stochastically varying amount R_{τ_K}, it follows that, conditioned on $(A_0, R_0) = (A, R)$,

$$\begin{aligned} B_0 &= \frac{C}{r} + \widetilde{\mathbb{E}}_0\left[e^{-r\tau_K}\left(R_{\tau_K} - \frac{C}{r}\right)\mathbb{1}_{\{\tau_K<\infty\}}\right] \\ &= \frac{C}{r} + \int_0^\infty e^{-rt}\left(\widetilde{\mathbb{E}}_0\left[R_{\tau_K} \mid \tau_K = t\right] - \frac{C}{r}\right) f_K(t)dt \\ &= \frac{C}{r}\left(1 - \int_0^\infty e^{-rt} f_K(t)dt\right) \\ &+ \int_0^\infty e^{-rt}R\left(\frac{K}{A}\right)^{\gamma} e^{((1-\gamma)r+\frac{1}{2}\gamma(1-\gamma)\sigma_A^2)t} f_K(t)dt. \end{aligned} \tag{114}$$

When rewritten, with $r^* := \gamma r - \frac{1}{2}\gamma(1-\gamma)\sigma_A^2$, the bond value is

$$B_0 = \frac{C}{r}\left(1 - \widetilde{\mathbb{E}}_0[e^{-r\tau_K}\mathbb{1}_{\{\tau_K<\infty\}}]\right) + R\left(\frac{K}{A}\right)^{\gamma}\widetilde{\mathbb{E}}_0[e^{-r^*\tau_K}\mathbb{1}_{\{\tau_K<\infty\}}]. \tag{115}$$

Using well known results for moment-generating functions of first-passage times of Brownian motions with drift, assuming $r^* > 0$, we obtain the closed form

$$\begin{aligned}
\widetilde{\mathbb{E}}_0[e^{-r\tau_K}1_{\{\tau_K<\infty\}}] &= \left(\frac{K}{A}\right)^{\frac{2r}{\sigma_A^2}} \\
\widetilde{\mathbb{E}}_0[e^{-r^*\tau_K}1_{\{\tau_K<\infty\}}] &= \left(\frac{K}{A}\right)^{y(r,r^*,\sigma_A)} = \left(\frac{K}{A}\right)^{\frac{2r}{\sigma_A^2}+\gamma-1} \\
y(g,z,\sigma) &:= \frac{g - \frac{1}{2}\sigma^2 + \sqrt{(g-\frac{1}{2}\sigma^2)^2 + 2z\sigma^2}}{\sigma^2}
\end{aligned} \tag{116}$$

which results in the closed-form expression for a perpetual bond with stochastic recovery

$$B_0 = \frac{C}{r}\left(1 - \left(\frac{K}{A}\right)^{\frac{2r}{\sigma_A^2}}\right) + R\left(\frac{K}{A}\right)^{\frac{2r}{\sigma_A^2}+2\gamma-1}. \tag{117}$$

By utilizing (102), (116), and Theorem 3, we see that if in addition to $r^* > 0$, we also have $r > \left(\frac{1}{2} - \gamma\right)\sigma_A^2$, then it follows that $\forall t \geq 0$

$$\begin{aligned}
\lim_{T\to\infty} \widetilde{\mathbb{E}}_t[\mathrm{PV}_{t,T}\,[\mathrm{Cpns}]] &= \frac{C}{r}\left[1 - \left(\frac{K}{A}\right)^{\frac{2r}{\sigma_A^2}}\right] \\
\lim_{T\to\infty} B_{t,T}^{\mathrm{SRBC}} &= R\left(\frac{K}{A}\right)^{\frac{2r}{\sigma_A^2}+2\gamma-1}
\end{aligned} \tag{118}$$

and so we achieve consistency in the passage to infinite horizon.

□

7. Conclusions

In this work we introduced the Stochastic Recovery Black-Cox (SRBC) model which is essentially a Black-Cox model with an extra recovery risk driver. We then consider pricing with recovery risk and in particular explicitly compute closed form prices for both bonds and CDS under this framework, as well as associated risk metrics. This framework allows us to compute the Recovery implies by bond and CDS prices as well as compute the recovery risk premium.

Acknowledgments: The authors would like to thank Joe Campolieti (Wilfrid Laurier) for making us aware of the Reference: Hua He, William P. Keirstead, and Joachim Rebholz (1998). as well as Peter Carr (NYU) and Steven Shreve (Carnegie Mellon) for useful discussions on pricing defaultable bonds and CDS. We are indebted to Harvey Stein (Bloomberg) for introducing us to the partial information perspective for credit modeling which forms the theoretical justification for our much of this work. Finally, we sincerely thank the anonymous reviewers for their careful reading and suggestions for improvement, which we have followed and implemented in this version of our work.

Author Contributions: The two authors contribute equally to this paper.

Conflicts of Interest: The authors declare no conflict of interest.

References

1. Altman, Edward I., Brooks Brady, Andrea Resti, and Andrea Sironi. "The Link Between Default and Recovery Rates: Theory, Empirical Evidence and Implications." *The Journal of Business* 78 (2005): 2203–28.

2. Jon Frye. "Depressing Recoveries." *Risk* 13 (2000): 108–11.
3. Guido Giese. "The Impact of PD/LGD Correlations on Credit Risk Capital." *Risk* 18 (2005): 79–85.
4. Amnon Levy, and Zhenya Hu. *Incorporating Systematic Risk in Recovery: Theory and Evidence, Modeling Methodology*. San Francisco: Moody's KMV, 2007.
5. Qiang Meng, Amnon Levy, Andrew Kaplin, Yashan Wang, and Zhenya Hu. *Implications of PD-LGD Correlation in a Portfolio Setting*. New York: Moody's Analytics, 2010.
6. Peter Miu, and Bogie Ozdemir. "Basel Requirement of Downturn LGD: Modeling and Estimating PD & LGD Correlations." *Journal of Credit Risk* 2 (2006): 43–68.
7. Michael Pykhtin. "Unexpected Recovery Risk." *Risk* 16 (2003): 74–78.
8. Amraoui, Salah, Laurent Cousot, Sébastien Hitier, and Jean-Paul Laurent. "Pricing CDOs with state-dependent stochastic recovery rates." *Quantitative Finance* 12 (2012): 1219–40.
9. Norddine Bennani, and Jerome Maetz. "A Spot Stochastic Recovery Extension of the Gaussian Copula." Working Paper. University Library of Munich, Germany, 2009. Available online: http://www.defaultrisk.com/pp_cdo_82.htm (accessed on 19 April 2017).
10. Damiano Brigo, and Massimo Morini. "CDS Calibration with tractable structural models under uncertain credit quality." *Risk Magazine* 19 (2006): 1–13.
11. Charaf Ech-Chatbi. CDS and CDO Pricing with Stochastic Recovery. 2008. Available online: http://dx.doi.org/10.2139/ssrn.1271823 (accessed on 19 April 2017).
12. Stephan Höcht, and Rudi Zagst. "Pricing distressed CDOs with stochastic recovery." *Review of Derivatives Research* 13 (2010): 219–44.
13. Martin Krekel. Pricing Distressed CDOs with Base Correlation and Stochastic Recovery. 2008. SSRN Preprint. Available online: http://dx.doi.org/10.2139/ssrn.1134022 (accessed on 19 April 2017).
14. Timo Schläfer, and Marliese Uhrig-Homburg. Is recovery risk priced? *Journal of Banking & Finance* 40 (2014): 257–70.
15. Cohen, Albert and Costanzino, Nick. "Bond and CDS Pricing with Recovery Risk I: The Stochastic Recovery Merton Model." 2015. Available online: http://dx.doi.org/10.2139/ssrn.2544532 (accessed on 19 April 2017).
16. Tomasz R. Bielecki, and Marek Rutkowski. *Credit Risk: Modeling, Valuation and Hedging*. Berlin: Springer, 2002.
17. John Hull, and Alan White. "Valuing Credit Default Swaps I: No Counterparty Default Risk." *Journal of Derivatives* 8 (2000): 29–40.
18. Dominic O'Kane. *Modelling Single-Name and Multi-Name Credit Derivatives*. Somerset: John Wiley & Sons, 2008.
19. Robert Merton. "On the Pricing of Corporate Debt: the Risk Structure of Interest Rates." *Journal of Finance* 29 (1974): 449–70.
20. Fischer Black, and John C. Cox. "Valuing Corporate Securities: Some Effects of Bond Indenture Provisions." *Journal of Finance* 31 (1976): 351–67.
21. Christopher Finger, Vladimir Finkelstein, Jean-Pierre Lardy, George Pan, Thomas Ta, and John Tierney. *CreditGrades*^{TM} *Technical Document*. New York: Risk Metrics Group, 2002.
22. C. H. Hui, C. F. Lo, and H. C. Lee. Valuation of Corporate Bonds with Stochastic Default Barriers. Preprint. Availabel online: http://www.phy.cuhk.edu.hk/~cflo/Finance/papers/EuroFinRev_paper.pdf (accessed on 19 April 2017).
23. I. H. Gökgöz, Ö. Uğur, Y. Yolcu Okur. "On the single name CDS price under structural modeling." *Journal of Computational and Applied Mathematics* 259 (2014): 406–12.
24. Paul Wilmott, Jeff Dewynne, and Sam Howison. *Option Pricing: Mathematical Models and Computation*. Oxford: Oxford Financial Press, 1993.
25. David Lando. *Credit Risk Modeling*. Princeton: Princeton University Press, 2004.
26. Hua He, William P. Keirstead, and Joachim Rebholz. "Double Lookbacks." *Mathematical Finance* 8 (1998): 201–28.
27. Viral V. Acharya, Sreedhar T. Bharath, and Anand Srinivasan. "Does industry-wide distress affect defaulted firms? Evidence from creditor recoveries." *Journal of Financial Economics* 85 (2007): 787–821.
28. Martin Hillebrand. "Modeling and Estimating Dependent Loss Given Default." *Risk* 19 (2005): 120–25.
29. Klaus Dullmann, and Monika Trapp. "Systematic Risk in Recovery Rates of US Corporate Credit Exposures." In *Recovery Risk The Next Challenge in Credit Risk Management*. Edited by Edward Altman, Andrea Resti and Andrea Sironi. London: Risk Books, 2005, pp. 235–52.

30. Jon Frye. "Collateral Damage: A source of systematic credit risk." *Risk* 13 (2000): 91–94.
31. Jon Frye. *Collateral Damage Detected*. Working Paper, Emerging Issues Series. Chicago: Federal Reserve Bank of Chicago, 2000, pp. 1–14.
32. William Perraudin and Yen Ting Hu. Dependence of Recovery Rates and Default. SSRN Working Paper. 2006. Available online: http://dx.doi.org/10.2139/ssrn.1961142 (accessed on 19 April 2017).
33. Chanatip Kitwiwattanachai. *The Stochastic Recovery Rate in CDS: Empirical Test and Model*. Working Paper. 2014. Available online: http://dx.doi.org/10.2139/ssrn.2136116 (accessed on 19 April 2017).
34. Todd C. Pulvino. "Do Asset Fire Sales Exist? An Empirical Investigations of Commercial Aircraft Transactions." *Journal of Finance* 53 (1998): 939–78.
35. Young Ho Eom, Jean Helwege, and Jing-Zhi Huang. "Structural Models of Corporate Bond Pricing: An Empirical Analysis." *Review of Financial Studies* 17 (2004): 499–544.
36. Jing-Zhi Huang, and Ming Huang. "How Much of the Corporate-Treasury Yield Spread is Due to Credit Risk?" *Review of Asset Pricing Studies* 2 (2012): 153–202.
37. E. Philip Jones, Scott P. Mason, and Eric Rosenfeld. "Contingent Claims Analysis of Corporate Capital Structures: An Empirical Investigation." *Journal of Finance* 39 (1984): 611–25.
38. Joseph P. Ogden. "Determinants of the Ratings and Yields on Corporate Bonds: Tests of the Contingent Claims Model." *Journal of Financial Research* 10 (1987): 329–40.
39. Gordon Gemmill. "Testing Merton's Model for Credit Spreads on Zero-Coupon Bonds." Paper presented at the European Financial Management Association 2002 Annual Meetings, London, UK, 26–29 June 2002.
40. Ioannis Karatzas, and Steven E. Shreve. *Brownian Motion and Stochastic Calculus*, 2nd ed. Berlin: Springer, 2004.
41. Andrei Shleifer, and Robert W. Vishny. "Liquidation values and debt capacity: A market equilibrium approach." *Journal of Finance* 47 (1992): 1343–66.
42. Dominique C. Badoer, and Chris M. James. "The Determinants of Long Term Corporate Debt Issuances." *Journal of Finance* 71 (2016): 457–92.
43. Thomas T. Vogel Jr. "Disney amazes investors with sale of 100-year bonds." *The Wall Street Journal*, 23 July 1993.
44. Hayne E. Leland. "Corporate debt value, bond covenants, and optimal capital structure." *The Journal of Finance* 49 (1994): 1213–52.

risks

MDPI

Article

Risk Management under Omega Measure

Michael R. Metel [1,*], Traian A. Pirvu [2] and Julian Wong [2]

[1] Laboratoire de Recherche en Informatique, Université Paris-Sud, 91405 Orsay, France
[2] Department of Mathematics and Statistics, McMaster University, 1280 Main Street West, Hamilton, ON L8S 4K1, Canada; tpirvu@math.mcmaster.ca (T.A.P.); julianwwong@gmail.com (J.W.)
* Correspondence: metel@lri.fr

Academic Editor: Albert Cohen
Received: 10 January 2017; Accepted: 27 April 2017; Published: 5 May 2017

Abstract: We prove that the Omega measure, which considers all moments when assessing portfolio performance, is equivalent to the widely used Sharpe ratio under jointly elliptic distributions of returns. Portfolio optimization of the Sharpe ratio is then explored, with an active-set algorithm presented for markets prohibiting short sales. When asymmetric returns are considered, we show that the Omega measure and Sharpe ratio lead to different optimal portfolios.

Keywords: risk management; portfolio optimization; Omega measure; Sharpe ratio; active-set algorithm; non-convex optimization

1. Introduction

In the modern world of finance and insurance, it is routine for investors, firms and companies to manage different financial/insurance assets in the hope of increasing their capital gain. The collection of such investments is known as a portfolio, and it is designed to match the investor's preference. Different compositions of varying assets allow for a diversity of combinations that suit distinct appetites. For example, a bulge bracket investment bank such as J.P. Morgan is willing to undertake more risk to compensate for a larger return, in comparison to a retiree who is overseeing his retirement fund. However, despite an individual's taste, investors face the challenge of balancing reward and risk, as a high reward investment is often tightly linked with high underlying risk, and thus the main goal of portfolio management is finding the optimal tradeoff between the two.

The mean-variance portfolio model, proposed by Harry Markowitz (1968) serves as the keystone to portfolio theory. He formalized the problem of a rational, risk adverse investor that faces the tradeoff between reward and risk as proposed above. In such a scenario, reward and risk are defined as the expected return from the portfolio and its variance. There are problems with the implementation of the Markowitz model when the universe of assets is large. In this situation, the assets' sample covariance matrix is not an efficient estimator of the assets' true covariance matrix. Therefore, using the sample mean and covariance matrix in the mean-variance optimization procedure will result in an optimal return estimate different from reality. A fix for this problem is proposed in Bai et al. (2009), by using the theory of the large-dimensional random matrix. Another reason for the poor performance of the optimal mean-variance portfolio is perhaps due to the symmetry of asset returns. Low et al. (2016) shows that it is possible to enhance mean-variance portfolio selection by allowing for distributional asymmetries. Portfolio optimization under skewed returns is performed in several papers such as in Low (2015); Hu et al. (2010).

Under the mean-variance framework, various major portfolio theories have sprouted, and one of the major developments proposed by Willian Sharpe (1966) is known as the Sharpe ratio. The Sharpe ratio is the most fundamental of performance measures, which are critical in the evaluation, management and trading of portfolios. Under the mean-variance portfolio framework, the Sharpe ratio compares the return of the portfolio with the risk-free interest rate, which serves as a significant benchmark, owing to the fact that if overall return of the portfolio ranks below the risk free rate, investors should put their capital in the money market and earn interest without bearing any risk. The Sharpe ratio is greatly incorporated as a modern investment strategy, and is highly appraised by investors. However, the Sharpe ratio only comprises and examines the first two moments of the return distribution, namely, the expected return and the variance in return, while distribution properties such as skewness and kurtosis, which measure asymmetry and thickness of the tail distribution at the third and fourth moments respectively, may profoundly impact the performance of the portfolio. DeMiguel et al. (2009) compares the optimal mean-variance portfolio with the naive $\frac{1}{N}$ portfolio. They found that the $\frac{1}{N}$ rule performs better than the optimal mean-variance portfolio in terms of the Sharpe ratio, indicating that the gain from optimal diversification is higher when compared to the offset produced by estimation error.

The failure of the Sharpe ratio to address higher moments motivated Keating and Shadwick (2002) to develop the Omega measure, which captures all moments of the return distribution, including the expected value and variance. The Omega measure serves as a universal performance measure as it can be applied to any portfolio that follows a well-defined return distribution.

Even though the Omega measure was developed over 10 years ago, little research has been done to address its compatibility with previous developments, namely, with distribution functions that only involve lower moments. This paper aims to explore and address the backward compatibility of the Omega measure. We consider a market (financial or insurance) encompassing several risks within a one period paradigm. The risks are first assumed to follow a jointly elliptical distribution. Under this framework, we prove that the Sharpe ratio and the Omega measure yield the same optimal portfolios. Next, Sharpe ratio portfolio optimization is explored. The quasi-concavity of the Sharpe ratio is employed to develop an active-set algorithm for markets banning short sales. The convergence of this algorithm is established and numerical results are presented. Moreover, we show that, in a model with asymmetric returns, the optimal Sharpe ratio portfolio fails to be optimal when Omega measure is considered.

The remainder of this paper is organized as follows: in Section 2, we present the model. Section 3 provides the Sharpe ratio and Omega measure equivalence within the class of elliptical distributions of returns. Portfolio optimization formulations are presented in Section 4. Numerical analysis is performed in Section 5, with numerical results displayed in Section 6. Section 7 presents a model with asymmetric returns. The conclusion is summarized in Section 8. The paper ends with an Appendix A containing the proofs.

2. The Model

We have a market (financial or insurance) model that encompasses several instruments denoted $S_1, ..., S_n$. We consider a single period model from time $t = 0$ to $t = 1$. For each instrument, let the arithmetic return be

$$R_i = \frac{S_i(1) - S_i(0)}{S_i(0)},$$

and

$$\mathcal{R} = (R_1, R_2, \cdots, R_n).$$

We assume the return of the portfolio follows an *elliptically symmetric* distribution. Then, the vector of means $E(\mathcal{R}) = \mu = (\mu_1, ..., \mu_n)^T$ and the $n \times n$ covariance matrix $Cov(\mathcal{R}) = \Sigma = (\sigma_{ij})_{i,j}$ exist, and we further assume that Σ is invertible. The density f, if it exists, is

$$f(x) = |\Sigma|^{-\frac{1}{2}} g\Big[(x-\mu)^T \Sigma^{-1} (x-\mu)\Big],$$

where $x \in \mathbb{R}^n$ and $g : \mathbb{R}^+ \to \mathbb{R}^+$ is called the *density generator* or *shape* of R, and we write

$$\mathcal{R} \sim EC_n(\mu, \Sigma; g),$$

where (μ, Σ) is called the parametric part and g is called the non-parametric part of the elliptical distribution. The characteristic function ψ of R is

$$\psi_{\mathcal{R}}(t) = E \exp(it^T \mathcal{R}) = \exp(it^T \mu) \phi(t^T \Sigma t),$$

for some scalar function ϕ, called the *characteristic generator*. For background on the elliptically symmetric distribution, which is also called elliptically countered, see Bingham and Kiesel (2002); Fang et al. (1990).

The class of elliptical distributions, which have densities and defined mean and covariance is rich enough to contain several common distributions of asset returns: the multivariate normal distribution, the multivariate t distribution, normal-variance mixture distributions, symmetric stable distributions, the symmetric generalized hyperbolic distribution, the symmetric variance-gamma distribution, and the multivariate exponential power family (and thus the Laplace distribution). One advantage of this class is that the non-parametric part g "escapes the curse of dimensionality" (cf. Bingham and Kiesel (2002)). This class is chosen to model the stock returns by Bingham et al. (2003); Chamberlain (1983); Owen and Rabinovitch (1983).

Elliptical distributions are appealing for portfolio analysis, since it is a closed class under linear combinations. A portfolio at times $t = 0$ and $t = 1$ will, respectively, be

$$X(0) = \Delta_1 S_1(0) + \cdots + \Delta_n S_n(0),$$
$$X(1) = \Delta_1 S_1(1) + \cdots + \Delta_n S_n(1).$$

Let the arithmetic return of the portfolio be

$$R = \frac{X(1) - X(0)}{X(0)}.$$

The following Lemma gives the distribution of R.

Lemma 1. *Let*

$$w_i = \frac{\Delta_i S_i(0)}{\Delta_1 S_1(0) + \cdots + \Delta_n S_n(0)}$$

be the proportion of the initial wealth invested in instrument i, and w be the vector with components w_i. Then, R follows an elliptical distribution

$$R \sim EC_1(\bar{\mu}, \bar{\sigma}; g),$$

where

$$\bar{\mu} := w \cdot \mu = \sum_{i=1}^{n} w_i \mu_i, \quad \bar{\sigma}^2 := w^T \Sigma w = \sum_{i=1}^{n} \sum_{j=1}^{n} w_i w_j \sigma_{ij}.$$

Proof. See the Appendix A □

Let us consider the Sharpe Ratio and Omega measure defined by the formal definitions.

Definition 1. *The Sharpe ratio of a portfolio with return R is defined as*

$$S(R) = \frac{\bar{\mu} - r_f}{\bar{\sigma}},$$

where $\bar{\mu}$ is the expected return of the portfolio, $\bar{\sigma}$ is the standard deviation of return, and r_f is the risk-free interest rate.

Definition 2. *The Omega measure of a portfolio with return R is defined as*

$$\Omega(R) = \frac{\int_L^\infty (1 - F(x))dx}{\int_{-\infty}^L F(x)dx},$$

where $F(x)$ is the cumulative distribution function of the return distribution R, and L is an exogenously satisfied benchmark index.

The intuition behind the Omega measure is simple; by selecting a benchmark L, which serves as a reference that our portfolio is aiming to beat, the Omega measure compares the area of the cumulative distribution function from the right of L to the area to the left of L. Under such a definition, the Omega measure encompasses the entire return distribution, therefore incorporating higher moment properties as discussed.

3. Sharpe Ratio and Omega Measure Equivalence

When holding a portfolio, an investor uses a performance measure such as the Sharpe ratio or the Omega measure to evaluate how well the portfolio is performing. Hence, it is a natural question to ask how one should distribute his wealth in order to maximize his portfolio under the Omega measure. The following theorem states that using the Sharpe ratio or the Omega measure to optimize portfolio performance leads to the same optimal portfolio within the class of elliptical distributions of returns.

Theorem 1. *Recall that, under our framework, the portfolio return R is elliptically distributed $R \sim EC_1(\bar{\mu}, \bar{\sigma}; g)$. If $r_f = L$, we claim that*

$$\max_{w_1,..,w_n} \Omega(R)$$

is equivalent to

$$\max_{w_1,..,w_n} S(R).$$

Proof. See the Appendix A □

4. Portfolio Optimization

Given Theorem 1, we are able to transform optimization problems of the Omega measure into optimization problems of the Sharpe ratio for elliptical distributions. Let $e = \mu - L$, the excess expected return above a selected benchmark index L. With no restrictions on short selling, our optimization problem is as follows:

$$\max \frac{w^T e}{\sqrt{w^T \Sigma w}}, \quad \text{s.t.} \quad \sum_{i=1}^n w_i = 1. \tag{1}$$

However, certain financial markets prohibit the act of short selling, especially during periods of financial upheaval. An example would be the U.S. securities market under the 2008 financial crisis, when the U.S. Securities and Exchange Commission prohibited the act of short selling to protect the integrity of the securities market. Hence, we are also interested in the following problem as well:

$$\max \frac{w^T e}{\sqrt{w^T \Sigma w}}, \tag{2}$$
$$\text{s.t.} \sum_{i=1}^{n} w_i = 1,$$
$$w_i \geq 0 \qquad i = 1, ..., n.$$

5. Numerical Analysis

The optimal solution to (1) can be found directly as described in the following proposition.

Proposition 1. *The optimal solution to (1) is* $w^* = \frac{\hat{w}}{\sum_i^n \hat{w}_i}$, *where* $\hat{w} = \Sigma^{-1} e$.

Proof. See the Appendix A □

We require the following properties of the Sharpe ratio in developing an algorithm for solving (2).

Proposition 2. *The Sharpe ratio* $S(w) = \frac{w^T e}{\sqrt{w^T \Sigma w}}$ *is a quasi-concave function and* $\nabla S(w) = 0$ *iff* $w = c\Sigma^{-1} e$ *for some* $c \neq 0$.

Proof. See the Appendix A □

If $\Sigma^{-1} e \geq 0$, then our optimal solution for (1) is also optimal for (2), so let us assume that for (2), our optimal solution $w^* \neq c\Sigma^{-1} e$ for any c. By our assumption, $\nabla S(w^*) \neq 0$ and the following theorem is applicable.

Theorem 2 (Arrow and Enthroven (1961)). *Let* $f(x)$ *be a differentiable quasi-concave function subject to non-negativity constraints. If* $\nabla f(x^*) \neq 0$ *and* x^* *satisfies the KKT conditions with constants* μ^*, *then it is a global optimal solution.*

The KKT conditions for (2), ignoring the equality constraint are as follows, where $\nabla S(w) = \frac{e}{\sqrt{w^T \Sigma w}} - \frac{w^T e \Sigma w}{(w^T \Sigma w)^{\frac{3}{2}}}$.

$$\frac{e}{\sqrt{w^T \Sigma w}} - \frac{w^T e \Sigma w}{(w^T \Sigma w)^{\frac{3}{2}}} + \mu = 0 \qquad \text{(stationarity)}, \tag{3}$$
$$w \geq 0 \qquad \text{(primal feasibility)},$$
$$\mu \geq 0 \qquad \text{(dual feasibility)},$$
$$\mu^T w = 0 \qquad \text{(complementary slackness)}.$$

Consider the sets P and W defined by

$$P := \{i \in \{1, \ldots, n\} : w_i > 0\},$$

$$W := \{i \in \{1, \ldots, n\} : w_i = 0\}.$$

Let us permute the data so that

$$e = [e_P; e_W], \qquad w = [w_P; w_W],$$

and let Σ_P be the covariance matrix of the instruments indexed by P. Let $|P|$ be the number of elements of P. At optimality, the first $|P|$ rows of (3) will equal

$$e_P - \frac{w_P^T e_P \Sigma_P w_P}{w_P^T \Sigma_P w_P} = 0,$$

with solution

$$w_P = c\Sigma_P^{-1} e_P, \text{ for } c \neq 0.$$

Therefore, the optimal solution of (2) is the optimal solution of (1) for some unknown subset of instruments P. For ease in what follows, we will always take $c = 1$.

Our main objective then is to find the optimal set P, after which the optimal solution can be found by solving a positive definite system of linear equations. We propose the use of the following active-set algorithm to solve (2), which is inspired by Algorithm 16.3 in Nocedal and Wright (2006).

Algorithm 1: Sharpe Ratio active-set (SRAS) algorithm.

1: $i = 0$
2: $w^i = \mathbf{0}$
3: $j = \text{argmax} \frac{e_j}{\sqrt{\Sigma_{jj}}}$
4: $w_j^i = \frac{e_j}{\sqrt{\Sigma_{jj}}}$
5: $W^i = \{j | w_j^i = 0\}$
6: $P^i = \{j | w_j^i > 0\}$
7: **loop**
8: $\quad x_{P^i}^i = \Sigma_{P^i}^{-1} e_{P^i}$
9: $\quad x_{W^i}^i = \mathbf{0}$
10: $\quad p^i = x^i - w^i$
11: $\quad$ **if** $p^i = 0$ **then**
12: $\quad\quad \mu_{W^i}^i = \frac{w^{iT} e (\Sigma w^i)_{W^i}}{(w^{iT} \Sigma w^i)^{\frac{3}{2}}} - \frac{e_{W^i}}{\sqrt{w^{iT} \Sigma w^i}}$
13: $\quad\quad$ **if** $\mu_j^i \geq 0 \; \forall j \in W^i$ **then**
14: $\quad\quad\quad w^* = \frac{w^i}{\sum_{j=1}^n w_j^i}$
15: $\quad\quad\quad$ **quit**
16: $\quad\quad$ **else**
17: $\quad\quad\quad k^i = \underset{j \in W^i}{\text{argmin}} \, \mu_j^i$
18: $\quad\quad\quad W^{i+1} = W^i \setminus \{k^i\}$
19: $\quad\quad\quad P^{i+1} = P^i \cup \{k^i\}$
20: $\quad\quad\quad w^{i+1} = w^i$
21: $\quad\quad$ **end if**
22: $\quad$ **else**
23: $\quad\quad \alpha^i = \min\{1, \underset{j \in P^i, p_j^i < 0}{\min} \frac{-w_j^i}{p_j^i}\}$
24: $\quad\quad$ **if** $\alpha^i < 1$ **then**
25: $\quad\quad\quad h^i = \underset{j \in P^i, p_j^i < 0}{\text{argmin}} \frac{-w_j^i}{p_j^i}$
26: $\quad\quad\quad W^{i+1} = W^i \cup \{h^i\}$
27: $\quad\quad\quad P^{i+1} = P^i \setminus \{h^i\}$
28: $\quad\quad$ **end if**
29: $\quad\quad w^{i+1} = w^i + \alpha^i p^i$
30: $\quad$ **end if**
31: $\quad i = i + 1$
32: **end loop**

We find the portfolio consisting of a single instrument that maximizes the Sharpe ratio to initialize the algorithm in lines 1–6. At iteration i, $x_{P^i}^i$ is set to maximize the Sharpe ratio, which in general is not feasible in (2), in line 8. If the current feasible solution $w^i = x^i$, we check if $\mu_{W^i}^i \geq 0$. If so, then

$$w^* = \frac{w^i}{\sum_{j=1}^n w_j^i}$$

is the optimal solution to (2), or else we remove the index of the minimum value of dual variables μ^i from W^i to form W^{i+1} in lines 11–21. If $w^i \neq x^i$, w^{i+1} is set by moving in the direction of x^i from w^i

while remaining feasible in (2). If $w^{i+1} \neq x^i$, the index of the first blocking constraint $j \in P^i$ is added to W^i to create W^{i+1} in lines 22–30.

Theorem 3. *The SRAS algorithm is convergent.*

Proof. See the Appendix A □

There is in fact a quadratic convex reformulation of this problem (see Durand et al. (2012)), which has the following formulation under the mild condition that there exists at least one stock with $e_i > 0$, where $z > 0$ is a free constant:

$$\begin{aligned} &\min\ w^T \Sigma w, \\ &\text{s.t.}\ \ w^T e = z, \\ &\qquad w_i \geq 0. \end{aligned} \tag{4}$$

After solving, the w_i simply have to be normalized to sum to one to obtain the optimal solution. The choice of z can affect solution quality, in particular when the number of instruments n becomes large and the algorithm used to solve (4) employs a stopping criteria of the form $|w^i - w^{i+1}| \leq$ tolerance. In practice, we have found that choosing $z = e^T 1$, ensuring the average value of elements of w^i equals 1, gives high quality solutions with virtually no optimality gap compared to the active-set algorithm, without having to alter default stopping criteria.

6. Numerical Results

A computational experiment was conducted where the SRAS algorithm was compared to Gurobi 7.0 using data derived from historical stock prices from two stock market indices. All computing was done using Matlab R2016a on a Windows 10 64-bit, AMD A8-7410 processor with 8 GB of RAM.

Six problems were used for testing. Historical stock prices of the Dow Jones Industrial Average and the S&P/ TSX 60 were used to calculate the expectation and covariance of instrument returns. For each index, the past year, two years and five years were used for estimation. This data was generated using the website InvestSpy (2017). Results are presented in Table 1 below. We observe that the mean computing time of SRAS is over an order of magnitude faster when compared to Gurobi.

Table 1. Numerical results.

	SRAS		Gurobi	
	Time (s)	**Solution**	**Time (s)**	**Solution**
Dow 1 Yr	0.0386	2.6769	0.6881	2.6769
Dow 2 Yr	0.0057	3.3883	0.5551	3.3883
Dow 5 Yr	0.0030	15.7604	0.5829	15.7604
S&P 1 Yr	0.0479	7.2073	0.6569	7.2073
S&P 2 Yr	0.0095	4.4550	0.6233	4.4550
S&P 5 Yr	0.0053	5.0557	0.5562	5.0557
Mean	0.0184		0.6104	

7. Model with Skewness

We show numerically that the Omega measure is not equivalent to the Sharpe ratio for skewed distributions. Our estimation of Omega measure uses the following proposition.

Proposition 3. *The Omega measure is equal to* $\frac{\bar{\mu}-L}{\mathbb{E}(\max(L-R,0))} - 1$, *i.e.,*

$$\Omega(R) = \frac{\bar{\mu} - L}{\mathbb{E}\left(\max(L-R,0)\right)} - 1.$$

Proof. See the Appendix A □

We consider the skew-normal distribution Azzalini (2005), which is closed under affine transformation and has probability distribution function

$$f(r) = \frac{2}{\omega}\phi(\frac{r-\epsilon}{\omega})\Phi\left(\alpha(\frac{r-\epsilon}{\omega})\right),$$

where $\phi(\cdot)$ and $\Phi(\cdot)$ are the standard normal probability distribution function and cumulative distribution function, respectively, with location paramter ϵ, scale ω and shape α.

For a given skewness γ_1, let

$$|\delta| = \sqrt{\frac{(\pi/2)|\gamma_1|^{2/3}}{((4-\pi)/2)^{2/3} + |\gamma_1|^{2/3}}},$$

where the sign of δ is chosen as negative for left skewness and positive for right skewness. Given δ,

$$\alpha = \frac{\delta}{\sqrt{1-\delta^2}},$$

and for a desired standard deviation,

$$\omega = \frac{\sigma}{\sqrt{1-2\delta^2/2}},$$

and mean,

$$\epsilon = \mu - \omega\delta\sqrt{2/\pi}.$$

We plot the Omega measure for $L = 0.01$, $\mu = 0.1$ and $\sigma = 0.3$, with γ_1 varying over the domain $[-0.99, 0.99]$ in increments of 0.01. Monte Carlo integration was used to estimate $\mathbb{E}\left(\max(L-R,0)\right)$ by taking 10 million samples of R and taking the mean of $\max(L-R,0)$.

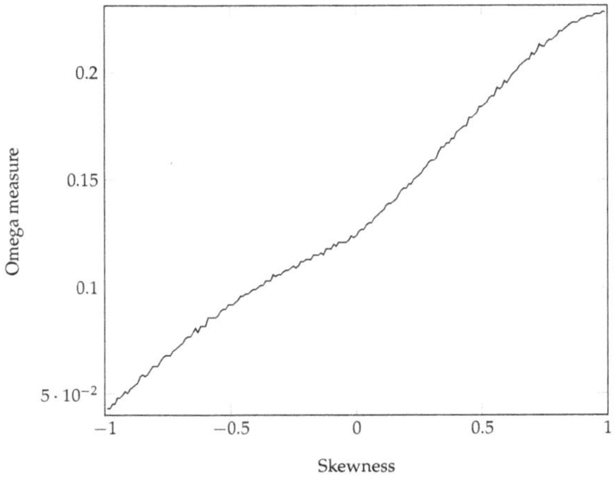

Figure 1. Omega measure versus skewness for a skew-normal random variable with $\mu = 0.1$, $\sigma = 0.3$ and $L = 0.01$.

Under the Sharpe ratio, we are indifferent to all of the plotted portfolios, each having a Sharpe ratio $S(R) = 0.3$, but under the Omega measure, taking into consideration higher moments, it is clear that we would prefer a portfolio with right skewness in this example.

8. Conclusions

In this paper, we have proved the equivalence of the Omega measure and the Sharpe ratio under jointly elliptical distributions of returns. The portfolio optimization of the Sharpe ratio with and without short sales was numerically analyzed. An active-set algorithm was presented for markets prohibiting short sales, with an improvement in average solution time of over an order of magnitude when compared to standard optimization techniques. Numerical experiments show that, when the return distributions are not symmetric, the Omega measure and the Sharpe ratio are not equivalent. Future research could be done to develop optimization methods for the Omega measure under more general distribution assumptions such as the skew-elliptical distribution.

Acknowledgments: This work is supported by NSERC grant 371653-09 and by the Digiteo Chair C&O program. The authors would like to thank the two anonymous referees for numerous valuable and helpful comments.

Author Contributions: The authors contributed equally to this paper.

Conflicts of Interest: The authors declare no conflict of interest.

Appendix A

Proof of Lemma 1.

$$
\begin{aligned}
R &= \frac{\Delta_1 S_1(1) + \cdots + \Delta_n S_n(1) - (\Delta_1 S_1(0) + \cdots + \Delta_n S_n(0))}{\Delta_1 S_1(0) + \cdots + \Delta_n S_n(0)} \\
&= \frac{\Delta_1 S_1(1) - \Delta_1 S_1(0)}{\Delta_1 S_1(0) + \cdots + \Delta_n S_n(0)} + \cdots + \frac{\Delta_n S_n(1) - \Delta_n S_n(0)}{\Delta_1 S_1(0) + \cdots + \Delta_n S_n(0)} \\
&= S_1(1) - S_1(0) \left(\frac{\Delta_1}{\Delta_1 S_1(0) + \cdots + \Delta_n S_n(0)} \right) + \cdots + S_n(1) \\
&- S_n(0) \left(\frac{\Delta_n}{\Delta_1 S_1(0) + \cdots + \Delta_n S_n(0)} \right) \\
&= \frac{S_1(1) - S_1(0)}{S_1(0)} \left(\frac{\Delta_1 S_1(0)}{\Delta_1 S_1(0) + \cdots + \Delta_n S_n(0)} \right) + \cdots \\
&+ \frac{S_n(1) - S_n(0)}{S_n(0)} \left(\frac{\Delta_n S_n(0)}{\Delta_1 S_1(0) + \cdots + \Delta_n S_n(0)} \right) \\
&= w_1 R_1 + \cdots + w_n R_n.
\end{aligned}
$$

Thus, the return of the portfolio R is a linear combination of $R_1, \cdots, R_n$. The closedness of elliptical distributions under linear combinations yields the claim. □

Proof of Theorem 1. Under our framework, we are now able to simplify the Omega measure. Recall the Omega measure is defined as

$$
\Omega(R) = \frac{\int_L^\infty (1 - F(x))dx}{\int_{-\infty}^L F(x)dx}.
$$

Here, $F(x) = \int_{-\infty}^x f(r)dr$ is the cumulative distribution function of the portfolio with arithmetic return R, with probability distribution function $f(r)$. Thus,

$$\Omega(R) = \frac{\int_L^\infty \left(1 - \int_{-\infty}^x f(r)dr\right) dx}{\int_{-\infty}^L \int_{-\infty}^x f(r)drdx}$$
$$= \frac{\int_L^\infty \int_x^\infty f(r)drdx}{\int_{-\infty}^L \int_{-\infty}^x f(r)drdx}.$$

We use Fubini's theorem to change the order of integration. Let D_1 be the integration region of the integral in the numerator and let D_2 be the integration region of the integral in the denominator, then

$$D_1 = \left\{(x,r)|x \in (L,\infty), r \in (x,\infty)\right\} = \left\{(x,r)|x \in (L,r), r \in (L,\infty)\right\}$$

and

$$D_2 = \left\{(x,r)|x \in (-\infty,L), r \in (-\infty,x)\right\} = \left\{(x,r)|x \in (r,L), r \in (-\infty,L)\right\}.$$

Thus, by Fubini's Theorem

$$\Omega(R) = \frac{\int_L^\infty \int_L^r f(r)dxdr}{\int_{-\infty}^L \int_r^L f(r)dxdr}. \tag{A1}$$

Under elliptical distributions

$$f(r) = \frac{1}{\bar{\sigma}} g\left(\left(\frac{r-\bar{\mu}}{\bar{\sigma}}\right)^2\right).$$

Evaluating the upper integral gives us

$$\int_L^\infty \int_L^r \frac{1}{\bar{\sigma}} g\left(\left(\frac{r-\bar{\mu}}{\bar{\sigma}}\right)^2\right) dxdr = \frac{1}{\bar{\sigma}} \int_L^\infty (r-L) g\left(\left(\frac{r-\bar{\mu}}{\bar{\sigma}}\right)^2\right) dr$$
$$= \frac{1}{\bar{\sigma}} \int_L^\infty r g\left(\left(\frac{r-\bar{\mu}}{\bar{\sigma}}\right)^2\right) dr - \frac{L}{\bar{\sigma}} \int_L^\infty g\left(\left(\frac{r-\bar{\mu}}{\bar{\sigma}}\right)^2\right) dr.$$

Let us perform the change of variable. Therefore, we let $u = \frac{r-\bar{\mu}}{\bar{\sigma}}$, then $\bar{\sigma}du = dr$ and $r = \bar{\sigma}u + \bar{\mu}$

$$\int_L^\infty \int_L^r \frac{1}{\bar{\sigma}} g\left(\left(\frac{r-\bar{\mu}}{\bar{\sigma}}\right)^2\right) dxdr = \int_{\frac{L-\bar{\mu}}{\bar{\sigma}}}^\infty (\bar{\sigma}u + \bar{\mu}) g(u^2) du - L \int_{\frac{L-\bar{\mu}}{\bar{\sigma}}}^\infty g(u^2) du$$
$$= \bar{\sigma} \int_{\frac{L-\bar{\mu}}{\bar{\sigma}}}^\infty u g(u^2) du + (\bar{\mu} - L) \int_{\frac{L-\bar{\mu}}{\bar{\sigma}}}^\infty g(u^2) du.$$

Thus,

$$\int_L^\infty \int_L^r \frac{1}{\bar{\sigma}} g\left(\left(\frac{r-\bar{\mu}}{\bar{\sigma}}\right)^2\right) dxdr$$
$$= \bar{\sigma}\left[-\frac{1}{2} H_1\left(\left(\frac{L-\bar{\mu}}{\bar{\sigma}}\right)^2\right) + \left(\frac{L-\bar{\mu}}{\bar{\sigma}}\right) H_2\left(\frac{L-\bar{\mu}}{\bar{\sigma}}\right) - K\left(\frac{L-\bar{\mu}}{\bar{\sigma}}\right)\right],$$

where

$$H_1'(x) = g(x), \;\; H_2'(x) = g(x^2), \;\; K = \int_{-\infty}^\infty g(x^2)\, dx.$$

We use the same methodology for the lower integral to obtain

$$\int_{-\infty}^L \int_r^L \frac{1}{\bar{\sigma}} g\left(\left(\frac{r-\bar{\mu}}{\bar{\sigma}}\right)^2\right) dxdr = \bar{\sigma}\left[-\frac{1}{2} H_1\left(\left(\frac{L-\bar{\mu}}{\bar{\sigma}}\right)^2\right) + \left(\frac{L-\bar{\mu}}{\bar{\sigma}}\right) H_2\left(\frac{L-\bar{\mu}}{\bar{\sigma}}\right)\right].$$

Let $z = \frac{L-\bar{\mu}}{\bar{\sigma}}$, then

$$\Omega(R) = G(z),$$

where

$$G(z) = 1 - \frac{Kz}{zH_2(z) - \frac{1}{2}H_1(z^2)}.$$

We claim that $\Omega(R)$ is a decreasing function of z. To see that, we first take the derivative of $G(z)$

$$G'(z) = -\frac{1}{2}\frac{KH_1(z^2)}{\left(zH_2(z) - \frac{1}{2}H_1(z^2)\right)^2} \leq 0,$$

since

$$H_1(x) = \int_{-\infty}^{x} g(u)\,du \geq 0,$$

due to the positivity of g. Therefore, $\Omega(R)$ is a decreasing function of z. Hence,

$$\begin{aligned}\max_{w_1,\ldots,w_n} \Omega(R) &\Leftrightarrow \min_{w_1,\ldots,w_n} \frac{L-\bar{\mu}}{\bar{\sigma}}, \\ &\Leftrightarrow \max_{w_1,\ldots,w_n} \frac{\bar{\mu}-L}{\bar{\sigma}}, \\ &\Leftrightarrow \max_{w_1,\ldots,w_n} S(R).\end{aligned}$$

Therefore, maximizing the Omega measure over $\{w_1, \ldots, w_n\}$ is equivalent to maximizing the Sharpe ratio over $\{w_1, \ldots, w_n\}$ with risk-free interest rate R_f equal to L. □

Proof of Proposition 1. The extended Cauchy–Schwarz inequality, see Johnson and Wichern (2002), states that for vectors b and d, and positive definite matrix B, $(b^T d)^2 \leq (b^T B b)(d^T B^{-1} d)$ with equality if and only if $b = cB^{-1}d$ for any constant c. It follows that, for the objective of (1), $\frac{w^T e}{\sqrt{w^T \Sigma w}} \leq \sqrt{e^T \Sigma^{-1} e}$ for $w \neq 0$, with the maximum attained by $\hat{w} = \Sigma^{-1}e$. In order to satisfy the constraint $\sum_{i=1}^{n} w_i = 1$, $\hat{w}$ is multiplied by the normalizing constant, $c = \frac{1}{\sum_i^n \hat{w}_i}$ to obtain the optimal solution to (1). □

Proof of Proposition 2. A function $f(x)$ is quasi-concave if its upper level sets $\{x | f(x) \geq t\}$ are convex. The upper level sets of $S(w)$ form second order conic constraints, $w^T e \geq t\sqrt{w^T \Sigma w}$, which define convex regions.

If $\nabla S(w) = \frac{e}{\sqrt{w^T \Sigma w}} - \frac{w^T e \Sigma w}{(w^T \Sigma w)^{\frac{3}{2}}} = 0$, then $w = c\Sigma^{-1}e$ for $c = \frac{w^T \Sigma w}{w^T e}$. Taking $w = c\Sigma^{-1}e$ for any $c \neq 0$, it follows directly that $\nabla S(w) = 0$. □

Proof of Theorem 3.

Lemma A1. *If $w^i = x^i$ but w^i is suboptimal for (2), then $\alpha^{i+1} > 0$ in the next iteration, unless there exists a $j \in P^i$ such that $w^i_j = 0$ and $p^{i+1}_j < 0$.*

Proof of Lemma A1. Let $P^{i+1} = P^i \cup \{k\}$ for some $k \in W^i$. In the ith iteration, consider the rows of P^{i+1} in (3), $e_{pi+1} - \frac{w^{iT} e \Sigma_{pi+1} w^i_{pi+1}}{w^{iT} \Sigma w^i} + \hat{\mu}^i_{pi+1} = 0$, where $\hat{\mu}^i = \sqrt{w^{iT} \Sigma w^i}\mu^i$. Given $w^i = x^i$, it follows that $w^{iT} e = w^{iT} \Sigma w^i$, and since $\hat{\mu}^i_{pi} = \mathbf{0}$, we get $\Sigma_{pi+1} w^i_{pi+1} = \begin{bmatrix} e_{pi} \\ e_k + \hat{\mu}^i_k \end{bmatrix}$. Taking the Cholesky decomposition, $\Sigma_{pi+1} = LL^T$, we can write $L \begin{bmatrix} y^i_{pi} \\ y^i_k \end{bmatrix} = \begin{bmatrix} e_{pi} \\ e_k + \hat{\mu}^i_k \end{bmatrix}$ with $L^T w^i_{pi+1} = y^i$. Since L^T is upper triangular, $L_{kk} w^i_k = y^i_k$, and so $y^i_k = 0$. Considering now the $i + 1th$ iteration, $\Sigma_{pi+1} x^{i+1}_{pi+1} = \begin{bmatrix} e_{pi} \\ e_k \end{bmatrix}$, and similarly if $L^T x^{i+1}_{pi+1} = y^{i+1}$, then $L \begin{bmatrix} y^{i+1}_{pi} \\ y^{i+1}_k \end{bmatrix} = \begin{bmatrix} e_{pi} \\ e_k \end{bmatrix}$. Since L is lower triangular,

$y_{Pi}^{i+1} = y_{Pi}^{i}$, $y_k^{i+1} = y_k^i - \frac{\hat{\mu}_k^i}{L_{kk}}$, and so $x_k^{i+1} = \frac{-\hat{\mu}_k^i}{L_{kk}^2} = -\hat{\mu}_k^i \Sigma_{kk}^{-1}$. As w^i is not optimal, $\hat{\mu}_k^i < 0$, so $p_k^{i+1} > 0$. Assuming now that $p_j^{i+1} \geq 0$ for all $j \in P^i$ with $w_j^i = 0$, $\alpha^{i+1} > 0$. □

Lemma A2. *If $w^i = x^i$ but w^i is suboptimal for (2), then $S(w^{i+2}) > S(w^i)$ $\forall \alpha \in (0, 1]$.*

Proof of Lemma A2.

$$\begin{aligned}
S(w^{i+2}) &= S\left(w^{i+1} + \alpha(x^{i+1} - w^{i+1})\right) = S\left(w^i + \alpha(x^{i+1} - w^i)\right) \\
&= \frac{\left(w^i + \alpha(x^{i+1} - w^i)\right)^T e}{\sqrt{\left(w^i + \alpha(x^{i+1} - w^i)\right)^T \Sigma(w^i + \alpha\left(x^{i+1} - w^i\right))}} \\
&= \frac{\left(w^i + \alpha(x^{i+1} - w^i)\right)^T e}{\left\|\Sigma^{\frac{1}{2}}(w^i + \alpha(x^{i+1} - w^i))\right\|_2}.
\end{aligned}$$

Focusing on the numerator,

$$\begin{aligned}
\left(w^i + \alpha(x^{i+1} - w^i)\right)^T e &= (1-\alpha) w^{iT} e + \alpha x^{i+1T} e \\
&= (1-\alpha)\left(\Sigma_{Pi+1}^{-1} \begin{bmatrix} e_{Pi} \\ e_k + \hat{\mu}_k^i \end{bmatrix}\right)^T \begin{bmatrix} e_{Pi} \\ e_k \end{bmatrix} + \alpha x^{i+1T} e \\
&= (1-\alpha) \begin{bmatrix} e_{Pi} \\ e_k + \hat{\mu}_k^i \end{bmatrix}^T x_{Pi+1}^{i+1} + \alpha x^{i+1T} e \\
&= x^{i+1T} e + (1-\alpha)\hat{\mu}_k^i x_k^{i+1}.
\end{aligned}$$

Focusing on the denominator,

$$\begin{aligned}
\left\|\Sigma^{\frac{1}{2}}(w^i + \alpha(x^{i+1} - w^i))\right\|_2 &= \left\|\Sigma^{\frac{1}{2}}\left((1-\alpha)w^i + \alpha x^{i+1}\right)\right\|_2 \\
&= \left\|\Sigma_{Pi+1}^{\frac{1}{2}}\left((1-\alpha)\Sigma_{Pi+1}^{-1} \begin{bmatrix} e_{Pi} \\ e_k + \hat{\mu}_k^i \end{bmatrix} + \alpha x_{Pi+1}^{i+1}\right)\right\|_2 \\
&= \left\|\Sigma_{Pi+1}^{\frac{1}{2}}\left(x_{Pi+1}^{i+1} + (1-\alpha)\Sigma_{Pi+1}^{-1} \begin{bmatrix} \mathbf{0} \\ \hat{\mu}_k^i \end{bmatrix}\right)\right\|_2 \\
&= \sqrt{x^{i+1T}\Sigma x^{i+1} + 2(1-\alpha)x_k^{i+1}\hat{\mu}_k^i + (1-\alpha)^2(\hat{\mu}_k^i)^2\Sigma_{kk}^{-1}} \\
&= \sqrt{x^{i+1T}\Sigma x^{i+1} + 2(1-\alpha)x_k^{i+1}\hat{\mu}_k^i - (1-\alpha)^2 x_k^{i+1}\hat{\mu}_k^i} \\
&= \sqrt{x^{i+1T}\Sigma x^{i+1} + (1-\alpha^2)\hat{\mu}_k^i x_k^{i+1}}.
\end{aligned}$$

Therefore,

$$
\begin{aligned}
S(w^{i+2}) &= \frac{x^{i+1T}e + (1-\alpha)\hat{\mu}^i_k x^{i+1}_k}{\sqrt{x^{i+1T}\Sigma x^{i+1} + (1-\alpha^2)\hat{\mu}^i_k x^{i+1}_k}} \\
&\geq \frac{x^{i+1T}e + (1-\alpha^2)\hat{\mu}^i_k x^{i+1}_k}{\sqrt{x^{i+1T}e + (1-\alpha^2)\hat{\mu}^i_k x^{i+1}_k}} \\
&= \sqrt{x^{i+1T}e + (1-\alpha^2)\hat{\mu}^i_k x^{i+1}_k} \\
&> \sqrt{x^{i+1T}e + \hat{\mu}^i_k x^{i+1}_k} \\
&= \sqrt{w^{iT}e} = \frac{w^{iT}e}{\sqrt{w^{iT}e}} = \frac{w^{iT}e}{\sqrt{w^{iT}_{pi}\Sigma_{pi}\Sigma^{-1}_{pi}e_{pi}}} \\
&= \frac{w^{iT}e}{\sqrt{w^{iT}_{pi}\Sigma_{pi}w^i_{pi}}} = \frac{w^{iT}e}{\sqrt{w^{iT}\Sigma w^i}} = S(w^i).
\end{aligned}
$$

□

The algorithm is monotone increasing as for all i, $S(x^i) \geq S(w^i)$, and by the quasi-concavity of $S(w)$, this implies that $S(w^i + \alpha(x^i - w^i)) \geq S(w^i)$. If w^0 is not optimal $S(w^2) > S(w^0)$ by Lemmas A1 and A2, and since $S(w^0) \geq S(w)$ for all portfolios w of size 1, $|P^i| \geq 2$ for all $i \geq 1$.

Assume now that $x^i \neq w^i$, and this holds until $x^{i+m} = w^{i+m}$, where $m \leq n-2$ and $|P^{i+m}| \leq n-m$. If the solution is not optimal, there exists $q \leq n-m-2$ indices of P^{i+m} such that $w^{i+m+1}_j = 0$ and $p^{i+m+1}_j < 0$. After q iterations, there exists no $j \in P^{i+m+1+q}$ such that $w^{i+m+1+q}_j = 0$ and $p^{i+m+1+q}_j < 0$, so by Lemma A1, $\alpha^{i+m+1+q} > 0$ and by Lemma A2, $S(w^{i+m+2+q}) > S(w^{i+m+q}) \geq S(w^i)$. Assuming that $m = 0$ considers the case where $x^i = w^i$, we have shown that the algorithm is strictly increasing after $m + 2 + q \leq n$ iterations.

Since the optimal value is bounded and the algorithm is strictly monotone increasing over intervals of n iterations, the algorithm converges. □

Proof of Proposition 3. Beginning from Equation (A1) of the proof of Theorem 1,

$$
\Omega(R) = \frac{\int_L^\infty \int_L^r f(r)dxdr}{\int_{-\infty}^L \int_r^L f(r)dxdr} = \frac{\int_L^\infty (r-L)f(r)dr}{\int_{-\infty}^L (L-r)f(r)dr} = \frac{\mathbb{E}(R) - L}{\mathbb{E}((L-R)^+)} - 1.
$$

□

References

Arrow, Kenneth J., and Alain C. Enthoven. 1961. Quasi-concave programming. *Econometrica: Journal of the Econometric Society* 29: 779–800.

Azzalini, Adelchi. 2005. The skew-normal distribution and related multivariate families *Scandinavian Journal of Statistics* 32: 159–88.

Bai, Zhidong, Liu Huixia, and Wong Wing-Keung. 2009. Enhancement of the Applicability of Markowitz's Portfolio Optimization by Utilizing Random Matrix Theory. *Mathematical Finance* 19: 639–67.

Bingham, Nicholas H., and Rüdiger Kiesel. 2002. Semi-parametric modelling in finance: Theoretical foundations. *Quantitative Finance* 2: 241–50.

Bingham, Nicholas H., and Rüdiger Kiesel, and Rafael Schmidt. 2003. A semi-parametric approach to risk management. *Quantitative Finance* 3: 426–41.

Chamberlain, Gary. 1983. A characterization of the distributions that imply mean-variance utility functions. *Journal of Economic Theory* 29: 185–201.

Durand, Robert B., Hedieh Jafarpour, and Claudia Klüppelberg. 2012. *Maximizing the Sharpe Ratio*. Lecture note for IEOR 4500. New York: Columbia University.

DeMiguel, Victor, Lorenzo Garlappi, and Raman Uppal. 2009. Optimal versus Naive Diversification: How Inefficient Is the 1/N Portfolio Strategy? *Review of Financial Studies* 5: 1915–53.

Fang, Kai-Tai, Samuel Kotz, and Kai Wang Ng. 1990. *Symmetric Multivariate and Related Distributions*. London: Chapman and Hall.

Harry M. Markowitz. 1968. *Portfolio Selection: Efficient Diversification of Investments*. Yale: Yale University Press.

InvestSpy. 2017. Portfolio Risk Analytics. Available online: http://www.investspy.com (accessed on 5 January 2017).

Johnson, Richard Arnold, and Dean W. Wichern. 2002. *Applied Multivariate Statistical Analysis*. Upper Saddle River: Prentice hall, 2002.

Keating, Con, and William F. Shadwick. 2002. A universal performance measure. *Journal of Performance Measurement* 6: 59–84.

Low, Rand Kwong Yew, Robert Faff, and Kjersti Aas. 2016. Enhancing Mean-variance Portfolio Selection by Modelling Distributional Asymmetries. *Journal of Economics and Business* 85: 49–72.

Low, Rand Kwong Yew. 2015. Vine Copulas: Modeling Systemic Risk and Enhancing Higher-Moment Portfolio Optimization. Available online: https://papers.ssrn.com/sol3/papers.cfm?abstract_id=2259076 (accessed on 1 May 2015).

Nocedal, Jorge, and Stephen J. Wright. 2006. *Numerical Optimization*. New York: Springer Science & Business Media.

Owen, Joel, and Ramon Rabinovitch. 1983. On the class of elliptical distributions and their applications to the theory of portfolio choice. *Journal of Finance* 38: 745–52.

Sharpe, William F. 1966. Mutual fund performance. *The Journal of Business* 39: 119–38.

Wenbo Hu, and Rüdiger Kiesel. 2010. Portfolio optimization for student t and skewed t returns. *Quantitative Finance* 10: 55–83.

risks

MDPI

Article

An Analysis and Implementation of the Hidden Markov Model to Technology Stock Prediction

Nguyet Nguyen

Faculty of Mathematics and Statistics, Youngstown State University, 1 University Plaza, Youngstown, OH 44555, USA; ntnguyen01@ysu.edu; Tel.: +1-330-941-1805; Fax: +1-330-941-3170

Academic Editor: Albert Cohen
Received: 20 April 2017; Accepted: 17 November 2017; Published: 24 November 2017

Abstract: Future stock prices depend on many internal and external factors that are not easy to evaluate. In this paper, we use the Hidden Markov Model, (HMM), to predict a daily stock price of three active trading stocks: Apple, Google, and Facebook, based on their historical data. We first use the Akaike information criterion (AIC) and Bayesian information criterion (BIC) to choose the numbers of states from HMM. We then use the models to predict close prices of these three stocks using both single observation data and multiple observation data. Finally, we use the predictions as signals for trading these stocks. The criteria tests' results showed that HMM with two states worked the best among two, three and four states for the three stocks. Our results also demonstrate that the HMM outperformed the naïve method in forecasting stock prices. The results also showed that active traders using HMM got a higher return than using the naïve forecast for Facebook and Google stocks. The stock price prediction method has a significant impact on stock trading and derivative hedging.

Keywords: hidden Markov model; stock prices; observations; states; predictions; AIC; BIC; likelihood; trading

1. Introduction

Stock investments can have a huge return or a significant loss due to the high volatilities of stock prices. An adaptable stock price prediction model would reduce risk and enhance potential return in financial derivative trading. Recently, researchers have applied the hidden Markov model for stock prices' forecasts. Hassan and Nath (2005) used HMM to predict the stock price for interrelated markets. Kritzman, Page, and Turkington (Kritzman et al. 2012) applied HMM with two states to predict regimes in market turbulence, inflation, and industrial production index. Guidolin and Timmermann (2006) used HMM with four states and multiple observations to study asset allocation decisions based on regime switching in asset returns. Nguyen (2014) used HMM with both single and multiple observations to forecast economic regimes and stock prices. Nobakht, Joseph and Loni (Nobakht et al. 2012) implemented HMM using various observation data (open, close, low, high) prices of stock to predict its close prices. In our previous work Nguyen and Nguyen (2015), we used HMM for single observation sequence for the S&P 500 to select stocks for trading based on performances of these stocks during the predicted regimes. In this study, we use HMM to predict stock prices and apply the results to trade stocks. We use HMM for multiple independent observation sequences in this study. Three stocks: Apple Inc., Alphabet Inc., and Facebook, Inc., were chosen to implement the model. We limit numbers of states of the HMM to a maximum of four states and use two goodness of fit tests to choose the best HMM model among HMMs with two, three, or four states. The prediction process is based on the work of Hassan and Nath (2005). The authors use HMM with the four observations: close, open, high, and low prices of some airline stocks to predict their future close price using four states. They used HMM to find a day in the past that was similar to the recent day and used the price change in date and price of the current day to predict future close price. However, in the paper, the authors did not explain why they chose HMM with four states. Our approach is different from their work in the three following modifications. The first difference is that we use the Akaike information criterion (AIC) and Bayesian information criterion (BIC) to test the HMM's performances with numbers of states from two to four to find the best HMM model. The second modification is that we apply HMM for stock returns to predict future close prices and compare the results with the naïve forecast method. The modification is based on the assumption of the HMM's algorithms presented in this paper: the observation sequences are independent. Applying the HMM to stock returns, our prediction method is simpler than the method in Hassan and Nath (2005), which will be explained in Section 3.1. Finally, we use stock prices predicted via the HMM and the naïve method to trade these three stocks and compare the results.

The paper is organized as follows: Section 2 gives a brief introduction to HMM and its algorithms for multiple observation sequences. Section 3 describes the HMM model selections and data collections for stock price prediction. Section 4 presents the results of stock price predictions and stock trading, and Section 5 gives conclusions.

2. Hidden Markov Model and Its Algorithms

The Hidden Markov Model, HMM, is a signal detection model that was introduced in 1966 by Baum and Petrie (Baum and Petrie 1966). HMM assumes that an observation sequence was derived from a hidden state sequence of discrete data and satisfies the first order of a Markov process. HMM was developed from a model for a single observation variable to a model for multiple observation variables. The applications of HMM also were expanded to many areas such as speech recognition, biomathematics, and financial mathematics. In our previous paper Nguyen and Nguyen (2015), we described HMM for one observation, its algorithms, and applications. In this section, we present HMM for multiple observations and its corresponding algorithms. We assume that the multiple observations data are independent and have the same length. The basic elements of an HMM for multiple observations are:

- Observation data, $O = \{O_t^{(l)}, t = 1,2,\ldots,T, l = 1,2,\ldots,L\}$, where l is numbers of independent observation sequences and T is the length of each sequence,
- Hidden state sequence of O, $Q = \{q_t, t = 1,2,\ldots,T\}$,
- Possible values of each state, $\{S_i, i = 1,2,\ldots,N\}$,
- Possible symbols per state, $\{v_k, k = 1,2,\ldots,M\}$,
- Transition matrix, $A = (a_{ij})$, where $a_{ij} = P(q_t = S_j | q_{t-1} = S_i)$, $i, j = 1,2,\ldots,N$,
- Initial probability of being in state (regime) S_i at time $t = 1$, $p = (p_i)$, where $p_i = P(q_1 = S_i)$, $i = 1,2,\ldots,N$,
- Observation probability matrix, $B = \{b_i(k)\}$, where

$$b_i(k) \equiv b_i(O_t = v_k) \equiv P(O_t = v_k | q_t = S_i),\ i = 1,2,...,N,\ k = 1,2,\ldots,M.$$

Parameters of an HMM are the matrices A and B and the vector p. For convenience, we use a compact notation for the parameters, given by

$$\lambda \equiv \{A, B, p\}.$$

If the observation probability assumes the Gaussian distribution, then we have a continuous HMM with $b_i(k) = b_i(O_t = v_k) = \mathcal{N}(v_k, \mu_i, \sigma_i)$, where μ_i and σ_i are the mean and variance of the distribution corresponding to the state S_i, respectively, and $\mathcal{N}$ is Gaussian density function. For convenience, we write $b_i(O_t = v_k)$ as $b_i(O_t)$. Then, the parameters of HMM are

$$\lambda \equiv \{A, \mu, \sigma, p\},$$

where μ and σ are vectors of means and variances of the Gaussian distributions, respectively. With the assumption that the observations are independent, the probability of observation, denoted by $P(O|\lambda)$, is

$$P(O|\lambda) = \prod_{l=1}^{L} P(O^{(l)}|\lambda).$$

There are three main questions that readers should consider when using the HMM:

1. Given an observation data O and the model parameters λ, can we compute the probabilities of the observations $P(O|\lambda)$?
2. Given the observation data O and the model parameters λ, can we find the best hidden state sequence of O?
3. Given the observation O, can we find the model's parameters λ?

The first problem can be solved by using forward or backward algorithms Baum and Egon (1967); Baum and Sell (1968), the second problem was solved by using Viterbi algorithm Forney (1973); Viterbi (1967) and the Baum–Welch algorithm Rabiner (1989) was developed to solve the last problem. In the paper, we only use the algorithms to solve the first and the last problem. We first use the Baum–Welch algorithm to calibrate parameters for the model and the forward algorithm to calculate the probability of observation to predict trending signals for stocks. In this section, we introduce the forward algorithm and the Baum–Welch algorithm for HMM with multiple observations. These algorithms are written based on Baum and Egon (1967); Baum and Sell (1968); Forney (1973); Petrushin (2000); Rabiner (1989).

2.1. Forward Algorithm

We define the joint probability function as

$$\alpha_t^{(l)}(i) = P(O_1^{(l)}, O_2^{(l)}, ..., O_t^{(l)}, q_t = S_i|\lambda), t = 1, 2, ..., T \text{ and } l = 1, 2, ..., L.$$

Then, we calculate $\alpha_t^{(l)}(i)$ recursively. The probability of observation $P(O^{(l)}|\lambda)$ is just the sum of the $\alpha_T^{(l)}(i)'s$.

The forward algorithm

1. Initialization $P(O|\lambda) = 1$
2. For $l = 1, 2, ..., L$ do
   (a) Initialization: for i = 1, 2,..., N
   $$\alpha_{t=1}^{(l)}(i) = p_i b_i(O_1^{(l)}).$$
   (b) Recursion: for $t = 2, 3, \ldots, T$, and for $j = 1, 2, \ldots, N$, compute
   $$\alpha_t^{(l)}(j) = \left[\sum_{i=1}^{N} \alpha_{t-1}(i) a_{ij}\right] b_j(O_t^{(l)}).$$
   (c) Calculate:
   $$P(O^{(l)}|\lambda) = \sum_{i=1}^{N} \alpha_T^{(l)}(i).$$
   (d) Update:
   $$P(O|\lambda) = P(O|\lambda) * P(O^{(l)}|\lambda).$$
3. Output: $P(O|\lambda)$.

2.2. Baum–Welch Algorithm

The Baum–Welch algorithm is an algorithm to calibrate parameters for the HMM given the observation data. The algorithm was introduced in 1970 Baum et al. (1970), in order to estimate the parameters of HMM for a single observation. Then, in 1983, the algorithm was extended to calibrate HMM's parameters for multiple independent observations, Levinson et al. (1983). In 2000, the algorithm was developed for multiple observations without the assumption of independence of the observations, Li et al. (2000). In this paper, we use HMM for independent observations, so we will introduce the Baum–Welch algorithm for this case. The Baum–Welch method or the expectation modification (EM) method is used to find a local maximizer, λ^*, of the probability function $P(O|\lambda)$.

In order to describe the procedure, we define the conditional probability $\beta_t^{(l)}(i) = P(O_{t+1}^{(l)}, O_{t+2}^{(l)}, .., O_T^{(l)}|q_t = S_i, \lambda)$, for $i = 1, ..., N, l = 1, 2, ..., L$. Obviously, for $i = 1, 2, ..., N$ $\beta_T^{(l)}(i) = 1$, and we have the following backward recursive:

$$\beta_t^{(l)}(i) = \sum_{j=1}^{N} a_{ij} b_j(O_{t+1}^{(l)}) \beta_{t+1}^{(l)}(j),\ t = T-1,\ T-2, ..., 1.$$

We then defined $\gamma_t^{(l)}(i)$, the probability of being in state S_i at time t of the observation $O^{(l)}$, $l = 1, 2, ..., L$ as:

$$\gamma_t^{(l)}(i) = P(q_t = S_i|O^{(l)}, \lambda) = \frac{\alpha_t^{(l)}(i)\beta_t^{(l)}(i)}{P(O^{(l)}|\lambda)} = \frac{\alpha_t^{(l)}(i)\beta_t^{(l)}(i)}{\sum_{i=1}^{N} \alpha_t^{(l)}(i)\beta_t^{(l)}(i)}.$$

The probability of being in state S_i at time t and state S_j at time $t+1$ of the observation $O^{(l)}, l = 1, 2, ..., L$ as:

$$\xi_t^{(l)}(i,j) = P(q_t = S_i, q_{t+1} = S_j|O^{(l)}, \lambda) = \frac{\alpha_t^{(l)}(i) a_{ij} b_j(O_{t+1}^{(l)}) \beta_{t+1}^{(l)}(j)}{P(O^{(l)}, \lambda)}.$$

Clearly,

$$\gamma_t^{(l)}(i) = \sum_{j=1}^{N} \xi_t^{(l)}(i,j).$$

Note that the parameter λ^* was updated in Step 2 of the Baum–Welch algorithm to maximize the function $P(O|\lambda)$ so we will have $\triangle = P(O, \lambda^*) - P(O, \lambda) > 0$.

If the observation probability $b_i(k)^*$, defined in Section 2, is Gaussian, we will use the following formula to update the model parameter, $\lambda \equiv \{A, \mu, \sigma, p\}$

$$\mu_i^* = \frac{\sum_{l=1}^{L} \sum_{t=1}^{T-1} \gamma_t^{(l)}(i) O_t^{(l)}}{\sum_{l=1}^{L} \sum_{t=1}^{T-1} \gamma_t^{(l)}(i)}$$

$$\sigma_i^* = \frac{\sum_{l=1}^{L} \sum_{t=1}^{T} \gamma_t^{(l)}(i)(O_t^{(l)} - \mu_i)(O_t^{(l)} - \mu_i)'}{\sum_{l=1}^{L} \sum_{t=1}^{T} \gamma_t(i)}.$$

3. Model Selections and Data Collections

The Hidden Markov Model has been widely used in financial mathematics area to predict economic regimes (Kritzman et al. 2012; Guidolin and Timmermann 2006; Ang and Bekaert 2002; Chen 2005; Nguyen 2014) or predict stock prices (Hassan and Nath 2005; Nobakht et al. 2012; Nguyen 2014). In this paper, we explore a new approach of HMM in predicting stock prices. In this section, we discuss how to use the Akaike information criterion, AIC, and the Bayesian information criterion, BIC, to test the HMM's performances with different numbers of states. We then will present how to use HMM to predict stock prices and apply the results to trade stocks. First, we will describe the chosen data and the AIC and BIC for HMM with selected numbers of states.

Baum–Welch for L independent observations $O = (O^{(1)}, O^{(2)}, ..., O^{(L)})$ with the same length T

1. Initialization: input parameters λ, the tolerance tol, and a real number $\triangle$
2. Repeat until $\triangle < tol$
   - Calculate $P(O, \lambda) = \Pi_{l=1}^{L} P(O^{(l)}|\lambda)$ using the forward algorithm (??)
   - Calculate new parameters $\lambda^* = \{A^*, B^*, p^*\}$, for $1 \le i \le N$

$$p_i^* = \frac{1}{L} \sum_{l=1}^{L} \gamma_1^{(l)}(i)$$

$$a_{ij}^* = \frac{\sum_{l=1}^{L} \sum_{t=1}^{T-1} \xi_t^{(l)}(i,j)}{\sum_{l=1}^{L} \sum_{t=1}^{T-1} \gamma_t^{(l)}(i)}, \ 1 \le j \le N$$

$$b_i(k)^* = \frac{\sum_{l=1}^{L} \sum_{t=1}^{T} |_{O_t^{(l)} = v_k^{(l)}} \gamma_t^{(l)}(i)}{\sum_{l=1}^{L} \sum_{t=1}^{T} \gamma_t^{(l)}(i)}, \ 1 \le k \le M$$

   - Calculate $\triangle = P(O, \lambda^*) - P(O, \lambda)$
   - Update

$$\lambda = \lambda^*.$$

3. Output: parameters λ.

3.1. Overview of Data Selections

We chose three stocks that are actively trading in the stock market to examine our model: Apple Inc. (AAPL), Alphabet Inc. (GOOGL), and Facebook Inc. (FB). The daily stock prices (open, low, high, close) of these stocks and information of these companies can be found from finance.yahoo.com. We used daily historical prices of these stocks from 4 January 2010 to 30 October 2015 in this paper.

3.2. Checking Model Assumptions

The HMM's algorithms presented in this paper are based on the assumption that the observation sequences are independent. However, the open, low, high, and close prices of a stock are highly correlated, which can be since from the matrix of correlation in Figure 1. On the other hand, stock returns of these four series prices are independent, which are shown in Figure 2.

We use the Autocorrelation function (ACF) to calculate the paired correlation between the series and plot in Figures 1 and 2. The ACF for the Facebook and Google stocks are presented in Appendix A. We can see clearly from the figures that the return price series have low correlations while the stock price series have very high correlations.

Furthermore, we conduct the Ljung–Box test to test the independence of each time series. We use the test with $lag = 1$ for returns of the three stocks: AAPL, FB, and GOOGL, from 1 October 2014 to 1 October 2015, and present results in Table 1. Note that the stock prices are not independent, and they failed the Ljung–Box test at significance level $\alpha = 5\%$, so Table 1 only displays results for stock returns.

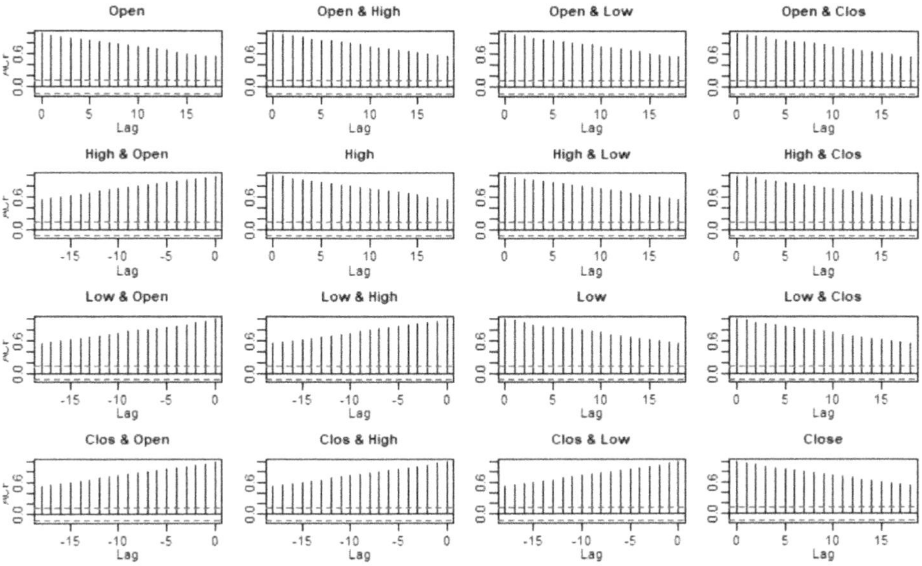

Figure 1. ACF test for correlation between open, low, high, and close of Apple stock daily prices from 1 October 2014 to 1 October 2015.

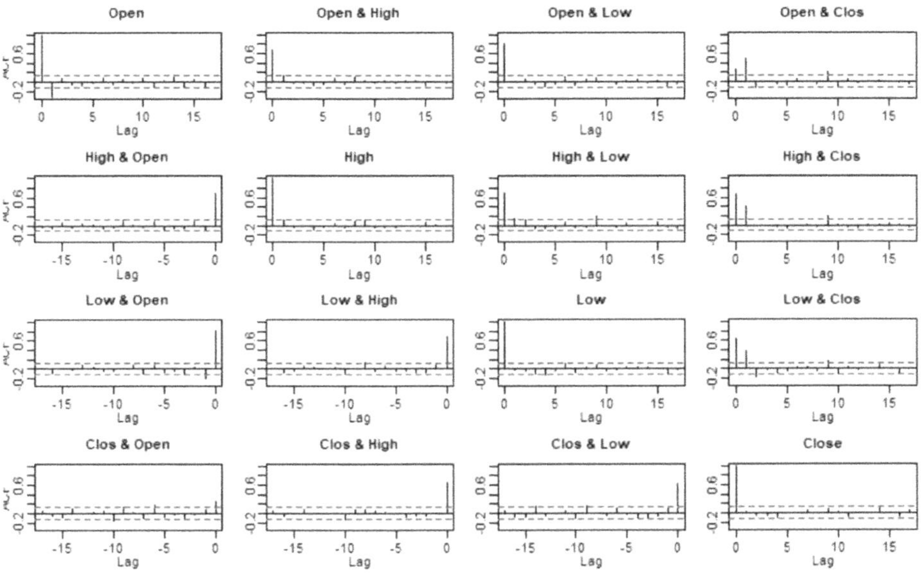

Figure 2. ACF test for correlation between open, low, high, and close of Apple stock daily return prices from 1 October 2014 to 1 October 2015.

Table 1. p-values from the Ljung–Box test for independencies of stock return series: Open, High, Low, and Close. "*" indicates that the p-value is statistically significant at $\alpha = 5\%$, "**" indicates that the p-value is statistically significant at $\alpha = 1\%$, and "***" indicates that the p-value is statistically significant at $\alpha = 0.1\%$.

Stock	Open	High	Low	Close
AAPL	0.0010 ***	0.0718	0.6584	0.6566
FB	0.2151	0.0153 *	0.3273	0.0094 **
GOOGL	0.5378	0.0214 *	0.0010 ***	0.0608

The null hypothesis of the Ljung–Box test is that the data are independently distributed. Thus, we will accept the null hypothesis if the p-value is bigger than the chosen significant level α. From Table 1, we can see that most of the stock returns series pass the independent test at the significant level $\alpha = 1\%$, and the only two series that do not pass the test at the significant level $\alpha = 0.1\%$ are APPL's open returns and GOOGL's low returns. The HMM works for dependent observation data with a modification in calculating probabilities of observations. We will explore the case in our future study. We will apply HMM for predicting the daily returns and then forecast future stock prices in the next section.

3.3. Model Selection

Choosing a number of hidden states for the HMM is a critical task. We first use two standard criteria: the AIC and the BIC to examine the performances of HMM with different numbers of states. The two measures are suitable for HMM because, in the model training algorithm, the Baum–Welch algorithm, the EM method was used to maximize the log-likelihood of the model. We limit numbers of states from two to four to keep the model simple and feasible for stock prediction. The AIC and BIC are calculated using the following formulas, respectively:

$$AIC = -2\ln(L) + 2k,$$

$$BIC = -2\ln(L) + k\ln(M),$$

where L is the likelihood function for the model, M is the number of observation points, and k is the number of estimated parameters in the model. In this paper, we assume that the distribution corresponding to each hidden state is a Gaussian distribution. Therefore, the number of parameters, k, is formulated as $k = N^2 + 2N - 1$, where N is numbers of states used in the HMM.

To train HMM's parameters, I use historical observed data of a fixed length T,

$$O = \{O_t^{(1)}, O_t^{(2)}, O_t^{(3)}, O_t^{(4)},\ t = 1, 2, ..., T\},$$

where $O^{(i)}$ with $i = 1, 2, 3,$ or 4 represents the daily returns of open, low, high or close price of a stock, respectively. For the HMM with single observation, we use only the returns of close price data,

$$O = O_t,\ t = 1, 2, ..., T,$$

where O_t is stock's return of close price at time t. We ran the model calibrations with different time lengths, T, and saw that the model worked well for $T \geq 80$. On the results below, we used blocks of $T = 100$ trading days of stock price data, O, to calibrate HMM's parameters and calculate the AIC and BIC numbers. Thus, the total number of observation points in each BIC calculation is $M = 400$ for four observation data and $M = 100$ for one observation data. For convenience, we did 100 calibrations for 100 blocks of data by moving the block of data forward, (we took off the price of the oldest day on the block and added the price of the following day to the recent day of the block). The calibrated parameters of the previous step are used as initial parameters for the new calibration. The training data set is from 16 January 2015 to 30 October 2015.

The first block of stock prices of 100 trading days from 16 January 2015 to 6 June 2015 was used to calibrate HMM's parameters and calculate corresponding AIC and BIC. Let $\mu^{(O)}$ and $\sigma^{(O)}$ be the mean and standard deviation of observation data, O, respectably. We chose initial parameters for the first prediction as follows:

$$\begin{aligned} A =&(a_{ij}),\ a_{ij} = \frac{1}{N}, \\ p =&(1,0,..,0), \\ \mu_i =&\mu^{(O)} + Z,\ Z \sim \mathcal{N}(0,1), \\ \sigma_i =&\sigma^{(O)}, \end{aligned} \tag{1}$$

where $i,\ j = 1,..,N$ and $\mathcal{N}(0,1)$ is the standard normal distribution.

The second block of 100 trading day data from 17 January 2015 to 7 June 2015 was used for the second calibration and so on. The HMM calibrated parameters from the current calibration are used as initial parameters for the next estimation. We continued the process until we got 100 calibrations. We plot the AICs and BICs of the 100 calibrations of these three stocks (AAPL, FB, and GOOGL) on Figures 3–5. On Figures 3–5, the graph of AIC is located on the left and BIC is located on the right. The lower AIC or BIC is the better model calibration. However, the Baum–Welch algorithm only finds a local maximizer of the likelihood function. Therefore, we did not expect to have the same AIC or BIC if we run the calibration twice. The results on Figures 3–5 showed that the calibration performances of the model with different numbers of states differ from one simulation to others. Based on the AIC results, the performances of HMM with two, three, or four states are almost the same. However, based on the BIC, the HMM with two states is the best candidate for all three of the stocks. Therefore, we choose the HMM with two states to predict prices of the three stocks in the next section.

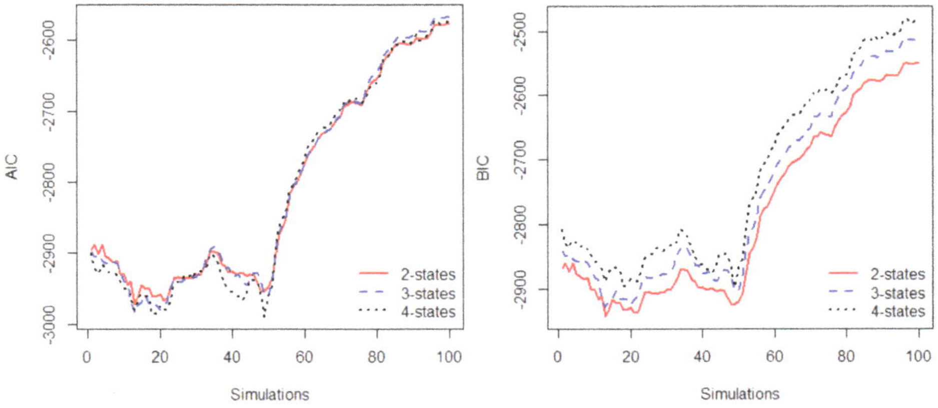

Figure 3. AIC (**left**) and BIC (**right**) for 100 parameter calibrations of HMM using Apple, AAPL, stock daily return prices.

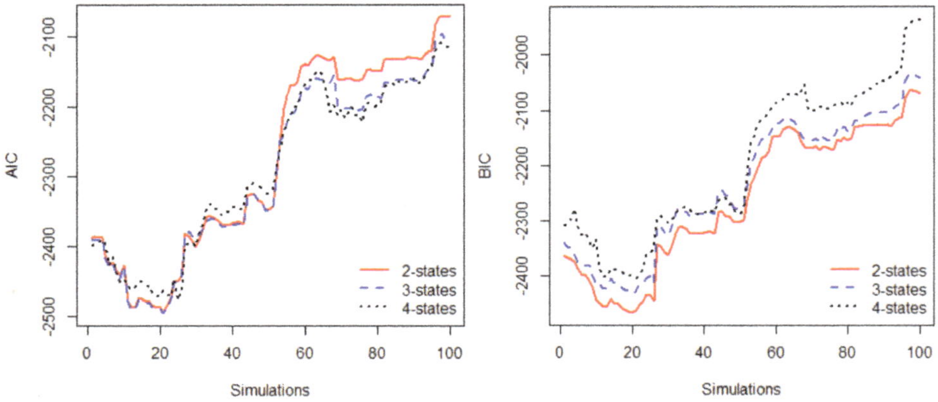

Figure 4. AIC (**left**) and BIC (**right**) for 100 parameter calibrations of HMM using Google, GOOGL, stock daily return prices.

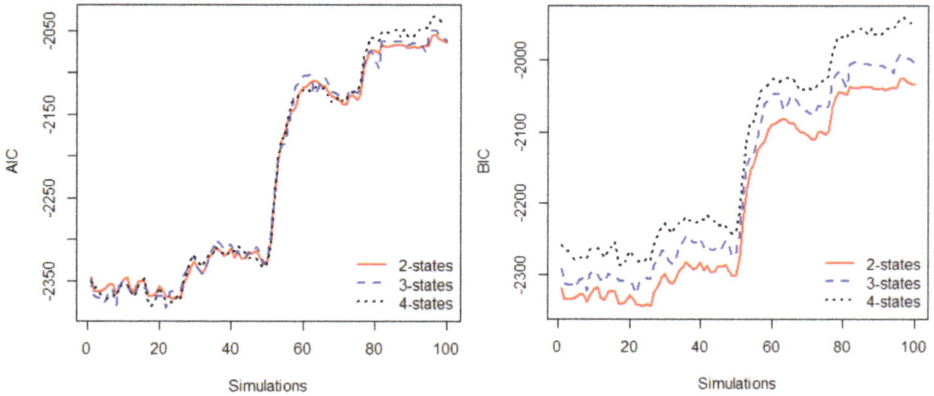

Figure 5. AIC (**left**) and BIC (**right**) for 100 parameter calibrations of HMM using Facebook, FB, stock daily return prices.

4. Stock Price Prediction and Stock Trading

In this section, we will use HMM to predict stock prices and compare the prediction with the real market prices. We will predict stock prices of GOOGL, APPL, and FB using HMM with two states, the best model selected from Section 3.3, and calculate the relative errors to the real market prices. The results will be compared with the naïve none change method. A trading strategy using HMM is also presented in this section.

4.1. Stock Price Prediction

We first introduce how to predict stock prices using HMM. The prediction process can be divided into three steps. Step 1: calibrate HMM's parameters and calculate the likelihood of the model.

Step 2: find the day in the past that has a similar likelihood to the recent day. Step 3: use the stock returns on the day after the "similar" day in the history to be the predicted return for tomorrow price. This prediction approach is based on the work of Hassan and Nath (2005). However, our procedure is different from their method in that we apply HMM for the returns of open, low, high, and close prices, which are independent, while the authors used the HMM directly to open, low, high, and close prices, which are not independent. Due to applying the HMM for stock returns, our method is simpler than their method in the third step. We use HMM with the returns of the four observation sequences (open, low, high, close price), as in Hassan and Nath (2005).

Suppose that we want to predict tomorrow's closing price of stock A, the prediction can be explained as follows. In the first step, we chose a block of T of the four daily return prices of stock A: open, low, high, and close, ($O = \{O_t^{(1)}, O_t^{(2)}, O_t^{(3)}, O_t^{(4)}, t = T-99, T-98, ..., T\}$), to calibrate HMM's parameters, λ, of the HMM. We then calculate the probability of observation, $P(O|\lambda)$. We assumed that the observation probability $b_i(k)$, defined in Section 2, is Gaussian distribution, so the matrix B, in the parameter $\lambda = \{A, B, p\}$, is a 2 by N matrix of means, μ, and variances, σ, of the N normal distributions, where N is numbers of states. In the second step, we move the block of data backward by one day to have new observation data $O^{new} = \{O_t^{(1)}, O_t^{(2)}, O_t^{(3)}, O_t^{(4)}, t = T-100, T-99, ..., T-1\}$ and calculate $P(O^{new}|\lambda)$. We keep moving blocks of data backward day by day until we find a data set O^*, ($O^* = \{O_t^{(1)}, O_t^{(2)}, O_t^{(3)}, O_t^{(4)}, t = T^*-99, T^*-98, ..., T^*\}$) such that $P(T^*|\lambda) \simeq P(O|\lambda)$. In the third step, after finding the past "similar" day, T^*, we estimate the return of close price at time $T+1$, by using the following formula:

$$O_{T+1}^{(4)} = O_{T^*+1}^{(4)}. \tag{2}$$

After the first prediction for stock return of day $T+1$ we update data window, O, by moving it forward one day, $O = \{O_t^{(1)}, O_t^{(2)}, O_t^{(3)}, O_t^{(4)}, t = T-98, T-97, ..., T+1\}$, to predict stock return for the day $T+2$. The calibrated HMM's parameters in the first prediction were used as the initial parameters for the second prediction. We repeat the prediction process as mentioned in the first prediction for the second prediction and so on. For HMM with a single observation sequence, we use $O = O_t^{(4)}$, where $O^{(4)}$ is the return of close price.

The predicted close price at time $T+1$, P_{T+1}, is calculated by the predicted stock returns:

$$P_{T+1} = P_T * (O_{T+1}^{(4)} + 1), \tag{3}$$

where P_T is close price at time T and $O_{T+1}^{(4)}$ is the return of close price calculated in (2).

The naïve none change method is applied for returns of the three stocks' close prices. The model simply takes the return of the close price today to use as the return of the tomorrow's close price

$$O_{T+1}^{(4)} = O_T^{(4)}.$$

After forecasting $O_{T+1}^{(4)}$, we predict the next day's close price by using Equation (3). We use the naïve method for stock returns instead of stock prices because, for trading purposes, if we assume no change in future stock prices, then there is no trade. We present results of using the HMM to predict these three stocks'—AAPL, GOOGL, and FB—closing prices for one year trading, 252 days, in Figures 6– 8. The results indicate that the HMM captures the trends of the three stocks well, while the naïve forecasts often go to the opposite directions of the real market trends. We can see from Figure 7 that the naïve forecast method had a few huge errors in predicting stock prices in February. The naïve model also showed its weakness when predicted prices of Google stock at the end of July 2015 are far from the actual prices.

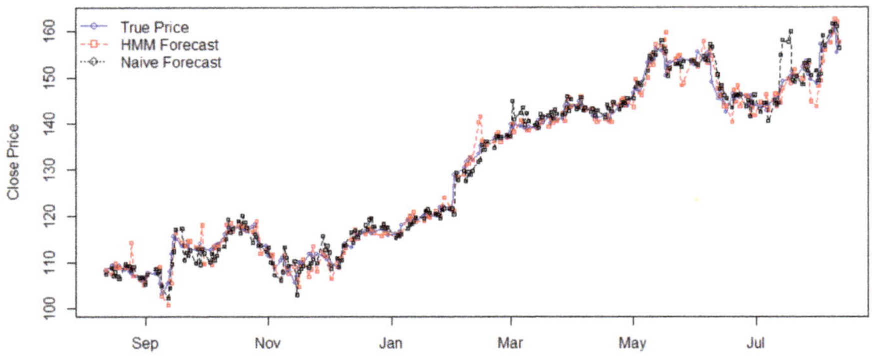

Figure 6. HMM prediction of Apple stock daily close prices from 15 August 2016 to 11 August 2017 using two-states HMM and the naïve model.

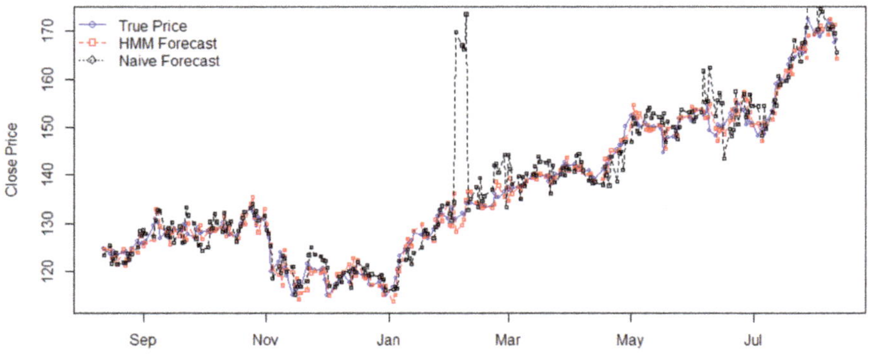

Figure 7. HMM prediction of Facebook stock daily close prices from 15 August 2016 to 11 August 2017 using two-states HMM and the naïve model.

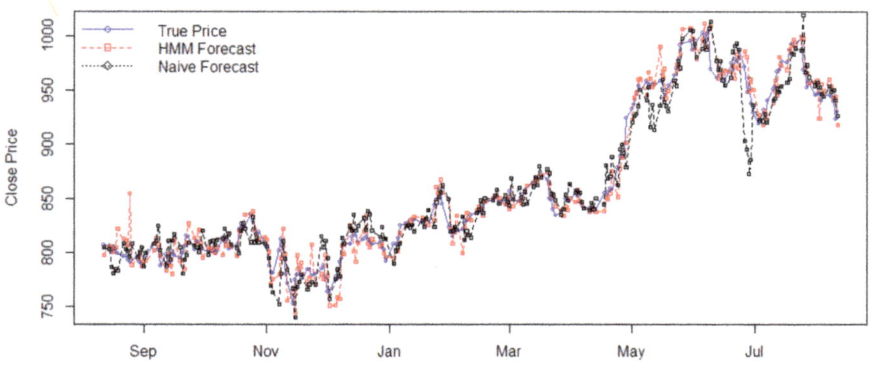

Figure 8. HMM prediction of Google stock daily close prices from 15 August 2016 to 11 August 2017 using two-states HMM and the naïve model.

We also compare the forecasting results of using the two-state HMM and the naïve method numerically by calculating the mean absolute percentage error, MAPE, of the estimations.

$$MAPE = \frac{1}{N}\sum_{i=1}^{N}\frac{|M_i - P_i|}{M_i},$$

where N is number of predicted points, M is market price, and P is predicted price of a stock. The results were shown in Table 2. In Table 2, the "Price Std." and "Return Std." are the standard deviation of the stock prices and stock returns, respectively, and the efficiencies are calculated by taking the errors of the naïve method divided by the errors of the HMM. All efficiencies in the table are bigger than one, showing that the HMM outperformed the naïve in forecasting stock prices.

Table 2. Comparison of MAPE of stock price predictions of Apple, Google, and Facebook from 15 August 2016 to 11 August 2017, between the HMM and the naïve forecast model.

Stock	Price Std.	Return Std.	HMM's MAPE	Naïve's MAPE	Efficiency
AAPL	17.0934	0.0113	0.0113	0.0133	1.1770
FB	14.4879	0.0111	0.0116	0.0213	1.8362
GOOGL	69.9839	0.0098	0.0107	0.0137	1.2804

Among these three stocks, GOOGL's prices have the highest volatility, but its returns have the lowest volatility. These factors will affect stock trading results so that we will present the results in the next section.

4.2. Stock Trading

In this section, we will use the predicted returns to trade these three stocks: AAPL, FB, and GOOGL. The trading strategy is: if HMM predicts that the stock price of AAPL will move up tomorrow, or its return is positive, we will buy this stock today and sell it tomorrow, assuming that we buy and sell with close prices. If the HMM predicts that the stock price will not increase tomorrow, then we will do nothing. We also assume that there is no trading cost. For each trade, we will buy or sell 100 shares of each of these three stocks. Based on the AIC and BIC results, we only use HMM with two states for the stock trading. Again, we will use a block of 252 trading days, one year, from 15 August 2016 to 11 August 2017 for model testing. We present the results of one year trading in the Table 3.

Table 3. Stock trading results from 15 August 2016 to 11 August 2017.

Stock	Models	Investment $	Earning $	Profit %
AAPL	HMM	10,908	3481	31.91
	Naïve	10,818	3513	32.47
FB	HMM	12,490	2939	23.53
	Naïve	12,488	2565	20.54
GOOGL	HMM	80,596	20,039	24.86
	Naïve	79,965	2715	3.40

In Table 3, the "Investment" is the price that we bought 100 shares of the stocks the first time. The "Earning" is the money gained, and the "Profit" is the percentage of return of the one-year trading. The results show that the HMM worked better than the naïve in trading the Facebook and Google stocks. Especially in the one year trading period, the GOOGL stock yielded a much higher return compared to the naïve forecast method. However, the results are reversed for AAPL stock. From Figures 6–8 and Table 2, we can see that, in the one period, the GOOGL prices have the highest volatility and lowest risk of returns among the three stocks. The naïve results are consistent with the risk of return levels, the "Return Std." in Table 2: the higher the risk, the better the return. The HMM followed close to the risk level theoretical. Based on the results in Table 3, using an HMM model, traders had returns of 32.00%, 24%, and 25% for AAPL, FB, GOOGL, respectively. Trading using HMM gave much higher returns than using the naïve for two stocks FB and GOOGL, but a likely lower return for the AAPL stock compare to the naïve.

5. Conclusions

Stock's performances are an essential indicator of the strength or weakness of the stock's corporation and economic viability in general. Many factors will drive stock prices up or down. In this paper, we use a Hidden Markov Model, HMM, to predict prices of three stocks: AAPL, GOOGL, and FB. We first use the AIC and BIC criterions to examine the performances of HMM numbers of states from two to four. The results showed that the HMM with two states is the best model among the two, three and four states. We then use the models to predict stock prices and compare the predictions with the naïve forecast results by plotting the forecasted prices versus the market prices and evaluating the mean absolute percentage error, MAPE. The prediction errors show that HMM worked better in predicting prices of the three stocks—AAPL, FB, and GOOGL—compared with the naïve method. In stock trading, the HMM outperformed the naïve for two stocks: FB and GOOGL. The graphs indicate that the HMM is the potential model for stock trading since it captures the trends of stock prices well.

Acknowledgments: I thank three anonymous referees at Risks, the editor Albert Cohen, and the assistant editor Shelly Liu for their comments and assistances.

Conflicts of Interest: The author declares no conflict of interest.

Appendix A

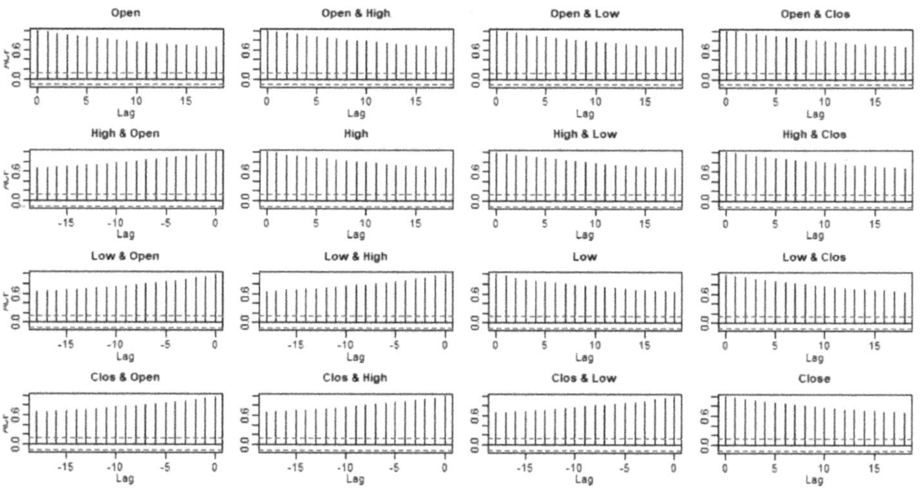

Figure A1. ACF test for correlation between open, low, high, and close of Facebook daily stock prices from 1 October 2014 to 1 October 2015.

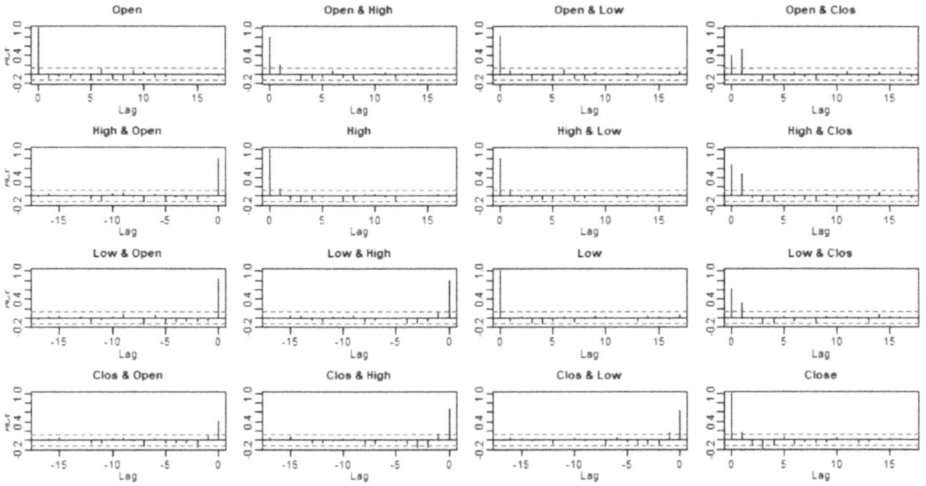

Figure A2. ACF test for correlation between open, low, high, and close of Facebook stock daily returns from 1 October 2014 to 1 October 2015.

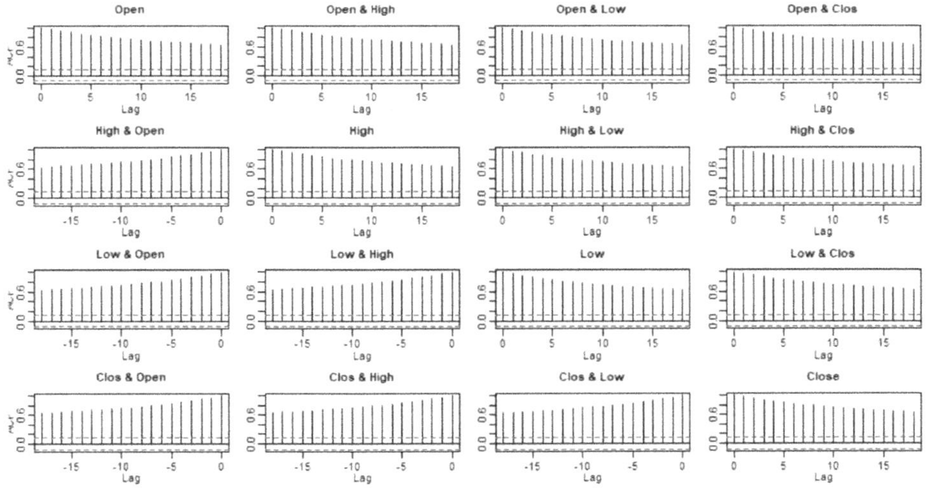

Figure A3. ACF test for correlation between open, low, high, and close of Google daily stock prices from 1 October 2014 to 1 October 2015.

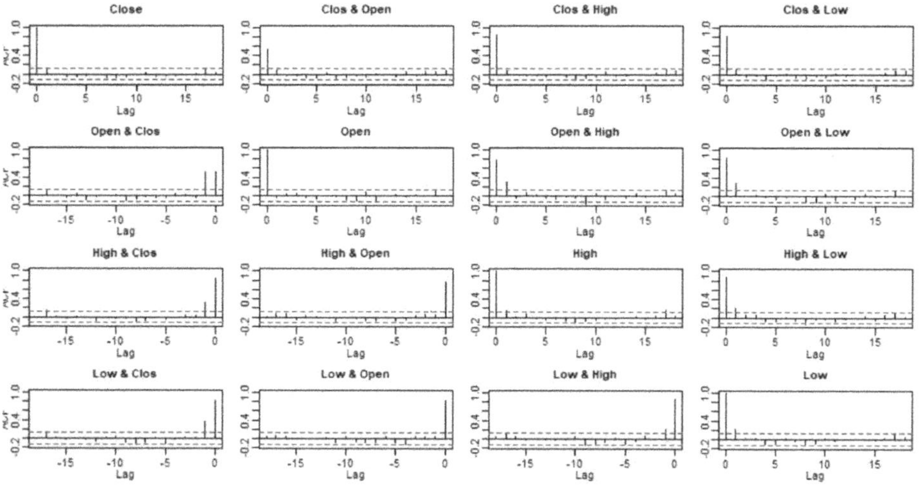

Figure A4. ACF test for correlation between open, low, high, and close of Google stock daily returns from 1 October 2014 to 1 October 2015.

References

Ang, Andrew, and Geert Bekaert. 2002. International Asset Allocaion with Regime Shifts. *The Review of Financial Studies* 15: 1137–87.

Baum, Leonard E., and John Alonzo Eagon. 1967. An inequality with applications to statistical estiation for probabilistic functions of Markov process and to a model for ecnogy. *Bulletin of the American Mathematical Society* 73: 360–63.

Baum, Leonard E., and Ted Petrie. 1966. Statistical Inference for Probabilistic Functions of Finite State Markov Chains. *The Annals of Mathematical Statistics* 37: 1554–63.

Baum, Leonard E., and George Roger Sell. 1968. Growth functions for transformations on manifolds. *Pacific Journal of Mathematics* 27: 211–27. doi: 10.2140/pjm.1968.27.211

Baum, Leonard E., Ted Petrie, George Soules, and Norman Weiss. 1970. A maximization technique occurring in the statistical analysis of probabilistic functions of Markov chains. *The Annals of Mathematical Statistics* 41: 164–71.

Chen, Chunchih. 2005. *How Well Can We Predict Currency Crises? Evidence from a Three-Regime Markov-Switching Model*. Davis: Department of Economics, UC Davis.

Forney, G. David. 1973. The Viterbi algorithm. *Proceedings of the IEEE* 61: 268–78.

Guidolin, Massimo, and Allan Timmermann. 2006. Asset Allocation under Multivariate Regime Switching. SSRN FRB of St. Louis Working Paper No. 2005-002C, FRB of St. Louis, MO, USA.

Hassan, Md Rafiul, and Baikunth Nath. 2005. Stock Market Forecasting Using Hidden Markov Models: A New approach. Paper presented at the IEEE fifth International Conference on Intelligent Systems Design and Applications, Warsaw, Poland, September 8–10.

Kritzman, Mark, Sebastien Page, and David Turkington. 2012. Regime Shifts: Implications for Dynamic Strategies. *Financial Analysts Journal* 68: 22–39.

Levinson, Stephen E., Lawrence R. Rabiner, and Man Mohan Sondhi. 1983. An introduction to the application of the theory of probabilistic functions of Markov process to automatic speech recognition. *Bell System Technical Journal* 62: 1035–74.

Li, Xiaolin, Marc Parizeau, and Réjean Plamondon. 2000. Training Hidden Markov Models with Multiple Observations—A Combinatorial Method. *IEEE Transactions on PAMI* 22: 371–77.

Nguyen, Nguyet, and Dung Nguyen. 2015. Hidden Markov Model for Stock Selection. Journal of Risks in special issue: Recent Advances in Mathematical Modeling of the Financial Markets. *Risks* 3: 455–73. doi:10.3390/risks3040455.

Nguyen, Nguyet Thi. 2014. Probabilistic Methods in Estimation and Prediction of Financial Models. Electronic Theses, Treatises and Dissertations Ph.D. dissertation, The Florida State University, Tallahassee, FL, USA.

Nobakht, B., C. E. Joseph, and B. Loni. 2012. Stock market analysis and prediction using hidden markov models. Paper presented at the 2012 Students Conference on IEEE Engineering and Systems (SCES), Allahabad, Uttar Pradesh, India, March 16–18, pp. 1–4.

Petrushin, Valery A. 2000. Hidden Markov Models: Fundamentals and Applications (part 2-discrete and continuous hidden markov models). Online Symposium for Electronics Engineer. Available online: http://citeseerx.ist.psu.edu/viewdoc/download?doi=10.1.1.378.3099&rep=rep1&type=pdf (accessed on 23 November 2017).

Rabiner, Lawrence R. 1989. A Tutorial on Hidden Markov Models and Selected Applications in Speech Recognition. *Proceedings of the IEEE* 77: 257–86.

Viterbi, Andrew J. 1967. Error bounds for convolutional codes and an asymptotically optimal decoding algorithm. *IEEE Transactions on Information Theory* IT-13: 260–69.

risks MDPI

Article

Effects of Gainsharing Provisions on the Selection of a Discount Rate for a Defined Benefit Pension Plan

Robert J. Rietz *, Evan Cronick, Shelby Mathers and Matt Pollie

Michigan State University, 220 Trowbridge Rd, East Lansing, MI 48824, USA; evancronick@gmail.com (E.C.); mathersshelby3@gmail.com (S.M.); polliematt@gmail.com (M.P.)

* Correspondence: dbactuary@hotmail.com; Tel.: +1-313-530-3071

Academic Editor: Albert Cohen
Received: 21 March 2017; Accepted: 12 June 2017; Published: 20 June 2017

Abstract: This paper examines the effect of gainsharing provisions on the selection of a discount rate for a defined benefit pension plan. The paper uses a traditional actuarial approach of discounting liabilities using the expected return of the associated pension fund. A stochastic Excel model was developed to simulate the effect of varying investment returns on a pension fund with four asset classes. Lognormal distributions were fitted to historical returns of two of the asset classes; large company stocks and long-term government bonds. A third lognormal distribution was designed to represent the investment returns of alternative investments, such as real estate and private equity. The fourth asset class represented short term cash investments and that return was held constant. The following variables were analyzed to determine their relative impact of gainsharing on the selection of a discount rate: hurdle rate, percentage of gainsharing, actuarial asset method smoothing period, and variations in asset allocation. A 50% gainsharing feature can reduce the discount rate for a defined benefit pension plan from 0.5% to more than 2.5%, depending on the gainsharing design and asset allocation.

Keywords: gainsharing; pension; discount rate; hurdle rate; asset smoothing; asset allocation

---

1. Introduction

This paper defines the cost of gainsharing as the reduction in the expected return on plan assets due to automatically removing a portion of excess investment gains for future gainsharing to plan participants. Even if some further action is required to actually distribute the excess investment gains, the cost event occurs when a portion of excess investment gains are removed from the pension plan assets. The cost is not dependent on whether the excess investment gains are provided to current retirees or another portion of the plan population, or whether the form of gainsharing is a 13th check or a permanent Cost-of-Living-Adjustment (COLA).

Gainsharing in a pension context is an asymmetric benefit; that is, benefits increase under favorable scenarios but do not decrease under unfavorable scenarios. There are many different pension gainsharing designs, such as a floor offset plan. Using excess pension fund returns for cash balance plan interest credit rates, perhaps with a minimum interest credit rate, is another example of gainsharing. Pension gainsharing is typically the sharing of unanticipated investment gains with some or all of the pension plan population—usually current retirees. Favorable (higher) mortality experience has also been discussed as a possible gainsharing design (Piggott et al. 2005), although that article anticipated decreases in annuity payments for unfavorable (lower) mortality experience.

Profit commissions in reinsurance provide a similar gainsharing analogy. Some brokers and reinsurance purchasers attempt to insert profit commission language in their contracts and they argue that these provisions are "free." Reinsurance underwriters and actuaries understand that profit commissions are in fact not free, and that their inclusion will increase the quoted price.

Several states appear to have or had some form of gainsharing in their retirement systems, among them Alaska, Arizona, Arkansas, Connecticut, Illinois, Indiana, Louisiana, Michigan, Minnesota, Mississippi, Oregon, and Texas, and quite possibly other states.

The *New York Times* cited gainsharing as a contributing factor to the underfunded status of Detroit's two large retirement systems (New York Times 2013). *Bloomberg* mentioned an analysis during Detroit's bankruptcy proceedings that said one of the systems paid about $951M in gainsharing benefits from 1985 to 2008, which would have accumulated to about $1.92B with the foregone interest (Bloomberg News 2013). This particular form of gainsharing required the city council's approval before it was paid, but gainsharing was approved 18 times during the 23 years of the analysis. Gainsharing was stopped in 2011, but the 2011 and 2012 payments were made retroactively due to provisions in Michigan's Constitution.

Washington State added a gainsharing provision to its retirement system in 1998. This provision gave members and retirees of certain state pension plans a share of "extraordinary investment returns" whenever the pension trust funds had average investment gains of more than 10% over the preceding four years (Department of Retirement Systems 2014a). Gainsharing events occurred in 1998 and 2000, for total gainsharing expenditures of about $1.0B (Washington State Court System 2014). The legislature repealed this gainsharing provision in 2007 and replaced it with other pension benefits, including options for early retirement (Department of Retirement Systems 2014b). The pensioners sued and the case worked its way through the courts and was argued before the Washington State Supreme Court in October 2013. That court ruled on August 14 2014 (Washington Education Association) that the repeal was allowable, because the enacting language contained a reservation of rights clause, stating that the legislature could repeal the benefits at a later date.

Yet, the actuarial literature on estimating the cost of gainsharing favorable pension investment experience is rather meager. Dr. Jeremy Gold, an actuary who co-authored (with Lawrence Bader) a seminal paper (Bader and Gold 2003) on the application of Financial Economics to pension plans, briefly mentioned "skim funds" in his September 2000 dissertation (Gold 2001). The Society of Actuaries published research papers on pension gainsharing in 2011 (Buchen et al. 2011), 2012 (New York Times 2013) and 2013 (Shang et al. 2013).

However, the current Actuarial Standard of Practice #4 (Actuarial Standards Board, 2013) *Measuring Pension Obligations and Determining Pension Plan Costs or Contributions*, requires actuaries to disclose the methods or procedures they used to estimate the cost of asymmetric benefits such as gainsharing, effective for measurement dates on or after 31 December 2014. The language of Section 3.5.3 of Actuarial Standards of Practice #4 (Plan Provisions that are Difficult to Measure), which specifically mentions gainsharing, states in part, "For such plan provisions, the actuary should consider using alternative valuation procedures, such as stochastic modeling, option-pricing techniques, or deterministic procedures in conjunction with assumptions that are adjusted to reflect the impact of variations in experience from year to year."

2. Results

The baseline asset allocation was 60% equities, 25% long-term government bonds, 10% alternative investments, and 5% treasury bills for the first three findings. There was no smoothing period used for the first two findings. Those two findings were then compared to the results using a two-, three-, four-, and five-year actuarial asset smoothing periods. The last finding used varying asset allocations with a five-year smoothing period and a 10% hurdle.

There were four primary findings from an analysis of the model's output:

1. The higher the hurdle rate, the lower the cost of gainsharing.
2. The cost of gainsharing is directly proportional to the percentage of favorable investment gains that are gainshared.
3. If excess investment gains are calculated from smoothed assets, the cost of gainsharing decreases as the smoothing period increases.

4. More aggressive asset allocations lead to greater "peak" returns for a given hurdle rate and smoothing period, which increases the cost of gainsharing. However, these greater returns also experience greater volatility, which further increases the cost of gainsharing.

2.1. Hurdle Rate

When an actuary assumes a future discount rate, such as 7.25%, the actuary knows that the fund will not earn exactly 7.25% every year. The fund may earn 15.54% in one year and the fund may lose 12.06% in another year. The actuary assumes that these investment gains and losses will offset each other over time, and the fund will earn an average of 7.25% over the life of the plan.

However, when a portion of investment returns above the hurdle rate are shared with plan participants, investment returns above 7.25% will not completely offset investment returns below 7.25% and the fund will not earn 7.25% over the life of the plan. If the fund earned 16.54% in some future year, and the pension plan provisions required sharing half of investment gains over a 10.00% hurdle, then plan participants would receive 3.27% of fund assets (half of the net of 16.54% minus the 10.00% hurdle rate) in that year. Thus, the fund would actually have earned only 13.27% in that year.

Figure 1 and the supporting data in Table 1 display one of the 5000 30-year simulations for a 10% hurdle, 50% gainsharing, no smoothing period, and the baseline asset allocation. It shows each year's total investment return and the investment return after gainsharing. In this simulation, the pension fund earned 10.19% before gainsharing, and gainsharing lowered the fund's 30-year return to 8.07%. Thus, the cost of gainsharing for this single simulation and these parameters was a reduction in the discount rate of 2.12%. For comparison, after 5000 simulations, the fund earned 9.38% before gainsharing, and gainsharing lowered the fund's 30-year return to 7.05%. The average cost of gainsharing was 2.33%. The corresponding standard deviations were 10.50%, 8.05%, and 2.90%. For comparison, the corresponding standard deviations after 5000 simulations were 2.40%, 1.88%, and 0.52%.

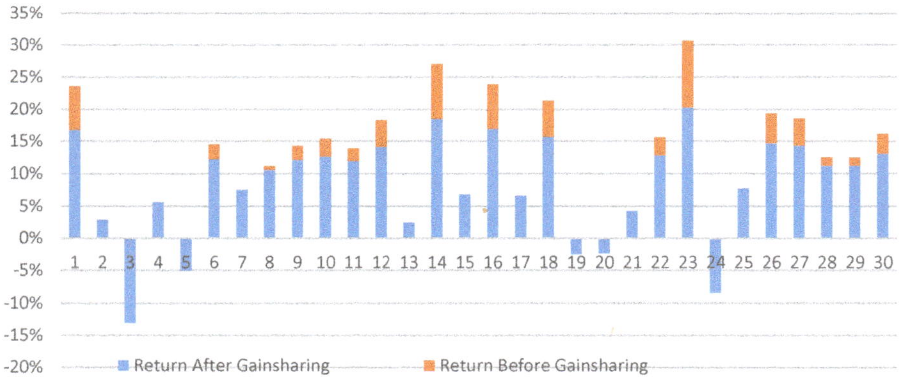

Figure 1. Annual returns before and after gainsharing.

Figure 2 displays the relationship between the hurdle rate and the cost of gainsharing for the baseline asset allocation and smoothing period. The cost of gainsharing, which is the decrease in the expected return on plan assets for this model, ranges from 2.57% for a 9.00% hurdle to 1.356% for a 15.00% hurdle rate. Thus, the actuary would lower the discount rate by these amounts for a 50% gainsharing design with these sample hurdle rates, no smoothing period, and the baseline asset allocation.

Table 1. Returns Before and After 50% Gainsharing in One of 5000 Simulations.

Year	Before G/S	After G/S	Year	Before G/S	After G/S	Year	Before G/S	After G/S
1	23.58%	16.79%	11	13.85%	11.93%	21	4.29%	4.29%
2	2.89%	2.89%	12	18.24%	14.12%	22	15.62%	12.81%
3	−13.10%	−13.10%	13	2.43%	2.43%	23	30.59%	20.30%
4	5.58%	0.00%	14	27.04%	18.52%	24	−8.44%	−8.44%
5	−5.08%	−5.08%	15	6.80%	6.80%	25	7.73%	7.73%
6	14.50%	12.25%	16	23.86%	16.93%	26	19.34%	14.67%
7	7.54%	7.54%	17	6.63%	6.63%	27	18.58%	14.29%
8	11.14%	10.57%	18	21.30%	15.65%	28	12.44%	11.22%
9	14.24%	12.12%	19	−2.52%	−2.52%	29	12.39%	11.19%
10	15.36%	12.68%	20	−2.34%	−2.34%	30	16.14%	13.07%

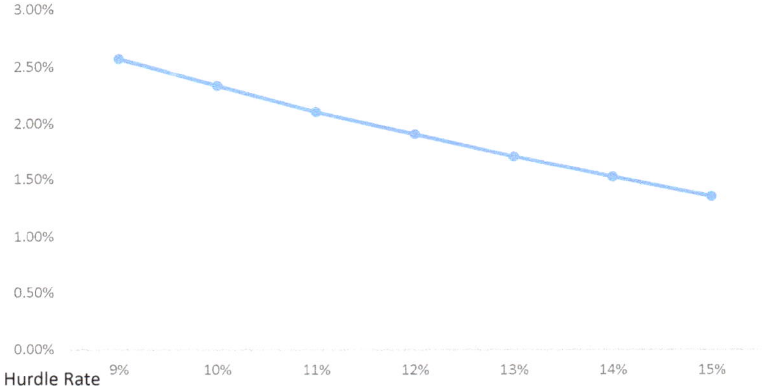

Figure 2. Cost of 50% gainsharing by hurdle rate.

2.2. *Percentage of Gainsharing*

Intuitively, the cost of gainsharing should be directly proportional to the percent of investment returns over the hurdle rate that are provided to pension plan participants. Figure 3 displays the model's results of varying the amount of gainsharing, confirming this intuitive conclusion.

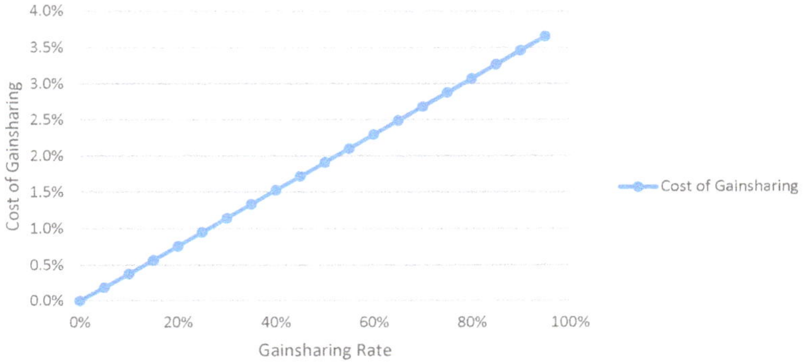

Figure 3. Gainsharing rate vs. cost of gainsharing.

2.3. Smoothing Period

An actuarial asset smoothing method averages investment gains and losses over a defined smoothing period, typically three to five years. Plan sponsors utilize a smoothed actuarial value of assets in the belief that this method will help stabilize their contributions, though this does not always occur to the extent that plan sponsors desire. This paper uses the term "smoothing period" for the longer "actuarial asset method smoothing period."

Suppose the fund earned 17.54%, −11.06%, 7.23%, 20.48%, and 17.27% over a five-year period. Without a smoothing period, the first, fourth, and fifth years would call for gainsharing a portion of investment gains over 10.00% with plan participants. However, if the gainsharing plan provisions required an investment gain to exceed a 10.00% hurdle rate for a rolling five-year period, then plan participants would receive only 0.292% of fund assets at the end of the fifth year.

$$(17.54\% - 11.06\% + 7.23\% + 20.48\% + 17.27\%)/5 - 10.00\% = 0.292\%$$

If the fund earned 16.08% or less in the sixth year, then plan participants would not receive gainsharing at the end of the sixth year.

$$(-11.06\% + 7.23\% + 20.48\% + 17.27\% + 16.08\%)/5 - 10.00\% = 0.0\%$$

Figure 4 and the supporting data in Table 2 display the relationship of the smoothing period on the cost of gainsharing with a 10.00% hurdle. The cost of gainsharing, which is the decrease in the assumed discount rate for this model, ranges from 1.83% for no smoothing period to 0.77% for a five-year smoothing period. Thus, the actuary should lower the discount rate by these amounts for these smoothing periods, given a 50% gainsharing design, a 10.00% hurdle rate, and the baseline asset allocation.

Table 2. Cost of 50% Gainsharing by Hurdle Rate and Smoothing Period.

Hurdle Rate	9.00%	10.00%	11.00%	12.00%	13.00%	14.00%	15.00%
no smoothing	2.56%	2.31%	2.10%	1.90%	1.69%	1.50%	1.35%
2 year smoothing	1.98%	1.74%	1.50%	1.29%	1.11%	0.94%	0.80%
3 year smoothing	1.74%	1.47%	1.23%	1.04%	0.85%	0.70%	0.57%
4 year smoothing	1.58%	1.30%	1.10%	0.88%	0.71%	0.58%	0.45%
5 year smoothing	1.48%	1.23%	0.99%	0.80%	0.63%	0.49%	0.39%

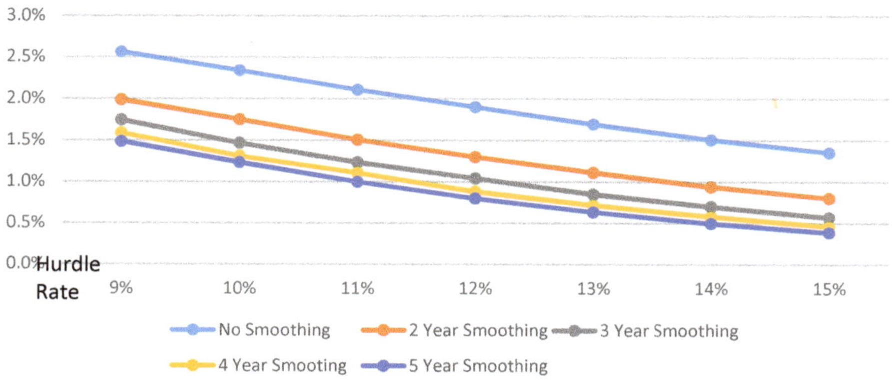

Figure 4. Cost of gainsharing by hurdle rate and smoothing period.

Figure 5 and Table 3 show the fund's returns before and after 50% gainsharing with a 10% hurdle rate for these smoothing periods.

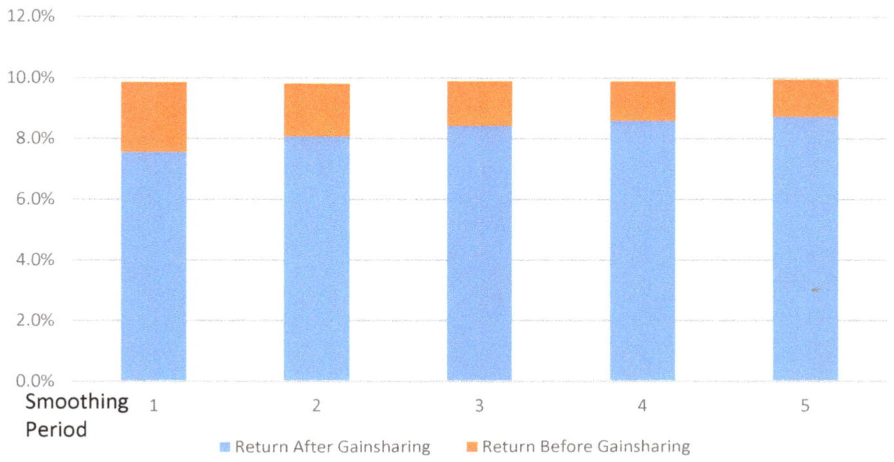

Figure 5. Cost of gainsharing by smoothing period.

Table 3. Returns Before and After 50% Gainsharing by Smoothing Period for 10% Hurdle Rate.

	Before G/S	After G/S	G/S Cost
no smoothing	9.84%	7.55%	2.30%
2 year smoothing	9.80%	8.06%	1.74%
3 year smoothing	9.88%	8.41%	1.47%
4 year smoothing	9.89%	8.59%	1.30%
5 year smoothing	9.94%	8.72%	1.22%

2.4. Asset Allocation

Four portfolios were constructed, ranging from conservative to aggressive. The allocations to stocks and alternative investments were increased in the aggressive portfolios, while the allocation to long-term government bonds decreased. Table 4 displays the asset allocation in each portfolio.

Table 4. Asset Allocation of the Four Portfolios.

	Large Company Stocks	Long-Term Government Bonds	Alternative Investments	Treasury Bills
Portfolio A	55	35	5	5
Portfolio B	60	25	10	5
Portfolio C	65	15	15	5
Portfolio D	70	10	15	5

Figure 6 and its supporting data in Table 5 display the fund's returns before and after 50% gainsharing for each of these asset allocations, a 10% hurdle rate, and a five-year smoothing period. As expected, the more aggressive portfolios yielded higher returns. These higher returns provided more favorable investment returns to be gainshared, thus increasing the cost of gainsharing for the more aggressive portfolios. Greater volatility of the more aggressive portfolios also increases the cost of gainsharing, as the investment return "peaks" are higher, leading to greater gainsharing. However, a five-year smoothing period tends to dampen the cost of gainsharing.

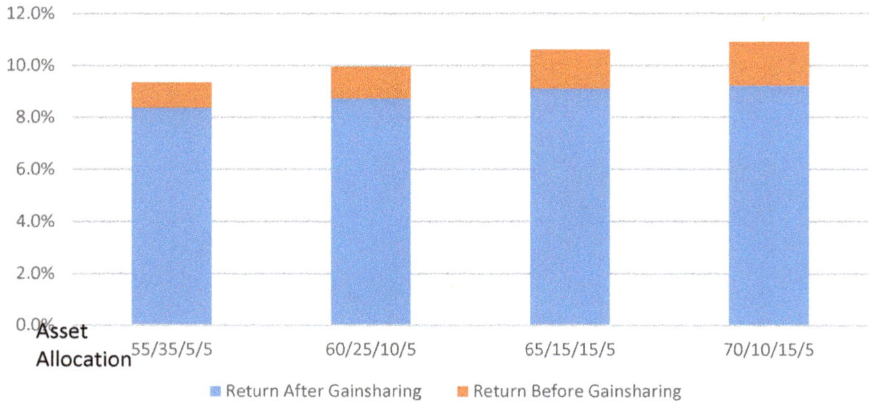

Figure 6. Returns and cost of gainsharing for four asset allocations.

Table 5. Effect of Asset Allocation on Returns Before and After 50% Gainsharing.

Asset Allocation	Before G/S	After G/S	G/S Cost
55/35/5/5	9.33%	8.36%	0.97%
60/25/10/5	9.94%	8.72%	1.22%
65/15/15/5	10.61%	9.11%	1.50%
70/10/15/5	10.90%	9.23%	1.67%

2.5. Limitations of the Model

This model has some limitations because it was a one semester independent study project. For example, inflation is a significant factor in investment returns, particularly long-term bond returns, but the model does not reflect current or future inflation in any of the future asset class returns. Also, current long-term bond returns are near historic lows, and the model ignores this when it generates bond returns in the early years of the projection. Many more sophisticated models have been developed to calculate discount rates with additional asset classes, beginning with the current investment environment.

The use of Ibbotson data, the alternative investment class, and treasury bills all produced a particular set of results. Using different sources of data for the historical returns or different historical periods would undoubtedly lead to different results. While this model used only four asset classes, most pension funds have several more asset classes, each with its own expected return and volatility. Using more asset classes would also lead to different results.

However, these limiting factors are all applied equally to the calculation of future returns without and with gainsharing. This paper focuses on the difference between these two returns, and not on the absolute value of either return, thus minimizing the impact of these limitations.

This model is intended to illustrate the impact of various gainsharing designs under different circumstances, and should not be used to calculate the cost of gainsharing in any specific situation.

3. Discussion

Many defined benefit pension plans, particularly public retirement systems, contain gainsharing provisions. Most of these designs provide gainsharing benefits to existing retirees, but gainsharing can also be provided to active participants. For example, a cash balance plan could provide additional interest credits to active participants in a year when investment earnings exceed the hurdle rate. Indeed, a few of these plans already exist. A career average plan could also provide an additional automatic retroactive accrual after a plan year of favorable investment experience. However, Actuarial Standards of Practice #4 requires an actuary to select a discount rate that reflects any gainsharing provision and to disclose how the impact was derived, or to disclose that the gainsharing benefit was not reflected in the calculations and the rationale for excluding it. This requirement is effective for measurement dates on or after 31 December 2014.

Note that some plan designs have been developed that may appear to be gainsharing designs, but are not. Participants in the New Brunswick Shared Risk Pension Plan (Munnell and Sass 2013) have a base benefit and an ancillary benefit. The base benefit does not change but the ancillary benefit can increase or decrease, depending on the funded status of the pension plan. Participants in a Retirement Shares Plan (Fuerst 2014) design might also have their benefits increase or decrease. Retirement Share Plan participants can elect certain investment choices, and their benefits are based on the investment experience of the underlying investments.

The distinguishing characteristic of these last two designs are their symmetry. That is, participants are exposed to the risk of their benefits increasing or decreasing. In asymmetrical gainsharing plan designs, participants' benefits can increase with no downside risk, and that risk is borne by plan sponsors or tax-payers in the case of public plans.

4. Materials and Methods

This section describes the development of a stochastic Excel model that demonstrates the cost of gainsharing favorable pension investment using stochastic techniques. Analyzing the output of the model, this paper makes certain observations on the estimated cost of gainsharing based on hurdle rates, the percentage of gainsharing applied to excess investment gains, the actuarial asset method smoothing period, and variations in asset allocation.

The stochastic model uses four asset classes:

- Large company stocks
- Long-term government bonds
- Alternative investments
- Treasury bills

The first three asset classes model future returns using Ibbotson (Ibbotson Associates 2010) data from 1926 through 2009. The historical data for the first two asset classes was fitted to a pair of three parameter lognormal distributions which were used for the model's asset return projections. Commercial software identified three parameter lognormal distributions as well fitting distributions to the underlying data according to Kolmogorov-Smirnov and Anderson-Darling criteria.

A lognormal distribution was used when the original data is positively skewed, but the natural logarithms of the original data tend to follow a normal distribution. In this distribution (Aristizabal 2012),

- μ is the scale parameter that stretch or shrink the distribution,
- σ is the shape parameter that affects the shape of the distribution, and
- γ is the threshold parameter or location parameter that defines the point where the support set of the distribution begins.

The third asset class (for example, real estate and private equity) was assigned parameters intended to imitate 2.0% higher yielding investments with 10.0% greater volatility than large company stocks. A constant treasury bill yield represented short term cash investments, typically a minor portion of the overall asset allocation. The asset allocation among these four asset classes was a user-controlled parameter, as was the hurdle rate, percentage of gainsharing, and asset smoothing period.

A stochastic model projected investment returns for 30 years without gainsharing and with gainsharing, and calculated those two geometric returns for the simulation. It then calculated the arithmetic average of 5000 such geometric averages without gainsharing and the arithmetic average of 5000 such geometric averages with gainsharing. The cost of gainsharing is the difference between these two arithmetic averages.

Several assumptions are used in the model, in addition to the ones already mentioned, such as:

- Future annual benefit payments equal future annual contributions
- No correlation between asset classes
- Returns are net of investment expenses
- No administrative expenses were payable from the trust
- Continuously compounded returns of each asset class follow a lognormal distribution with mean $(r - \delta - 0.5\sigma^2)$ and variance σ^2, where
  - ○ r is based on the average continuously compounded rate of return of each asset class over the indicated historical data,
  - ○ δ is the dividend rate, and
  - ○ σ is based on historical prices of each asset class over the indicated historical data.
- Each year, the asset class return evolves according to the model:
  - ○ $S_h = S_{h-1}e^{(r-\delta-0.5\sigma^2)h+\sigma\sqrt{h}Z}$
  - ○ where Z is a lognormal random variable, whose expected value is $E(Z) = e^{\mu+\frac{1}{2}\sigma^2} + \gamma$,
  - ○ and μ, σ, γ are parameters that fit the lognormal distribution to the underlying historical returns for each asset class.

The model for large company stocks was defined by:

- ○ $Z \sim lognormal(\mu = 6.588,\ \sigma = 0.02834,\ \gamma = -714.18)$
- ○ and $E(Z) = e^{(6.588)+\frac{1}{2}(0.02834)^2} + (-714.18) = 12.148$.

And for long-term government bonds, the model was defined by:

- ○ $Z \sim lognormal(\mu = 3.576,\ \sigma = 0.024905,\ \gamma = -31.033)$
- ○ and $E(Z) = e^{(3.576)+\frac{1}{2}(0.024905)^2} + (-31.033) = 5.823$.

5. Conclusions

Despite its characterization in some media reports, gainsharing is neither good nor evil. It is merely a design of some pension plans, like early retirement reduction factors. However, asymmetrical gainsharing features are not free; they have an underlying cost. This model demonstrates how a stochastic method could be used to estimate the cost of gainsharing.

Acknowledgments: There were no funds or grants received for this article.

Author Contributions: This paper is based on work done by Evan Cronick, Shelby Mathers and Matt Pollie in a one semester independent study actuarial science class at Michigan State University in 2014–2015. The corresponding author thanks them for developing the stochastic EXCEL gainsharing model and their suggestions on various drafts of this paper, before they joined their respective employers. The author also thanks anonymous reviewers whose advice greatly improved this paper.

Conflicts of Interest: The authors declare no conflict of interest.

References

Aristizabal, Rodrigo J. 2012. Estimating the Parameters of the Three-Parameter Lognormal Distribution. Master's Thesis, Florida International University, Miami, FL, USA, March 30.

Actuarial Standards Board. 2013. *Measuring Pension Obligations and Determining Pension Plan Costs or Contributions*. Washington: American Academy of Actuaries.

Bader, Lawrence, and Jeremy Gold. 2003. Reinventing Pension Actuarial Science. *The Pension Forum* 14: 2.
Bloomberg News. 2013. Detroit Union Seeks to Revive 13th Pension Check Policy. *Bloomberg*, September 27.
Buchen, Isaac, David R. Cantor, Jared Forman, Sheldon Gamzon, and PricewaterhouseCoopers LLP. 2011. *Embedded Options in Pension Plans*. Schaumburg: Society of Actuaries Pension Section.
Department of Retirement Systems. 2014a. *Supreme Court Rulings Issued on Gain Sharing*. UCOLA Lawsuits. Tumwater: Washington State Department of Retirement Systems.
Department of Retirement Systems. 2014b. *Supreme Court Rulings Issued on Gain Sharing*. UCOLA lawsuits. Tumwater: Washington State Department of Retirement Systems.
England, Colin, Thomas Bolton, and Ann Sturner. 2012. *Considerations in the Evaluation of Gain Sharing Designs*. Schaumburg: Society of Actuaries Research Project.
Fuerst, Donald E. 2014. *Retirement Shares Plan: A New Model of Risk Sharing*. Philadelphia: Pension Research Council of the Wharton School of the University of Pennsylvania.
Gold, Jeremy. 2001. *Assumed Rates of Discount for Valuations of Publicly Sponsored Defined Benefit Plans*. Pension Research Council, Philadelphia: The Wharton School of the University of Pennsylvania, WP2001-06.
Ibbotson Associates. 2010. *Ibbotson 2010 Classic Yearbook*. Hoboken: Ibbotson Associates.
Munnell, Alicia H., and Steven A. Sass. 2013. *New Brunswick's New Shared Risk Pension Plan*. Chestnut Hill: Center for Retirement Research at Boston College.
New York Times. 2013. Case in Detroit Highlights Cost of 'Extra' Pension Payments. *New York Times*, October 22.
Piggott, John, Emiliano Valdez, and Bettina Detzel. 2005. The Simple Analytics of a Pooled Annuity Fund. *Journal of Risk and Insurance* 72: 497–520. [CrossRef]
Shang, Kailan, Jen-Chieh Huang, and Hua Su. 2013. *Pension Plan Embedded Option Valuation*. Schaumburg: Society of Actuaries Research Project.
Washington State Court System. 2014. Case #87424-7. Olympia, WA, USA.
Washington Education Association. *Washington Department of Retirement Systems 2014*. Olympia: Washington Department of Retirement Systems.

risks

MDPI

Article

Model Uncertainty in Operational Risk Modeling Due to Data Truncation: A Single Risk Case

Daoping Yu [1] **and Vytaras Brazauskas** [2,*]

[1] School of Computer Science and Mathematics, University of Central Missouri, Warrensburg, MO 64093, USA; dyu@ucmo.edu
[2] Department of Mathematical Sciences, University of Wisconsin-Milwaukee, P.O. Box 413, Milwaukee, WI 53201, USA
* Correspondence: vytaras@uwm.edu; Tel.: +1-414-229-5656

Academic Editor: Albert Cohen
Received: 27 April 2017; Accepted: 1 September 2017; Published: 13 September 2017

Abstract: Over the last decade, researchers, practitioners, and regulators have had intense debates about how to treat the data collection threshold in operational risk modeling. Several approaches have been employed to fit the loss severity distribution: the empirical approach, the "naive" approach, the shifted approach, and the truncated approach. Since each approach is based on a different set of assumptions, different probability models emerge. Thus, model uncertainty arises. The main objective of this paper is to understand the impact of model uncertainty on the value-at-risk (VaR) estimators. To accomplish that, we take the bank's perspective and study a single risk. Under this simplified scenario, we can solve the problem analytically (when the underlying distribution is exponential) and show that it uncovers similar patterns among VaR estimates to those based on the simulation approach (when data follow a Lomax distribution). We demonstrate that for a fixed probability distribution, the choice of the truncated approach yields the lowest VaR estimates, which may be viewed as beneficial to the bank, whilst the "naive" and shifted approaches lead to higher estimates of VaR. The advantages and disadvantages of each approach and the probability distributions under study are further investigated using a real data set for legal losses in a business unit (Cruz 2002).

Keywords: asymptotics; data truncation; delta method; model validation; operational risk; VaR estimation

1. Introduction

Basel II/III and *Solvency II* are the leading international regulatory frameworks for banking and insurance industries, and mandate that financial institutions build separate capital reserves for operational risk. Within the advanced measurement approach (AMA) framework, the loss distribution approach (LDA) is the most sophisticated tool for estimating the operational risk capital. According to LDA, the risk-based capital is an extreme quantile of the annual aggregate loss distribution (e.g., the 99.9th percentile), which is called value-at-risk or VaR. Some recent discussions between the industry and the regulatory community in the United States reveal that the LDA implementation still has a number of "thorny" issues (AMA Group 2013). One such issue is the treatment of data collection threshold. Here is what is stated on page 3 of the same document: "Although the industry generally accepts the existence of operational losses below the data collection threshold, the appropriate treatment of such losses in the context of capital estimation is still widely debated."

Various assumptions about the data collection threshold have been considered in the existing literature: known threshold (Baud et al. 2002; Shevchenko and Temnov 2009), threshold as unknown parameter (Baud et al. 2002), stochastic threshold whose distribution has to be modeled (Baud et al. 2002; de Fontnouvelle et al. 2006), and time varying threshold that may scale according to inflation and business factors (Shevchenko and Temnov 2009). In this paper, we will assume that the threshold is known. Given (external) operational risk databases (which often collect losses exceeding, for example, $1 million), such an assumption is appropriate.

Further, the annual aggregate loss variable is a combination of two variables—loss frequency and loss severity—and there are different ways to estimate risk-based capital. One way is to estimate the untruncated severity and truncation-adjusted frequency and then compute VaR. This approach follows directly from the results described by Brazauskas, Jones, and Zitikis (Brazauskas et al. 2015). Another way is to estimate the truncated severity and unadjusted frequency to compute VaR. For a comprehensive review of analytic techniques for truncated data in the context of operational risk modeling, see Cruz, Peters, Shevchenko (Cruz et al. 2015, sct. 7.9). Furthermore, as is known in practice, the severity distribution is a key driver of the capital estimate (Opdyke 2014). This is the part of the aggregate model where initial assumptions about the data collection threshold are most influential. A number of authors have examined some aspects of this topic in the past (e.g., Cavallo et al. 2012; Chernobai et al. 2007; Ergashev et al. 2016; Luo et al. 2007; Moscadelli et al. 2005). The modeling approaches they (collectively) considered include: the empirical approach, the "naive" approach, the shifted approach, and the truncated approach. Since each approach is based on a different set of assumptions, different probability models emerge. Thus, model uncertainty arises.

The main objective of this paper is to understand the impact of model uncertainty on risk measurements, and (hopefully) help settle the debate about the treatment of data collection threshold in the context of capital estimation. Solving such a problem under a general setup (i.e., by considering many interdependent risks and multiple stakeholders) is only possible through extensive simulations, but that would not produce much insight. Therefore, we simplify the problem by taking the bank's perspective and by studying a single risk. Under this simplified scenario, we can solve the problem analytically (when the underlying distribution is exponential), and show that it uncovers similar patterns among VaR estimates to those based on the simulation approach (when data follow a Lomax distribution). We demonstrate that for a fixed probability distribution, the choice of the truncated approach yields lowest VaR estimates, which may be viewed as beneficial to the bank, whilst the "naive" and shifted approaches lead to higher estimates of VaR. As for the choice of severity distributions, besides the Lomax distribution (which is heavy tailed and hence appropriate in operational risk modeling), we intentionally select the light-tailed exponential distribution to show what happens to VaR estimates when incorrect assumptions are made. Moreover, our step-by-step analysis not only shows "what happens" to VaR estimates, but it helps understand the questions of "how" and "why" it happens. Additionally, perhaps surprisingly, our numerical illustrations reveal why the shifted approach is still popular. That is because it is flexible enough to pass standard model validation tests and thus cannot be discarded from practical use based on such tools alone. In summary, this paper contributes to the existing literature by performing an extensive investigation of the impact that model uncertainty has on the VaR estimators, justifies the soundness of the regulatory recommendation (i.e., use the truncated approach), and paves the way for a number of research problems in this important area.

It is worth noting here that the model uncertainty considered in this paper is an epistemic one, not a random uncertainty. It can be reduced—but not completely eliminated—by employing sound model validation tools, and in some cases (e.g., when the shifted approach is used) may require out-of-model knowledge. In a more general context, model uncertainty is an important topic within the model risk governance framework as regulated by the OCC and the Federal Reserve Bank in the U.S. and the Basel Committee on Banking Supervision for the G20 countries (e.g., Basel Coordination Committee 2014; Office of the Comptroller of the Currency 2011).

The rest of the paper is structured as follows. In Section 2, we describe how model uncertainty emerges and study its effects on VaR estimates. This is done by employing theoretical results (presented in Appendix A) and via Monte Carlo simulations. Next, in Section 3, these explorations are further illustrated using a real data set for legal losses in a business unit. Finally, concluding remarks are offered in Section 4. Additionally, in Appendix A we provide some technical tools that are essential for analytic treatment of the problem. In particular, key probabilistic features of the generalized Pareto distribution are presented, and several asymptotic theorems of mathematical statistics are specified.

2. Model Uncertainty

We start this section by introducing the problem and describing how model uncertainty arises. Then, in Section 2.2, we review several typical models used for estimating VaR. Finally, using the theoretical results of Appendix and Monte Carlo simulations, we finish with two parametric examples, where we evaluate the probability of overestimating true VaR for exponential and Lomax distributions.

2.1. Motivation

In order to fully understand the problem, in this paper we will walk the reader through the entire modeling process and demonstrate how our assumptions affect the end product, which is the estimate of severity VaR. Since the problem involves collected data, initial assumptions, and statistical inference (in this case, point estimation and assessment of estimates' variability), it will be tackled with statistical tools, including theoretical tools (asymptotics), Monte Carlo simulations, and real-data case studies. Let us briefly discuss data, assumptions, and inference. As noted in Section 1, it is generally agreed that operational losses exist above and below the data collection threshold. Therefore, this implies that choosing a modeling approach is equivalent to deciding on how much probability mass there is below the threshold.

In Figure 1, we provide graphs of truncated, naive, and shifted probability density functions of two distributions (studied formally in Section 2.3): *Exponential*, which is a light-tailed model; and *Lomax*, with the tail parameter $\alpha = 3.5$, which is a moderately-tailed model (it has three finite moments). We clearly see that those models are quite different below the threshold $t = 195,000$, but in practice that would be unobserved. On the other hand, in the observable range (i.e., above $t = 195,000$), the plotted density functions are similar (note that the vertical axes are in very small units, 10^{-6}) and converge to each other as losses get larger (note how little differentiation there is among the curves when losses exceed 1,000,000). Moreover, it is even difficult to spot a difference between the corresponding exponential and Lomax models, though the two distributions possess distinct theoretical properties (e.g., for one all moments are finite, whereas for the other only three are). Additionally, since probability mass below the threshold is one of the "known unknowns," it will have to be estimated from the observed data (above t). As will be shown in the case study of Section 3, this task may look straightforward, but its outcomes vary and are heavily influenced by the initial assumptions.

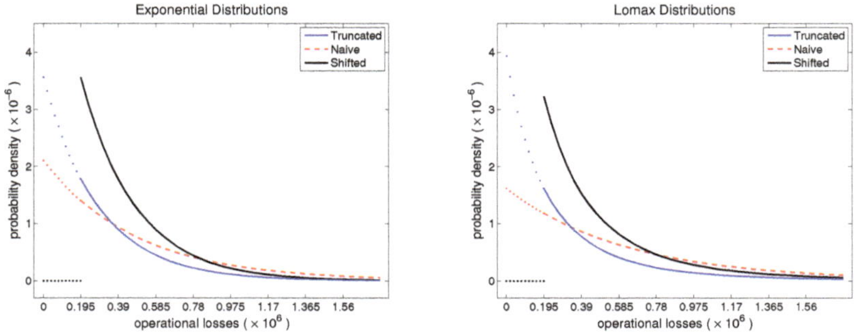

Figure 1. Truncated, naive, and shifted *Exponential* (σ) and *Lomax* $(\alpha = 3.5, \theta_1)$ probability density functions. Data collection threshold $t = 195,000$, with 50% of data unobserved. Parameters σ and θ_1 are chosen to match those in Tables 2 and 3 (see Section 2.3).

To formalize this dicussion, suppose that $Y_1, \ldots, Y_N$ represent (positive and *i.i.d.*) loss severities resulting from operational risk, and let us denote their probability density function (pdf), cumulative distribution function (cdf), and quantile function (qf) as f, F, and F^{-1}, respectively. Then, the problem of estimating VaR-based capital is equivalent to finding an estimate of qf at some probability level (e.g., $F^{-1}(\beta)$). The difficulty here is that we observe only those Y_i's that exceed some known data collection threshold $t \gg 0$. That is, the actually observed variables are X_i's with

$$X_1 \stackrel{d}{=} Y_{i_1} \mid Y_{i_1} > t, \; \ldots, \; X_n \stackrel{d}{=} Y_{i_n} \mid Y_{i_n} > t, \tag{1}$$

where $\stackrel{d}{=}$ denotes "equal in probability" and $n = \sum_{j=1}^{N} \mathbf{1}\{Y_j > t\}$. Their cdf F_*, pdf f_*, qf F_*^{-1} are related to F, f, F^{-1}, and given by

$$F_*(x) = \frac{F(x) - F(t)}{1 - F(t)}, \quad f_*(x) = \frac{f(x)}{1 - F(t)}, \quad F_*^{-1}(u) = F^{-1}\big(u + (1-u)F(t)\big) \tag{2}$$

for $x \geq t$ and $0 < u < 1$, and for $x < t$, $f_*(x) = F_*(x) = 0$.

Further, let us investigate the behavior of $F_*^{-1}(u)$ from a purely mathematical point of view. Since the qf of continuous random variables (which is the case for loss severities) is a strictly increasing function and $(1-u)F(t) \geq 0$, it follows that

$$F_*^{-1}(u) = F^{-1}\big(u + (1-u)F(t)\big) \geq F^{-1}(u), \quad 0 < u < 1,$$

with the inequality being strict unless $F(t) = 0$. This implies that any quantile of the observable variable X is never below the corresponding quantile of the unobservable variable Y, which is true VaR. This fact is certainly not new (for example, see the extensive analysis by Opdyke (2014), about the effect of Jensen's inequality in VaR estimation). However, if we now change our perspective from mathematical to statistical and take into account the method of how VaR is estimated, we could augment the above discussion with new insights and improve our understanding.

A review of existing methods shows that, besides estimation of VaR using Equations (1) and (2) under the truncated distribution framework, there are other parametric methods that employ different strategies, such as the naive and shifted approaches (described in Section 2.2.2). In particular, those two approaches use the data $X_1, \ldots, X_n$ and either ignore t or recognize it in some other way than Equation (2). Thus, model uncertainty emerges.

2.2. Typical Models

2.2.1. Empirical Model

As mentioned earlier, the empirical model is restricted to the range of observed data. So, it uses data from Equation (1), but since the empirical estimator $\widehat{F}(t) = 0$, Formulas (2) simplify to $\widehat{F}_*(x) = \widehat{F}(x)$, $\widehat{f}_*(x) = \widehat{f}(x)$, for $x \geq t$, and $\widehat{F}_*^{-1}(u) = \widehat{F}^{-1}(u)$. Thus, the model cannot take full advantage of Equation (2). In this case, the VaR(β) estimator is simply $\widehat{F}^{-1}(\beta) = X_{(\lceil n\beta \rceil)}$, and as follows from Theorem A1,

$$X_{(\lceil n\beta \rceil)} \text{ is } \mathcal{AN}\left(F_*^{-1}(\beta), \; \frac{1}{n}\frac{\beta(1-\beta)}{f_*^2(F_*^{-1}(\beta))}\right).$$

We now can evaluate the probability of overestimating the true VaR by a certain percentage; i.e., we want to study function $H(c) := \mathbf{P}\{X_{(\lceil n\beta \rceil)} > c\,F^{-1}(\beta)\}$ for $c \geq 1$. Using Z to denote the standard normal random variable and Φ for its cdf, and taking into account Equation (2), we proceed as follows:

$$H(c) = \mathbf{P}\{X_{(\lceil n\beta \rceil)} > c\,F^{-1}(\beta)\} \approx \mathbf{P}\left\{ Z > \left[c\,F^{-1}(\beta) - F_*^{-1}(\beta)\right] \times \left(\frac{1}{n} \frac{\beta(1-\beta)}{f_*^2(F_*^{-1}(\beta))} \right)^{-1/2} \right\}$$
$$= 1 - \Phi\left(\sqrt{\frac{n}{\beta(1-\beta)}} \left[c\,F^{-1}(\beta) - F^{-1}(\beta + (1-\beta)F(t))\right] \times \frac{f\,(F^{-1}(\beta + (1-\beta)F(t)))}{1-F(t)} \right).$$

From this formula, we clearly see that $0.50 \leq H(1) < 1$, with the lower bound being achieved when $F(t) = 0$. Additionally, at the other extreme, when $c \to \infty$, we observe $H(c) \to 0$. Additional numerical illustrations are provided in Table 1.

Several conclusions emerge from the table. First, the case $F(t) = 0$ is a benchmark case that illustrates the behavior of the empirical estimator when data is completely observed (and in that case $X_{(\lceil n\beta \rceil)}$ would be a consistent method for estimating VaR(β)). We see that $H(1) = 0.5$, and then it quickly decreases to 0 as c increases. The decrease is quickest for the light-tailed distribution, exponential($\sigma = 1$), and slowest for the heavy-tailed Lomax ($\alpha = 1, \theta_2 = 1$), which has no finite moments. Second, as less data is observed (i.e., as $F(t)$ increases to 0.5 and 0.9), the probability of overestimating true VaR increases for all types of distribution. For example, while the probability of overestimating VaR(0.995) by 20% ($c = 1.2$) for the light-tailed distribution is only 0.226 for $F(t) = 0$, it increases to 0.398 and 0.811 for $F(t) = 0.5$ and 0.9, respectively. If severity follows the heavy-tailed distribution, then $H(1.2)$ is 0.444, 0.612, 0.734 for $F(t) = 0$, 0.5, 0.9, respectively. Finally, in practice, typical scenarios would be near $F(t) = 0.9$ with moderate- or heavy-tailed severity distributions, which corresponds to quite unfavorable patterns in the table. Indeed, function $H(c)$ declines very slowly, and the probability of overestimating VaR(0.995) by 100% seems like a norm (0.577 and 0.715).

Table 1. Function $H(c)$ evaluated for various combinations of c, confidence level β, proportion of unobserved data $F(t)$, and severity distributions with varying degrees of tail heaviness ranging from light- and moderate-tailed to heavy-tailed. The sample size is $n = 100$.

c	β	$F(t) = 0$			$F(t) = 0.5$			$F(t) = 0.9$		
		Light	*Moderate*	*Heavy*	*Light*	*Moderate*	*Heavy*	*Light*	*Moderate*	*Heavy*
1	0.95	0.500	0.500	0.500	0.944	0.925	0.874	1.000	1.000	0.981
	0.995	0.500	0.500	0.500	0.688	0.672	0.638	0.949	0.884	0.738
	0.999	0.500	0.500	0.500	0.587	0.579	0.563	0.767	0.703	0.612
1.2	0.95	0.085	0.178	0.331	0.585	0.753	0.824	1.000	1.000	0.978
	0.995	0.226	0.349	0.444	0.398	0.551	0.612	0.811	0.840	0.734
	0.999	0.331	0.424	0.475	0.414	0.517	0.550	0.615	0.668	0.610
1.5	0.95	0.000	0.010	0.138	0.032	0.326	0.726	0.968	0.996	0.975
	0.995	0.030	0.167	0.362	0.083	0.364	0.571	0.403	0.756	0.727
	0.999	0.137	0.317	0.437	0.191	0.424	0.532	0.358	0.613	0.606
2	0.95	0.000	0.000	0.015	0.000	0.009	0.523	0.056	0.930	0.968
	0.995	0.000	0.026	0.240	0.001	0.127	0.501	0.017	0.577	0.715
	0.999	0.014	0.170	0.376	0.025	0.280	0.500	0.073	0.516	0.600

Threshold t is 0 for $F(t) = 0$ and 195,000 for $F(t) = 0.5, 0.9$. Distributions: *Light* = exponential(σ), *Moderate* = Lomax($\alpha = 3.5, \theta_1$), *Heavy* = Lomax($\alpha = 1, \theta_2$). For $F(t) = 0$: $\sigma = \theta_1 = \theta_2 = 1$. For $F(t) = 0.5$: $\sigma = 281,326$, $\theta_1 = 890,355$, $\theta_2 = 195,000$. For $F(t) = 0.9$: $\sigma = 84,687$, $\theta_1 = 209,520$, $\theta_2 = 21,667$.

2.2.2. Parametric Models

We discuss three parametric approaches: truncated, naive, and shifted.

Truncated Approach: The truncated approach uses the observed data $X_1, \ldots, X_n$ and fully recognizes its distributional properties. That is, it takes into account Equation (2) and derives maximum likelihood estimator (MLE) values by maximizing the following log-likelihood function:

$$\log \mathcal{L}_T(\theta_1, \ldots, \theta_k \,|\, X_1, \ldots, X_n) = \sum_{i=1}^{n} \log f_*(X_i) = \sum_{i=1}^{n} \log\left(\frac{f(X_i)}{1 - F(t)}\right), \tag{3}$$

where $\theta_1, \ldots, \theta_k$ are the parameters of pdf f. Once parameter MLEs are available, VaR(β) estimate is found by plugging those MLE values into $F^{-1}(\beta)$. □

Naive Approach: The naive approach uses the observed data $X_1, \ldots, X_n$, but ignores the presence of threshold t. That is, it bypasses Equation (2) and derives MLE values by maximizing the following log-likelihood function:

$$\log \mathcal{L}_N(\theta_1, \ldots, \theta_k \,|\, X_1, \ldots, X_n) = \sum_{i=1}^{n} \log f(X_i). \tag{4}$$

Notice that since $f(X_i) \leq f(X_i)/[1 - F(t)] = f_*(X_i)$, with the inequality being strict for $F(t) > 0$, the log-likelihood of the naive approach will always be less than that of the truncated approach. This in turn implies that parameter MLEs of pdf f derived using the naive approach will always be suboptimal, unless $F(t) = 0$. Finally, VaR(β) estimate is computed by inserting parameter MLEs (the ones found using the naive approach) into $F^{-1}(\beta)$. □

Shifted Approach: The shifted approach uses the observed data $X_1, \ldots, X_n$ and recognizes threshold t by first shifting the observations by t. Then, it derives parameter MLEs by maximizing the following log-likelihood function:

$$\log \mathcal{L}_S(\theta_1, \ldots, \theta_k \,|\, X_1, \ldots, X_n) = \sum_{i=1}^{n} \log f(X_i - t). \tag{5}$$

By comparing Equations (4) and (5), we can easily see that the naive approach is a special case of the shifted approach (with $t = 0$). Moreover, although this may only be of interest to theoreticians, one could introduce a class of shifted models by considering $f(X_i - s)$, with $0 \leq s \leq t$, and create infinitely many versions of the shifted model. Finally, VaR(β) is estimated by applying parameter MLEs (the ones found using the shifted approach) to $F^{-1}(\beta) + t$. □

2.3. Parametric VaR Estimation

2.3.1. Example 1: Exponential Distribution

Suppose $Y_1, \ldots, Y_N$ are *i.i.d.* and follow an exponential distribution, with pdf, cdf, and qf given by Equations (A1), (A2), and (A4), respectively, with $\gamma = 0$ and $\mu = 0$. However, we observe only variable X, whose relation to Y is governed by Equations (1) and (2). Now, by plugging exponential pdf and/or cdf into the log-likelihoods Equations (3)–(5), we obtain

$$\begin{aligned} \log \mathcal{L}_T(\sigma \,|\, X_1, \ldots, X_n) = \sum_{i=1}^{n} \log\left(\frac{f(X_i)}{1 - F(t)}\right) &= \sum_{i=1}^{n} \log\left(\frac{\sigma^{-1} e^{-X_i/\sigma}}{e^{-t/\sigma}}\right) \\ &= -n \log \sigma + \sum_{i=1}^{n} \frac{-(X_i - t)}{\sigma}, \end{aligned} \tag{6}$$

$$\begin{aligned} \log \mathcal{L}_N(\sigma \,|\, X_1, \ldots, X_n) = \sum_{i=1}^{n} \log f(X_i) &= \sum_{i=1}^{n} \log\left(\sigma^{-1} e^{-X_i/\sigma}\right) \\ &= -n \log \sigma + \sum_{i=1}^{n} \frac{-X_i}{\sigma}, \end{aligned} \tag{7}$$

$$\log \mathcal{L}_S(\sigma \mid X_1, \ldots, X_n) = \sum_{i=1}^{n} \log f(X_i - t) = \sum_{i=1}^{n} \log\left(\sigma^{-1} e^{-(X_i - t)/\sigma}\right) \\ = -n \log \sigma + \sum_{i=1}^{n} \frac{-(X_i - t)}{\sigma}, \tag{8}$$

where the subscripts T, N, S (for $\mathcal{L}$) denote "truncated", "naive", and "shifted", respectively. Then, by maximizing the log-likelihoods (6)–(8) with respect to σ, we get the following MLE formulas for parameter σ under the truncated, naive, and shifted approaches:

$$\widehat{\sigma}_T = \overline{X} - t, \quad \widehat{\sigma}_N = \overline{X}, \quad \widehat{\sigma}_S = \overline{X} - t,$$

where $\overline{X} = n^{-1} \sum_{i=1}^{n} X_i$.

Next, by inserting $\widehat{\sigma}_T$, $\widehat{\sigma}_N$, and $\widehat{\sigma}_S$ into the corresponding qf's as described in Section 2.2.2, we get the following $\mathrm{VaR}(\beta)$ estimators:

$$\widehat{\mathrm{VaR}}_T(\beta) = -\widehat{\sigma}_T \log(1-\beta), \quad \widehat{\mathrm{VaR}}_N(\beta) = -\widehat{\sigma}_N \log(1-\beta), \quad \widehat{\mathrm{VaR}}_S(\beta) = -\widehat{\sigma}_S \log(1-\beta) + t.$$

Further, a direct application of Theorem A2 for $\widehat{\sigma}_T$ (with obvious adjustment for $\widehat{\sigma}_N$), yields that

$$\widehat{\sigma}_T \text{ is } \mathcal{AN}\left(\sigma, \frac{\sigma^2}{n}\right), \quad \widehat{\sigma}_N \text{ is } \mathcal{AN}\left(\sigma + t, \frac{\sigma^2}{n}\right), \quad \widehat{\sigma}_S \text{ is } \mathcal{AN}\left(\sigma, \frac{\sigma^2}{n}\right).$$

Furthermore, having established $\mathcal{AN}$ for parameter MLEs, we can apply Theorem A3 and specify asymptotic distributions for VaR estimators. They are as follows:

$$\widehat{\mathrm{VaR}}_T(\beta) \text{ is } \mathcal{AN}\left(-\sigma \log(1-\beta), \frac{\sigma^2 \log^2(1-\beta)}{n}\right),$$

$$\widehat{\mathrm{VaR}}_N(\beta) \text{ is } \mathcal{AN}\left(-(\sigma + t) \log(1-\beta), \frac{\sigma^2 \log^2(1-\beta)}{n}\right),$$

$$\widehat{\mathrm{VaR}}_S(\beta) \text{ is } \mathcal{AN}\left(-\sigma \log(1-\beta) + t, \frac{\sigma^2 \log^2(1-\beta)}{n}\right).$$

Note that while all three estimators are equivalent in terms of the asymptotic variance, they are centered around different targets. The mean of the truncated estimator is the true quantile of the underlying exponential model (estimating which is the objective of this exercise) and the mean of the other two methods is shifted upwards; in both cases, the shift is a function of threshold t.

Finally, as was done for the empirical VaR estimator in Section 2.2.1, we now define function $H(c) = \mathbf{P}\{\widehat{\mathrm{VaR}}(\beta) > c\, F^{-1}(\beta)\}$ for $c \geq 1$, the probability of overestimating the target by $(c-1)100\%$ for each parametric VaR estimator and study its behavior:

$$H_T(c) \approx 1 - \Phi\left((c-1)\sqrt{n}\right), \quad H_N(c) \approx 1 - \Phi\left((c-1)\sqrt{n} - \sqrt{n}(t/\sigma)\right),$$

$$H_S(c) \approx 1 - \Phi\left((c-1)\sqrt{n} + \sqrt{n}(t/\sigma) \log^{-1}(1-\beta)\right).$$

Table 2 provides numerical illustrations of functions $H_T(c)$, $H_N(c)$, $H_S(c)$. We select the same parameter values as in the light-tailed cases of Table 1. From Table 2, we see that the case $F(t) = 0$ is special in the sense that all three methods become identical and perform well. For example, the probability of overestimating true VaR by 20% is only 0.023 for all three methods, and it is essentially 0 as $c \geq 1.5$. In this case, parametric estimators outperform the empirical estimator (see Table 1) because they are designed for the correct underlying model. However, as the proportion of unobserved data increases (i.e., as $F(t)$ increases to 0.5 and 0.9), only the truncated approach maintains its excellent performance. Additionally, while the shifted estimator is better than the naive, both methods perform poorly and even rarely improve the empirical estimator. For example, in the extreme case of $F(t) = 0.9$, the naive and shifted methods overestimate true VaR(0.95) by 50% with probability 1.000 and 0.996, respectively, whereas the corresponding probability for the empirical estimator is 0.968.

Table 2. Functions $H_T(c)$, $H_N(c)$, $H_S(c)$ evaluated for various combinations of c, confidence level β, and proportion of unobserved data $F(t)$. (The sample size is $n = 100$.)

c	β	$F(t) = 0$			$F(t) = 0.5$			$F(t) = 0.9$		
		T	N	S	T	N	S	T	N	S
1	0.95	0.500	0.500	0.500	0.500	1.000	0.990	0.500	1.000	1.000
	0.995	0.500	0.500	0.500	0.500	1.000	0.905	0.500	1.000	1.000
	0.999	0.500	0.500	0.500	0.500	1.000	0.842	0.500	1.000	1.000
1.2	0.95	0.023	0.023	0.023	0.023	1.000	0.623	0.023	1.000	1.000
	0.995	0.023	0.023	0.023	0.023	1.000	0.245	0.023	1.000	0.991
	0.999	0.023	0.023	0.023	0.023	1.000	0.159	0.023	1.000	0.909
1.5	0.95	0.000	0.000	0.000	0.000	0.973	0.004	0.000	1.000	0.996
	0.995	0.000	0.000	0.000	0.000	0.973	0.000	0.000	1.000	0.257
	0.999	0.000	0.000	0.000	0.000	0.973	0.000	0.000	1.000	0.048
2	0.95	0.000	0.000	0.000	0.000	0.001	0.000	0.000	1.000	0.010
	0.995	0.000	0.000	0.000	0.000	0.001	0.000	0.000	1.000	0.000
	0.999	0.000	0.000	0.000	0.000	0.001	0.000	0.000	1.000	0.000

NOTE: Threshold t is 0 for $F(t) = 0$ and 195,000 for $F(t) = 0.5, 0.9$. Exponential(σ), with $\sigma = 1$ (for $F(t) = 0$), $\sigma = 281{,}326$ (for $F(t) = 0.5$), $\sigma = 84{,}687$ (for $F(t) = 0.9$).

2.3.2. Example 2: Lomax Distribution

Suppose that $Y_1, \ldots, Y_N$ are *i.i.d.* and follow a Lomax distribution, with pdf, cdf, and qf given by Equations (A1), (A2), and (A4), respectively, with $\alpha = 1/\gamma$, $\theta = \sigma/\gamma$, and $\mu = 0$. However, we observe only variable X whose relation to Y is governed by Equations (1) and (2). Now, unlike the exponential case, maximization of the log-likelihoods (3)–(5) does not yield explicit formulas for MLEs of a Lomax model. So, in order to evaluate functions $H_T(c)$, $H_N(c)$, $H_S(c)$, we use Monte Carlo simulations to implement the following procedure: (i) generate a Lomax-distributed data set according to pre-specified parameters; (ii) numerically evaluate parameters α and θ for each approach; (iii) compute the corresponding estimates of VaR; (iv) check whether the inequality in function $H(c)$ is true for each approach and record the outcomes; and (v) repeat steps (i)–(iv) a large number of times and report the proportion of "true" outcomes in step (iv). To facilitate comparisons with the moderate-tailed scenarios in Table 1, we select simulation parameters as follows:

- Severity distribution Lomax($\alpha = 3.5, \theta_1$): $\theta_1 = 1$ (for $F(t) = 0$), $\theta_1 = 890{,}355$ (for $F(t) = 0.5$), $\theta_1 = 209{,}520$ (for $F(t) = 0.9$).
- Threshold: $t = 0$ (for $F(t) = 0$) and $t = 195{,}000$ (for $F(t) = 0.5,\ 0.9$).
- Complete sample size: $N = 100$ (for $F(t) = 0$); $N = 200$ (for $F(t) = 0.5$); $N = 1000$ (for $F(t) = 0.9$). The *average* observed sample size is $n = 100$.
- Number of simulation runs: 10,000.

Simulation results are summarized in Table 3, where we again observe similar patterns to those of Tables 1 and 2. This time, however, the entries are more volatile, which is mostly due to the randomness of the simulation experiment (e.g., all entries for the T and $c = 1$ cases theoretically should be equal to 0.5, because those cases correspond to the probability of a normal random variable exceeding its mean, but they are slightly off). The $F(t) = 0$ case is where all parametric models perform well, as they should. However, once they leave that comfort zone ($F(t) = 0.5$ and 0.9), only the truncated approach works well, with the naive and shifted estimators performing similarly to the empirical estimator. Since Lomax distributions have heavier tails than exponential, function $H(c)$ under the truncated approach is also affected by that and converges to 0 (as $c \to \infty$) slower. In other words, for a given choice of model parameters, the coefficient of variation of VaR is larger for the Lomax model than that for the exponential model, thus resulting in larger overestimating probabilities than those in Table 2. The difference between the T entries in Tables 2 and 3 is also influenced by the fact that the numerically found MLE does not often produce very stable or trustworthy parameter estimates for the truncated approach, which is a common technical issue. Nonetheless, the overall message here does not change: we observe certain patterns among functions $H_T(c)$, $H_N(c)$, and $H_S(c)$, which are no different from those of Section 2.3.1, which were found using the theoretical tools.

Table 3. Functions $H_T(c)$, $H_N(c)$, $H_S(c)$ evaluated for various combinations of c, confidence level β, and proportion of unobserved data $F(t)$. The *average* sample size is $n = 100$.

c	β	$F(t) = 0$			$F(t) = 0.5$			$F(t) = 0.9$		
		T	N	S	T	N	S	T	N	S
1	0.95	0.453	0.453	0.453	0.459	0.951	0.982	0.547	0.908	1.000
	0.995	0.433	0.433	0.433	0.435	0.692	0.734	0.444	0.891	0.998
	0.999	0.426	0.426	0.426	0.437	0.149	0.624	0.331	0.867	0.944
1.2	0.95	0.131	0.131	0.131	0.095	0.945	0.791	0.356	0.904	0.999
	0.995	0.247	0.247	0.247	0.184	0.208	0.518	0.170	0.889	0.993
	0.999	0.297	0.297	0.297	0.272	0.059	0.484	0.121	0.845	0.864
1.5	0.95	0.009	0.009	0.009	0.002	0.626	0.270	0.112	0.879	0.998
	0.995	0.097	0.097	0.097	0.044	0.044	0.278	0.021	0.875	0.872
	0.999	0.178	0.178	0.178	0.123	0.016	0.313	0.019	0.843	0.708
2	0.95	0.000	0.000	0.000	0.000	0.032	0.010	0.002	0.865	0.984
	0.995	0.025	0.025	0.025	0.004	0.004	0.090	0.000	0.851	0.563
	0.999	0.075	0.075	0.075	0.032	0.002	0.147	0.001	0.224	0.459

NOTE: Threshold t is 0 for $F(t) = 0$ and 195,000 for $F(t) = 0.5, 0.9$. Lomax($\alpha = 3.5, \theta_1$), with $\theta_1 = 1$ (for $F(t) = 0$), $\theta_1 = 890,355$ (for $F(t) = 0.5$), $\theta_1 = 209,520$ (for $F(t) = 0.9$).

3. Real-Data Example

In this section we illustrate how all the modeling approaches considered in this paper (empirical and three parametric) perform on real data. We go step-by-step through the entire modeling process, starting with model fitting and validation, continuing with VaR estimation, and completing the example with model-based predictions for quantities below the data collection threshold. Note that for the parametric approaches we employ both exponential and Lomax models, although exponential is clearly not a viable model for operational risk data (because its tail is too light for such data). However, the exponential distribution is a model for which all relevant formulas are explicit and can be easily verified by the reader. Moreover, the data analysis exercise also serves as an example of how to identify inappropriate models (e.g., exponential), and if the model validation step is ignored, to illustrate how wrong the predictions based on such models can be.

3.1. Data

We will use the data set from Cruz (2002, p. 57), which has 75 observations and represents the cost of legal events for a business unit. The cost is measured in U.S. dollars. To illustrate the impact of data collection threshold on the selected models, we split the data set into two parts: losses that are *at least* \$195,000, which will be treated as observed and used for model building and VaR estimation, and losses that are *below* \$195,000, which will be used at the end of the exercise to assess the quality of model-based predictions. This data-splitting scenario implies that there are 54 observed losses. A quick exploratory analysis of the observed data shows that it is right-skewed and potentially heavy-tailed, with the first quartile 248,342, median 355,000, and the third quartile 630,200; its mean is 546,021, standard deviation 602,912, and skewness 3.8.

3.2. Model Fitting

We fit exponential and Lomax models to the observed data and use three parametric approaches: truncated, naive, and shifted. The truncation threshold is $t = 195,000$. For the exponential model, MLE formulas for σ are available in Section 2.3.1. For the Lomax distribution, we perform numerical maximization of the log-likelihoods (3)–(5) to compute parameter values. For the data set under consideration, the resulting MLE values are reported in Table 4. Additionally, the corresponding estimates for parameter variances and covariances were computed using Theorem A3.

Table 4. Parameter maximum likelihood estimators (MLEs, with variance and covariance estimates in parentheses) of the exponential and Lomax models, using truncated, naive, and shifted approaches.

Model	*Truncated*	*Naive*	*Shifted*
Exponential	$\widehat{\sigma} = 351,021$ (2.28×10^9)	$\widehat{\sigma} = 546,021$ (5.52×10^9)	$\widehat{\sigma} = 351,021$ (2.28×10^9)
Lomax	$\widehat{\alpha} = 1.91$ (0.569)	$\widehat{\alpha} = 22.51$ $(5,189.86)$	$\widehat{\alpha} = 1.91$ (0.569)
	$\widehat{\theta} = 151,234$ (3.84×10^{10})	$\widehat{\theta} = 11,735,899$ (1.54×10^{15})	$\widehat{\theta} = 346,234$ (3.84×10^{10})
	$(\widehat{cov}(\widehat{\alpha},\widehat{\theta}) = 138,934)$	$(\widehat{cov}(\widehat{\alpha},\widehat{\theta}) = 2.82 \times 10^9)$	$(\widehat{cov}(\widehat{\alpha},\widehat{\theta}) = 138,934)$

3.3. Model Validation

To validate the fitted models, we employ quantile–quantile plots (QQ plots) and two goodness-of-fit statistics: Kolmogorov–Smirnov (KS) and Anderson–Darling (AD).

In Figure 2, we present plots of the fitted-versus-observed quantiles for the six models of Section 3.2. In order to avoid visual distortions due to large spacings between the most extreme observations, both axes in all the plots are measured on a logarithmic scale. That is, the points plotted in those graphs are the following pairs:

$$\left(\log\left(\widehat{G}^{-1}(u_i)\right),\ \log\left(X_{(i)}\right)\right), \quad i = 1, \ldots, 54,$$

where $\widehat{G}^{-1}$ is the estimated parametric qf, $X_{(1)} \leq \cdots \leq X_{(54)}$ denote the ordered losses, and $u_i = (i - 0.5)/54$ is the quantile level. For the truncated approach, $\widehat{G}^{-1}(u_i) = \widehat{F}^{-1}(u_i + \widehat{F}(195,000)(1 - u_i))$; for the naive approach, $\widehat{G}^{-1}(u_i) = \widehat{F}^{-1}(u_i)$; for the shifted approach, $\widehat{G}^{-1}(u_i) = \widehat{F}^{-1}(u_i) + 195,000$. Additionally, the corresponding cdf and qf functions were evaluated using the MLE values from Table 4.

We can see from Figure 2 that Lomax models show a better overall fit than exponential models, and especially in the extreme right tail. That is, most of the points in those plots do not deviate from the 45° line. The naive approach seems off, but the truncated and shifted approaches do a reasonably good job for both distributions, with Lomax models exhibiting slightly better fits.

The KS and AD goodness-of-fit statistics measure, respectively, the maximum absolute distance and the cumulative weighted quadratic distance (with more weight on the tails) between the empirical cdf $\widehat{F}_n(x) = n^{-1}\sum_{i=1}^{n} \mathbf{1}\{X_i \leq x\}$ and the parametrically estimated cdf $\widehat{G}(x)$. Their respective computational formulas are given by

$$\mathrm{KS}_n = \max_{1 \leq i \leq n} \left\{ \left|\widehat{G}(X_{(i)}) - \frac{i-1}{n}\right|, \left|\widehat{G}(X_{(i)}) - \frac{i}{n}\right| \right\}$$

and

$$\mathrm{AD}_n = -n + n\sum_{i=1}^{n} (i/n)^2 \log\left(\frac{\widehat{G}(X_{(i+1)})}{\widehat{G}(X_{(i)})}\right) - n\sum_{i=0}^{n-1} (1 - i/n)^2 \log\left(\frac{1 - \widehat{G}(X_{(i+1)})}{1 - \widehat{G}(X_{(i)})}\right),$$

where $195,000 = X_{(0)} \leq X_{(1)} \leq \cdots \leq X_{(n)} \leq X_{(n+1)} = \infty$ denote the ordered claim severities. Additionally, $\widehat{G}(X_{(i)}) = \widehat{F}_*(X_{(i)})$ for the truncated approach, $\widehat{G}(X_{(i)}) = \widehat{F}(X_{(i)})$ for the naive approach, and $\widehat{G}(X_{(i)}) = \widehat{F}(X_{(i)} - 195,000)$ for the shifted approach. Note that $n = 54$ and the corresponding cdf's were evaluated using the MLE values from Table 4. The p-values of the KS and AD tests were computed using parametric bootstrap with 10,000 simulation runs. For a brief description of the parametric bootstrap procedure, see, for example, Klugman, Panjer, and Willmot (2012, sct. 20.4.5).

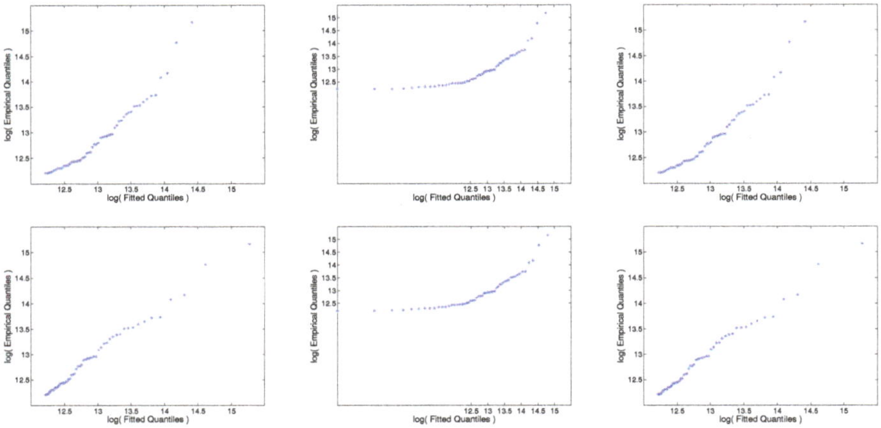

Figure 2. Fitted-versus-observed *log*-losses for exponential (**top row**) and Lomax (**bottom row**) distributions, using truncated (**left**), naive (**middle**), and shifted (**right**) approaches.

As the results of Table 5 suggest, both naive models are strongly rejected by the KS and AD tests, which is consistent with the conclusions based on QQ-plots. The truncated and shifted exponential models are also rejected, which strengthens our "weak" decisions based on QQ-plots. Unfortunately, for this data set, neither KS nor the AD test can help us with differentiating between the truncated and shifted Lomax models, as both of them fit the data very well.

Table 5. Values of KS and AD statistics (with p-values in parentheses) for the fitted models, using truncated, naive, and shifted approaches.

Model	**Kolmogorov–Smirnov**			**Anderson–Darling**		
	Truncated	*Naive*	*Shifted*	*Truncated*	*Naive*	*Shifted*
Exponential	0.186 (0.004)	0.307 (0.000)	0.186 (0.004)	3.398 (0.000)	4.509 (0.000)	3.398 (0.000)
Lomax	0.072 (0.632)	0.316 (0.000)	0.072 (0.631)	0.272 (0.671)	4.696 (0.000)	0.272 (0.678)

3.4. VaR Estimates

Having fitted and validated the models, we now compute several point and interval estimates of VaR(β) for all six models. The purpose of calculating VaR(β) estimates for all—"good" and "bad"—models is to see the impact that model fit (which is driven by the initial assumptions) has on the capital estimates. The results are summarized in Table 6, where empirical estimates of VaR(β) are also reported for completeness. The confidence intervals for the exponential models are derived using Theorem A3 and based on the variance estimates from Table 4. For the Lomax models, the confidence intervals are obtained using parametric bootstrap with 10,000 simulation runs.

Table 6. Value-at-risk (VaR)(β) estimates (with 95% confidence intervals in parentheses), measured in millions and based on the fitted models, using truncated, naive, and shifted approaches.

Model	β	*Truncated*	*Naive*	*Shifted*
	0.95	1.052 (0.771; 1.332)	1.636 (1.199; 2.072)	1.247 (0.966; 1.527)
Exponential	0.995	1.860 (1.364; 2.356)	2.893 (2.121; 3.665)	2.055 (1.559; 2.551)
	0.999	2.425 (1.778; 3.071)	3.772 (2.766; 4.778)	2.620 (1.973; 3.266)
	0.95	0.576 (0.071; 1.160)	1.670 (1.134; 2.206)	1.514 (0.978; 2.755)
Lomax	0.995	2.281 (0.413; 4.758)	3.114 (2.257; 5.023)	5.417 (2.213; 20.604)
	0.999	5.504 (1.100; 13.627)	4.214 (3.019; 8.586)	12.797 (3.649; 89.992)

Empirical estimates of VaR(β): 1.416 (for $\beta = 0.95$) and 3.822 (for $\beta = 0.995$ and 0.999).

We see from the table that the VaR(β) estimates based on the naive approach significantly differ from the rest. The difference between truncated and shifted estimates at the exponential model is $t = 195,000$. For the Lomax model, these two approaches—which exhibited nearly perfect fits to data—produce substantially different estimates, especially at the very extreme tail. Finally, in view of such large differences between parametric estimates (which resulted from models with excellent fits), the empirical estimates do not seem completely off.

3.5. Model Predictions

As the final test of our models, we check their out-of-sample predictive power. Table 7 provides the "unobserved" legal losses, which will be used to verify how accurate our model-based predictions are. To start with, we note that the empirical and shifted models are not able to produce meaningful predictions because they assume that such data were impossible to occur (i.e., $\widehat{F}(195,000) = 0$ for these two approaches). So, we now work only with the truncated and naive models.

Table 7. Unobserved costs of legal events (below $195,000).

142,774.19	146,875.00	151,000.00	160,000.00	176,000.00	182,435.12	191,070.31
143,000.00	150,411.29	153,592.54	165,000.00	176,000.00	185,000.00	192,806.74
145,500.50	150,930.39	157,083.00	165,000.00	180,000.00	186,330.00	193,500.00

Source: Cruz (2002, p. 57).

Firstly, we report the estimated probabilities of losses below the data collection threshold, $\widehat{F}(195,000)$. For the exponential models, it is 0.300 (naive) and 0.426 (truncated). For the Lomax models, it is 0.310 (naive) and 0.794 (truncated). Secondly, using these probabilities we can estimate the total, observed, and unobserved number of losses. For the exponential models, $\widehat{N} = 77.2 \approx 77$ (naive) and $\widehat{N} = 94.1 \approx 94$ (truncated). For the Lomax models, $\widehat{N} = 78.3 \approx 78$ (naive) and $\widehat{N} = 262.1 \approx 262$ (truncated). Note how different from the rest the estimate of the truncated Lomax model is. (Recall that this model exhibited the best statistical fit for the observed data).

For predictions that are verifiable, in Table 8 we report model-based estimates of the number of losses, the average loss, and the total loss in the interval $[150{,}000; 175{,}000]$. We also provide the corresponding 95% confidence intervals for the predictions. The intervals were constructed by using the variance and covariance estimates of Table 4 in conjunction with Theorem A3. Notice that by using the data points from Table 7 it is straightforward to verify that the actual number of losses is eight, the average loss is 156,627, and the total loss is 1,253,017. We see from Table 8 that, with the exception of the average loss measure, there are large disparities in predictions between different approaches. This mostly has to do with the quality of model fit for the given data set, which is good for the truncated Lomax model but bad for the other models and/or approaches. As a consequence, 95% confidence intervals based on the truncated Lomax model cover the actual values of two important measures—number of losses (eight) and total loss (1,253,017)—but those based on the truncated exponential model do not. Moreover, both naive models fit the data poorly and produce point and interval predictions that are even further from their respective targets than those of the truncated exponential model. In addition, if one chose to ignore the model validation step and proceeded directly to predictions based on the naive models, they would be (falsely) reassured by the consistency of such predictions (number of losses: 2.6 and 2.7; total loss: 426,197 and 441,155).

Table 8. Model-based predictions (with 95% confidence intervals in parentheses) of several statistics for the unobserved losses between $150,000 and $175,000.

Model	*Truncated*			*Naive*		
	Number of Losses	Average Loss	Total Loss	Number of Losses	Average Loss	Total Loss
Exponential	4.2 (3.0; 5.5)	162,352 (162,312; 162,391)	685,108 (452,840; 917,376)	2.6 (1.9; 3.4)	162,405 (162,379; 162,430)	426,197 (141,592; 710,802)
Lomax	9.9 (3.3; 16.5)	162,017 (161,647; 162,388)	1,609,649 (543,017; 2,676,281)	2.7 (1.8; 3.7)	162,397 (162,343; 162,451)	441,155 (288,324; 593,985)

4. Concluding Remarks

In this paper, we have studied the problem of model uncertainty in operational risk modeling, which arises due to different (seemingly plausible) model assumptions. We have focused on the statistical aspects of the problem by utilizing asymptotic theorems of mathematical statistics, Monte Carlo simulations, and real-data examples. Similar to other authors who have studied some aspects of this topic before, we conclude that:

- The naive and empirical approaches are inappropriate for determining VaR estimates.
- The shifted approach—although fundamentally flawed (simply because it assumes that operational losses below the data collection threshold are impossible)—has the flexibility to adapt to data well and successfully pass standard model validation tests.
- The truncated approach is theoretically sound when appropriate fits data well, and (in our examples) produces lower VaR-based capital estimates than those of the shifted approach.

The research presented in this paper invites follow-up studies in several directions. For example, as the first and most obvious direction, one may choose to explore these issues for other—perhaps more popular in practice—distributions such as lognormal or loggamma. If the chosen model lends itself to analytic investigations, then our Example 1 (in Section 2.3) is a blueprint for analysis. Otherwise, one may follow our Example 2 for a simulations-based approach. Second, VaR can be replaced by a different risk measure. For instance, the Expected Shortfall (also known as Tail-VaR or Conditional Tail Expectation) has some theoretical advantages over VaR (e.g., it is a coherent risk measure), and is a recommended measure in the *Swiss Solvency Test*. Third, due to the theoretical soundness of the truncated approach, one may try to develop model-selection strategies for truncated (but not necessarily nested) models. However, this line of work may be quite challenging due to the "flatness" of the truncated likelihoods—a phenomenon frequently encountered in practice (see Cope 2011). The fourth venue of research that may also help with the latter problem is robust model fitting. There are several excellent contributions to this topic in the operational risk literature (e.g., Chau 2013; Horbenko et al. 2011; Opdyke and Cavallo 2012), but more work can be done.

Acknowledgments: The authors are very appreciative of valuable insights and useful comments provided by two anonymous referees, which helped to substantially improve the paper.

Author Contributions: The two authors contribute equally to this paper.

Conflicts of Interest: The authors declare no conflict of interest.

Appendix A

In this appendix, we provide some theoretical results that are key to the analytic derivations in the paper. Specifically, in Appendix A.1, the generalized Pareto distribution (GPD) is introduced, and a few of its special and limiting cases are discussed. In Appendix A.2, the asymptotic normality theorems for sample quantiles (equivalently, value-at-risk or VaR) and the maximum likelihood estimators (MLEs) of model parameters are presented. The well-known delta method is also provided in this section.

Appendix A.1 Generalized Pareto Distribution

The cumulative distribution function (cdf) of the three-parameter GPD is given by

$$F_{\text{GPD}(\mu,\sigma,\gamma)}(x) = \begin{cases} 1 - (1+\gamma(x-\mu)/\sigma)^{-1/\gamma}, & \gamma \neq 0, \\ 1 - \exp\left(-(x-\mu)/\sigma\right), & \gamma = 0, \end{cases} \tag{A1}$$

and the probability density function (pdf) by

$$f_{\text{GPD}(\mu,\sigma,\gamma)}(x) = \begin{cases} \sigma^{-1}(1+\gamma(x-\mu)/\sigma)^{-1/\gamma-1}, & \gamma \neq 0, \\ \sigma^{-1}\exp\left(-(x-\mu)/\sigma\right), & \gamma = 0, \end{cases} \tag{A2}$$

where the pdf is positive for $x \geq \mu$, when $\gamma \geq 0$, or for $\mu \leq x \leq \mu - \sigma/\gamma$, when $\gamma < 0$. The parameters $-\infty < \mu < \infty$, $\sigma > 0$, and $-\infty < \gamma < \infty$ control the location, scale, and shape of the distribution, respectively. Note that when $\gamma = 0$ and $\gamma = -1$, the GPD reduces to the shifted exponential distribution (with location μ and scale σ) and the uniform distribution on $[\mu; \mu+\sigma]$, respectively. If $\gamma > 0$, then the Pareto-type distributions are obtained. In particular:

- Choosing $1/\gamma = \alpha$, $\sigma/\gamma = \theta$, and $\mu = \theta$ leads to what actuaries call a single-parameter Pareto distribution, with the scale parameter $\theta > 0$ (usually treated as known *deductible*) and shape $\alpha > 0$.
- Choosing $1/\gamma = \alpha$, $\sigma/\gamma = \theta$, and $\mu = 0$ yields the Lomax distribution with the scale parameter $\theta > 0$ and shape $\alpha > 0$. This is also known as a Pareto II distribution.

For a comprehensive treatment of Pareto distributions, the reader may be referred to Arnold (2015), and for their applications to loss modeling in insurance, see Klugman, Panjer, and Willmot (2012).

A useful property for modeling operational risk with the GPD is that the truncated cdf of excess values remains a GPD (with the same shape parameter γ), and it is given by

$$\mathbf{P}\{X \leq x \,|\, X > t\} = \frac{\mathbf{P}\{t < X \leq x\}}{\mathbf{P}\{X > t\}} = 1 - \left(1 + \gamma \frac{x-t}{\sigma + \gamma(t-\mu)}\right)^{-1/\gamma}, \quad x > t, \tag{A3}$$

where the second equality follows by applying Equation (A1) to the numerator and denominator of the ratio.

In addition, besides the functional simplicity of its cdf and pdf, another attractive feature of the GPD is that its quantile function (qf) has an explicit formula. This is especially useful for model diagnostics (e.g., quantile–quantile plots) and for risk evaluations based on VaR measures. Specifically, for $0 < u < 1$, the qf is found by inverting Equation (A1) and given by

$$F^{-1}_{\text{GPD}(\mu,\sigma,\gamma)}(u) = \begin{cases} \mu + (\sigma/\gamma)\left((1-u)^{-\gamma} - 1\right), & \gamma \neq 0, \\ \mu - \sigma\log(1-u), & \gamma = 0. \end{cases} \tag{A4}$$

Appendix A.2 Asymptotic Theorems

Suppose $X_1, \ldots, X_n$ represent a sample of *independent and identically distributed* (*i.i.d.*) continuous random variables with cdf G, pdf g, and qf G^{-1}, and let $X_{(1)} \leq \cdots \leq X_{(n)}$ denote the ordered sample values. We will assume that g satisfies all the regularity conditions that usually accompany theorems such as the ones formulated below (for more details on this topic, see, e.g., Serfling 1980, Sections 2.3.3 and 4.2.2). Note that a review of modeling practices in the U.S. financial service industry (see AMA Group 2013) suggests that practically all the severity distributions in current use would satisfy the regularity assumptions mentioned above. In view of this, we will formulate "user-friendly" versions of the most general theorems, making them easier to work with. Additionally, throughout the paper, the notation $\mathcal{AN}$ is used to denote "asymptotically normal."

Since VaR measure is defined as a population quantile, say $G^{-1}(\beta)$, its empirical estimator is the corresponding sample quantile $X_{(\lceil n\beta \rceil)}$, where $\lceil \cdot \rceil$ denotes the "rounding up" operation. We start with the asymptotic normality result for sample quantiles. Proofs and complete technical details are available in Section 2.3.3 of Serfling (1980).

Theorem A1 (Asymptotic Normality of Sample Quantiles). *Let $0 < \beta_1 < \cdots < \beta_k < 1$, with $k > 1$, and suppose that pdf g is continuous, as discussed above. Then, the k-variate vector of sample quantiles $\left(X_{(\lceil n\beta_1 \rceil)}, \ldots, X_{(\lceil n\beta_k \rceil)}\right)$ is $\mathcal{AN}$ with the mean vector $\left(G^{-1}(\beta_1), \ldots, G^{-1}(\beta_k)\right)$ and the covariance–variance matrix $\left[\sigma_{ij}^2\right]_{i,j=1}^{k}$ with the entries*

$$\sigma_{ij}^2 = \frac{1}{n} \frac{\beta_i(1-\beta_j)}{g(G^{-1}(\beta_i))g(G^{-1}(\beta_j))}.$$

In the univariate case ($k = 1$), the sample quantile

$$X_{(\lceil n\beta \rceil)} \text{ is } \mathcal{AN}\left(G^{-1}(\beta), \frac{1}{n}\frac{\beta(1-\beta)}{g^2(G^{-1}(\beta))}\right).$$

Clearly, in many practical situations the univariate result will suffice, but Theorem A1 is more general and may be used, for example, to analyze business decisions that combine a set of VaR estimates.

The main drawback of statistical inference based on the empirical model is that it is restricted to the range of observed data. For the problems encountered in operational risk modeling, this is a major limitation. Therefore, a more appropriate alternative is to estimate VaR parametrically, which first requires estimates of the distribution parameters and then those values are applied to the formula of $G^{-1}(\beta)$ to find an estimate of VaR. The most common technique for parameter estimation is MLE. The following theorem summarizes its asymptotic distribution. Description of the method, proofs, and complete technical details are available in Section 4.2 of (Serfling 1980).

Theorem A2 (Asymptotic Normality of MLEs). *Suppose pdf g is indexed by k unknown parameters, $(\theta_1, \ldots, \theta_k)$, and let $\left(\widehat{\theta}_1, \ldots, \widehat{\theta}_k\right)$ denote the MLE of those parameters. Then, under the regularity conditions mentioned above,*

$$\left(\widehat{\theta}_1, \ldots, \widehat{\theta}_k\right) \text{ is } \mathcal{AN}\left((\theta_1, \ldots, \theta_k), \frac{1}{n}\mathbf{I}^{-1}\right),$$

where $\mathbf{I} = \left[I_{ij}\right]_{i,j=1}^{k}$ is the Fisher information matrix, with the entries given by

$$I_{ij} = \mathbf{E}\left[\frac{\partial \log g(X)}{\partial \theta_i} \cdot \frac{\partial \log g(X)}{\partial \theta_j}\right].$$

In the univariate case ($k = 1$),

$$\widehat{\theta} \text{ is } \mathcal{AN}\left(\theta, \frac{1}{n}\frac{1}{\mathbf{E}\left[\left(\frac{\partial \log g(X)}{\partial \theta}\right)^2\right]}\right).$$

Having parameter MLEs, $\left(\widehat{\theta}_1, \ldots, \widehat{\theta}_k\right)$, and knowing their asymptotic distribution is useful. Our ultimate goal, however, is to estimate VaR—a function of $\left(\widehat{\theta}_1, \ldots, \widehat{\theta}_k\right)$—and to evaluate its properties. For this we need a theorem that would specify the asymptotic distribution of functions of asymptotically normal vectors. The *delta method* is a technical tool for establishing asymptotic normality of *smoothly* transformed asymptotically normal random variables. Here we will present it as a direct application to Theorem A2. For the general theorem and complete technical details, see Serfling (1980, Section 3.3).

Theorem A3 (The Delta Method). *Suppose that* $\left(\widehat{\theta}_1, \ldots, \widehat{\theta}_k\right)$ *is* $\mathcal{AN}$ *with the parameters specified in Theorem A2. Let the real-valued functions* $h_1(\theta_1, \ldots, \theta_k), \ldots, h_m(\theta_1, \ldots, \theta_k)$ *represent m different risk measures, tail probabilities, or other functions of model parameters. Then, under some smoothness conditions on functions* $h_1, \ldots, h_m$*, the vector of MLE-based estimators*

$$\left(h_1\left(\widehat{\theta}_1, \ldots, \widehat{\theta}_k\right), \ldots, h_m\left(\widehat{\theta}_1, \ldots, \widehat{\theta}_k\right)\right) \text{ is } \mathcal{AN}\Big(\left(h_1(\theta_1, \ldots, \theta_k), \ldots, h_m(\theta_1, \ldots, \theta_k)\right), \frac{1}{n}\mathbf{D}\mathbf{I}^{-1}\mathbf{D}'\Big),$$

where $\mathbf{D} = [d_{ij}]_{m \times k}$ *is the Jacobian of the transformations* $h_1, \ldots, h_m$ *evaluated at* $(\theta_1, \ldots, \theta_k)$*, that is,* $d_{ij} = \partial h_i / \partial \widehat{\theta}_j \Big|_{(\theta_1, \ldots, \theta_k)}$. *In the univariate case* $(m = 1)$*, the parametric estimator*

$$h\left(\widehat{\theta}_1, \ldots, \widehat{\theta}_k\right) \text{ is } \mathcal{AN}\Big(h(\theta_1, \ldots, \theta_k), \frac{1}{n}\mathbf{d}\mathbf{I}^{-1}\mathbf{d}'\Big),$$

where $\mathbf{d} = \left(\partial h / \partial \widehat{\theta}_1, \ldots, \partial h / \partial \widehat{\theta}_k\right)\Big|_{(\theta_1, \ldots, \theta_k)}$.

References

AMA Group. 2013. *AMA Quantification Challenges: AMAG Range of Practice and Observations on "The Thorny LDA Topics"*. Munich: Risk Management Association.

Arnold, Barry C. 2015. *Pareto Distributions*, 2nd ed. London: Chapman & Hall.

Basel Coordination Committee. 2014. Supervisory guidance for data, modeling, and model risk management under the operational risk advanced measurement approaches. *Basel Coordination Committee Bulletin* 14: 1–17.

Baud, Nicolas, Antoine Frachot, and Thierry Roncalli. 2002. Internal Data, External Data and Consortium Data for Operational Risk Measurement: How to Pool Data Properly? Working Paper, Groupe de Recherche Opérationnelle, Crédit Lyonnais, France.

Brazauskas, Vytaras, Bruce L. Jones, and Ričardas Zitikis, R. 2015. Trends in disguise. *Annals of Actuarial Science* 9: 58–71.

Cavallo, Alexander, Benjamin Rosenthal, Xiao Wang, and Jun Yan. 2012. Treatment of the data collection threshold in operational risk: A case study with the lognormal distribution. *Journal of Operational Risk* 7: 3–38.

Chau, Joris. 2013. *Robust Estimation in Operational Risk Modeling*. Master's thesis, Department of Mathematics, Utrecht University, Utrecht, The Netherland.

Chernobai, Anna S., Svetlozar T. Račev, and Frank J. Fabozzi. 2007. *Operational Risk: A Guide to Basel II Capital Requirements, Models, and Analysis*. Hoboken: Wiley.

Cope, Eric. 2011. Penalized likelihood estimators for truncated data. *Journal of Statistical Planning and Inference* 141: 345–58.

Cruz, Marcelo G. 2002. *Modeling, Measuring and Hedging Operational Risk*. Hoboken: Wiley.

Cruz, Marcelo G., Gareth W. Peters, and Pavel V. Shevchenko. 2015. *Fundamental Aspects of Operational Risk and Insurance Analytics: A Handbook of Operational Risk*. Hoboken: Wiley.

de Fontnouvelle, Patrick, Virginia Dejesus-Rueff, John S. Jordan, and Eric S. Rosengren . 2006. Capital and risk: New evidence on implications of large operational losses. *Journal of Money, Credit, and Banking* 38: 1819–46.

Ergashev, Bakhodir, Konstantin Pavlikov, Stan Uryasev, and Evangelos Sekeris. 2016. Estimation of truncated data samples in operational risk modeling. *Journal of Risk and Insurance* 83: 613–40.

Horbenko, Nataliya, Peter Ruckdeschel, and Taehan Bae. 2011. Robust estimation of operational risk. *Journal of Operational Risk* 6: 3–30.

Klugman, Stuart A., Harry Panjer, and Gordon E. Willmot. 2012. *Loss Models: From Data to Decisions*, 4th ed. Hoboken: Wiley.

Luo, Xiaolin, Pavel V. Shevchenko, and John B. Donnelly. 2007. Addressing the impact of data truncation and parameter uncertainty on operational risk estimates. *Journal of Operational Risk* 2: 3–26.

Moscadelli, Marco, Anna Chernobai, and Svetlozar T. Rachev. 2005. Treatment of missing data in the field of operational risk: The impacts on parameter estimates, EL and UL figures. *Operational Risk* 6: 28–34.

Office of the Comptroller of the Currency. 2011. Supervisory guidance on model risk management. *SR Letter* 11: 1–21.

Opdyke, John Douglas. 2014. Estimating operational risk capital with greater accuracy, precision, and robustness. *Journal of Operational Risk* 9: 3–79.

Opdyke, John Douglas, and Alexander Cavallo. 2012. Estimating operational risk capital: The challenges of truncation, the hazards of maximum likelihood estimation, and the promise of robust statistics. *Journal of Operational Risk* 7: 3–90.

Serfling, Robert J. 1980. *Approximation Theorems of Mathematical Statistics*. Hoboken: Wiley.

Shevchenko, Pavel V., and Grigory Temnov. 2009. Modeling operational risk data reported above a time-varying threshold. *Journal of Operational Risk* 4: 19–42.

MDPI AG
St. Alban-Anlage 66
4052 Basel, Switzerland
Tel. +41 61 683 77 34
Fax +41 61 302 89 18
http://www.mdpi.com

Risks Editorial Office
E-mail: risks@mdpi.com
http://www.mdpi.com/journal/risks

www.ingramcontent.com/pod-product-compliance
Lightning Source LLC
Chambersburg PA
CBHW051844210326
41597CB00033B/5772
* 9 7 8 3 0 3 8 4 2 7 3 3 9 *